Anthropology through
the looking-glass

Anthropology through the looking-glass

Critical ethnography in the margins of Europe

Michael Herzfeld

Associate Professor of Anthropology and Semiotics, Indiana University

CAMBRIDGE
UNIVERSITY PRESS

Published by the Press Syndicate of the University of Cambridge
The Pitt Building, Trumpington Street, Cambridge CB2 1RP
40 West 20th Street, New York, NY 10011-4211 USA
10 Stamford Road, Oakleigh, Melbourne 3166, Australia

First published 1987
First paperback edition 1989
Reprinted 1992, 1993, 1995

Printed in Great Britain by
Athenæum Press Ltd, Gateshead, Tyne & Wear

British Library cataloguing in publication data

Herzfeld, Michael
Anthropology through the looking-glass :
critical ethnography in the margins of
Europe.
1. Greece—Civilization
I. Title
306'.09495   DF77

Library of Congress cataloguing in publication data

Herzfeld, Michael, 1947–
Anthropology through the looking-glass :
Bibliography.
Includes index.
1. Anthropology.   2. Ethnology—Europe.
I. Title
GN33. H47   1987   306   87–9341

ISBN 0 521 34003 9 hardback
ISBN 0 521 38908 9 paperback

RB

For John Campbell

Of the conceit of nations we have heard that golden saying of Diodorus Siculus, that nations, whether Greek or barbarian, have each had the foolish conceit of having been ahead of all the others in discovering the good things of human life and of having memories of their affairs that go back to the beginning of the world. (....) To this conceit of nations we may add here the conceit of the learned, who want whatever they know to be as old as the world.

Giambattista Vico (1668–1744)
(1,2,3–4 [1977:174–5] [B/F 125, 127])

Contents

Preface

I came to anthropology through my early fascination with modern Greece, rather than the other way round. The route was ethnographic and experiential; theory, though useful, was a means to an end. As a student, I nevertheless also felt the heady lures of theoretical formalism. Symbolic opposition pitted its claims of rigor and precision against the very different intellectual ascetism of strictly empirical approaches and considerations. But here lay a huge irony, one that I only slowly began to perceive: the very tension between empirical description and structured formalism was itself both a symbolic form and a pragmatic experience.

It gradually became apparent to me that, despite their alluring neatness, structuralist techniques were in practice the expressive paraphernalia of a symbolism that we shared with the people we studied. They were not so much misguided, as the fashionable overreaction against their use would have it, as grimly embedded in the objectivism that allowed Us to study Them. The fact that this was a symbolic opposition in its own right was ignored, or deemed irrelevant. After all, since structuralism (like its many predecessors) made claims to global explanatory capacities, it was *obvious* that we could, if we wanted, study ourselves. But this was usually regarded as trivial at best, pure narcissism in the less generous view; "reflexivity" – a very different concept – was not yet part of the day-to-day vocabulary.

Meanwhile, I continued to work "on" Greek materials, to live in Greece over long periods, and to think about my own fascination with Greek culture and society. Educated Greek friends would sometimes intimate a sense of unease at the application of methods and ideas derived from the study of "primitives" to their European culture. This was a prejudice, certainly; but could I claim that my own approach was any less ethnocentric unless I encouraged its application to "my own" culture – whatever that was?

Such were the beginnings of this book. In it, I argue that anthropology is as much a symbolic system, and as concerned with the differentiation of identities, as any of the social groups that it reifies and studies. But this is emphatically not a rejection of anthropology, any more than it is a denial of theory. These extremes do not improve upon the blindness of positivism.

Rather, I believe that an anthropology that makes an ethnographic problem of itself offers pragmatic insight into the social worlds that it examines and to which it belongs. Above all, it permits access to the *rhetoric* of social life, not as some spurious gloss on reality (which is how the vulgar positivism of everyday talk treats rhetoric), but as the accessible dimension of social reality itself. Anthropology has already demonstrated a remarkable capacity for reflexive criticism, as the practitioners of other disciplines increasingly recognize. The status of theory is an issue in many areas, but fieldwork forces the anthropologist to come to immediate terms with its frail provisionality. This enforced dialectic between theory and practice may give anthropology an unusually powerful relevance for other disciplines, ranging from the eminently practical field of law to the most monastic forms of philology.

I do not know how probable that is; I only know that many Greek friends have taught me to see the provisionality of my own frameworks of interpretation. As they struggle with the anxieties of being Greek, so I struggle with the pettier but often surprisingly parallel dilemmas of being an anthropologist – and especially of being an anthropologist in the country that, more than any other, Europe has imperiously commandeered as its ancestor. In this book, my goal is to seek out the fractured ethnographic reflections of this concern, and the dim image of its spreading ideological roots, in the disturbed and muddy waters that swirl around the margins of European identity.

These Greek friends include the members of two village communities – "Pefko" on Rhodes and "Glendi" on Crete – where I did most of my field research to date. My intellectual as well as my personal gratitude to these people is immense. I have retained the pseudonyms here for reasons of both a practical and an ethical nature.

It is perhaps appropriate that I finally began to write at a literal distance. As a Visiting Fellow of the Humanities Research Centre of the Australian National University in Canberra and then as a Visiting Scholar in the Department of Anthropology at the University of Sydney (under the aegis of the Sydney Association for Studies in Society and Culture), for a total of nearly three months in mid 1985, I was able to contemplate European "aboriginality" with an increasing sense of historical irony. I shall always be grateful to my genial hosts in both institutions – Graeme Clark in Canberra, and Michael Allen, Michael Halliday, and Terry Threadgold in Sydney – as well as to many others who made my travels in Australia intellectually stimulating and personally warming.

At Indiana University, where departmental colleagues and others have supported my interests with friendship and warmth, I also have to express my gratitude for grants-in-aid received for summer research in 1984 from the Office of Research and Graduate Development, Russian and East European Studies, and West European National Resource Center. At Cambridge University Press I am indebted to Susan Allen-Mills, Susan Conn, and Liz Graham for their extraordinary patience and helpfulness at various stages in the gestation of the book.

Many friends offered valuable advice and suggestions, and moved me to renewed efforts with their lively interest and good talk. I would particularly like to thank those who read the manuscript of this book at various levels of completion and articulation: Loring M. Danforth, J. Michael Holquist, Michael Jackson, Gregory Jusdanis, George Marcus, Vassilis Lambropoulos, Anthony Seeger, Gregory Sifakis, and Bonnie Urciuoli. They all went to immense trouble, and I owe any clarity there may be in the exposition and ideas to their constructively critical encouragement. Cornelia Mayer Herzfeld has been unsparing of inspiration, support, insight, and critical good sense.

It was under the kindly, tolerant, and perceptive guidance of John Campbell at Oxford that I learned to appreciate the complexities of ethnographic research and writing. My debt to him is the personal refraction of a condition shared by all who have studied the society and culture of modern Greece. It is also the personal reflection mirrored in the looking-glass of this book, which I offer him in gratitude and affection. This book brings into specific focus concerns and approaches that his own work has made accessible to critical analysis. In dedicating the book to him, I am trying to make some small return for his profound and sympathetic guidance through the pitfalls of anthropological exploration, in which his example has always fused theory and ethnography in an intensely pragmatic search for understanding.

Key to symbols

Two linguistic symbols are used in this book:

*   at the head of a word or phrase means that it is not an ordinarily used form;

x < y   indicates etymological derivation (i.e., x is derived from y).

Extensive reference is made to the 1744 edition of G. B. Vico, *La Scienza nuova*. Page nos. and book/section/paragraph nos. are taken from the critical edition by Paolo Rossi (Milan: Rizzoli, 1977). In addition, paragraph nos. are provided in accordance with the English language translation by Thomas Godard Bergin and Max Harold Fisch (Ithaca: Cornell University Press, 1948) and these are prefixed by the abbreviation B/F.

Transliteration of modern Greek terms has followed a modified phonemic system, except that names are given in a form that should be more accessible to library searches, etc. Further modifications, based on the International Phonetic Alphabet, have been adopted for dialect variants.

Acknowledgment

The passage from Graham Greene's *The Ministry of Fear* is reproduced by kind permission of the publishers, William Heinemann Ltd, and Viking Penguin Inc.

1 Romanticism and Hellenism: burdens of otherness

The dilemmas of marginal identity: anthropology as ethnographic object

Ancient Greece is the idealized spiritual and intellectual ancestor of Europe. Anthropology, the study of humankind that emerged from the heyday of European dominance, has nevertheless found disproportionately little theoretical use for the Greece of today. This is all the more noteworthy in that anthropologists have worked productively in contemporary Greek communities, and because issues in the development of anthropological theory closely and instructively parallel ideological conflicts in modern Greece. A curious silence enfolds the connections between modern Greek culture and the practice of anthropology.

Probing that silence is an investigation of anthropology and its assumptions. More specifically, the labile boundary between the exotic and the familiar in Greek ethnography illuminates the problem of exoticism in anthropological thinking generally. The present project is political as well as epistemological; ethnographic as well as anthropological; and descriptive as well as analytical. Indeed, these are not mutually exclusive or radically polar opposites, any more than are modern anthropological theory and the ethnographic study of modern Greece, although such pairs may have been so treated in the past.

The task is a comparative one. The poles of the comparison are, respectively, the culture of modern Greece, and the discourse of anthropology. By taking as its touchstone a society that brings together the stereotypes of the exotic and the European, this approach highlights the symbolic character of anthropology as the exploration and expression, not of exotic societies, but on the contrary of the cultural identities of those globally dominant societies that themselves created the discipline. It will thus allow us to explore the relationship between theory and the cultural practices in which it is embedded. This relationship has always represented a pragmatic issue for anthropologists, whose task is *empirical* but who are themselves not necessarily *empiricists*.

The relationship between theory and practice troubles scholars in vir-

1

tually all fields of cultural analysis and criticism: art, literature, aesthetics, linguistics, and legal studies, to name a few prominent areas. The empirical concerns of anthropology, however, may make a distinctive contribution. By selecting Greece for special attention, we shall be paying particularly close attention to an *absence*, to a topical, geographical, and cultural entity whose unquestionable marginality to the development of general theory in this discipline provokes some productively embarrassing questions about what that theory is supposed to be and to do. Because a number of literary and other non-anthropological scholars are also asking related questions about Greece specifically, moreover, the very narrowness of the Greek example will help to broaden the implications of the inquiry beyond the self-determined boundaries of one particular subject.

Such a project challenges some familiar habits of thought. Anthropologists who read this book may hitherto have thought of the ethnography of Greece as a charming but theoretically secondary field. They should now suspend both their scepticism about the broader anthropological significance of modern Greece, and their suspicion of the deep involvement of modern Greek studies with the traditionally Eurocentric disciplines (philology, folklore, and history come particularly to mind). And scholars whose major focus is modern Greece, many of them accustomed to treating that country in the established frame of reverence (as it were), must now instead redirect their attention to its practical irrelevance to the development of much social and humanistic theory. These two adjustments of perspective are closely interrelated. Anthropology is as marginal to Greece as Greece is to anthropology. This tendency to mutual exclusion suggests that prevalent ideas about the Greeks' role in the modern world may mirror, in some ironical fashion, ideas about the ways in which anthropologists – and their compatriots everywhere – go about understanding that world.

In a European tradition that takes its Classical heritage for granted, the neglect of Greek ethnography is both surprising and significant. It emphasizes the besetting ambivalence of a country that falls disconcertingly between the exotic and the familiar. Modern Greece does not fit comfortably into the duality of Europeans and Others, especially as Greeks are themselves ambivalent about the extent to which they are European; conversely, the ethnography of European societies in general is uncomfortably beset by an ambiguity of purpose, caught between grand impersonal surveys of 'folk culture' and ethnographies of communities intimate enough to seem acceptably exotic in their own right (Zonabend 1985:34). In this ethnographic record, the Greeks' perplexities – which situate them in a historically common discourse with the cultures of Western Europe – can become a productive irritant. Both from without and from within the world of the anthropological observer, these perplexities of identity doubly challenge the goals of a discipline that rejects *exoticism* (the sensationalizing of cultural difference) but nevertheless paradoxically pursues the study of cultural *otherness.*

This is not merely an academic nicety. It is an intimation of disturbing links between the goals of anthropology and the hard facts of international politics. The Greeks of today, heirs – so they are repeatedly informed – to the glories of the European past, seriously and frequently ask themselves if perhaps they now belong politically, economically, and culturally to the Third World. Whether as the land of revered but long dead ancestors, or as an intrusive and rather tawdry fragment of the mysterious East, Greece might seem condemned to a peripheral role in the modern age. The marginality of modern Greece to both western anthropological theory and the centers of modern international power highlights, if we will only allow it to do so, the Eurocentric ideology that both spawned anthropology and now elicits its most pious ire.

Taking anthropology itself as an ethnographic object is both a logical consequence and a valuable tool of a discipline that claims above all to be comparative. As an intellectual strategy, it forces us to note that all the hoary dualisms of rule and strategy, of structure and process, of competence and performance, even of Radcliffe-Brown's (1952:1) time-worn contrast between nomothetic and idiographic methods, are not merely poles in a theoretical debate. They are social phenomena, and their contrasted meanings come into especially dramatic focus when they take the form of a clash between ideological nation-statism and the pragmatic vagaries of everyday life. The Greece of today is an accessible setting in which to examine this parallel critically, since many facets of Greek national and cultural ideology share common historical sources with the assumptions of anthropological theory, and encounter comparable difficulties in accommodating the unpredictability and indeterminacy of social existence. Here, then, is a suitable context in which to ponder Giambattista Vico's cutting observation on the parallel conceits of nations and scholars.

As Strathern (1985:192) remarks, the examination "of the limits of our own representational devices ... provides information on how these devices might be contextualized and compared with those of other societies" (see also Boon 1982:231). Such a scheme, with its focus on representation as a means of creating otherness (see also Said 1978), portrays anthropology as a discourse about how the societies that gave it birth differ from the exotic cultures that fed its growth. It is, in short, an antidote to exoticism.

Louis Dumont has already offered his study of traditional Indian hierarchy as an appropriately – because absolutely – contrasted pole to what he calls the "modern ideology" (1966, 1977). On this basis – not without its own risks of exoticism – Dumont (1977:27) argues that "to isolate our ideology is a *sine qua non* for transcending it, simply because otherwise we remain caught in it as the very medium of our thought." It is a strangely Utopian optimism, perhaps, that can seriously contemplate transcending "our own" ideology, because it is not clear who "we" are: that is the fundamental problematic (see especially Boon 1982:47–8, 107–8, 236). But only a restless effort along these lines can bring the hitherto immanent principles of Eurocentrism into open comparison with other cultural ideologies – with hierarchy in India in Dumont's own research, for example, or, as here, with the statist and nationalistic doctrines of Europe. It may be that similarities will emerge as generously as differences. But this is a question to be asked repeatedly, not begged once and for all. Otherwise, taxonomic *form* ("they/we") suppresses reflection on what difference and similarity *mean*.

Unlike India or (to cite another popular example of an "ethnographic area") sub-Saharan Africa, modern Greece has been conspicuous mainly by its absence from the development of anthropological theory.[1] This perhaps owes something to Greece's ambiguous suspension between the exotic and the familiar, between the historically formulated symbolic poles of the European and the oriental; but that same ambiguity, and its emergence from Eurocentric preoccupations with otherness, are then precisely what make the ethnography of modern Greece an indispensable and distinctive source of perspective on the discipline of anthropology itself.

Above all, Greece furnishes an ethnographic foil beyond as well as within the immediate purview of the village community. Greek ethnography is neither just a haphazard collection of unrelated ethnographic sketches, nor the drearily uniform portrait of "a culture." Because Greece is a nation-state, and cannot conveniently be studied as a whole using the traditional methods of participant observation, it has so far escaped the sort of authoritative reduction that a generic title like "the Greeks" might suggest (cf. Clifford 1983:119).

Without simply reverting to the village ethnography genre, then, a critical ethnographic project still beckons, and one that offers far more scope to the goal of examining the discipline that makes it possible. Such an approach entails making a problem out of what is supposed to be wholly unproblematical: it shifts the emphasis from *the Greeks "themselves"* to *"the Greeks."* This book, then, remains an ethnographic study; but is an ethnography of concepts and identities rather than of institutions. Its immediate focus, tentative and provisional throughout, is on the discursive constructs that have actualized *both* modern Greek identity *and* a theoretical anthropology. On the Greek side, it concentrates specifically on the effects of state attempts to control and reshape the refractions of that identity in social life. On the anthropological side, it addresses the difficulties that anthropology – as a product of related ideological traditions – must face in resisting the temptation to do the same.

Greece and "Mediterranean society": ethnography against anthropology

Open any survey of anthropological theory: modern Greece rarely appears, and even here, away from the rarefied air of Classical scholarship, the total-izing rubric of "the Greeks" usually excludes all but those of the ancient past. Even when anthropologists turn their attention directly to Europe, modern Greece – the land to which they trace their own spiritual ancestry as well as that of European culture in general – gets astonishingly short shrift. In what must be the most comprehensive anthropological account now available of European national identity and state ideology (Grillo 1980), Greece does not merit so much as a paragraph to itself, let alone a separate chapter on its peculiar vicissitudes.

This is especially odd in a book that deals with the nation-state, an entity whose origins western Europeans conventionally trace back to their Greek heritage along with so much else. Of course, as Collingwood long ago observed (1939:61), Plato did not mean the same as Hobbes when both talked about "states"; and, certainly, the modern product of nineteenth-century romanticism is something else again. But this never prevented the West from parading Greece as the intellectual and political source. Yet the volume, while including essays on Israel and Turkey, tells us of Greece no more than that a historical legacy "may be... used to sustain the present, as... in modern Hellenism" (Grillo 1980:11). *Why* the Greeks should have found it necessary to appeal to the past in this way is never clarified. The absence of further comment, here or virtually anywhere else in the literature, is ideologically self-serving: it perpetuates the impression that the Greeks freely opted to concoct their history, dismisses the issue as uninteresting and parochial, and sidesteps the question of what is implied by the parallel involvement of several western nations in the fashioning of Greek nationalism and in the invention of modern anthropology.

Greece is of course not unique in the rarity with which it appears in theoretical discussions. Most obviously, it appears to be a special case of that more general failure to generate new theory with which John Davis, in *The People of the Mediterranean* (1977:5–10), chides his fellow Mediter-raneanists. But Davis's own offering, subtitled "an essay in comparative social anthropology" and pitched at a point intermediate between local eth-nography and global generalization, does not really bridge these ill-matched levels. Mediterranean anthropology is a second-best enterprise, an attempt to create a parochial theory in the absence of sustained interest on the part of practitioners of the more grandly exotic ethnographies. In the attempt to generate abstract theory about a geographically defined entity, moreover, "Mediterranean *anthropology*" overlooks its own *ethnographic* status both as a collection of descriptive unities and as a product of stereotypes existing in the societies from which social and cultural anthropology emerged. In responding to these broad assumptions, we must use ethnography, not as a servant of anthropological theory, but as the source for a critique of anthropological practice – of what theory *does*.

In an apparent retreat from his promising observation that "anthropology has helped create the history of the mediterranean [*sic*]" (1977:3), Davis's subsequently reiterated desire (1980) to reinsert Mediterranean ethnography into history overlooks the anthropologists' own active role in constructing the rules for the management of that same history. This role is no different from that played by the people whom anthropologists study (Appadurai 1981). But theory has always claimed a degree of creative originality; this is what elevates it over its object, suppressing the (historical) circumstance that it is itself a historically constituted construction (Said 1975:362). In this regard, it closely resembles the claims of nation-statism to the "eternal" status of national identities embodied in bureaucratic systems and sanctified by myths of origin. The Mediterranean is a region of nationalisms one of which – the Greek – is held to have originated the very idea of Europe, and, in the writings of Herodotus, the discipline of anthropology itself. In this context, it is more than usually difficult to maintain the separation of theory from its local object, as other regional ethnographies have tended to do, or to pretend that the absolute claims of nationalism bear no resemblance whatever to those of anthropological theory.[2] A historically conscious Mediterranean ethnography therefore challenges the traditional separation of theory from ethnography; in doing so, however, it also fatally punctures the project of creating a discrete theoretical subdiscipline of Mediterranean anthropology.

This dilemma goes some way toward explaining the strangely irrelevant status of Mediterranean ethnography within the discipline as a whole. Davis is only partially correct when he attributes to "[t]he desire to be as primitive as every other colleague" (1977:7–8) the typically Mediterraneanist decision to do fieldwork in a marginal community, in isolation from its regional and national contexts. This is a methodological issue; but there is also an epistemological problem that can best be elucidated by turning the searchlight of anthropological theory on to its own categories.

We have already seen that Davis's program calls for comparison within the region, not outside it, thereby begging the fundamental question of whether there is a clearly defined region at all. In the global comparative context, however, Mediterranean cultures create a problem of category ascription: they are neither exotic nor wholly familiar, and the embarrassment their presence creates is scarcely assuaged by the current fashion for discussing exoticism as a central issue.

Mary Douglas's (1966) model of ritual pollution as "matter out of place" is richly suggestive here. She has argued that ritual pollution and sanctity are analogous to each other in that both represent exclusion from the normative and ordinary; entities that cut across or stand outside everyday categories symbolize either uncleanliness or holiness, being potentially dangerous violations of normal expectations. Mediterranean ethnographies not only frequently address such category violations in indigenous systems; they also themselves, as an ethnographic phenomenon in their own right, confuse the symbolic boundary that defines anthropological activity. Ernestine Friedl (1962:5), for example, expresses wonderment at the blend of cultural familiarity with strange detail that she found soon after her arrival in the Greek village where she was to work. This sense of contradictory first impressions reveals some of the specific assumptions that anthropologists entertain as members of their own cultures, and that inevitably color their reactions to an alien environment. In terms of the ideology of Eurocentrism, at once the source and the foe of modern anthropology, Greece is symbolically both holy and polluted. It is holy in that it is the mythic ancestor of all European culture; and it is polluted by the taint of Turkish culture – the taint that late medieval and Renaissance Europe viewed as the embodiment of barbarism and evil.

To varying degrees, the same paradox applies to the entire Mediterranean region, the "cradle of civilization" from which (western) Europe considers itself to have emigrated long since (see also Chabod 1964:23–47). If this region is ancestral to "us," it is removed from us through mythic time; if merely exotic, then its distance is one of cultural space. In either case, it is "not us," even though we claim it as "our own." Its paradoxical status lies in the Eurocentric ideology rather than in anything intrinsic to the region itself. In a discipline constantly trying to escape its own ethnocentrism, the ethnography of a Mediterranean trapped in this sort of logic can hardly be anything other than embarrassing.

Honor and the state:
practical and theoretical triumphs of survivalism

Less inclined than Davis to make a theoretical unity of the Mediterranean, or indeed to privilege theory at all, is Pierre Bourdieu in his *Outline of a Theory of Practice* (1977). This justly influential work, despite a diagnostic concern with "honor and shame," avoids the trap of presenting itself primarily as a Mediterraneanist essay. On the contrary, it is thoroughly grounded in the local ethnography of the Kabylia region of Algeria. In its criticisms of the anthropological tendency to reduce all observation of human activity to formalized rules, moreover, it is an important contribution to any discussion of the relations between anthropological theory and ethnographic practice, as is the same author's more recent discussion of the relationship between language and power (Bourdieu 1982).

As a result of its local focus, however, the *Outline* also misses the chance to address one of the principal points of theoretical interest shared by virtually all circum-Mediterranean societies (and many others besides): although the author has evinced deep interest in the complexities of the relations between local community and nation-state in Algeria (see particularly Bourdieu 1962, 1979), he systematically excludes any such conjuncture between local-level ethnography and nationalist or regionalist ideologies in the *Outline*. The ethnographic props of his argument are treated monolithically as Kabyle material, rather than in any identifiable sense as part of the larger Algerian picture. This has consequences for, and is a consequence of, his categorical distinction between societies of greater and lesser internal differentiation, a refraction of the Eurocentric division between bureaucratic and informal concepts of social action that informs the entire *Outline*. Most seriously, it loses the chance of examining possible parallels between the ways in which nation-state ideology and anthropological theory respectively treat the pragmatics of everyday life.

In fact Bourdieu's uncritical acceptance of the notion of "honor" is symptomatic of this omission, in that it hermetically separates the values of the local community from those of the encompassing bureaucratic and religious institutions. In other words, it presupposes the conventional separation of official from informal discourse. Bourdieu clearly regards honor as a feature of local societies dominated by strategic competition rather than by the effective legal regulation of state systems. His thesis turns on the assumption that local societies lack permanent hierarchy, much as early Indologists assumed the egalitarianism of the Indian "village community" (see Dumont 1966; 1975:112) and for comparable reasons. Hidden behind this asymmetrical distinction between local and national societies lies at least a vestigially survivalist thesis – that is, an argument that treats the values of local societies as relatively simple features surviving from a prestatist era.

The characteristic view of honor in the Mediterraneanist literature allows for much less stable internal differentiation as well as for a much lower degree of actual variation than are to be found in the formal structures of the encompassing state systems. This notion consigns peasant concepts of prestige to an evolutionarily earlier phase. In India, the virginal Indo-European culture created by Sanskritic scholarship played this role, thereby permitting the conquering Europeans to treat their Indian contemporaries as premodern (see also Said 1978). In Europe, in addition to the moral values of a simpler age, local-level studies sought out the remnants of bygone social institutions, as in what Davis (1977:197) revealingly dubs "residual patriliny" – the "debris of traits and peoples surviving from the wreckage of deceased civilizations," to quote another equally survivalist argument (Quigley 1973:320).[3]

This assumption of local archaism within the modern nation-state belongs to a long, Eurocentric tradition. Its appearance here is ironical, however, in that modern anthropologists commonly reject historicist forms of philology and linguistics; these disciplines, with their diachronic emphasis on etymology and on the survival of particular forms and nuclei of meaning, have seemed to offer scant help to a field whose concern was supposedly with ahistorical societies. But before the golden age of romantic nationalism, in the eighteenth century, Giambattista Vico proposed a *critical* science of etymology that would rebuff the foolish claims of states and scholars alike to possession of the most ancient and therefore the most certain forms of knowledge. Read his stricture again: "To this conceit of nations we may add here the conceit of the learned, who want whatever they know to be as old as the world."

Vico's thoughts provide an incisive start to any critique of statism, and of its effects on the constitution of knowledge and society. But it is the expropriation of his ideas over two centuries following his death in 1744 that most ironically illuminates their present relevance. The ideologues of romantic statism, though often respectful of Vico, used him for precisely the vainglorious rewriting of history in terms of modern political needs that he had critically rejected. The path taken by his own fame confirmed his most pessimistic expectations.

Since we shall be looking at nineteenth-century nationalism and its effects on modern discourse, the fate of Vico's ideas in the heyday of romantic statism is a striking object lesson. Vico has been claimed as the ancestor of both nationalism and anthropology; modern scholarship suggests that he also prefigured many of the *criticisms* currently levelled at both, and particularly at their respective formalisms. Vico's critique of both scientism and statism was at the same time an appreciation of the value of ordinary discourse, which romantic statism treated with the regulatory dead hand that it also laid to Vico's own flexible view of society.[4]

The anthropological contemporary of systematic nationalism was the doctrine known as survivalism. It is best known from the work of E. B. Tylor, author of the revealingly titled *Researches into the Early History of Mankind and the Development of Civilization* (1865) and *Primitive Culture* (1871). It was an unabashedly Eurocentric doctrine of cultural survivals, which Tylor treated as cases of arrested development in a broadly universal pattern of evolution. He argued that the European peoples of his day represented the apogee and culmination of this process. In this respect, survivalism was nationalism writ large, a claim to the moral and cultural superiority of Europe over the entire world.

Conversely, the survivalist argument could be transferred to more parochial nationalisms. European statists used Tylor's general schema to argue that the modern state rested on an ancient foundation that had survived, relatively undamaged if also unappreciated, amongst the uneducated rural populations. There was thus a close relationship between global models of evolution and nationalistic doctrines of cultural continuity. Many European nationalists intentionally coopted the rhetoric of survivalism for their own ends. The Greek intelligentsia, in particular, found it useful to treat the local peasantry internally as a backward population while simultaneously presenting folk culture to the outside world as evidence of the glorious common heritage of all Greeks. Tylor's own respect for modern Greek civilization was not very deep, however, and nationalistic survivalisms masked a radical difference between domestic and international readings of their significance.

At that time, what are now folklore and anthropology were methodologically almost the same discipline, sharing a common ideology, but pointed in different directions; folklore studied the *domestic* exotics, as it were. The grand comparative studies of such scholars as Tylor and J. G. Frazer mixed European and exotic folk practices with instances from the ancient civilizations of East and West. European peasants appeared to validate the survivalist thesis in two complementary ways: first, by demonstrating the persistence of traits from the childhood of the human race even in the most civilized countries; and second, by showing that only the intellectual independence of the educated classes could achieve final escape from the burden of superstition and ignorance. This created a double hierarchy: the European intellectual emerged as the peasant's superior; but the European peasant claimed pride of place over all exotic peoples.

The subsequent drifting apart of anthropology and folklore merely let that hierarchy ossify. In post-War Greece, however, they again found a common object, and today Greece is one of the few terrains where a largely foreign anthropology and an indigenous though foreign-inspired survivalist folklore continue to be practiced side by side. The by now rather rare coexistence of the two disciplines in a single territory is a fair index of the ambiguity that surrounds Greek identity – a tension between European and exotic stereotypes.

Anthropology has never fully succeeded in escaping the intimations of inequality and Eurocentrism that we associate with nationalist folklore studies. Its failure to do so is of course, in some ultimate sense, inevitable. But there has been a remarkable blindness to the persistence of ideas whose specific embodiments in Victorian ethnology are now considered hopelessly ethnocentric. Survivalism, for example, informs modern anthropological theory much more extensively than current histories of the discipline claim. This is notably true of the emergent "subspecialty" (Gilmore 1982:176) of Mediterranean anthropology. Just as Victorian survivalism translated the Eurocentric hierarchy of cultures into a global historical sequence (Hodgen 1964:511), Mediterranean anthropology has done the same on a more parochial scale: the extension of ethnography to the circum-Mediterranean has created a need for exoticizing devices to justify research in what is otherwise a familiar cultural backyard.

One of these devices is a complex literature that presents honor and shame as *the* moral values of Mediterranean society (e.g. Peristiany 1965; Pitt-Rivers 1977). By concentrating the weight of its attention on these values, Mediterraneanist anthropology suggests a pervasive archaism. This reinforces the hierarchical relationship between nation-state and village culture that is such a prominent feature of nationalistic folklore studies also. The nation-state – by its own reckoning, the ultimate symbol and embodiment of modernity – serves as the touchstone against which Mediterranean society and culture acquire their distinctive characteristics, their fundamental otherness, and above all their removal to a more primitive age.

It is the state, according to Anton Blok (1981), a committed Mediterraneanist, that usurped the code of honor in the northern and western parts of Europe – that is, in precisely those European cultures from which anthropology emerged as a by-product of colonial rule and exploration. In the Mediterranean lands, so his essentially survivalist argument runs, the code remained relatively unaffected, a testimony to older values and virtues. But since the Mediterranean state bureaucracies were largely modelled on Great Power prototypes, we could just as easily assume that the ideology of honor was transferred back to the Mediterranean as a component of these new structures. It was the rise of bourgeois nationalism in northern and western Europe, after all, that elevated the medieval chivalric code to the status of a generic morality (Mosse 1985:13), and there is at least some Balkan evidence that the extreme sexual pudicity of rural folk is a phenomenon of the nineteenth century or not much before (on Greece: Llewellyn Smith 1965:91; Herzfeld 1983a; on Bulgaria: Lodge 1947).

Sexual self-control was certainly a major component of the Victorian ethos. We also know that is was often violated, but it has taken a long withdrawal from Victorian rhetoric to make that clear. Mediterranean nation-states that began their existence in an atmosphere where this ethos still prevailed throughout Europe are understandably reticent about drawing back the veil in turn. It begins to look as though the Mediterraneanist argument represents a suppression of history, and especially of the critical rôle of the anthropologists' own cultures in forming the defensive ideology that they now dub "Mediterranean."

At the broadest level, treating honor and shame as Mediterranean (or Greek) overlooks the extraordinary resemblance that this pair of idealized values bears to the public rhetoric of international relations. The village focus of most ethnography in the area has tended to obscure the complex web of relations between local, national, and international politics and economics (see Mouzelis 1978:68–9; Wolf 1982:4–5). By paying exclusive attention to these relatively functional links, however, we risk obscuring the ways in which local values mirror larger *ideational* structures, with their prominent history in our own "cultivated" arts. *Onore* rings out in many an Italian grand opera of the *Risorgimento*, and "national honor" quietly persists throughout folkloristic writing in Greece and Italy throughout the nineteenth and early twentieth centuries. Anthropologists have been reluctant to take such texts as germane to their task – indeed, Wagner (1975:30) specifically names opera as a component of the sense of culture that anthropologists will *not* tackle – and they have largely ignored the attendant historical connections between local-level interaction and the values of the nation-state.

Blok has tried to remedy the omission. According to his argument (1981), the powerful nation-state societies of industrialized Europe bureaucratized a code of honor that is still preserved in its localized and pristine form in Mediterranean societies. This scenario, however, is little more than a corollary of Banfield's (1956) earlier claims that "amoral familism" (a judgmental *denial* of morality) characterized the "backward society" (a clearly survivalist concept) of the Italian village he studied. For Banfield, the definitive failure of the Italian peasants lay in their preference of family allegiance over bureaucratic values. He thus endorsed one of the key assumptions of the nation-state concept, which makes the formal political structure the highest incarnation of national aspirations. If we take the positions of Banfield and Blok together, the resemblance between them becomes apparent. The state both usurps the distinctive ethos of the local community and uses it to proclaim the latter a backward rendition of the national culture.

This process also informs the professional discourse of anthropology. The study of a constructed phenomenon such as "the Mediterranean code of honor and shame" is a study of our own relationship to the cultures in question. For this reason, the honor and shame argument, which was originally designed to tease out the coherent uniqueness of Mediterranean societies, ultimately undermines itself: it shows how these societies share with the ideology of the western nation-state a set of values that we have nonetheless tried to treat as unique to them. It makes our claim to be studying "them" curiously unconvincing. We, too, are in the picture.

Otherness, absolute and relative

From such a perspective, otherness appears as a relative quality. It is not at all clear that this realization solves any problems, except in the sense that it *initiates* a critique of exoticism, and so of the power relations that exoticism entails. Anthropologists have conventionally made two, mutually opposed kinds of statements about their discipline: first, that it establishes the essential unity of human intellection; and second, that it explores the uniqueness of each culture and society in its own terms. (It is between these two levels that "Mediterraneanism" somehow fails to find a satisfactory identity as a theoretical construct.) Supposedly, in studying other cultures, we also study ourselves. But these pieties express little more than a sense of irreducible contradiction – the stuff of myth, in Lévi-Strauss's view – and they actually conceal the imbalance of the relationship between "them" and "us." Inasmuch as important areas of anthropology historically derive from the history of colonialism, moreover, the discipline's commitment to a universalistic appreciation of humankind must always represent a struggle against its own origins. For this reason, a critical history of anthropology must always be a disjunctive account of revelatory failures honestly confronted, rather than a cumulative list of successes.

This uncomfortable awareness reproduces in miniature Vico's conviction that, at the moment when scholars lose sight of the material and social metaphors on which their abstract ideas are based, they also lose the essence of knowledge and fall back into a "second barbarism," just as do states that forget their humble origins. Such critical reflexion must atrophy with each attempt to privilege theory or positivize a discipline's theoretical capital. In this regard, the intrinsic Eurocentrism of anthropology resembles the parochial statism of nationalistic ethnologies – modern Greek folkloristics being an excellent case in point – that have sought to subordinate everyday practices to an all-embracing official discourse. Such discourses deny their own social and historical contexts, claiming instead the status of absolute truths; they contradict Vico's dictum that "the truth is constructed." Empirical description gives way to empiricism; history to historicism; and folklore to a bureaucratically regulated "folklorism" (German *Folklorismus*), which paradoxically makes a sophisticated organization serve images of spontaneity and *naïveté* (see Damianakos 1985; Karnoouh 1985a, 1985b; Kiriakidou-Nestoros 1985).

It is no coincidence that the nineteenth century saw the rise of empiricism and the emergence of folklorism at roughly the same time. Indeed, a series of similar terms – scientism, literalism, historicism, legalism, sociologism – points back to a pattern of belief in the possibility of absolute, context-free knowledge. The national state became the ultimate verity, validated by a view of human science perhaps most fully expressed in

Auguste Comte's *Positivist Catechism*. Natural laws presided over an efficient, predictable universe; and, in their mould, the laws of society (as well as the laws *governing* society) were progressively naturalized too. The state, the ultimate reification of social and cultural identity, displaced folklore by the rhetoric of *Folklorismus*. In short, the totalizing ideologies of the era reduced the vagaries of social *experience* (Greek *empeiria*) to an intransigently invariant cultural *form*. Like the more familiar domains of literature and aesthetics (see Ong 1982), the natural and social sciences have still not fully emerged from these romantic preoccupations with the absolute: the emergence of a discrete anthropology of the Mediterranean is one example of this tendency to "anthropologism."

The presumption of absolute knowledge, moreover, assumes the utter irrelevance of the observer's own context. Context-dependency, when it emerged specifically into anthropological thought, did so as a mark of otherness, of the ethnographic subject rather than of the anthropological observer (e.g. Malinowski 1935:325–6). Fieldwork is the excursion from culture into nature, the attempt to domesticate a rampant contextuality (Beattie 1964:4):

For the past half-century or so social anthropologists have been investigating at first hand the social lives and cultural backgrounds of other peoples, especially though by no means only those peoples who still lack, or lacked until very recently, written literatures and histories and advanced technologies. If such peoples are to be studied at all, they must be studied in the living context of their own societies. For their social and cultural institutions are not, like those of Western civilizations, enshrined in mountains of documents, which would enable us to study them at a distance, as an American scholar can study Russia, say, without ever visiting that country.

In this view, access to meaning in literate cultures does not depend on an appreciation of context; the scholar does not have to claim to have *been there* as a basis for what Clifford (1983) calls "ethnographic authority." So-called preliterate cultures, on the other hand, lack this achievement of absolute significance; they constitute what Bernstein (1971) has called a "restricted code" – one that can only be read with the help of contextual cues, and that for this reason is inappropriate for the rendering of abstract, timeless propositions. Beattie admits that anthropology is also concerned with some literate cultures; but this is a pre-text for the recognition of *imperfectly* literate societies such as those of Greek and Italian villages, where the anthropologist can still claim to "know more" about the national history and culture. In participant observation, survivalism survives.

Literate self-absolution from the exigencies of context does indeed belong unambiguously to the romantic tradition. Ironically, it employs decontextualized symbols of otherness to convey the sense of a primitive world characterized by caprice, mysticism, and vague principles. In localized terms and concepts, torn from their ethnographic settings, it conflates phenomena found amongst quite varied non-western peoples (see also Beidelman 1971, 1980; Crick 1976). Despite early complaints against this practice by Max Müller (e.g. 1878:52–127, 1885:109–32, 1897:7; Dorson 1968:166), the practice died hard. Today, the massive generalization of honor and shame as "the code" of "Mediterranean society" lacks even the grand universalism of early anthropology to justify it.

Lévi-Strauss (1963b) has directed a devastating critique at the case of the totem – at "totemism." In his view, we have generalized the Ojibwa term *totam* into a metaphor of otherness: when Linton sought evidence of it in the nickname of the Rainbow Brigade (an American military unit) and its members' fascination with rainbows, the extended use of the concept to cover a domestic phenomenon made little sense to American scholars and their interest rapidly faded (Lévi-Strauss 1963b:75). Massively conceived, invariant totemism was the antithesis of European variety and intellect; in the context of European culture, its use is almost always derogatory – much, indeed, as Greeks faced with a choice of nouns will still often use the "Turkish" alternative to signify deprecation. Otherness in the self is a categorical confusion, "matter out of place." In like manner, discussions of honor and shame signify the restricted otherness of "Mediterranean society"; Pitt-Rivers's (1977:13) comparison of honor with the Melanesian concept of *mana* (itself a further example of the displaced ethnocentrism that has generalized *totam* and *tabu*; see Crick 1976:27, 76) has the understated but significant virtue of exposing the risks of exoticism in Mediterranean ethnography.

Exoticism of this sort is a mode of boundary creation, and should be seen as a problem in the ethnography of anthropological theory. Attempts to move in that direction have been few and far between. Over two decades ago, I. A. Hallowell (1965) proposed to treat the history of anthropology as an anthropological (read: ethnographic) problem; and much more recently Lee Drummond has offered a penetrating comparison of anthropological approaches to ethnicity with indigenous myths of origin (1981). Despite these challenges, however, most studies of Euro-American society as such rarely contemplate anthropological (or any other) epistemology as an ethnographic object. To do so is to muddy the categorical distinction that privileges academic discourse over its object.

Indeed, categorical fuzziness appears as a mark of *otherness* (Bourdieu 1977:109).[5] Honor and shame, for example, resist exact definition, and their impermanence contrasts with the ascription of roles in bureaucratic ideologies. In this way, we idealize clarity as scientific, and measure other cultures in terms of how far they fail to live up to this *exacting* standard. But clearly Mediterranean societies threaten to expose fuzziness in *our* categorical system. Anthropological categories serve as the collective representation of the Eurocentric ideology abroad. In the Mediterranean context, which broaches the modern edges and past center of Europe, they reproduce the ambiguities of identity – European or oriental, familiar or exotic? – that the local populations directly experience for themselves. In this way, anthropological theory and indigenous experience come together in an accessible framework of comparison.

Nationalism and anthropology: a suppressed link

Modern Greek nationalism, like many similar movements in Europe and elsewhere, resembles anthropology in the degree to which it is historically embedded in romantic ideology, as well as with its concern to distinguish clearly between identity and otherness. They also share a concomitant ability to suppress *internal* contradictions between unity and variety.[6] Nineteenth-century folklore studies conceived the paradox of an educated Mind formulating a folk culture in which it claimed participatory rights, but to which it was at the same time both exterior and superior. In anthropology, the same oxymoronic claim appears as "participant observation," an intervention in people's daily lives legitimized by claims of both a humanity that is shared and a sophistication that sets the observer apart.

Participant observation can indeed be seen as a historically specialized product of objectivism, in which "man has distanced himself from nature *and the universe of which he was a part*, and has asserted his capacity to remodel things according to his will" (Dumont 1982:233; my italics). Anthropological theory is thus not necessarily a radical departure from the irredentist proclamations of nineteenth-century folklore. Indeed, the separation of the two disciplines is partly a scientist denial of intellectual and political history, an attempt to "remodel things" in Dumont's sense, and especially to background the irony of close parallels between a universalist anthropology and various avowedly Eurocentric nationalisms.

Anthropology did gradually evolve a systematic, global critique of prejudice. On the other hand, it has been less successful in coming to terms with its origins in a cultural formation in which particular forms of prejudice are deeply embedded. Any revolutionary code, whether political or epistemological, may be seriously embarrassed by a structure that encodes some of the conservative principles from which it emerged (Sahlins 1976; Bourdieu 1977; Giddens 1981:85; B. S. Jackson 1982:154–5). Even an active, organized revolutionary movement finds it hard to slough off its conservative matrix (Michel Foucault, in Friedrich and Burton 1981:148) – and, we might add, can only hope to do so by first frankly acknowledging it. For anthropology, the problem is to realize that it can never definitively eradicate ethnocentrism. Anthropology is an institutionalized discipline, with roots that go far back in the occidental academy; and its appearance in the

Greek setting, like that of certain forms of "radical" literary criticism (Jusdanis 1985:178–80), could merely coopt critical discourse for establishment ends both within and outside Greece (e.g. by hypostatizing *Greek culture*). But in a framework that insists on its own provisionality, anthropology's critical potential stands to gain, rather than lose, from an awareness of its historical entailment in the ethnocentric ideologies against which it has since turned. Historical self-awareness is Vico's antidote to the relapse into intellectual as well as political "barbarism" (see also Holmes 1981:213–14).

To see the origins of anthropology in colonialism alone is certainly a gross oversimplification. On the other hand, any attempt to explore "otherness" has always and everywhere implied a moral discrimination, easily translated into the terms of a power inequality between "them" and "us." To begin with, asking questions – a definitive facet of the observer-participant's role – is itself a status-related activity; the higher the questioner's status, the greater the range of available modes of interrogation (E. Goody 1978:37). Anthropologists may appear deferential to their informants, but this is merely the privilege of power inasmuch as it is optional. Structurally, the ethnographer's self-appointed right to adopt the entire range of interrogative modes, from the humblest to the haughtiest, reproduces at the level of immediate social interaction the twin paradoxes of participant observation and national Mind: the privileged observer in each case is both *a* member of the culture and yet can operate the privileges of *all* its members.

As Dumont (1982:238–9) has argued with respect to the slogan "separate but equal" that in America "marked the transition from slavery to racism," insistence upon difference necessarily entails hierarchy; but this in turn directly contradicts the ideological thrust of anthropology. Dumont is blunt in his view of anthropology as a hierarchizing activity. At least since its incarnation in the "noble savage," the oxymoron of a qualitative moral difference transcended by commonality has beset anthropological thought (cf. also White 1978:191). In various guises, the question persists throughout the contemporary literature of the discipline. For how long will Beattie's (1964:4–5) contention that "pre-literate" is less condescending and less offensive than "primitive" satisfy the critics of anthropology? Has cultural relativism *failed* in some ultimate sense (e.g. Hanson 1979; Fabian 1983), or is the failure located merely in the complacency that it sometimes induces? In writing of a "science of the concrete" and of "ethnoscience," have Lévi-Strauss (1966) and the ethnosemanticists included their informants in an intellectual arena merely to prove them inferior, much as their folklorist colleagues have done with "folk literature"?

Every escape from judgmentalism turns out, sooner or later, to have been illusory; but each attempt confers a new kind of insight in its own time. It therefore seems a good deal less productive to vilify the discipline for its inevitable bias, than to insist instead on the provisionality of all its apparent escapes from ethnocentrism and hegemony. A perspective that recognizes anthropology as the symbolic elaboration of an ideology of collective identity necessarily also acknowledges its ethnocentrism; and this, ironically, makes it directly comparable to all the ideologies of identity of *other cultures* (in Beattie's [1964] phrase).

For all ethnography is in some sense an account of a social group's ethnocentrism.[7] To write a comprehensive ethnography of anthropology, in these or other terms, is a virtually impossible task, and I would not presume to claim it as a feasible goal here. But anthropological thought lives off the tension between common humanity and cultural difference, and so inevitably produces hierarchical classifications of identity rather like those reported by many anthropologists as ethnographic case studies. As a European-originated discipline, moreover, anthropology cannot evade the Eurocentric character of its criteria of comparison. It oscillates between this cultural heritage on the one hand, and an equally potent yearning to escape the constraints of bias altogether on the other.

Modern Greek culture and the dilemmas of anthropology

The tension I have just described is ironically recaptured in the predicament of being Greek. Some Greeks, some of the time, claim a European identity that other Greeks claim they have either never attained or never desired. Greeks thus live out the tension between similarity and difference, or inclusion and exclusion, in an *inhabited* replay of anthropology's central dilemma. For this reason, an approach to the cultural construction of anthropology could do worse than to begin from a direct and deliberately ethnographic comparison with the record of Greek ethnography.

In fact, anthropology is often rather specific in claiming an origin that belongs to the same ideological tradition as early western European philhellenism – the political doctrine that supported the creation and maintenance of an independent Greek national state, and that today often provokes frequent derision from foreigners unwilling to contemplate its origins (e.g. Holden 1972). In her magisterial study of early anthropology, for example, Margaret Hodgen (1964:20–9, etc.) constructed a Herodotean genealogy for modern anthropological comparativism. She was not the first to see Herodotus as the "first anthropologist" or this genealogy as epitomizing the larger Hellenism of European culture (e.g. Penniman 1974:24–6; cf. also Pandian 1984:102–3). But she intensified the link by cheerfully and anachronistically slighting the intervening years of medieval cosmography as lacking in the scientific acumen displayed by the "father of anthropology." For her, ironically, the first post-Classical, partially modern ethnologist was Columbus (Hodgen 1964:20); she too literally anticipated the current *critical* interest in the New World's impact on the development of images of the Other (see Bucher 1981; Todorov 1984). Through another irony that seems to have escaped Hodgen's notice, Herodotus himself very aptly prefigured the ideological uses of the concept of Europe where she instead treated it as a literal entity: he vacillated on the question of whether the Scythians – a buffer zone between Greeks and true barbarians – were truly European in a cultural or even a geographical sense (Hartog 1980). Yesterday's Scythians are today's Greeks; and such, too, are the ambiguities of the modern Greeks' preoccupations with "Europe."

Survivalist anthropology and romantic Hellenism grew to maturity in the same century. At first sight, they appear to have been diametrically opposed projects – the one a grandiose dream of generalization, the other a parochial attempt to give a small and politically weak entity a foothold in the scramble for international recognition. But this contrast is more apparent than real: romantic statism, which in Hegel's hands was to treat history as possible only within the political state (Hegel 1857:62–3; Cassirer 1946:263), often also credited the Greeks with universal significance. Absolute compounded absolute: the West supported the Greeks on the implicit understanding that the Greeks would reciprocally accept the role of living ancestors of European civilization – the standard, for most romantic writers, of civilization in the most general and absolute sense.

And yet the terms of this tacit agreement were unequal in the extreme. Whereas the Greeks sought genetic confirmation of their cultural destiny in the link with the ancient past, western observers, operating on the basis of a self-fulfilling prophecy, more often saw in it the evidence of Greek backwardness and "obsession." The Greeks of today are still living out the consequences of that imbalance, which recent political hostility to western hegemony discloses where earlier romanticism had effectively disguised it; and this circumstance enhances the relevance of the ethnography of Greece to an understanding of anthropological ideology in general.

The ethnography of Greece cannot and should not claim to be either unique or comprehensive in this regard. Many other cultures are no less significantly absent from the grand theoretical formulations, while anthropologists who have worked elsewhere will recognize problems of Greek ethnography as familiar from their own fieldwork. Many countries also exhibit a comparable ambiguity in their relationship with the concept of Europe, while yet others present entirely different nation-state frameworks.

But Greece may be unique in the degree to which the country as a whole has been forced to play the contrasted roles of *Ur-Europa* and humiliated oriental vassal at one and the same time. These two roles might seem mutually incompatible, were it not for the fact that both imply inferiority to the "true' Europeans of today. This conceptual and ideological trap has marked both anthropological practice and the larger political scene in which it is embedded. The very marginality of Greek ethnography in the development of anthropological theory reproduces the marginalization of the Greeks in international affairs. For many west Europeans, the Greeks of today are a people neither dramatically exotic nor yet unambiguously European. They are supposedly the willing servants of western interests, yet they are frequently disobedient to that role. In consequence, they receive public chastisement from journalists and politicians alike, not as the parent of all Europe, but as the political West's poorly socialized and wayward offspring.[8]

The fall from cultural grace: sources of symbolic pollution

Although the West often invokes images of the spoiled child in order to complain of Greece's "ingratitude," there is another potent trope that especially permeates the rhetoric of Greek identity. This is a secular version of the fall from Paradise. If the loss of Eden is partly a charter for male domination, the story of a fallen nation may similarly reflect an attempt to explain and justify its lowly status. In Greece, as well as amongst its nominal admirers, the Turkish (and some would add the Byzantine) influence on its cultural heritage constitutes a deep-veined imperfection in the marmoreal Hellenic image. European writings of the nineteenth century are full of attempts to explain why the Classical culture collapsed, what fatal flaws doomed it to such a humiliating twilight: its lack of internal debate and differentiation, the effete Greeks' supposed inability to withstand the might of sundry (European) empires that consequently succeeded to their cultural heritage, the squabbles of the Byzantine clergy and royalty and their inability to unite in the face of the infidel.

There is something profoundly self-serving in all these justificatory formulae, and it is reflected in the complacent self-congratulation with which the West expropriated the Classical antiquities, an orgy of acquisition that continued – with serious consequences for the current international relations of Greece[9] – into the age of Lord Elgin, and it has since resurfaced in some no less unpleasant modern guises.[10] Along with material relics, the West has also expropriated all rights to the understanding of the Classical past, or to define its very nature. It "saved" the Elgin Marbles, then completed the process discursively by naming them after their possessor. In criticizing their medieval precursors for being content with a virtual caricature of the ancient writers (e.g. Hodgen 1964; cf. also Loomis 1906), modern observers have drawn attention away from the ideological implications of their own more complete and therefore more successful recasting of the Classics. In this they doubtless found support in the deeply entrenched conservativism of Classical philology (on which, see Peradotto 1983). Classical "anthropology" is little more than an exercise in legitimation within a general canon of European identity, a canon that also included political philhellenism among its practical manifestations.

By the standards of that canon, Greece was indeed Byron's "sad relic of departed worth." Significantly, however, Byron's archaeological metaphor contrasts vividly with the reconstructive sense of what has been called the "patriotic or archaeological" character of nineteenth-century folklore studies (Orlandos 1969:6). The romantic love of ruins converts into visual images the sense of a Hellas irrevocably fallen beyond any hope of redemption. While the Greeks largely acquiesced in the *rhetoric,* with its intimations of a fall from cultural gracefulness, their *interpretation* of it was not that of the tutelary Powers. On the contrary, they saw it as a powerful argument for self-redemption through the active purification of language, customs, social institutions, and the moral character of the nation itself.

Etymologies of power: against legitimation

Ironic echoes of the Greeks' ancestral sins of culture haunt ethnographic fieldwork and theory. Settling in a rural Greek community for the first time, an ethnographer is liable to experience this frustrating response: as a "literate" (*ghrammatismenos*) individual and a "scholar" (*epistimon[as]*[11]), someone who surely knows much more than the villagers about their customs and history, should the visitor not be telling *them* about such matters? Their attitude encapsulates two fundamental themes of this book.

First, what may superficially strike one as an almost abject regard for literacy pervades the idiom of social inequality, an idiom that enfolds anthropologists as easily as any other willing or unwilling representatives of external power. Such humility may look distinctly odd in a country with an unusually high rate of functional literacy: we should beware, therefore, of literal interpretation. Reading the statement instead as symbolic reveals the essence of the second theme: that the stance of humility masks a resistance. It expresses the resentment and rejection of a prying order, and the moral inversion of an inequality defined by political power. This is quite evident from the analogies of social interaction. Formal politeness, for example, can generate a boundary of silence to keep the ethnographer out, on the grounds that unseemly behavior would be insulting; and lavish hospitality can reduce the ethnographer to the status of a dependent ("You don't have anything of your own here!"). In exactly the same way, the most fulsome expressions of regard for the visitor's scholarly status protect and conceal local values from effective penetration.[12]

Given the grace with which Greek villagers thus incorporate anthropologists into their moral universe, it would be all too easy to accept the rhetoric of literacy at face value. Just as the participant-observer's right to ask questions is only rarely challenged, so too the rhetoric of literacy feeds the creation of a hierarchical relationship, which may subsequently be reflected in assumptions that underlie the published ethnography. Although a literal reading of the villagers' deference may seem to take what they say seriously, it also turns a deaf ear to irony (as when one is told that one speaks Greek "better" than the villagers): the ethnographer, in effect, condescends to accept a monopoly of knowledge. In a national culture in which the state has invested heavily in the establishment of universal literacy, this further identifies the ethnographer's position with an official system of values, and with the official reassurance that the villagers truly concur with those values. Indeed, both official and informal discourses render such relationships in terms of the pervasive image of the power of the written word. That power has also had a drastic influence on the development of theories about language itself,[13] as, we may presume, has the development of printing (on which, see Anderson 1983:47–8; Eisenstein 1983:66–70): academic authority reflects – and participates in – the play of power in the experienced social world.

My plan in this book is to pursue the *etymology of power* to which the image of writing belongs: to play philology against its own embodiment in the literate symbolism that anthropologists share with the communities they study. This, again, is a Vichian project: it uses etymology as a means of dramatizing the socially and historically contingent character of institutions, rather than treating those institutions as givens waiting to be studied. It means examining, in the first place, the uses of the idea of literacy as a symbol; in the second, it challenges the ways in which the symbol of literacy can be used to reify social experience as a code of etiquette. Much has been written about the importance of literacy in transforming perception, and its role in the increasing homogenization of culture.[14] Rather less has been said about the social implications and effects of the *concept* of literacy – effects that surely flow, at least in part, from the perceptible benefits that literacy bestows, but that then work to confirm the hegemony of the literate. Other images that call for etymological examination include the pervasive one of a fall from grace. This motif provides a rhetoric to explain current imperfections; at the local level, it articulates the delicate relationship between knowing that Greece has suffered at the hands of foreign powers, eastern and western alike, and assessing the effects of this sad history in moral terms. In a discourse of culture where the highest accolade is to be called "European," it provides a justification of the frequently alleged national failure to live up to that demanding model.

Etymology has a long history in linguistics, where it often served to establish the "original" meanings of words. By extension, it acquired a similar lease of life in art history, where the possibility of establishing etymological links between motifs became a rhetoric for the historical legitimation of style (see Gombrich 1984:180–90). Its more purely linguistic applications also spilled over into the study of figures of speech, notably in J. L. Austin's (1956–7) study of how excuses deploy etymological allusion in order to gain effect. Such etymological allusions may not be purely linguistic; one can also deploy etymologies of *imagery*, as, for example, when the behavior of a powerful politician or bureaucrat is taken to resemble the operation of fate.

Both linguistic and other etymologies represent important arenas of interpretative contest. While some linguists (e.g. Bolinger 1975:406–9) have posited a distinction between philological and "folk" etymology, "a people's own linguistic glosses provide a significant mode of analysing a lexical category" (Ardener 1971b:lxxiii); the scholarly as well as the popular choice of etymologies is also significantly determined by aesthetic considerations (B. Joseph 1985). The distinction between folk and scholarly is thus itself a problematical product of the constructed otherness of ethnographic "subjects." Finally, "folk etymology" is almost always a passive category, something to be analyzed and then dismissed by scholars whose own etymologizing is purportedly active and self-conscious; passivity is a definitive attribute of dominated otherness. By calling what ordinary people do with words and images "etymology," the dominant tradition is able to represent it as inferior into the bargain.

But we can reverse the conventional pattern by subjecting the etymological roots of our own disciplinary vocabulary and practices to equally critical analysis. Etymology is traditionally a legitimizing device; challenges to etymology must therefore be seen as initiating battles over the determination of canonical truth. Renaissance etymology claimed to reveal truth (Classical Greek *etumon*), and this made it attractive to political systems attempting to establish the aboriginality of their power. If, as Hegel argued, the state was indeed the ultimate reality, the etymologies of statist imagery would establish that reality in the minds of all its subjects. In this regard, there is no obvious discrimination to be made between the way in which the East African Iteso people explain their name (Karp 1978:16), the Roman usurpation of a Classical etymology in order to lay claim to a remote district in Asia Minor (Lane 1975:239), or the Greek junta's notorious use of *dhimokratia* ("republic") to legitimize their abolition of the monarchy and their own dictatorial usurpation of power in the land where philhellenism situates the actual birth of *dhimokratia* (see Clogg 1972).

But if etymology can legitimate, its study can by the same token generate a critique of legitimacy, and this reversal supports the parallel upheaval of turning anthropology into an ethnographic object. The idea is not a new one. Struever (1976, 1983) has argued that it motivated Vico's extensive reliance on etymological analysis. Vico's subsequent appropriation by the forces of statism – with all their thirst for legitimacy – may have obscured this aspect of his thought. Outwardly, too, his concentration on etymology follows a pattern in the scholarship of rhetoric that had long been developing along well established lines by the time he published the first edition of his celebrated *New Science* in 1724. But beneath the respectable exterior, Struever suggests, there lay a truly subversive plan that "stipulates the essential continuity between barbarism and civility, between the primitive and the rationally organized" and thus "creates uncomfortable but challenging parameters for social or ethical theory" (1983:120).

Vico may well have adopted a conventional framework on purpose. The *New Science* is not only replete with the full panoply of Classical erudition (although many scholars have objected to his flagrant imagination), but it makes its object a revelation of the workings of Divine Providence. Vico's aim is to criticize the "unnatural" abuse of power. The first humans, he says, able only to communicate through symbols ("hieroglyphs") and still lacking the power of speech, had been unable to depart from the absolute, divinely ordained truth. With the emergence of "poetic wisdom" – tropological discourse – and then of increasingly literal language, it became correspondingly easier to practice deception, and in consequence to exercise a baseless and brutal dominion over the oppressed. For Vico, then, as for Foucault, knowledge *was* power. In this spirit, Vico charts the emergence of a rapacious aristocracy, its popular overthrow, and the emergence of a monarchy that tolerates neither plebeian nor aristocratic excess but rules on behalf of all. He thus bows respectfully to an ideal of enlightened but absolute monarchy (4,9,3 [1977:608] [B/F 953]; 4,13,2–3 [1977:644–52] [B/F 1007–19]; *Conchiusione* [1977:703] [B/F 1104–6]).

One scholar has argued that Vico dissembled his radical notions mainly in order to escape the likely ire of both the Inquisition and the Bourbon rulers of his native Naples (Vaughan 1972). But this conclusion does not necessarily follow from Vico's monarchist enthusiasms as such. Certain kinds of monarchy, specifically those associated with emergent national identities, were to acquire genuinely revolutionary implications in the succeeding century. It would therefore be anachronistic to revile Vico's monarchism as reactionary, even though its later uses by Italian Fascism in particular might well tempt us to do so.

In any case, Vico's work is a radical critique of power in a more general sense. Specifically, it documents the *impermanence* of social institutions – hardly an establishment message. In particular, his view that "national identity... is a traditional civil disability, rather than an unproblematic native genius" (Struever 1983:123) ran directly counter to the ideal national identities propagated by statist ideologies: recall the shift of emphasis that I signalled at the beginning of this chapter from an unproblematical entity called "the Greeks" to the highly problematical conceptual category thus signified. The entire project of this book follows the critical trajectory thus suggested by Vico.

Vico treats institutions as products of the same human propensity for structuring as the history that records their rise and fall. This undermines the scientistic program of reifying the history of all social institutions, of giving these institutions objective permanence. It is true that a violently reactionary reading of Vico is also possible. His adoption by the Italian *Risorgimento* led to the further reification of his thought and deification of his person by later Fascist propagandists, who saw in him a philosophical founder of totalitarian statism. But this is truly an irony, worthy of Vico's own critical view that all facts are mental constructs. The fate of his thought exemplifies the power of the state to coopt the *discursive idioms* of potential sources of opposition; but once we see that this is what has happened, we derail the statist program of controlling the *meaning* of discourse.

Anthropology, identity, power

I shall return more systematically to the uses of (verbal) etymology in the final chapter. Throughout the book, however, in a Vichian mode as I have just sketched it, we shall constantly be in search of the etymologies of the dominant images, of the symbols whereby one social group legitimizes its power over others at multiple levels: international bloc over constituent small nation, state over local community, one sex or class over another. These etymologies of power and subordination are the means whereby anthropology has reacted against inclusion in the same framework as its object, and through which we may now initiate a critique of that reaction. They include the myriad reincarnations of the fall motif, as well as of that of the incontestable written edict of fate and of the bureaucratic state.

They also include the rhetoric of European aboriginality. As the price of independence, the Greeks found themselves expected to play the part of the revenant, primordial ancestor of Europe itself. Whether as primordial ancestor or as corrupt bastion of the East, moreover, Greece internalized the problem of *otherness* that anthropology, under the heading of exoticism, has objectified as peculiarly its own. The ethnography of Greece preserves etymologies of conflict between European and exotic (especially "oriental") self-images, much as it also maintains in daily speech a vocabulary of social concepts that shows up surprisingly often as etymological cognates in formal anthropological terminology. Greek ethnography, then, taken in its historical context, offers a looking-glass to the discipline: it records the effects on everyday life in one country of at least some of the ideological tensions and pressures that also generated anthropology itself.

But this does not mean that the present study is intended primarily as a survey of Greek ethnography. That has already been attempted (Dimen and Friedl 1976; Piault 1985; see also Davis 1977; Mouzelis 1978), and a repeat performance would merely beg the crucial question. The key issues to which this book speaks concern the *constitution* of Greece and Greekness, and the involvement of anthropological writing in that process; for only in this way will we learn something about the constitution of anthropology as practiced in Greece and throughout the world. Moreover, my goal is less to elucidate Greek ethnography as such than to comment on the significance of its marginality in the development of anthropological thought.

These questions are all about identity, and about how it is created. What is the status of regional and national cultures? If the concept of a "Greek culture" strikes us as too obviously ideological, how different is "Mediterraneanism"?[15] The emergence of Greek folklore as a recognized "national discipline" unquestionably has important ideological implications. To pretend, however, that "Mediterranean anthropology" does not similarly speak to ideological interests simply reifies the distinction between "them" and "us," to argue that we are objective where they are merely ideological. To chart the constitution of that boundary is certainly the task of a symbolic ethnography of cultural scholarship.

I therefore also do not propose here to tackle the status of "Mediterraneanism" as a discrete and isolated problem, as the recent debate on this subject may have seemed to do. Like "Greek folklore," "Mediterranean anthropology" is part of the larger, discipline-wide text that all anthropologists are necessarily engaged in writing. The commonly heard attack on folklore, that it "lacks theory," may be a reflection of the popular view of folklore as a trivial mythology of modern life, or as a study of merely peripheral social groups. Furthermore, the internal marginalization of peasant societies reproduces the larger political marginalization of Greece and other circum-Mediterranean countries; and the theoretical irrelevance of Greek ethnography serves as a collective representation of that marginality.[16]

If then the theory-ethnography distinction often merely glosses a difference between our intellectual selves and our "subject" informants, the exclusion of folklore studies on these grounds emerges as a more intrinsic part of the ideological bias of anthropology. In some respects, the evolutionist rhetoric of anthropology's own historiography – as in Marvin Harris's *The Rise of Anthropological Theory* (1968) – closely parallels the rhetoric of nineteenth-century statism and nationalism – the very movements whose folkloristics it rejects, and whose parochial interests it despises in relation to its own universalistic claims.

It is in the exploration of that common rhetorical tradition that I ground the present study. As we have already seen, the adulation of literacy conjoins Greek villagers to scholars. The difference is that scholars are on the side of the literate. It is the "others," the villagers, who must confront the literate controllers of their destiny, and come to terms with "this scholarly code as the principle of the production and evaluation of every utterance (*de la parole*)" (Bourdieu 1982:52). For, like fate, of which Greek villagers say that "what it writes, it cannot unwrite," scholars, bureaucrats, and Great Powers wield a pen that is demonstrably mightier than the sword. These are compelling, pervasive images of inequality.

The same tropological tradition also gives us the specter of an aboriginal fall from the Classical Greek heritage, a cataclysmic disinheritance from cultural purity, out of which the burdens of social and historical experience emerged. This is a fitting image with which to turn, now, to the main investigation. For if history derives from the fallen condition of humanity, or of particular human societies, then the discourse in which we engage with our informants is the product of that moment, and we are heirs to the same original sin, identified by following its etymological tracks,[17] as they.

2   A secular cosmology

Rules and imperfections: some comparisons

The tension between idealized Greek culture and the direct experience
of Greek social life provides an instructive parallel with some of the
fundamental symbolic oppositions of anthropological discourse. In order
to make that comparison more useful, we must now examine in some
detail the workings of the dominant tropes through which Greeks explore
the tension between grand abstract ideals and social and historical
experience.[1] Both constructed .

Prominent among these is the theologically derived metaphor of a fall
from cultural grace. This metaphor is familiar from the anthropology of the
mid-Victorian period, which had inherited from its medieval and Renaissance theological roots the image of a humanity struggling toward ultimate
redemption from the consequences of original sin. Whether the so-called
savages of this world were corrupt backsliders from the great evolutionary
destiny, or were simply retarded in progress toward it, the imagery
remained firmly judgmental.

The symbolism of the fall, in both the theological and the secular senses,
affirmed European civilization as the ultimate cultural touchstone.
Europe, the secular Eden, brought humanity within sight of perfection. In
Greece, a country that owed its independence in large measure to the
romantic desire to resuscitate antiquity, national self-images of all kinds
acquired meaning only in direct relation to this hegemonic standard. Since
Europe claimed ancient Greece as its spiritual ancestor, Europe also
decided what was, or what was not, acceptable as Greek culture in the
modern age.[2]

The complementary opposite of this standard was a monolithic image of
oriental barbarism, for which the Turks were the most potent living
symbol. The secularization of the medieval conflict between Islam and the
crusading West brought a narrowed focus of western contempt on the
Turks in particular. What then would become of an entire culture that bore
the indelible marks of its Turkish bondage? The presence of obviously
Turkish-derived elements in Greek culture was bound to become problem-

atical when Greek political and intellectual leaders looked to western Europe for the definition of Greekness.

Neither in the more distant nor in the recent past, however, did Greeks unanimously accept the external standard of the West. Some, notably in seventeenth-century Crete, initially welcomed the Turks as deliverers from Frankish – in other words, western European – oppression. But by the nineteenth century, the European standard of cultural excellence had become central to official nationalism. Perhaps the best measure of western cultural and political hegemony was its eventual success in persuading the Greeks to adopt the Turks as their natural enemies, and to treat Turkish elements in Greek culture as its worst failing – as a source of cultural pollution. But everyday culture and social values remained obdurately resistant to the call of Europe: Greeks who were quite willing to condemn the Turks on religious grounds nevertheless would not purge all the secular traces of a Turkish-dominated past.

The resulting tensions in Greek social life provide a historical basis for the present comparison with the tension between formalism and ethnographic observation in anthropology. The flaws that the Turks supposedly brought to the Hellenic perfection included shiftiness, double-dealing, illiteracy, influence-peddling and rule-bending, disrespect for norms and admiration for cunning individuals who could twist them to their own advantage. These sources of symbolic pollution represent the subversion of structure by unpredictable event or mischievous strategy. Here, then, is a direct analogy with the anthropological paired symbols such as structure and process, or rule and strategy.

A bridge between these two comparativist poles is provided by Greek folklore studies, which are both a scholarly antecedent to modern anthropology and an important dimension in the creation of a Greek national culture. Greek folklorists often rejected the seemingly Turkish-derived elements that they identified in particular variants of folk texts, on the grounds that such elements were extraneous and ugly, "matter out of place." In the nineteeth century, Greek folklorists, following and elaborating a western European scholarly tradition, treated all apparently oriental elements in folksongs or legends as evidence of "corruption." Their typologies and reconstructions had the effect of obliterating specific, recorded texts – the "variants" of *Urtexten* (the German folklorists' term for "originary texts"). They created a moralistic canon of texts that reduced diversity to uniformity.

In statist ideologies, diversity is a threat, because it signifies change and especially fragmentation. In Italy, for example, the profession of criminal anthropology was engaged for many years in studying banditry in order both to eradicate its localized peculiarities and to salvage its romanticized generality (Moss 1979:488; see also, more generally, De Mauro 1979). Historical divergence thus becomes synchronic convergence; Italian folklorists of the Fascist era insisted on regional diversity as evidence of a *unifying versatility*, and even mounted folk art exhibitions to prove it (e.g. Bona 1940). Even though these are extreme examples, they illustrate the contribution of scholarship, not only in folklore but also in linguistics and anthroplogy, to the homogenization of diversity. The general concept of structure takes precedence over process, system over event, competence over performance, rule over strategy, *langue* over *parole*. In short, *structure* elaborated the notion of *Urtext*, *event* that of "textual variant." For this reason, romantic nationalism curiously anticipated some of the more reductive effects of modern structuralism. As Foucault (1979:33) has observed, structuralism "was the most systematic attempt to evacuate the concept of event not only from ethnology but also from a whole series of other sciences and even, at the limit, from history." The irony is huge: in abolishing historical specificity in the name of global concerns, structuralism reproduces the very historicism that it has tried to put behind it.

It is this reflection of a historicist conceptual heritage that makes anthropological writing so immediately comparable to romantic nationalism. The analogy here is between, on the one hand, the relation between an undying Greekness and the allegedly transient disfigurement of Turkish influence; and, on the other, eternal structure and passing event. Of course, process and Turkishness are also both idealizations, albeit negative ones. Foucault rightly (ibid.) emphasizes that "what is important is not to do for the event what was done for structure." It is entirely possible to reify event and process, as well as other useful notions such as indeterminacy. To avoid that trap means rejecting the Cartesian real-ideal antinomy (see also Galaty 1981). The task is instead to examine as social rhetoric the dialectic between homogeneity and the recognition of individuality, unpredictability, and indeterminacy;[3] or, at the other pole of the comparison, between the national unity of the Hellenes and the untidy fractiousness of Greek social experience.

The fall: a pervasive metaphor

The image of the fall embodies these dialectics. It has informed the most intractable antinomy that anthropology faces – the tension between common humanity on the one hand, and inequality and difference on the other. It is an etiology of *both* faces, the unified and the divided. As anthropology emerged from its medieval and Renaissance stirrings, the story of Eden furnished a pre-text for theories of a common human origin, while Babel served as an allegorical confirmation of human diversity and unreliability. On a smaller scale, the Bible also provided models for the secular explanation of tensions between idealized national identities and the abundant evidence of internal diversity and disunity that contradicted every national stereotype, every attempt to talk about "*the* Greeks" or "*the* African mind."[4]

The fall is an etiology of original sin. It is perhaps the oldest, and beyond doubt the most pervasive, means of explaining the tension between the unity and diversity of humankind in the Judaeo-Christian hermeneutic canon. The expulsion from Paradise provided an explanation for the weary grind of human life; it is replicated in the stories of the Noachian Flood and of the Tower of Babel. The Babel narrative focusses more specifically on the persistent and inconvenient diversity of cultural forms, which was a punishment for disobedience to the Divine Will; it begins the process of converting divinely ordained imperfection into cultural autonomy that was to reach its greatest secular elaboration in the nationalisms of the nineteenth century. Conversely, the story of Genesis retraces humanity's unified origin, while the ecumenicalism of Christ's message proclaims an eventual redemption in unity rediscovered. Successive discoveries brought readjustments in their train. Before the European discovery of Australia, any thought of an antipodean race would have required "an intolerably heretical polygenetic theory of the origin of mankind" (Hodgen 1964:52); after it, new arguments were marshalled to assert monogenesis. In short, unity is the ideal condition, from which all cultural and political differences are earthly aberrations.

The use of the fall image to explain human sinfulness and difference appears to be a comparatively late reworking of the Genesis story. There, Adam is inherently capable of sin, and the fall is merely a punishment for realizing that capacity. The biblical story, which attributed to Adam and Eve "absence of shame at the fact that they were naked," meant only that "they shared the ignorance of childhood" and that they lacked "even the most elementary characteristics of civilisation" (Tennant 1968[1903]:9–10). The modern distinction according to which the events described in Genesis actually precipitated the possibility of intentional rather than merely inadvertent sin seems to represent a recasting of that earlier perspective, with the result that the doctrine of original sin now absolves humanity of responsibility for those actions that spring from social rather than individual weakness. This distinction, which appears at least as early as the fourth century in the writings of St. Gregory of Nazianzus (Ellverson 1981:62), initiated an increasingly historicist conception of human depravity that reached explicit formulation in St. Augustine. The centuries of the Enlightenment and Romanticism recast original sin still further, as Europe assumed immediate responsibility for its intellectual weaknesses as a precondition for historical perfectibility, and transmuted the polyglot agonies of Babel into a cult of transcendent European erudition. Some of the most dramatic expressions of this secular reading of original sin came from writers such as Herder and Hegel, who were deeply implicated in the rise of national and statist ideologies. Hegel thought that the state, being historically constituted, was marred by sundry imperfections that it would nevertheless eventually transcend, just as "the most deformed human being, the criminal, the invalid, and the cripple are still always living human beings" (Hegel 1896:247 [no.258], cited in Cassirer 1946:266–7). Here, starkly, is the ahistorical reality of historicism – the perfect *Urtext*, the abolition of contingency, for which mere mortals constantly yearn.

Hegel's position offers a salutary lesson. Like Herder in Germany and Vico in Italy, Hegel was to become a symbol of philosophies very unlike what he preached. The transcendent love that the romantics preached was to turn into a bitter hatred, culminating in the horrors of Fascism and Nazism (see Cassirer 1946:186,276; Barnard 1965). The romantic nationalists had not yet lost sight of the implications of the fall: that imperfection is itself human. But the embodiment of romantic philosophy in state practices rapidly turned away from that realization, and toward the *repressive circumscription* of imperfection – a striking example of representation as the exercise of power. It was always the state that defined what perfection was.

The metaphor of the (cultural) fall, which played a significant role in the moral self-justification of the early New World colonists (Bucher 1981:166–7), is mainly present in anthropological discourse in the highly generalized sense of the imperfect variants of structure and *Urtext* that we have just inspected; additionally, the biblical fall serves as an ironical echo of theoretical backwardnesses and backslidings (e.g. Kuper 1985). Redemption, conversely, is very much a message of romantic nationalism, with its emphasis on bourgeois models of respectability. Nationalism attempted to repress time by regaining Edenic perfection: "By becoming a part of the nation and nature, Paradise Lost might be regained" (Mosse 1985:183).

The romantic preoccupation with human perfectibility is both a secular recasting of the fall and a significant part of the heritage of anthropology. Indeed, *anthropologia* itself is a category of theological discourse. Gregory of Nazianzus's "anthropology," for example (Ellverson 1981:22), treats the soul as divine in origin; its goal was thus the return to origin that he called *theosis* ("divinization"). *Theosis* represents the achievement of perfection; like both nationalist history and abstract theory, it entails the repression of time and contingency, the recapturing of an original state of being. The historicist claims of statism and anthropology, and their search for legitimate *Urtexten* and general theories, thus indirectly reproduce the theology that equates actual social and historical experience with spiritual or cultural imperfection.

The distinction between ideal structures and actual events is thus a hierarchical one, expressed by Vico as the distinction between "divine" and "gentile" history.[5] In the theological argument, historically grounded imperfection separates humankind from its original perfect *state* for the time being; but unremitting effort may eventually overcome it. These optimistic projections have persisted in the millenarian goals of statist ideologies, and in the anthropological search for the basic structures of human thought.

Greek refractions of the fall

The theological version of the fall, with its attendant doctrine of original sin, is a prominent feature of Orthodox Christian teaching. In Greece, it has also undergone numerous popular refractions. Campbell's (1964) ethnography of the Sarakatsani, a transhumant shepherd people of northern Greece, examines that group's peculiar understanding of the doctrine with particular sensitivity and respect.

The Sarakatsani inhabit an unfriendly social and material environment in which they constantly need to reconcile social practice with the very different teachings of church and state. Condemned by the state bureaucracy for their "nomadism" (itself a characteristic of "Turkish" culture according to Eurocentric stereotypes), despised by their neighbors for their poverty and illiteracy, and at war with officialdom because of their propensity for taking the law into their own hands in all matters regarding family prestige, they also engage in a problem-fraught symbiosis with sedentary villagers on whom they are dependent for the renting of grazing lands. As seminomads, they inhabit the margins of Greek society, although their rough lifestyle has also attracted a considerable burden of romantic speculation about their origins and ethnic purity. Polluted and pure at one and the same time, they reproduce the international dilemmas of Greek identity on a homelier stage.

They are Greek-speaking, unlike most of the other, still more heartily despised transhumant populations of northern Greece.[6] For this reason, they serve particularly well as a Hellenic version of the "noble savage." Campbell's account, however, does not directly partake in this romantic view of the Sarakatsani; on the contrary, instead of presenting them as close to the aboriginal state of innocence, he records their weighty preoccupation with the sinful condition of their lives and with the harsh circumstances that perpetuate it.

For the Sarakatsani, original sin is a *categorical* absolution for those crimes and defects which they have come to regard as a normal outcome of social existence: envy, gossip, violent disposition, self-regard, and even – when circumstances demand it – killing for vengeance. At the same time, of course, it is an admission that these problems exist, and indeed that they are endemic. Sarakatsani cannot expect to appeal to this doctrine for those delicts that are not socially sanctioned, and Campbell's account suggests that a good deal of energy is invested in representing one's own misdemeanors as inevitable consequences of the general state of disharmony, while others' wickedness is truly sinful in that it is deliberate and personal. In this regard, the balance between original and individual sin is somewhat like that between luck and personality: throughout rural Greece, others' successes and one's own failures are attributable to luck (*tikhero*), others' failures and one's own successes to innate personality (*fisiko*).

The Sarakatsani define sinfulness as rebellion against God but attribute its existence to the Divine Will (Campbell 1964:325–6). Yet Sarakatsani do not give up their struggle against temptation any more than they give up struggling with one another; and they certainly do not forget to vote. The predetermination of human, national, or personal affairs is a matter of course; but this does not render less contemptible those who passively surrender the right to resist it.[7] That right defines being a "human being" (*anthropos*), a Greek, and is the direct opposite of what we normally understand by "fatalism." This rhetoric has direct political consequences. West Cretan villagers of Glendi, for example, told me that the Socialist party leader Andreas Papandreou, an American-trained economist who nevertheless strongly criticized U.S. policy toward Greece, could only win elections as long as the Americans supported him; yet this did not prevent many of them from casting their votes for Papandreou as a way of *resisting* American influence. One does what one can, and only blames a superior agency after the event. In the twilight and aftermath of the Byzantine Empire, the western European states seemed to offer some hope of freedom from the Turkish yoke, but often failed to deliver. Indeed, disappointment became a formulaic experience,[8] and Greeks could only rail against the treachery of the "blond races" of the West. But that never stopped them from appealing to the Great Powers for help first.

I have slithered here from an initial focus on the Sarakatsani to ethnographic observations from elsewhere in Greece, and even to historical sources from a distant era. There is always a certain degree of danger in so generalizing out from a particularistic ethnography. Pushed to an extreme, it could easily result in the collective portrayal of all Greeks as Sarakatsani, a risk that clearly animates some of the objections to the anthropological habit of focussing on small, out-of-the-way populations. But the trait of *efthinofovia* ("fear of responsibility") is one that Greeks themselves often decry in their own political culture (e.g. Dimou n.d.). It is an acknowledgment of a flawed social and political world. Its superficial resemblance to the stereotype of fatalism, moreover, lends a spurious force to foreign criticisms of Greek civic behavior, and thus reinforces the self-fulfilling prophecies that circulate abroad about Greek national character. Once again, my intention is to show that Sarakatsan relations with the official Greek world reproduce, on a smaller scale, those between the Greeks and the West.[9]

If, then, there is a point of resemblance between Sarakatsan and general Greek attitudes to responsibility, it may reflect something of the relations of power in which the stereotype is implicated at both levels. The Sarakatsani, lacking an effective voice in the direction of their own communal future, adopt a rhetoric that harmonizes with the dominant view of them as shiftless, violent, and egotistical. This is a local-level rendition of the anthropological stereotype of Mediterranean rural people as willing to put personal and family interests over general moral considerations (Banfield's [1958] "amoral familism"). Like that description, it is strongly indicative of the imbalance of power between those who confer such stereotypes and those to whom they are applied. Similarly, at a more general level, when Greeks criticize their own alleged proclivity of *efthinofovia*, they reinforce a stereotype that the Great Powers have long used both to justify intervening in Greek affairs and to cover their disregard for Greek aspirations.

The fall of the City: culture and imperfection

These implications of inequality reappear in the refractions of the doctrine of original sin that characterize the cultural ideologies of modern Greece. Greek is no longer a "pure" tongue; adulterated by the oriental taint of Turkish and Arabic, it has failed to provide the universal code that its classical beginnings had led the world to anticipate, and that human divisiveness constantly subverts. Glendiot villagers describe the multiplicity of the world's languages – the heritage of Babel – as a terrible collective burden that would disappear if only all humanity would worship a single deity.

The sack of Constantinople, with its effect on Greek language and culture, reproduced the cataclysm of Babel. The ancestral purity of the Greek tongue and of Greek culture was sullied and adulterated. Cultural disunity produced political disarray: the Greeks' persistent fractiousness inspired the rueful proverb, "Twelve Greeks [make] thirteen captains" (see Friedl 1962:105), by which is meant that no two Greeks can ever agree on any plan of action. This reproduces the view from outside: at the time of the struggle for independence, for example, western observers saw in the Greeks' lack of organization and political unity a typically oriental character trait (see St. Clair 1972:35–8, 75–7).

Then again, the absence of linguistic uniformity in spoken Greek became the butt of an aptly named nineteenth-century satire, *Vavilonia* ("Babylon" < Babel) (Vizandios 1840). Popular and dialect linguistic forms are often attributed to Turkish influence on the virtually automatic assumption that anything that undermined the purity of the Hellenic heritage must be a consequence of Turkish dominion. The pure Hellenic morality, so the argument went, had given way to feuding, vengeance, animal-theft, and political pettiness, thereby guaranteeing further and infinite reproductions of the same essential fall from grace; and language, culture, and morals had all gone the same way. The Greeks now found themselves condemned to an endless repetition in everyday life of that same divisive pride (*eghoismos*) that the Sarakatsani, in Campbell's account, both admire as an individual trait and yet decry as an exigency of social life.

Greek ethnography thus encounters a Europe fallen to the Orient. An impure tongue, bad habits, "Turkish" practices and etymologies, fractiousness, fatalism before the course of events and the might of government, and an insuperable reluctance to dwell together in harmony: these are the wages of a secular original sin. The Greek capacity for self-criticism has long been noted (e.g. Burn 1944:2–4); but how can we see it as anything other than the expression of political subordination, when some Greeks "accepted" the military junta of 1967–74 on the grounds that they "needed" discipline (see Herzfeld 1980b), or bowed before repeated Nazi claims that they were "degenerate" (Burn 1944:2)? In the United States and Australia, negative stereotypes of Mediterranean peoples, embodied in immigration laws and backed by fashionable eugenic theories, provoked a considerable suppression of Greek ethnicity *by its bearers* for many decades (Price 1963:205–6; see also Haller 1963:54). What, too, is one to make of frequent affirmations that Greece has "lost the light" to "Europe"? While it is true that most anthropologists do not voluntarily share these attitudes, the countries from which the discipline largely originates represent the origins of the stereotypes as well.

One of the most characteristic traits that the Greeks deny in themselves, but attribute to others more "oriental" than themselves, is that of *fatalism*. As ordinarily understood, this term means passive and total resignation to future events. It is extremely doubtful whether such a philosophy characterizes an entire population anywhere in the world. It does enjoy a certain vogue, however, as a popular, western stereotype of the "oriental mentality" (see, e.g., Kabbani 1985:30), and its occasional application to Greece – as well as the Greeks' negative reaction to it – is a fair indication of its association with the idea of a torpid, immoral, and dull oriental mind. Indeed, Vico thought that fatalism, like atheism and belief in simple chance, could never be the basis of civil life (2,5,2 [1977:429] [B/F 602]; cf. 2,5,5 [1977:450] [B/F 629]); and it is worth noting that Greek villagers (with much less respect for Islam than Vico showed) regard the Turks, not only as lazy and fatalistic, but also as an "atheistic people." Otherness, as we shall see again and again, appears as a lack or a deficiency of some supposedly immanent quality such as individualism or belief.

The use of fatalism as a discursive instrument of domination is illustrated by the fall of Constantinople, which, as we have already seen, explained Greek cultural "inferiority" from an occidental perspective. By that time, western writers no longer viewed Byzantium as even conceptually a part of Europe; the Greeks, although "geographically included in Europe, were leaving the moral sphere of Europe" (Chabod 1964:37). With the return of direct western interest in Greek affairs in the nineteenth century, the paternalism of the tutelary Powers sought to perpetuate this separation, and one of the means at their disposal was to characterize the Greeks as oriental fatalists and evaders of blame.

The Greeks themselves, however, as well as some of their admirers (e.g. Lawson 1910:123), took a very different stance. For N. G. Politis (1918), the leading Greek folklorist of his age and the generally acknowledged founder of the discipline in Greece, the very suggestion of fatalism was a threat: were the Greeks supposed to submit passively to the occupation of their beloved city, Constantinople? In a resounding rejection, Politis tried to show that the folk traditions of Greece had kept alive the determination to take back that lost pinnacle of their cultural and political universe. For the Greeks, academic and peasant alike, it was the struggle that offered redemption: refracted since the Turkish invasion through a shattered social universe, struggle reappears everywhere – as the relentless need to stand up to one's fellows (Peristiany 1965:14), as resistance to ever encroaching nature (Friedl 1962:75), as a search for allies amongst an often unsympathetic officialdom (Campbell 1964:238–47; Loizos 1975:121), and in general as a commitment to combat everything that would otherwise make life miserable.

The concept of fatalism has resurfaced in anthropological writings about Greece, notably in an evocative ethnography of gender relations in the Thessalian village of Pouri (Handman 1983). Its author directs the brunt of her critical attention to the role of male domination within the community in shaping the entire range of power relations and responses. Thus, an important aspect of her argument concerns the sources and forms of submission. Except in the domain of physical labor, Handman claims that the Pouriani are fatalists about everything. While she accepts that what she has chosen to view as fatalism is the product of a power imbalance, however, she does not acknowledge that the very attribution of fatalism is itself a significant part of the power dynamic, in that outsiders use it as a discursive tool of oppression. Her meticulous ethnographic description nonetheless shows clearly that the Pouriani do not *submit* to superior power; they *resent* its repeated success in imposing itself upon them (Handman 1983:194–5). Thus, the apparent exception of work as the one domain in which the Pouriani do not seem fatalistic simply shows that here alone the authority of others has had a negligible impact, with the result that one hears less grumbling by hindsight. Simple resignation is nowhere apparent within the community; indeed, Handman points out explicitly that laziness is con-

sidered unforgivable. A villager always th   a self-
image as the very paragon of industry, and   ment
only when all efforts have failed. It is for   ndi-
vidual's failures to indolence; and it is always   tri-
bution of blame as fatalism or irresponsibility.

Thus, too, at the level of national history, the   to
the Greeks always seems to have originated from the
nated Greek interests. The Greeks' varied explanations of
stave off Turkish subjugation are always retrospective, while
folklorists' active efforts to reverse the picture are anything but
Not only did the folklorists try to prove that immediately after th
Greeks began to think of the City's recovery (Politis 1918), there
ferentiating the Greek attitude from that of the "fatalistic" Turks;
through a combination of selective editing and effective popularization of
folksong texts – they actively recreated a tradition of popular irredentism in
which the folk tradition was made to cry out for the *re*-establishment of the
Greek state (an entity that only came into existence in the nineteenth
century).

This scholarly use of popular ideology for its own ends locally reproduces a non-Greek orchestration of discourse; this time, however, those in
power are Greeks, drafting the voices of other Greeks into the service of
independence. The Greeks saw clearly that they had to resist the imputa-
tion of fatalism to them by western Europeans; but, in so resisting it, they
played a game not of their own invention. As with brothers in Kabyle
society (Bourdieu 1977:63), the price of a subordinate honor is an encompassing shame: such is the nature of hegemony.

But it is not simply the nationalist folklorists who adopt and recast
popular ideology in this way. Whether or not the ethnographers who describe rural Greeks attribute fatalism to them directly, the discourse of ethnography is part of a larger pattern whereby fatalism – often, for
anthropologists, in the guise of "rule-governedness" – represents both the
description and the justification of hegemony. As conformists to
"custom," peasants are as passive in anthropological as in statist eyes; and
that passivity, through an implicit circular argument, appears to justify
their reduction to homogeneous categories. The instrument of conceptual
control is the pen. Greeks, who historically wielded considerable power as
bureaucrats even when their every decision was subject to the edicts of the
Turkish Sultan, and who looked for learning to a West that professed to
admire their ancestors for the very gift of letters, are again entangled in
multiple ambiguities of identity: they have wielded the pen even as both the
Turks and the West, as well as fate itself, wielded it over them. Bureaucracy in Greece is *ghrafiokratia*, "the rule of places of writing [offices]." To
an anthropology that is beginning to accept the consequences of its own

writerliness, then, the Greeks' historically tempered fascination with the image of the pen offers an especially ironic insight into the status of the writing ethnographer.

Literacy as power

Attributions of fatalism provoke resentment because they imply a passive acceptance of subordinate status. Fate is the symbolic realization of power, and provides a rich source of imagery for expressing it. Greeks express this relationship by conflating fate with power in the most efficacious performative act of all, that of writing. As fate "writes" the irrevocable future, so the Great Powers "program" (*proskhediazoun*) the wars between Greece and her neighbors, and bureaucrats sign documents that cannot be reversed. Power is control of discourse; and the act of writing, itself at once an index and a metonym of the power of the literate over the rest of the world, reorganizes experience to suit the whims of the powerful. The powerless are symbolically illiterate: once again, deficiency defines them.

This symbolic use of the written word has important consequences for epistemology as well. The literalization of oral traditions subjects them to political reinterpretation in any situation of inequality.[10] More than that, however, fiat by writing subordinates the imagery of the folk texts to a larger version of itself, making "oral literature" and "oral" or "folk poetry" (e.g. Finnegan 1970, 1977; Beaton 1980) a pre-historic (and ahistorical) pre-text for histories of national literature defined in strictly literary terms (e.g. Dimaras 1972). We may also again recall Beattie's well-meant proposal to gloss "primitive" with "pre-literate" on the grounds that the latter term is less offensive. In all these formulae – for academic incantations are as formulaic as any – the analysis of culture is exclusively calibrated to a model of literacy (see also Ong 1982:12–13). R. Harris (1980) for linguistics and J. Goody (1977a, 1977b) for anthropology have both robustly denounced the sweeping reduction of alien cultural forms to the diagrammatic habits of a single literate canon.

The literate standard is thus an ethnocentric and anachronistic basis of comparison. Worse, it forces indigenous ideas to *compete* according to extrinsic standards in an unfamiliar arena. Moreover, writing has been associated historically with vast leaps in the reach of centralized power, and provides one of the most potent tropes of domination.[11]

As social dogma, this becomes a self-fulfilling prophecy: as a "fatalist," the victim can be treated as an inferior. The lazy villager fails to live up to social norms; the client succumbs to the bureaucrat's scriptist bullying; and the entire nation is seen as weak and fatalistic by those international giants to whose predestinations it is forced to succumb. Losers deserve to lose. This is also the logic whereby "oral poetry" represents a primitive

version of "literary poetry": its achievements are almost invariably represented as prefigurements of literate brilliance. Herein lies the circularity
of the prophecy: the pen is both the *instrument* and the *image* of social domination at every hierarchical level of everyday experience. Writing is the
objectification of discourse, *Logos*; and *Logos* is the divine source of all
authority, the Word of God.[12] The Word was "in the Beginning [*archē*],"
which is also the name of Authority (*archē*).

In Greece today, the status of literacy coincides with that of "Europe."
Note once again the representational circularity: Europe is both the image
of high culture, and the instrument that imposes it. Sometimes, the Greeks
represent themselves as being European and therefore as possessing literacy. In their ascribed role of living ancestors of the European ideal, they
can deride the Turks as both illiterate and fatalistic, reproducing in the
process some of the favorite jibes of Greek nationalist scholarship. But the
price of claiming literacy must always be the acceptance of European identity; in contexts where Greeks speak of Europe as an inimitable cultural
exemplar, they must themselves be "illiterate." Similar hierarchies,
involving the same pattern of self-deprecation, appear elsewhere: Greeks
often say that (Greek) women are "illiterate" (i.e. in relation to men), and
the fact that women themselves often reiterate such remarks shows how
easily a truly powerful imagery can reproduce itself wherever hierarchy
appears. Its very circularity has practical social consequences: women,
being traditionally discouraged from all but the most rudimentary schooling, can then hardly fail to match the stereotype in some degree (e.g.
Handman 1983:116).

Literacy, then, is a relative good (Herzfeld 1980b:296-8). When Greek
villagers wistfully remark to visiting foreigners that "we gave the light [of
the intellect] to Europe and have lost it ourselves," they *exclude* themselves from "Europe." The shifter-like propensities of this language[13] illustrate the relativities of a power relationship in which literate Europe, by
providing the dominant symbolism of power, thereby also assures its own
encompassing cultural and political domination. In this discourse, moreover, the ethnographer, pen and paper in hand, appears as a representative
of some powerful entity – political, cultural, or religious – that, like the
grim fates themselves, defines ("writes") an impossible perfection while
simultaneously creating the obstacles to its attainment. The ethnographer
is dependent on the goodwill of the local population, and this gives the inhabitants the chance to effect a symbolic reversal of the status relationship.
It can be done with hospitality, accompanied by remarks to the effect that
"you don't own anything here." Or it may be achieved by rougher
methods.

In Rhodes, for example, I found myself translated from the status of pol-
itely respected foreign visitor to that of national outcast at the moment of

the Turkish invasion of Cyprus in 1974.[14] The fact that I seemed to be interested in Turkish elements in the local dialect, and that I was observing life-as-lived rather than simply writing down moral precepts, can hardly have helped. Anthropologists have proposed honor and shame as the key terms for Mediterranean ethnography;[15] yet honor as defined in this literature resides in resisting the penetration by outsiders of domestic conflict (Campbell 1964:326). There is certainly nothing fatalistic about either the hostile or the hospitable reactions that anthropologists have encountered in rural Greek communities; both stances are reciprocities, and as such preclude the fixed inequality that charges of fatalism imply.

The encounter between villager and anthropologist reproduces on a small scale the relations of power in which both are enmeshed. The questions of honor and shame are thus not merely issues in village morality; they also concern the protection and penetration of an intimate view of communal and even national identity. These identities face in two directions at once; they represent a continual tension between self-presentation and self-knowledge. Self-presentation adopts the rhetoric of a cultural perfection already achieved; self-knowledge surveys the range of departures from that perfection in daily social experience. Greece is torn between two opposing stereotypes, the holy one of timeless Hellas and the unclean one derived from the historical *Tourkokratia*. This is a tension between a state of perfection on the one hand, and a post-fall alienation from the idealized collective self on the other. The metaphor of the fall, however, always expresses the power of those who define excellence: perfect understanding – whether as "the structures of the mind" or as "Classical perfection" – is only perfect from a particular point of view. For this reason, I devote the rest of this chapter to a cursory but necessary examination of the principles directing the Eurocentric reading of Greek culture.

History against histories:
the state and the problem of social and cultural difference

In the cosmology of the Edenic fall, knowledge, under the twin forms of history and social experience, results from a flaw. As history, it becomes the legitimation of political and cultural differences; as social experience, it becomes the knowledge of otherness, alienation, estrangement. Each subsequent event is a source of a new imperfection, and an insight into how that flaw came about; and dominating the whole confusion, confirming once and for all time the Greeks' identity as *Romii* (Byzantine and Turkish Christians) rather than as *Ellines* (idealized Hellenes of the Classical past), is the original, catastrophic collapse of 1453. Europe, the product of Classical Greece, is the antithesis of history thus conceived. Greeks today express their ambivalence about their cultural affiliations by a variable use of "Europe" both to include and to exclude themselves. Inclusion alludes to the founding role of Classical Greece in Europe, while exclusion represents the adoption of a self-view as oriental and illiterate.

To this picture we can compare the two kinds of history discussed in the last chapter in connection with the status of anthropology. A progressivist view that heaps success upon success as anthropology throws off the shackles of an outdated and primitive ethnocentrism reproduces its own history of human progress toward a scientistic paradise. It also denies its own historicity; totally predictable progress of this sort lacks any sense of engagement with the sheer difficulty of the enterprise, or with the social context in which it is conceived. It is, in short, a romantic history; and it contrasts with the disjunctive re-course to a history of instructive failures that I advocate here.[16]

Greek usage offers us a revealing ethnographic parallel to this choice between different ways of reading the history of anthropology. This is the contrast between "history in general," an instrument of the state's ideology, and "histories" (*istories*) of social disharmony. In ordinary usage, *istories* are "differences" (*dhiafores*) – quarrels or differences of rank or opinion. (Compare the derogatory English idiom, "telling stories.") History is thus a roster of the consequences of original sin. In the religious sphere, this is predominantly pride, leading to the social need for self-assertion (Campbell 1964:326–7); in the secular, it is the long account of Greek failures to unite against common foes, of villagers' professed inability to achieve cooperation over the use of resources (e.g. McNall 1974:62; but cf. Loizos 1975:99–102), of the absence of trust in all social relations. *This* history is a cause as well as a consequence of each fall; it is made up of the worldly-wise imperfections of *Romiossini* and of *anthropia* (common humanity). It is what makes possible the recognition of a domestic alterity – of Turkish elements in Greek life, for example, or of the supposedly Turkish practices of animal-theft and bride abduction in Crete.

Within the descriptions of Greek life, every encounter between unequal partners reproduces this alterity. Officials deride the Sarakatsani, for example, as *skinites* (tent-dwellers) – a sneer directed at their transhumant mode of life. Nomadism, perhaps through its association with the post-Classical invasions of Europe, has long been considered the antithesis of European life. In Herodotus's account, the Scythians' nomadism defines their alterity: the Classical Athenians, who function in modern Greek nationalist discourse as the *Urtext* for the entire culture and for Europe at large, opposed their jealously guarded autochthony to the nomadic indefinition of the Scythians (Hartog 1980:30). Doubtless reinforced by the experience of local conflict, distrust of nomadism as an "Asiatic" habit subsequently returned to Greece through the channels of neo-Classical ideology. As a result, in the modern Greek struggle to break free of Turkish regional domination, the supposedly ancestral nomadism of the stereotypical Turk – for which he "shares the odium of the Scythian, the Mongol, and the Hun" – could be used to undermine European support for Turkish aspirations (see Toynbee 1922:334). At the same time, it was supremely important for Greek territorial claims to show that the Sarakatsani, whose lifestyle is not at all European when judged in these terms, share fundamental cultural elements with the Classical past. Only internally, in direct dealings between themselves and the bureaucratic state, are the Sarakatsani treated as flawed and *different*: the imagery of the fall is an etiology of *intimate* knowledge, knowledge that one conceals from prying outsiders.

Not surprisingly, in the light of the present argument, the collective situation of the Sarakatsani in the bureaucratic Greek state reproduces the communal status of Sarakatsan women – partners whose sexual incontinence both justifies their enforced passivity and yet also allows the men to boast of their genetically inherited chastity and hence of the moral purity of their families and of the Sarakatsani in general. The Sarakatsani are regarded as untamed and uncivilized, and as requiring a strong guiding hand from the bureaucratic administration. These are the essential lineaments of the symbolism of political domination in Greece – a symbolism in which the search for European identity on the international stage also reinforces patterns of internal differentiation and inequality. As the rather Orwellian (Greek) saying has it: "Not all the fingers are [of] equal [length]." Intimate knowledge again: difference, a domestic weapon, is a public weakness, through which misfortune may renew the original fall again and again; and what anthropologists have called "honor" in the Greek context is the never-ending attempt to arrest that process. For this reason, anthropologists frequently find strong sentiment marshalled against their interest in internal divisions; I well remember assurances that "nothing had happened" in Glendi when I inquired why half the village seemed to be streaming along the street. In fact they were going to witness a fierce confrontation involving about fifteen armed men! *Istories* are the very antithesis of official History.

For history can also be generalized: in Greek, the definite article-prefix (i.e. *i istoria*, "history in general") implies a conflation so total, so schematic, that it is in fact entirely ahistorical. The same argument that excludes certain folksongs from scholarly collections because they are "just about local events" also means that they are not "historical": they do not serve the national entity, but, on the contrary, treacherously reveal its internal fragmentation. Such texts do not even appear in the collections of so-called "humorous" songs (e.g. Politis 1914:244–8), since the aim of that taxon is to generate admiration for the wit of Greek rhymesmiths *in general* rather than for their ability – so crucial to their own understanding of the meaning of the songs[17] – to match words to specifically remembered events, the stuff of which *istories* (rather than *i istoria*) are made. The distinction between "historical" and other traditions, which has been perpetuated in quite recent scholarship on Greek folklore (especially Beaton 1980:151–78), may conceivably be justified on stylistic grounds. But it is not clear whether the distinction corresponds to any perception on the part of the villagers who perform these songs; and the label "historical" certainly traduces indigenous ideas about the nature of events, recognizing as historical only what the academic tradition of the West has already accepted into its own acceptation of history.[18]

The generalization of history is a repression of history: it literalizes irony. It belongs to the class of tropes that includes protestations of discursive innocence (Valesio 1980:48). The generalization of history, its unity, is essential for the generation of a rule-like structure in social life. For history does not just ideologically legitimize the *status quo*; it also generates an atemporality that validates the seeming permanence of the *status quo* (see also Foucault 1971:112). (Note that our own convention permits the removal of the last term in *status quo ante*, thereby obliterating the last faint hint of temporality.) In this regard, history is, like myth in Lévi-Strauss's (1964:24) celebrated definition, a "machine suppressing time": the distinction between myth and history is merely a way of banishing "others" from "history."

Myths of origin, as Drummond (1981) has remarked, closely resemble anthropological theories of ethnogenesis in this respect: they deny historicity to those they regard as the embodiment of otherness. For the academic discipline of folklore, directed as it was by ideological commitments to statism and nationalism, the difficulty was that of marginalizing a cultural entity – the *Volk* – which was also part of the culture of the dominant group. Identity encapsulated alterity: but what if the alterity got out?

History came to the rescue here, by suggesting a golden age since when the purity of the original Hellenic culture had suffered endless contamination and enfeeblement. This was an effective argument because it coincided with the rural population's use of the idealized past as part of its own cosmology: earlier generations were always more peaceful, more prone to neighborly love, purer in mind and spirit (see du Boulay 1974:213, 249; Herzfeld 1983a). Where the Hellenic ideal seemed to coincide with rural mores, as in the matter of female chastity or family solidarity, folklore studies simply expropriated the discourse of village virtue for official purposes. Where, on the other hand, contrary values and actions intruded on this idyll, as when blood feuds and epidemics of animal theft erupted, officialdom took such embarrassments as indices of an *extrinsic, intrusive* influence; and here again the local value system was amenable to such an interpretative strategy.

An excellent example is provided by the institutionalized forms of animal-theft in Crete. While officials are quick to praise the patriotism and pride of the local shepherds, both they and the shepherds themselves conventionally attribute the incidence of rustling to Turkish influence, or describe it as a remnant of the response to Turkish oppression. Thus, the shepherds can go on raiding, taking pride in individual exploits as emblematic of Cretan daring and of the Greeks' unquenchable love of independence; and the officials who have to deal with this discomfiting use of patriotic stereotypes can represent their task as that of eradicating an evil for which the shepherds are not, collectively at least, responsible. The Turks have replaced the serpent in Eden; the job of officialdom is to eradicate it and so wrest back the lost cultural and legal paradise.

Another example, this time from Rhodes, similarly shows how local values, though often pitched against official ones, may nevertheless exploit the rhetoric of official morality and history. Villagers who openly accepted the existence of the evil eye in general, calling it by its Classical name of *vaskania* and legitimizing it still further by pointing to the Virgin Mary as its paradigmatic victim, nevertheless baulked at admitting to the presence of *ghrousouzia* – even though they also told me that this term was synonymous with *vaskania*. A *social* difference explains the distinction: unlike *vaskania*, *ghrousouzia* was person-specific, as well as an element in the assessment of one's covillagers' moral standing, so that to admit its presence was to let me, an outsider, penetrate communal *dhiafores*. One would not be able to identify *ghrousouzia* easily in someone from another community, simply because that person would be insufficiently "known" to permit a reliable moral assessment. The villagers were also thoroughly aware that *ghrousouzia* was a word of Turkish origin,[19] and decried it as "something the Turks are used to." They thus made an explicit connection between the act of moral discrimination between insiders and outsiders on the one hand, and linguistic origins on the other. Nor is this an isolated case: linguists have noted that words of Turkish, Arabic, Slavic, and Albanian origin are often semantically marked, with the foreign importations predominantly less highly valued than their recognizably Greek equivalents (Kazazis 1981b; B. Joseph 1983).

Difference, then, is the mark of otherness, a distinctive *istoria* that flaws the general *istoria* of the *ethnos*. In folklore, it takes the form of treating "variant" texts as "corrupted" or "altered" versions of a putative *Urtext*. Villagers' embarrassment over their non-standard, "uncouth" speech (see also Stirling 1965:283–5, on Turkish parallels) exhibits the same yearning for unity. But this is the attitude of self-display, of conformity to official values; it is not the villagers' only attitude. Indeed, "Turkishness" and *Romiossini* can also be marks of *intimacy*, for what official discourse marks as foreign and evil can, by a characteristic reversal of value, become profoundly familiar and therefore good. Thus, for example, Macedonian villagers use the acknowledged Turkism *moukhabet* to indicate conversation of a kind that they recognize as both "gossipy" and "intimate" (J. K. Cowan, personal communication, 1985).

Such a ready acceptance of the chequered past as the symbolic capital of a divided present fully reverses the statist ideology. More important still, it opposes that ideology, as the official face that denies conviviality and intimacy, to social experience. In everyday life, being morally and culturally perfect is no way to win friends. One who is socially acceptable must be by turns a cuckold (*keratas*), a bastard (*bastardhos*), a trickster (*baghasas*), a dog (*skilos*). All these literally unpleasant designations can be used with affection and admiration – a familiar enough phenomenon to speakers of English – precisely because they denote fellowship in an imperfect world, differences that translate personal history into personal relationships. Indeed, the more intimate the relationship, the ruder the description: in a truly close friendship, one can even call the other *atimos*, "lacking in social worth" – the ultimate denial. To call someone *Khristianos*, "Christian," curiously conveys these intimacies, rather than any literal religiosity: all Christians are heirs to the flawed world in which ordinary decency and fellowship count for more than the posturings of any official ideology. Within an unpenetrated intimacy, sin is a sign of one's basic humanity, however one may represent it to intruders. Seaminess is preferable to seamlessness.

The demands of social life – such as procreation and good fellowship – commit human beings to embodying ancestral sin in their personal actions. These same demands also require frequent violations of secular morality. One should not steal; but how should a proud Cretan shepherd, determined to hold his own in the competition for survival, deal with the theft of some of his best animals? Had the Turks not invaded Crete, perhaps the whole cycle of reciprocal theft would never have taken hold. One should not cast the evil eye; but one does so involuntarily (*athela tou*), as a consequence of the Turkish defilement of Greek culture. One should use "good" language, a pure Greek cleansed of its Turkish elements; but to do so invites ridicule, because one's neighbors know no better and so are full of envy. A man in a Rhodian village regretted the sexual penetration of his wife: he hoped to maintain perfection for longer than society deemed normal or acceptable.[20] He was essentially laying symbolic claim to an Edenic perfection that denied the very fabric of social life; and he found himself, through this and other actions, an outcast in his own village. And so it goes on. To be absolutely virtuous is a denial of humanity, because it denies participation in the tension between otherness and fellowship that is the lot of *Romiossíni* and all humankind. A social anthropology that strives too exclusively for system and rule is apt to forget these essential imperfections of true sociality.

Babel in Europe

The unattainable Eden of the Greeks is that of European culture, defined in terms of a neo-Classical ideal that also, as we have seen, legitimizes anthropology itself. In the next chapter, we shall look at some of the sources of the European image, and at the ways in which it reconciled a notion of transcendant style with the recognition of pervasive internal variation. It was this transcendence that enabled the fractious European nation-states to claim the pinnacle of cultural virtue as their own, despite the extensive and intensive differences that separated them from one another.

It is also the basis of the equation of knowledge with translation offered by perhaps the most eloquent modern apostle of European culture, George Steiner (1975). While Steiner argues that the very necessity of translation is a consequence of Babel – the linguistic fall, as it were – he practically restricts that activity to the confines of European culture. The European ideology that Steiner espouses recasts the biblical story of Babel in such a way that Europe provides a cultural redemption for the consequences of social sin. This reading of Babel replaces moral virtue with cultural virtuosity. It allows knowledge, biblically the fruit of sin, to stand for the new redemption, and a transcended difference to return Europe to an Edenic state of perfection. Steiner's heavy dependence on the biblical metaphor of Babel provides a suggestive mediation in our comparison of Greek cultural ideology and the practices of a discipline often described as the "translation of culture" (e.g. Beidelman 1971; Crick 1976).[21]

In Greece, European identity confronts alterity *in itself*, in the form of all the cultural flaws that I have described in the prevalent stereotypes. This results in a double-sided vision of the collective self that closely approaches the position of the anthropologist caught between two cultures. To some extent, all social groups exhibit a tension between self-display and intimate self-recognition. In Greece, however, this tension came to an extreme. The very negation and Antichrist of Europe – later its "sick man" – had taken over the Greek national character for his own nefarious ends. The Greeks' experience is one of tension between the European and the exotic, an inverted view of the romantic travellers' perspective (on which, see St. Clair 1967; Tsigakou 1981; Constantine 1984), and an internalization of what the anthropologist experiences in the brief passage of fieldwork.

To say that Greece has fallen from European grace is not to deny the relevance of Europe to the national identity. But unlike, say, contemporary France or Germany, Greece was in no position to claim to represent Europe at its best. In a game of power where the first Greek political groups were known as the "French," "English," and "Russian" parties (Couloumbis, Petropulos, Psomiades 1976:19), the definition of perfection was clearly not in Greek hands.

More to the point, nor was the definition of Greekness – which was, after all, a yardstick of cultural self-definition for all of Europe. The early anthropologists sought to define their own cultures on the basis of a romanticized heritage of Classical Greekness by comparison with which the exotic cultures were merely savage. The modern Greeks – caught between the condescending familiarity of Europe and the humiliation of their internalized alterity – were, on the contrary, corrupt deviants from that pristine state of cultural grace. In their endlessly attributed imperfections, they are still atoning politically for a fall defined as such by the hard hand of occidental power. The uncertainties and ambiguities of Greek identity decorate the reverse face of a coin that bears on its obverse the imperial heads of folklore and anthropology.

3　Aboriginal Europeans

Age-old Europe?

The image of fallen Hellenism separates a time of historical travail from a timeless past glory. As a tale of lost innocence, it reproduces both the corrupted *Urtexte* of the folklorists, and the grand mental schemata that structuralists discern behind the untidy accretions of conscious thought. The thesis of a Hellenism fallen from grace incorporates both the "holy" and the "polluted" visions of modern Greece. It portrays the aboriginal embodiment of the European ideal fallen to the evil corruption of anti-Europe. Like all such historicist visions, as we saw in the last chapter, it actually represents a present divested of time; the terms of the relevant symbolic opposition are eternity and history, not two phases of human development (see also Ardener 1971c:231–2). The supposedly historical *loss* of culture is transmuted into a synchronic *lack* of culture. But both perspectives, by treating the modern Greeks either as living ancestors or as wretched orientals, deny them the absolute essence of culture itself.

Literacy is the hallmark of culture conceived in these Eurocentric terms; and literacy confers effective power at many levels. Although rural Greeks satirize the literate, and regard them as deceivers of the poor, such attitudes are at base a grudging recognition of the power that literacy confers; they may also signal the emergence of a clear class differentiation (Meraklis 1984:73–4). In addition to illiteracy, nomadism and uncouthness are attributes of a stereotypical Turkishness that marks an absence of what enables a European to live, as Greeks say, "like a human being" (*san anthropos*); and these hackneyed traits legitimize the power of those who define the content of the national (or European) culture. It is judged on the basis of supposedly objective criteria of taste – of *discrimination* – that actually represent the political success of one group or society in enforcing its hegemony over another (see Bourdieu 1984:475–81). In this sense charges of fatalism, too, are attributions of cultural failure. Fatalism conveniently appears to explain surrender to totalitarian power, which creates it as a *means* to that end (see also Innis 1951:129).

All these traits are signs of an alleged incompleteness, of a denial of

49

people's human worth by outsiders who have arrogated to themselves the authority to define what human worth is (see also Freire 1970:41–2). Fatalism, for example, represents an absence of self-regard and initiative in a (Eurocentric) world view that demands these traits. Absences of this sort, *attributed* (and therefore *passive*) traits of an Other already defined by its passivity, are *actively constituted* by the discourse of the collective cultural self. As such, they include the incompletenesses that anthropologists, who by and large belong to culturally Eurocentric elites, attribute to societies lacking the western modes of political organization (see Clastres 1974; Kuklick 1984); the laziness that colonists thought they discerned in native populations; or the recurrently perceived fatalism of the oriental world at large.

The issue here is not the boasts of a particular cultural tradition, but social and cultural discourse in general as an exercise of power. Western empires were by no means unique in adopting the device of fatalism to brand the alterity of conquered peoples. After the annexation of Manchuria in 1931, for example, the Japanese remarked on the Lamaist "resignation" and lack of a "sense of self-interest" of their newly conquered Mongol subjects (*Asahi* 1932:148). When fatalism appears to play a role in anthropological theory, as in the predictive idiom of rules and structures, it always does so in regard to the ethnographic subject, never to the self-perception of the observer. Incompleteness is always the mark of the other, even at the individual level. In a comparison of rather different scale, the ultimate insult of the Greek villager is to accuse another of *lacking* social worth, and more particularly of refusing all social responsibility. What a Greek peasant says in order to gain social advantage is, at least in this respect, significantly similar to the discourse of cultural contempt amongst nations.

The rôle of fatalism in the ethnography of Greece is similarly that of an *attributed* trait. As Politis pointed out, explanations based on the concept of fate were always cited after the events in question. The Gospels "wrote" the fall of cities to the Turkish infidel, for example, but we only know this from poems and legends that appear to have gained currency *after* each collapse.[1] Moreover, other oracles and omens also portended future liberation, especially that of Constantinople (see also Clogg 1985). All these refusals to submit to destiny were *active attempts at collective self-assertion*.[2]

This is a major departure from the fatalistic stereotype, and it calls for elaboration. Unlike their European patrons, the Greeks were not seeking a return to the Classical *past*; they were instead seeking inclusion in the European *present*. The cultural policies of the Greek state appeared to outsiders to represent a sweeping concession to western European sensibilities: the Greeks had meekly submitted to the demand that they act out the role of living ancestors to the European cultural tradition. From within, however, matters looked quite different.

Greek leaders were not necessarily any more willing in practice to surrender politically to the dictates of Europe than they were in daily matters to accept those of fate, although both the Great Powers and fate have always furnished useful retrospective explanations when their attempts to assert an independent stance failed. While the Greek elite may have adopted the neo-Classical codes in language and other cultural domains for internally repressive ends, they also deployed these same codes in an active and continual struggle to wrest the definition of Greek culture from the hands of foreigners.

The "language question": context and dependence

This struggle is especially evident on the all-important linguistic front, where the extreme archaizers – who had hoped to reintroduce Classical Greek in its fifth century B.C. Attic form – had already met defeat by the time the new state came into being. Had they succeeded, it would have been far easier for European critics to represent the Greeks as the living ancestors that they refused to become. The modified purism that did triumph deflected most attempts at imposing the Classical Attic language by pre-empting the middle ground (Babiniotis 1979). Syntactically as well as in the use of extensive calquing, this language owed much to western European models as well as to the Classical tongue (for early accounts see Tozer 1869,II:115–17; *Spectator*, Nov. 3, 1900; and see Mackridge 1985:308, 312–13). Educated urban Greeks, around the middle of last century, even tried to introduce the French *u* as a means of refining the language while supposedly also restoring it to a better approximation of its ancient sound. The use of a French model illustrates their desire for inclusion in modern Europe, their antiquarian pretext the price of that goal. Europe was now the absolute measure of excellence (Tozer 1869,II:116; see also Burn 1944:28):

The progress which has been made in improving this language by eliminating all Turkish words, expurgating barbarous forms, and enriching the vocabulary, is truly wonderful; and there can be little doubt that it will ultimately be made an admirable vehicle of thought, from its plastic nature, its capability of forming new words to express new ideas by derivation and composition, and the resources it has to draw from in the ancient tongue.

Given such humiliating condescension, it is hardly surprising that Greek scholars gave high priority to the creation of a language that would at one and the same time prove to be an indisputable product of Classical erudition and yet also a ringing announcement of the only true kind of European modernity – independence *from* Europe. This language would have to shed the dependence on context that marked the oral language (*romeika*) of the people. Once again we see that context-dependence is a mark of subordinate otherness, and thus both indexes and models actual political dependence. As long as language lacked clarity of definition, it could not be used for scientific purposes. By appealing to the existence of a Classically trained European intelligentsia, moreover, Greek scholars were able to represent the purist language as a means of entering that international arena, arguing (as one university professor assured me during the period of the military regime) that non-Greek scholars in any humanistic field could be expected to understand *katharevousa* since they would surely know ancient Greek.

By placing *katharevousa* on this plane, Greek scholars treated it as supracultural: it was to serve as a completely unambiguous code for international scholarly communication. In other words, it was to be a *context-free code* – an imaginary construct as far as ordinary language is concerned, but one for which science has always yearned. In Bernstein's (1971) terms, *katharevousa* was to be an "elaborated code"; this relegated ordinary spoken Greek to the level of a "restricted code," one that depended heavily on contextual cues for interpretation. The distinction is essentially one that separates educated or, especially, scientific language from what is used in everyday situations. Just as Bernstein has been criticized for suggesting that his so-called restricted codes were unsuitable vehicles for abstract thought (Labov 1972; but cf. Threadgold 1986:25), however, so too the assumption that the ordinary Greek tongue could not adequately express the precision of science and philosophy must be seen as a consequence of the elite view that the educated are in some way themselves independent of their context. The notion of the abstract anthropological theorist whose ideas rise above all considerations of ideology or social setting is equally close to Eurocentric statism in its separation of scholar from informant, "us" from "them," Eurocentric intellectuals from preliterate tribespeople.

From the standpoint of the Eurocentric Greek intelligentsia at the time of early statehood, demotic (vernacular) Greek thus became another instance of cultural incompleteness, and one that required drastic corrective action. To the extent that the leadership succeeded in promoting *katharevousa*, the romantic vision of a scientific state would be matched by a scientific national language. Language, no longer dependent on the exigencies of context, would now become an absolute and precisely calibrated tool. *Katharevousa* would be the means of liberating the Greeks, not only from the cultural corruption that was the legacy of the Turkocracy, but also from the shackles of their humiliatingly dependent status in the European community. The projected freedom of the language from its erstwhile dependence on context would reproduce the Greeks' liberation from their dependence on the condescension of the European Powers.

By identifying with the absolute values of European romanticism, Greek scholars sought to gain admittance to Europe as cultural as well as political equals. They therefore both condemned the demotic language as a Turkish abomination and later (especially during and after the Civil War) as a Slavic invention, and at the same time continued to tolerate its use as a means of blocking the majority of the populace from access to the power that literacy confers (see Sotiropoulos 1977, 1982; Mouzelis 1978:136). They tried to make Greece more independent of Europe, and yet more acceptable to it, by denying at the level of state cultural policy the same parochiality and ephemerality in which they kept the populace at home. *Katharevousa* and the several other neo-Classical codes (notably in architecture) did not represent a passive acceptance of foreign neo-Classicism; on the contrary, it was an attempt to take internal and external control in a game where the definition of Greek culture was still largely in foreign hands.

Hellas, philhellenism, and the simplicity of the past

Greek neo-Classicism was thus an attempt at *reclamation*. If the European heritage was truly grounded in Greek philosophy and art, the Greeks of today argued, they had an ancestral, participatory right to the new modernity. As Greeks first and foremost, they were also Europeans; for the emergent ideology of European identity demanded that to be European in the modern sense, one also had to be a loyal member of a modern nation-state: the distinctiveness of each European culture was the guarantee of the collectively European character of them all (e.g. Guizot 1856; Cuoco 1924; see also Chabod 1964:137–8).

This idea, which contrasted the European cultures against the constructed homogeneity of "oriental" culture (see Said 1978; Kabbani 1986:10), is dramatically exemplified by the paradoxical emergence of nationalistic folklore as a discipline that symbolized a collective European identity (Cocchiara 1952:303). Anthropology has meanwhile perpetuated a similar division through its creation of a discrete category of "complex societies" (e.g. Banton 1966); in Europe, moreover, the barbarian may now sometimes come from the West instead of the East, as the commercial and homogenizing American of European popular fancy (e.g. Le Lannou 1977:81–2) and – note the convergence again – of anthropology (notably Lévi-Strauss 1974, 1985:ch. 21).[3]

Any attempt by the Greeks to gain admittance to a Europe thus defined had to rest both on national individuality and on the purity of the people's European heritage. But the oriental taint precluded the second part of this claim, while the exclusion of Classical Greece from the *modern* European cultural community appeared to present another insuperable difficulty. Thus, for example, the French politician François Guizot, who perhaps more than any other writer (and in more Gallocentric fashion) articulated the European ideology, explicitly consigned the Classical past to the rank of undifferentiated culture. As such, it was therefore ancestral but inferior to the modern western world (Chabod 1964:143). Ancient Greece, argued Guizot, while undoubtedly a great civilization – as indeed were the India and China of Guizot's own day – imposed a general conformity that must seem repressive to the modern western sophisticate. Guizot (1856:32–7) also maintained that the absence of alternative social forms caused the eventual collapse and stagnation of all the great civilizations of antiquity (1856:36) – an interesting precursor of Lévi-Strauss's cybernetic view of the history of human societies (1966; Charbonnier 1969), as well as a pre-text for the west European view that modern Greece, as the reincarnation of its Classical forebears, had scanty claims on a truly modern European identity (on Guizot, see D. Johnson 1963).

In Greece, local claims to European identity clashed with European claims of Greek otherness. The commonly held nineteenth-century view of Greece as an outpost of the Orient (or as a mere survival of the Classical age) clashed with the Greeks' own aspirations for recognition as a modern European nation. One possible resolution, suggested at least by analogy in Guizot's treatment of the ancient past, lay in presenting Greece as fixed in time before modern history, the definitive locus of European *aboriginality*.

The philhellenes, for example, western admirers of Classical culture whose political support was essential to the establishment of an independent modern Greek state, claimed the Greeks for the European past. They saw the Greece of their own time, not as an integral part of *modern* Europe, but as a passive reincarnation of its ancient self, and usually as a not terribly felicitous reincarnation at that (see St. Clair 1972). They somewhat resembled those Europeans who viewed India as the fossil of a society thought to have been internally uniform from the first (see Dumont 1975:51, 140). Above all, they viewed modern Greece as an *imperfect* reincarnation – an inevitable consequence of dependence upon a context defined by others. Context-dependency is itself a form of necessary imperfection when the *political* context treats definition as absolute, or defines culture as its own "high" culture (see also Wagner 1975).

The French writer Houssaye, more sympathetic than many better-known and self-styled philhellenes, captures the unfairness of it all (1879:131–2):

The French have the fault of forever basing their judgments on comparison, never forgetting Paris, whether they be in Athens, Cairo, or Lisbon. It has been said that they expect to find the café anglais in some oasis of the Great Desert, the Variétés theatre amidst the izbas of a Cossack village, and commissions of parliamentary inquiry amongst the Hottentots. Greece, more than any other country, is the victim of this feature of the French national character, for in Greece it is not just with modern France, but also with ancient Greece that comparison is forced upon the attention of the tourist, of the writer, or the politician. Greece has to suffer from a too distant antiquity and a too recent rebirth. People are astonished that Athens is not still the Athens of Pericles spreading civilization around herself, and that

Greece is not already a little France, with France's industry, commerce, agriculture, activity, and wealth. Hence the severe judgments, the unfair criticisms, the undeserved complaints.

Visitors to Greece expected an antique world, equipped with all modern conveniences, and inhabited by humble natives ready to accept every criticism of their failure to measure up to expectations. Having earlier remarked that "it was fashionable in 1825 to be a philhellene, [but] in 1875 it is good taste to be a turcophile," Houssaye satirizes the idiom of this prejudice (1879:147):

Athens is expected to become a little Paris, but people wish that Constantinople should remain Constantinople. Gas lamps in Stamboul! that would be a character slur; but Athens should be lit by electricity. In Turkey, dilapidation is beauty, ugliness picturesque, neglect local color, laziness dignity, indifference fatalism, tyranny authority.

Greece, delivered from its oriental yoke, was a child of its antique past, one that had failed to mature in the manner of the West. And in such a child, fatalism was so unforgivable that it had to be attributed instead to wilful "indifference."

Even the sympathetic Houssaye, however, although he describes the Greeks as a "free and proud people who think, work, and are ready to fight" (1879:134), ultimately succumbs to the prevailing perspective. Writing of the folksongs, he observes, "Grammar would find a good deal to criticize in them, as would good taste. ... They are not works of art at all. They are the tears, the smiles, and the sighs of a people" (1879:174). In an age that extolled personal genius and authorship, and that lauded elegant language over the merely direct expression of emotion (premonitions of the restricted code again!), this was a thoroughly backhanded compliment. It also shows that the standards of excellence were those of codified systems – in this case grammar, a curiously bureaucratic criterion for poetry. Like the English folklorist J. C. Lawson (1910:106; see also Tozer 1869,II:237), Houssaye apparently saw in the folk traditions something that predated even the great literary traditions of Classical times, surviving intact despite its elaboration by the great Attic poets. These traditions therefore belong to a lower social environment than the masterpieces of Classical or modern European literature; and such few more recent cultural influences as they showed lay in "a tone of exaggeration which is Oriental rather than Hellenic" (Tozer 1869, II:235). The peasant cultures of both ancient and eastern worlds are inferior to modern sophistication.

The class-conscious survivalism was also able to draw on the racial anthropology then dominating European thought.[4] As one traveller-anthropologist observed (Mahaffy 1913:7):

A long and careful survey of the extant literature of ancient Greece has convinced
me that the pictures usually drawn of the old Greeks are much idealized; and that
the real people were a very different – if you please, of a much lower – type.

The decay of romanticism thus served the Greeks ill; while survivalist
ideas, replete with their implications of cultural hierarchy, still infuse the
discourse of European attitudes to Greece. Prominent among these is the
conviction that ancient Greece was actually a much simpler place than its
European heirs. That simplicity, marred now and held forever in place by
the oriental taint of Turkish culture, was to be found still in the Greek land
and its people themselves. In commenting upon an age when the term "aboriginal" was already in general use for the inhabitants of distant and exotic
places, it may seem inappropriate to speak of the European aboriginality of
Greece. But collective, passive aboriginality was what the West discerned
there, in contrast to its own individualistic and modern *originality*.

Aboriginality and sophistication

The assumption of an aboriginal, prehistoric European identity persists in
quite recent ethnological work on Greek themes. A juxtaposition of older
and newer writings about Greece will show just how entrenched that ideology has been. For example, a frequently viewed and cited ethnographic
film of Greek island life, *Kypseli: Women and Men Apart – A Divided
Reality* (Hoffman, Cowan, Aralow 1974), opens with the proposition that,
at different periods, settlers came to the volcanic Cycladic island of Thira
(Santorini) "to weave a continuous thread of European tradition." Thira
must have seemed an especially good subject for this kind of treatment. It
boasts antiquities that include extensive witness to the cultural influence of
Crete during the Minoan period, archaeological remains from other major
phases of the area's cultural history, and a domestic architecture that furnishes a dramatic setting for the villagers' social life.

Kypseli also invites treatment as a serious ethnography to the same extent
as any book. It presents an overview of village life, but builds it around
several central themes. These include gender role differentiation, the symbolic analysis of time and space, and a fairly orthodox structuralist methodology that organizes the material in terms of a symbolic binarism keyed by
the fundamental opposition between men and women. These themes are all
closely interwoven in the film with the central thesis that island life represents a cumulative reinforcement of values rooted in the European past,
particularly those concerned with gender, dating back to the time of the
Minoans who created the "earliest" European civilization. Since Thira's
culture is made up of the "same traditions" as those that "have also formed
the rest of European culture," a delicately antinomic dissection of Thira's

value system will give us the clue to our own origins. That the film's concern is indeed with origins should be clear from the claim that the village of Kypseli represents "a less sophisticated outgrowth of the same heritage that has produced our complex cities."

Challenging though these assertions may be as ethnography, their interest is especially enhanced by the attempt to demonstrate the value of a structuralist approach, in which structure ultimately corresponds to aboriginal European forms of thought. Structuralist methods have rarely been brought to bear on the supposed cradle of European civilization; and the result, set out in film, is a dramatically inadvertent demonstration of how European, and Eurocentric, structuralism is. For when this approach is directed to a society claimed as the embodiment of the European quintessence, it sounds disturbingly like the rhetoric of romantic nationalism: a simple past has generated the present complex modernity, which "we" represent in its fullest flowering while denying its bucolic survivors any independent historical status of their own.

The concern to demonstrate the European essence of rural Mediterranean culture is not new. To understand it more fully as it appears in the film *Kypseli*, we can compare its presence there with its very different embodiment in one of the canonical written ethnographies. In his *Honour, Family, and Patronage*, Campbell (1964:34, 185) provides a broad context for notions of time and blood relationship among the Sarakatsani, one of Greece's most isolated and romanticized populations. Although he cites Onians's *The Origins of European Thought*, he does not thereby imply that the Sarakatsani represent an arrested earlier stage in the development of a distinctively European culture. Indeed, like Friedl, Campbell declines to enter the lists for or against the ever tender issue of continuity with the Classical Greek past. It is true that other writers – notably Walcot (1970) and Blum and Blum (1970) – have cheerfully adapted these ethnographers' materials to an uncritically survivalist argument. For Walcot in particular, the survivalist argument permits the use of parallels from *any* Mediterranean culture, not merely Greece alone, with Classical antiquity. Such arguments sail close both to Greek nationalist folklore and to the structuralist survivalism of *Kypseli*, but they make use of ethnographies intended to support very different ends. Before returning to *Kypseli* and to our exploration of the conceptual links between structuralism and nationalism, it would therefore be helpful to examine Campbell's study of the Sarakatsani in more detail, in order to show how and why these subsequent expropriations have obfuscated its peculiar achievement in bringing the tools of social anthropology to bear on a European society.

Campbell (1964:6) describes the Sarakatsani as "a people without history." At the level of nationalist discourse, they are denied any control over their own historical status; history itself is a property that those who

exercise power jealously guard and hedge around with rules for its ownership (Appadurai 1981).[5] Campbell's ironic observation, which could easily
be misrepresented in literal terms, implies rather a resistance to such officially inspired attitudes. He explicitly acknowledges that folksongs
remind the Sarakatsani of the heroes they contributed to the Greek Revolution as well as of local events that simply "do not belong" to history.[6] It
appears that Sarakatsan insistence on the qualities of their own revolutionary heroes represents a continual attempt to gain admittance to the national
entity on the limited terms made available by officially inspired schooling,
much as the Greek nationalists struggled to win their way into Europe.
Campbell's characterization of the Sarakatsani is thus clearly far more of an
allusion to the absence of written records, and to the official control of what
little is recorded about the Sarakatsan past, than an attempt to exclude
them from any participation in historically recorded events. Doubtless, his
initial choice of a "people without history" reflects the preoccupations of
his discipline and his teachers (see Campbell 1964:vi–vii). But he does in
fact discuss the historical memories and stereotypes that Sarakatsani entertain about their own heroic past; the supposed ahistoricity of the Sarakatsani is a product of the same semi-official exploitation as their helpless
insertion into a pervasive and unequal system of patronage.

A closely related topic is the treatment of kinship. Two partially opposed
accounts emerge. The foreign scholar, Campbell, while acknowledging the
strong preference that Sarakatsani show for agnatic kin in specific types of
situations, treats Sarakatsan kinship as based primarily on the cognatic
kindred (1964:36–58), while most Greek scholars insist that the Sarakatsani are organized in segmentary patrilineages. Campbell's detailed argument for the cognatic kindred places the Sarakatsani firmly within official
and ecclesiastical norms. It also adumbrates Sarakatsan social life to a European prototype that contrasts strikingly with the Africanist studies written
by his most immediate associates and teachers. Campbell's study is modelled on Evans-Pritchard's *The Nuer* (1940), both textually and methodologically, to a significant degree.[7] Thus, Campbell's subtly nuanced
treatment of agnatic kinship among the Sarakatsani stands out all the more
strongly. It represents an intellectual resistance to the temptation to represent the Sarakatsani as Nuer who had somehow wandered into Europe.

Greek writers insist that the Sarakatsani are basically patrilineal in their
social organization; and they also claim that the Sarakatsani possess a
history of their own, which is a special refraction of the national history of
Greece. Indeed, Garoufas, himself a Sarakatsanos, maintains that the difficulty is that "none of the researchers [who have previously studied Sarakatsan ethnology] was a Sarakatsanos" (1982:11). Kavadias (1965:149–51), in
the most detailed Greek account, presents the Sarakatsani as possessing a
classically segmentary, agnatic social organization, and this dimension has

been stressed anew in more recent publications (Garoufas 1982; Meraklis 1984:59–67; both these studies omit any mention of Campbell's still untranslated study). This view exoticizes the Sarakatsani in specifically Greek terms, giving them an "odd" kinship system that links them with the ancient past; Kavadias (1965:175) says explicitly that "the peculiarities of their family structure and their kinship system have been influenced by the Hellenic value systems of antiquity and of Byzantium." In short, the Sarakatsani are truly Greek, but, like the heroes of the struggle for independence, do not live in the modern world defined by bureaucratic and ecclesiastical definitions of social relations. They are "Greek others," conscripted into a struggle for national distinctiveness. Campbell's account, by contrast, shows that it is possible to study a European population anthropologically without denying its European character or even making an issue of it. His Sarakatsani are "other Europeans."

An anthropology that "comes part-way home" (Cole 1977) shares some history with its subjects, much as its colonial forebears did. Campbell's achievement lies in using the techniques of *The Nuer* to chart a delicate course between the Scylla of official romanticism and the Charybdis of anthropological exoticism, and thereby to bring ethnographically grounded critical insight to bear on historically self-conscious Europe. What emerges is a disjuncture, not an identity, between reified statist history and the social and cultural self-image of the Sarakatsani.[8]

The argument of *Honour, Family, and Patronage* must, then, be distinguished with care from the exoticism that the book itself philosophically opposes. In perhaps the most extreme case, the film *Kypseli* grasps a superficially similar rhetoric of European quintessence but reifies it as the explicit fulcrum of the entire presentation. Campbell's account remains faithful to a tradition of major emphasis on ethnographic description (on which, see Kuper 1985:528), and takes a cautious position in the historical debate about origins. By contrast, Susannah Hoffman's goal in *Kypseli* is more determinedly theoretical, and seeks a level of explanation that is at once both historical and structural (see also Hoffman 1976b, for amplification). This may seem paradoxical. But Hoffman, the anthropologist whose original fieldwork provided the basis for the film, seeks therein to deploy a structuralist methodology in order to explore gender relationships. She organizes these relationships as a series of congruent symbolic oppositions, in which the villagers seem entrapped.[9] She then avers that the structural blueprint is a part of our own, European heritage; it is thus a history that we need to know in order to achieve liberation from inherited sexual stereotypes. And it is here that her attempt to equate structure with aboriginality points up the Eurocentric character of a theoretical framework chosen for its universalistic goals. The equation of universal truth with European identity is disturbingly close to Guizot: "European civilization entered, we may say, into *eternal verity*, in the plan of Providence; it walks in the paths of God. This is the rational principle of its superiority" (Guizot 1856:41; my italics). Differentiation is superiority. The structural survivalism of *Kypseli* evokes the strength and the complexity ("sophistication") of an industralized West in contrast to a peasant Other who is constrained by simplicity and social fractiousness.

Similarly, when Lévi-Strauss argues (1963a) that conscious models are impoverished ones, he means *their* conscious models. *Our* models, being procedural (active) rather than processual (passive), must be made as *conscious* as possible. We can turn the structuralist mode of analysis on itself:

THEY	WE	
+	−	*unconscious*
−	+	*conscious*

This is Guizot's argument in disguise. *Their* conscious models simplify the processual complexity of which they are the unwitting bearers, and that only *our* minds can, procedurally, appreciate. It is an echo of an old claim: that *our* political commonality and cultural differences are the object of conscious enrichment ("democracy" – a concept that the conservative Guizot regarded as a crucial European achievement), whereas *their* egotism and cultural homogeneity – the hallmarks of the savage – make them the passive servants of circumstance and system:

THEY	WE	
−	+	
similar	different	*culture*
different	similar	*society/polity*

All this emerges with startling clarity when Hoffman tries to conjoin ahistorical structuralism with a supposedly historical argument about the relationship between the observed village culture of Thira and that of her own, Euro-American world. She explicitly declares that she seeks to locate Kypseli in "European" culture. She then, however, negates the sense of "sameness" that this tactic produces, by representing the villagers as unsophisticated survivors from an outdated past. They turn out to be unwitting automata, guided by structures that we share with them but that we are able, through our conscious wit, to transcend. Her epistemological tactic is to reverse what she apparently sees as the ahistoricity of previous ethnographic research. In this, her stance harmonizes with Davis's far from structuralist call for greater historical awareness, and betrays similarly survivalist assumptions. But she deploys history to very different ends: she identifies gender bias in Kypseli as the survival of more primitive values in her own culture, and thus as something to be objectified as a prelude to its eradication.

If, then, Hoffman's effort appeals to history, it is still not historical. This arises, in large measure, from her attempt to conjoin history with generalizations derived from structuralism. One of the commonest complaints against structuralism is that, like nationalism, it *suppresses* history. A discursively historical progression whose residue is "traditional peasants" pursuing an "age-old" lifestyle – a lost Eden, not so much prehistoric as outside history – *denies* historicity by telescoping a present identity with that of an identical past. It represents the Greek village as aboriginally European, and therefore as neither distinctive nor European in any modern sense at all. By bolting the generalized Greek village that emerges to a deterministic version of structuralism – one that makes all aspects of village life symbolize the male-female opposition in a set of immovable, cast-iron correlations – Hoffman has locked the people of the village out of historical time.

Eurocentrism and structuralism: a continuity?

The significance of *Kypseli* is thus in part its evocation of an ideology that we can identify in nineteenth-century romantic philhellenism and twentieth-century structuralism alike. Both pursue original forms; in *Kypseli*, these forms come together as a single configuration – aboriginal Europe. The effect is to deny that the villagers belong to Europe at all, or at least to modern Europe. The argument belongs to the philhellenic ideology, which expropriated ancient Greek culture as a timeless heritage for the values of an essentially bourgeois nationalism. In the eighteenth century, Winckelmann presented (Classical) Greek art in a fashion that allowed it to represent "the supposed *immutability* of morals and of the nation" (Mosse 1985:14; my italics). Yet Winckelmann never even went to Greece, despite his frequently expressed intentions (see Constantine 1984:125). Modern Greece, as so often in the halcyon days of Classical travel, was simply shoved aside. Western European historiography could treat all recent Greek history as a triumph of episodic oriental backwardness over the timeless Classical heritage.

Insofar as the traces of the ancient culture survived in Greece, if the arguments of Victorian philhellenism and *Kypseli* alike are to be believed, they did so mechanically. Greece had returned to what Lévi-Strauss calls a

"cold" state of society (1966; and in Charbonnier 1969:33). Greek nationalists, by treating the "foreign" Byzantine court and church as obstacles that
the Hellenic spirit successfully surmounted, preserving its wisdom in the
minds of the rural folk (Zambelios 1859), tried to champion the essential
modernity of the modern Greek state; but their dependence on the priority
of Classical culture continually subverted their claims on a central cultural
role in Europe. The cultural marginality of Greece persisted, reflected to
this day in its status in anthropological theory. In *Kypseli*, the ideological
parallel between philhellenism and structuralism is finally realized, as both
banish their object to a timeless past.

In this rhetoric, Greek culture reproduces a state of pure structure,
equivalent to the aboriginal and preconscious forms of thought (Said
1975:327):

> Structure is nonrational: it is not thought thinking about anything, but thought
> itself as the merest possibility of activity. It can offer no rationale for its presence,
> once discovered, other than its primitive *thereness*. In a most important way, then,
> as an ensemble of interacting parts, structure replaces the Origin with the play of
> orderly relationships.

The object of structural analysis is revealed as the essence of aboriginality.
The much vaunted emphasis on synchronic at the expense of diachronic
analysis threatens merely to replace one mode of historicism with another.
Kypseli superficially seems to furnish the historical sequence that conventional structuralism so often lacks. In the end, however, its historicity is
merely rhetorical, since its primary commitment is to a structuralist model
of the aboriginal European mind.

In *Kypseli*, the key male-female opposition – while oddly but significantly treated as a European rather than as a panhuman theme – transcends
the diachronic roster of invasions from East and West. Only the irrepressible presence of the villagers themselves undermines their banishment to a
time before time: the woman who remarks on the photographing in
process; the churches said to be segregated "even more rigidly than the
houses" as though like the latter the churches also belonged to the local-
level order alone; a shot of cupping, a cure (see Blum and Blum 1970:150–
5) that the film much too vaguely yokes to the general observation that
women deal with the occult; a washday scene linked to solemn allusions to
female pollution; shots of old women addressed to the crudest clichés in the
commentator's remark, "Some women carry the Devil inside their bodies.
They can give the evil eye . . ." (Can men not do so? They can in most
Greek villages; if they cannot do so here, the argument for Kypseli's
typicality collapses [see also Allen in Allen *et al.* 1978:132].)

But most telling of all is the contrast between the initial shot of a *briki*
(coffee-pot) to illustrate the extraordinary contention that the villagers

have "a set of notions that *tells them how and when to utilize the objects that make up their lives*." This bit of structuralist orthodoxy, in which the organization of ideas directs the actions of unresisting subjects, represents the aboriginal state of the European mind – the "*unobjecting* affirmation of its own originality" (Said 1975:327; my italics). It contrasts dramatically with the conclusion, in which we are told: "To a degree, *all of European culture participates* in these same assumptions." Note the reproduction here of the oxymoronic "*participant* observation," Europe looking in on something that it both includes *within* itself and yet also relegates to a position *below* itself: this again is the guiding Mind of the nineteenth-century folklorists. Yet the makers of the film defend it precisely as "an attempt to dredge up assumptions about life from the core of Euroamerican culture" (in Allen *et al.* 1978:141). *Kypseli*, intended as a critique of male domination, finally also falls prey to irony, by reproducing an almost identical hegemony at the international level: the film represents an oft conquered populace as passive victims of its own cognition, in contrast to the wilful but more actively – participatively – intelligent West.

The irony is instructive. As we shall see, the Greek stereotypes of womanhood – including the potential disobedience of all women to which *Kypseli* alludes – reproduce the popular stereotypes of the oppressed Greek. Is it the men or the women who demand a display of sexual passivity from young married women (cf. Campbell 1964:276–7)? Whose stereotype is under discussion? And, concurrently, whose interests are served, what hierarchy of values is fortified, when structure is seen to dominate the "less sophisticated" objects of an exercise that occasionally – though almost as though by accident – lets them speak and gesticulate for themselves? Does this exercise offer any hope for the women of Kypseli itself? And if it does not offer them hope, to what superior advantages can their western counterparts appeal, if the claim of a common European identity is valid?

That claim is initially disarming, just as – on the grand scale of cultural relativism – are all declarations of panhuman commonality (see Fabian 1983:62). In practice, the evocation of commonality is a rhetorical strategy.[10] It actually creates cultural and moral distance: the aboriginally European Greek village is not, in any modern sense, European at all. It is presumably a sense of this problem that has prompted some sociologists to attack the anthropological practice of studying small, often out-of-the-way communities (Vlachos in Dimen and Friedl 1976:277; Mouzelis 1978:68). Friedl (1976:277–8) has persuasively argued that typicality is not the issue (see also Zonabend 1985:35 on the same issue in the ethnography of France). In a sense, however, it is very much so; the question, however, has to be rewritten. It is no longer, "Is this community typical?" or even "What does it mean to call this community typical?" Those are strictly statistical questions (see Clarke 1968:29). It is a question of discursive history:

whose interests are served by representing this community as typical, and what must it be typical *of* (Greece? the Mediterranean?) in order for those interests to be served? We thus return to the curious discursive formation of "Mediterraneanism."

Mediterraneanists and the Mediterranean: the dishonor of national shame

"Mediterraneanism" is a term that I quite deliberately offer on the model of historicism, positivism, and Said's (1978) equally ironical coinage of "Orientalism." Both terms suggest the reification of a zone of cultural difference through the ideologically motivated representation of otherness. The creation of a Mediterraneanist "subspecialty" (Gilmore 1982) affords a clear political identity to its practitioners within the discipline (Galt 1985), but it also legitimizes the representation of the ancestral core of Europe as a sufficiently exotic subject of anthropological analysis. But folklore scholarship, unlike anthropology, was an attempt to *resist* exoticism, in Greece and elsewhere in the Mediterranean. The emergence of a Mediterranean focus in anthropology thus generated a new symbolic antinomy, in which the discourses of anthropology and nationalistic folklore have begun to compete for the control of cultural description.

There are good grounds for insisting on the symbolic character of the distinction between folklore and anthropology . In the comparativist spirit of this discussion, let us consider the distinction between folklore and anthropology in the light of the honor–shame antinomy so central to Mediterranean ethnography. The one common thread that appears to unite quite disparate authors who have dealt with the honor and shame debate is an agreement that these categories deal with the lines of social inclusion and rejection. In short, the categories glossed by these words are categories of self-presentation and self-concealment, the sexual aspects of which – though predominant in the anthropological literature – are but one facet. "Shame" centers on the revelation of matters considered as unfit for wider consumption (e.g. Wikan 1984; Abu-Lughod 1985); "honor" has to do with the aggressive presentation of an idealized self. As Duerr (1985:15) has argued with regard to the character of witchcraft in Renaissance Europe, the dark or weak side that appears as otherness is "the countenance of the guardians of the social order"; it is a concealed interiority, represented as completely alien or exterior. This is as true of the various sexual stereotypes that the northern Great Powers attributed to circum-Mediterranean peoples, notably in the attribution of oriental effeminacy (Kabbani 1986), as it is, in turn, of the very similar stereotypes that Greek men attach to Greek women. The antinomy of *covering* and *exposure* is so general to the cases described as "honor and shame" that we might realistically effect the substitution in our own terminology.

Approximately the same contrast between display and fear of exposure undergirds both "honor" and "shame" and the opposition between the two principal self-images of Greek culture. One of these, usually glossed as "Hellenism" (*Ellinismos*), tailors a grandiose and dehistoricized Classical past to external consumption; the other, *Romiossini*, expresses an ideology of intimacy. Since women have been more closely linked with the intimacy of the home, they have tended to become associated with anthropologists' notions of "shame," in contrast to men; they have also, for parallel reasons, *tended* to become stereotyped in terms that recall the *Romios* rather than the Hellene (Herzfeld 1986a). *Ellinismos* is a grammatically masculine noun, *Romiossini* a feminine one; like other Indo-European languages, Greek sometimes uses the masculine-feminine polarity to symbolize both the active-passive and the public-interior distinctions.[11]

All these polarities are *symbolic* oppositions. It makes no sense to argue that the Greeks are "really" either Hellenes or *Romii*, that women "have shame" while men "have honor" (see also Danforth 1983a), or, to recross the symbolic boundary between scholars and informants, that folklore and anthropology deal with distinct, mutual exclusive topics. For folklore and anthropology also express the theme of tension between display and penetration. Anthropological concern with Mediterranean sexual morality on the one hand and the political and ethnological penetration of Mediterranean societies on the other contrasts with the defense of national "honor" (*filotimo*) undertaken by nationalistic folklore. If the values glossed as honor and shame mark an arena of local-level strategic competition, the clash of disciplines offers a close analogy on the international scale.

It is all too easy to attribute one rather glaring aspect of nationalistic folklore, the concoction of texts, to "feelings of national or cultural inferiority" (Dundes 1985:13). This sort of psychoanalytic dismissal echoes the persistent characterizations of Mediterranean peasant cultures as familistic, amoral, and self-centered. In the Greek context, attempts to interpret the manufacture of folklore as evidence of a national inferiority complex must additionally bear an unfortunate resemblance to other, less scholarly western stereotypes of the Greeks as socially irresponsible and as politically immature. Some writers who adopt this stance also deride the Greeks for their excessive dependence on the Classical past (e.g. Holden 1972).

But others, by relating that same past to their otherwise very similar appraisals of the modern Greeks, make its ideological significance and origins much clearer. C. M. Woodhouse, who is on record with the view that the Greeks are "culturally mature but politically immature" (reported in *Neos Kosmos*, Melbourne, Sydney, Adelaide, 29 August 1985), *also* insists on "the unbroken continuity of the Greek race [*sic*]" (1986). Clearly, one does not have to share in the alleged national inferiority complex in order to adopt this survivalist argument. On the contrary, the conflation of a self-appointed right to judge the Greeks' maturity and self-confidence with authoritative pronouncements on their historical origins shows how persistently the political philosophies of the West continue to motivate the passive pedigree of the modern Greeks. Ideally "mature" Greeks would, we may presume, accept the political destiny they have been allocated on the grounds of a national history imposed upon them from the same source. Beware of neo-Classicists bearing gifts!

Folklore scholarship was a kind of discursive clothing of historical embarrassment, an act of expressive self-control and respectability: note again the close parallel between the antinomies of folklore/anthropology and honor/shame. European nationalism played continually on the metaphors of bodily and mental self-control, as well as on the contrasted representation of oriental and Mediterranean peoples as effeminate, degenerate, and loose (see Said 1978; Kabbani 1985; Mosse 1985:9, 20, 85, 89, 143). The Greeks had little choice but to show a thoroughly restrained and continent cultural face to the West. But so utterly had the West expropriated the ancient Greek identity for its own purposes that – in a truly astonishing irony – sexual degenerates and Mediterranean people alike appeared to be "[t]he spawn of dark, dank alleys, estranged from the healing power of nature, *alien to the world of Greece*" (Mosse 1985:36; my italics). In the tragic suppuration of this long festering ideology, the Nazis pursued it to the point where other western societies turned against it. For, while condemning modern Greeks as contemptibles fit only for servitude and death, the Nazi propagandists insisted that "the present-day Germans and the ancient Greeks were . . . the twin pillars of the Aryan race" (Mosse 1985:171; cf. also Constantine 1984:214).

When the powerful call the shots, collective self-defense – admirable as bravery or loyalty from the underdog's point of view – becomes the grovelling *defensiveness* ("inferiority complexes") of despised weaklings. What anthropologists call "shame" is an expressive response to inequality within a supposedly common cultural framework, and may generate deferential conventions toward those who possess greater power (see Aguilar 1982).[12] Even the more articulate members of an oppressed population may strategically adopt the negative features attributed to it by those of higher status (e.g. Mosse 1985: 36, 134). But this may be little more than a means of adapting to the practical realities of discrimination, of decoding the oppressors' world in order to resist from within. The shadow plays about the trickster-figure Karagiozis, for example, show an extraordinarily unctuous Greek who manages to throw his Turkish and wealthy targets perpetually off balance; and it is precisely that kind of status reversal, however temporary, that enables audiences to laugh uproariously at his exploits (Danforth 1979). This is social discourse; but it is the kind of discourse that often vanishes when it comes under too close a scrutiny from outside.

In much the same way, Greek folklorists (at least in their own estimation, which is what counts here) were neither grovelling nor defensive. They promoted a claim of national "honor," not admissions of "shame." These parallels between local-level and international contestation are not fortuitous: both, though at different levels, represent the effects of inequality on the interpretation of discourse, and consequently on the shape of social knowledge.

Each level, moreover, translates easily to the others. Campbell's reluctance to have *Honour, Family, and Patronage* published in Greek stems in part from a feeling that the sexual materials might cause offense, notably the observation that Sarakatsan women do not run for fear that they might accidentally expose themselves and thereby lose their honor forever (Campbell, personal communication; see 1964:287). This sensitivity to Greek feelings strongly suggests the fear many ethnographers have of "violating" their friends' – and, in a sense, the whole country's – confidence. It is matched by the anonymity often conventionally accorded to both individuals and their communities through the use of pseudonyms, a practice that again contrasts tellingly with many folklorists' equally ethical insistence that informants should be made as identifiable as possible. In anthropology, it was only when the community itself had ceased to exist that, in one tragic instance, it seemed right to reveal its real name in a further ethnographic study. After the destruction of his own ancestral village during the 1974 Turkish invasion of Cyprus, Loizos transmutes the pseudonym of "Kalo" ("Good [Place]") into the real name of the community, Argaki (Loizos 1975, 1981). Here, by throwing out a convention best adapted to standard situations, a scholar has enfolded us in the haunting embrace of memory and the awareness of a special horror.

In normative practice, the decision to name or not to name encodes assumptions about informants that anthropology and folklore share. The nationalist folklorist conventionally assumes that the singer or narrator is passively transmitting a text, and treats any embellishments added by the performer as extraneous. Naming, far from commemorating the performers, has the effect of denying their individuality; this is a rhetorical tactic that conforms to the general pattern of nationalistic and colonialist discourse, as we shall see. The performer's age is often given as the one additional salient datum: the older the performer, this suggests, the closer to its *Urtext* the performed version must be. Note, too, that folklorists give their informants' *age*, rather than actual dates. This has the effect of further deindividuating the informants: as tokens of a stage of textual evolution, they cease to be active participants in textual production.

By reducing performances to imperfect renditions of verbal *Urtexte*, moreover, the nationalist tradition dismembered the singers' own notions of history, meaning, and authorship. Since Greek rural notions of meaning (*simasia*) do not make a clear distinction between text and context, but attri-

bute authoriality to a performer who brings a situation into new focus re-
gardless of how original the verbal text is,[13] both the arid verbal folklore
collections and the anthropological reifications of "types of context" take
the stylization of performance to lengths undreamed of by the supposedly
"typical" and "traditional" performers themselves (see also Caraveli 1980,
1982). The literalism of romantic discourse holds the political and cultural
insubordination of performance at bay by turning the specificity of event
and performance into patterns of typicality instead. While this holds true
for colonial encounters with "obviously" aboriginal cultures such as those
of Australia (see Muecke 1983:88, 100), it also applies to European intellec-
tualist responses to the domestic aboriginality of the Greeks.

Small wonder, then, that rural Greeks are so often thought to have "no
history": their own *istories* are ignored as ahistorical by folklorists, or again
as reduced to typicality through the adumbration of "case histories" by
anthropologists. These strictures do not deny the real ethical concerns that
motivate many scholars in both disciplines. Both, however, are traditionally reductive: folklore as a restoration of textual history that transcends individual creativity, social anthropology as the elicitation of a social *langue*
that explains personal actions. Indeed, the two disciplines play out the opposition between history and society, diachrony and synchrony, long-term
process and structure. These differences, now gradually fading,[14] generate
the divergent ethical codes that respectively govern their relations with the
people on whose generosity and tolerance they depend. Although born of
different levels of social control, folklore and anthropology share a commitment to historicism – the romantic reading of history – that far too often effectively drowns out the argumentatively different historical voices of
individual rural Greeks.

The dilemma reflects the wider context in which the cultural disciplines
do their work. A cynic might well see the anthropologist's diffidence about
naming informants and communities as merely an expropriation of data at
the expense of the exploited rural Greek; but the cynic would then have
failed to see the ethnographer as trapped in a dilemma for which absolute
ethical prescriptions offer little help. The anthropologist does not only
have to consider the feelings of the local population; family and local community are both concentric with national identity (see also Friedl 1962:105;
Campbell 1976), and Greekness is the level at which the further association
with "being European" becomes salient. Whereas the villager who sings a
well-known folksong appears in the folklorist's recension as a bearer of
"national" tradition, the sheep thief or vengeance killer of ethnographic
repute poses a threat to the idealization of that image. This immediately
involves the ethnographer in the rhetoric of exposure and concealment.
Are such deeds expressions of Hellenic individualism, or of an embarrass-

ing criminality that should be blamed as far as possible on the history of foreign domination? Perhaps most significant of all, is jealously guarded sexuality "European," for example, in the way that "chastity" is? What Campbell describes, after all, differs from the romantic respectability of Eurocentric nationalist writers who discuss purity and obedience but never sex. Yet his penetration is always respectful; and in his gentle text (1964:277, 287) the "shapeless," sexually dissembling costume of the Sara-katsan women also becomes a tactful covering for the ambiguities of Greek identity. It is a negation of difference – a difference that is sexual at one level but cultural at another.

If Greece is the dominated woman in this metaphor, she is elsewhere a childlike figure from an era before the achievement of European maturity. The often heard, paternalistic image of Greece as a "child" of the western Powers recalls the survivalist association of national character with prac-tices from the childhood of the human past (Tylor 1871). The assumption of a supposedly homogeneous Mediterranean moral system attributes to Mediterranean people in general what Mediterranean men allegedly attri-bute to Mediterranean women – childlike social incontinence, requiring repressive tutelage. The Mongols under Japanese rule come to mind again: "children of the wild," they seemed to their new masters to be "sometimes most passionate, getting angry to no purpose; yet they are easy to please" (Asahi 1932). It would be easy to parallel these remarks in Victorian travel-lers' accounts of Greece and Turkey.

Much the same stance can also be found within Greece, as a mark of patronage and of paternalistic relations. Prince George of Greece, ap-pointed by the Great Powers as High Commissioner of the temporarily (1898–1913) autonomous island of Crete, was astonished when two animal-thieves voluntarily kept their promise to him that they would surrender to the prison authorities if he agreed to call off the foreign gendarmes (in Pallis 1959:53):

The naïve, not to say child-like, trustfulness made a great impression on me and touched me deeply. I knew now where I stood with my Cretans, and how to handle them. Their sense of honour is intensely strong.

And the prince concludes with a bitter aside, that the Cretans "are sterling men when they do not get mixed up in politics" – a clear allusion to the liberal statesman Eleftherios Venizelos, later to become prime minister of Greece, who eventually managed to have the prince removed from Crete. From the point of view of those in power, childishness is an admirable trait in a subject, since it counterbalances such impertinence – and it is charac-terized by an uncomplicated sense of honor!

The logic of otherness defined by childlike propensities is the hallmark of a survivalism that, thinly disguised, permeates much of the Mediterraneanist literature. In attributing the characteristics of preindustrial northern and western European culture to "the Mediterranean code of honor" – a significantly unitary notion, admitting none of the differentiation that stereotypically characterizes "European" societies – Blok (1981:435–6) discursively relegates the collectivity of circum-Mediterranean peoples to a premodern age, one already defined by the researches of Norbert Elias (1978). Not only does this tactic "deny coevalness" in an unusually specific way; it also contrasts starkly with the Greek folklorists' use of antiquity to claim a share of European modernity

The ownership of history

And so back once again to the film *Kypseli*, with its claim that the village's traditions are the "same" as those that "have also formed the rest of European culture." This is an unequivocal claim to identity, that of the anthropologist and film-maker as much as that of the villagers. But the villagers are also "less sophisticated," a people on whom the dominant West can inscribe history at will. How did this imbalance happen?

The film-makers' own explanation lies in a long historical account: successive conquerors function metonymically and cumulatively as a means of establishing the fact that Kypseli is a community that does not make history, but merely receives it: "The Minoans, who created the earliest European civilization, began Thera's recorded history." Then came Phoenicians, Dorians, Romans, the Christian religion, the Byzantine Empire, the Venetians (who "replaced the Byzantine lords with their own nobility"), the Turks (who "influenced the island's music, and introduced men's coffee-houses"); and, finally, when all the invaders have passed on, there remain the "traditional peasants" of Greece, "who maintain an age-old, European cultural pattern" – not as intellectually active Europeans, but as fossilized and patterned ancestors.

This account of historical change is no less ahistorical than the neo-Classicism of nationalist historians. Danforth (1984), adopting Fabian's (1983) posture, has already skillfully shown how Greek folklorists "denied coevalness" to the rural people by insisting on their blind continuity (or virtual identity, in this case) with the Classical past. But anthropological usage is full of similar distancing devices, which in turn suggest that it treats the national disciplines themselves much as both in turn treat the peasantry.

Kypseli is certainly an extreme case, made all the more dramatic by its attempt to portray a theoretical issue in terms that belong to the idiom of European nationalism. It attempts to argue a culturally specific study as a model for European identity while at the same time implying, through its application of structuralist methods, a higher universality. In this, it displays the key internal contradiction of the European ideology – the view that European culture is typified by its internal diversity, although it models the ultimate characteristics of human identity. This is as ironical now as it was in the nineteenth century: literacy, the definiens of European superiority, arguably makes for greater internal conformity through the imposition of bureaucratic control (Innis 1951, 1972; McLuhan 1972:ix). But homogeneity, like illiteracy, has long served as a collective representation of political subordination, and hence, when applied to European peasants or to non-Europeans of any kind, of otherness. The savage unconscious bespeaks both cognitive universality and intellectual subordination; the unsophisticated Greek peasant demonstrates European diversity by serving as its dullest and most disenfranchised representative.

Advocates of the European ideology resolved the paradox of a unity defined by internal diversity by appealing to an idealized past out of which grew all the variety of the present. This was the *Urtext* of European culture, so to speak, as revealed in the cultures of Classical Antiquity as well – in a much broader sense – as in the growing wealth of ethnographic texts about cultural survivals from a prehistoric era. Just as English and French peasants played the role of domestic exotics to the scholars of their countries, the Greeks found themselves cast in the role of European aboriginals in relation to these same scholars, acting now as representatives of the European mind.

Haunting the chimney: marginality as marginalization

That ancient Greek civilization shared certain of its characteristic understandings with modern "primitive" cultures is today perhaps best known from the historical and comparative studies of Jane Harrison (1912) and E. R. Dodds (1951). Classical civilization represented a triumph of rationality over superstition, the latter being nonetheless, in these authors' unabashedly survivalist terms, an ineradicable relic of the past. But the broad theme is much older. In the writings of J. G. Frazer and E. B. Tylor especially, the extraordinarily free intermixture of cultural elements from all over the world and from every known period of history sprang from the deep-seated conviction that human nature was fundamentally uniform (e.g. Bell 1877). Only European civilization had complicated matters through its plethora of rationalities, individualisms, and strivings for ever greater knowledge.

This is most startlingly revealed in Frazer's grandiose essays, notably that on the "primitive theory of the soul," which juxtaposes modern Greek materials, often very anachronistically, with examples from China, Germany, ancient Rome, Sumatra, Madagascar, Scotland, the Kachins, ancient

Mexico, and Siberia (Frazer 1886:67), as well as with the ancient culture of Greece itself. Frazer pre-emptively reorders time so as to bracket the ancients together with the modern primitives. This act of classification *disciplines* what would otherwise be an impossibly wild collection of cultural sources for what Frazer wants to present as an essentially unified cosmology. The beliefs in question, which Frazer examines in the hope of shedding light on Plutarch's question as to why a Roman who had been given up for dead had to enter his house through the roof, provide evidence of a sort of cosmological *Urtext* in which it is incongruous only for the rational western European to express implicit belief:

> Imagine a modern Englishman, whom his friends had given up for dead, rejoining the home circle by coming down the chimney, instead of entering by the front door. In this paper, I propose to show that the custom *originated* in certain primitive beliefs and observances touching the dead – *beliefs and observances by no means confined to Greece and Rome*, but occurring in similar if not identical forms in many parts of the world.   (Frazer 1886:64; my emphases)

The English, and perhaps some other northern Europeans, have detached themselves from the superstitions of that homogeneous otherness, and would consequently find it strange to behave in such a manner. Having deduced from his comparative analysis that the behavior in question is a survival from primitive fears of revenants and from the measures taken to prevent them from haunting their former homes, Frazer (1886:97) concludes that a man who had wrongly been supposed dead, and for whom the appropriate funerary rituals had therefore been carried out, had to find a special way of returning:

> he had to overcome the initial difficulty of getting into his own house. For the door was as ghost-proof as fire and water could make it, and *he* was a ghost. As such, he had to go as ghosts do; in fact, not to put too fine a point on it, he had to come down the chimney. And down the chimney he came – and this is an English answer to a Roman question.

This rather smug closure unveils Frazer's prior assumptions: that only a sensible Englishman, being himself free of such superstitious practices and beliefs, could provide an answer to a question that had baffled even a Classical author.

For the Victorian survivalists, there was nothing "impossible" about comparative research, since they believed that the degree of spiritual and intellectual individuation achieved by modern Europeans was such as to permit the absolute separation of scholar from subject. Symptomatic of this position is Frazer's confidence that modern as well as ancient Greek parallels, as well as a medley of instances taken from many other sources, would serve not only to explain the Roman custom, but also the peculiar genius that permitted a "modern Englishman" to provide the definitive answer.

The bracketing together of ancient and modern Greek material played an important part in the development of survivalism, since the parallels this procedure elicited provided an apparent if ultimately circular demonstration of the survivalist position. Hodgen (1936:48, n.1) has argued that Tylor's version of the survivalist hypothesis was often misunderstood: folklorist-travellers like Theodore Bent and Rennell Rodd inverted the Tylorean formula, regarding Classical survivals as evidence of a "high culture" rather than of a more primitive era. But this stricture certainly does not apply to Frazer, or to the eccentric J. S. Stuart-Glennie (1896), for whom even the glories of ancient Greece were still premodern in the sense of being internally homogeneous; and even the more simplistic among the survival-hunters in Greece hardly considered the Classical era to have been the equal of their own. Rather, by mythologizing both that era and its local incarnations in modern Greece as a form of cultural ancestry, they discursively banished the modern Greek "folk" to a position both anterior in time and inferior in political space. In that sense, Hodgen's distinction between them and the true Tyloreans must now be regarded as too literal.

Yet this does not mean that there were no contradictions at all between the two modes of survivalism. On the contrary, the one clear demonstration that the internal inconsistencies could not be repressed entirely is the case of Cyprus, a British colony largely inhabited by Greeks (and the subject of two of the best Greek studies of Classical survivals [Loukas 1874; Sakellarios 1890–1]). The Europeans' ancestors may have been primitive in comparison to their modern heirs; but primitivity is itself a relative concept. On the occasion of the 1886 Colonial and Indian Exhibition, for example, we distinctly hear the embarrassment that the inclusion of Greeks as colonial subjects must have occasioned (Lang 1887:186; my emphasis):

Mr. Hamilton Lang said he had been asked by the Chairman to give *a very brief description* of art and customs in Cyprus. His greatest difficulty was to maintain selections, for nearly all present art in Cyprus is a survival, and, at every turn, in present customs of the island, we meet survivals.

Furthermore, the contradictions threatened to become more obvious rather than less. Survival can only be attributed to "isolation," but "the clouds are breaking, and British rule will soon dispel them altogether" (Lang 1887:187). But that event, one presumes, would bring the tension between colonialism and respect for the Cypriots' ancestry to breaking point. A survivalist thesis, which had the effect of isolating the Cypriots in a *cordon sanitaire* of antiquity, was the only viable and available solution.

Thus, in Cyprus, colonialist and neo-Classical forms of survivalism necessarily fused, though the tension does not entirely disperse. Survivalism, used to justify colonial rule, is awkwardly equipped to deal with "a survival of an ancient race reputedly far advanced in civilisation when we in

Britain were still half-naked savages," and can only be salvaged by a close identification between rulers and ruled (Lang 1887:186):

Nothing has occurred to Cyprus, since the British occupation, so calculated to quicken this civilising motion as the Colonial and Indian Exhibition. It is the first direct touch between the Cypriotes and the great British public, and the warmth of that touch cannot fail to produce an electrifying influence upon the dry bones which, in Cyprus, have been pulverising during centuries of neglect and oppression.

In short, the British mission in Cyprus is less to civilize than to *restore*, through "contact with the science and intelligence of our nineteenth century" (Lang 1887:187). Benevolent British rule will generate a warm and productive contact between "the height of our present civilisation" and its living ancestors; but there is never any doubt as to who is directing the action, and resistance is not lightly forgiven. In consequence, the British – not unlike the French travelers so heartily castigated by Houssaye – romanticized the Turks as independent and proud, and recast the vaunted "European" independence of the Greeks as a form of obduracy. This attitude lives on in the history of official American reactions to the various Greco-Turkish conflicts to an extraordinary degree and for much the same ideological reasons (Coufoudakis 1985). The Greek's role is to serve, in the literal sense of that word, as a passive ancestor (Lang 1887:188):

The Cypriote of to-day is still a counterpart of the man of the past, but I greatly mistake if you do not find it very different at the next grand Exhibition to which His Royal Highness may invite him. The youth who visits to-day many objects in the Cyprus Court will probably, long before his head is grey, have to search for them in museums of antiquities.

The equation of physical with cultural isolation in Cyprus is symptomatic of this kind of survivalism; elsewhere, as in Bent's Cycladic researches, it became a means of finding the pure roots of European identity (1886:401; my emphasis):

In their daily life, in their methods of catching fish, in their planting of crops, in their medical and religious lore, endless parallels can be found to antiquity, which prove beyond a doubt that in these islands, *remote from civilisation and alien governments*, a race of people live of pure Hellenic blood, unadulterated by admixture with other races; they are not numerous, it is true, and for a pure Greek, as for a pure Celt, you must search in mountain villages and unfrequented bye-paths.

The Celtic parallel carries a clear message: marginal populations can more easily sanctify the dominant population's consumption of history than its own (see also Chapman 1978, on images of the Scot; on island Greeks,

Mears 1929:39). Even this is not always sufficient; the comparatively skeptical De Quincey, for instance, while conceding that one might conceivably expect to find "true-blooded" Greeks only "in the most sterile of the Greek islands," nonetheless doubted the probability that such a population would be genuinely untainted (1863:319). But inasmuch as remoteness did signify cultural aboriginality, it reproduced a favorite theme of empire. Yet once more, the Japanese view of their new Mongol subjects – "off the path of civilization" and "*therefore* outside worldly competition" (*Asahi* 1932; my italics) – serves to indicate the generality of the principle in question. The exemplary choice of marginal populations is an effective way – through metonymy – of marginalizing an entire subordinate nation. *Kypseli* exemplifies the further transmutation into modern anthropological terms of the motif of isolation as a museum of European identity. Remoteness is a symbol of aboriginality, and hence of exoticism; and it is this, rather than the literal fact of remote location, that so irritates Greek critics of anthropological work.

Neo-Classical survivalism thus privileged the concerns of western European states at least as much as those of the Greeks. However inchoately, Toynbee's (1922) study of the cultural and social background to the Asia Minor war of 1922 attempted to make this same point – that the issue was a western, not an eastern, question. His attempt foundered because he tried to argue from stereotypes of European, Near Eastern, and Middle Eastern cultures, blaming the débâcle Kipling-fashion on the cultural miscegenation implied by the neo-Classical ideology. In this, of course, he argued from the very same stereotypes that had engendered the neo-Classical argument against which he wrote. The Greeks were not, as he claimed, passive recipients of an ideology that the West had taught them, but a complex nation some elements of which sought to deploy the dominant ideology of Eurocentrism for its own strategic ends. However justified Toynbee may have been in denying the historicity of nationalist historiography, his own writings, no less than those of anthropologists hostile to national folklore scholarship, thus founder on the same treacherous rock: stereotypes necessarily deny temporality, while predictions based on "types" of culture are in practice nothing more than an affirmation of existing etiologies.

The defining characteristics of the stereotypical European of this debate are precision, legality, and individual genius. Such features, far from representing actual traits, must be treated as the elements of an international rhetorical contest. In the absolute language of nineteenth-century nationalism and anthropology, some people were European in this sense while others, just as categorically, were not. Categorical ascription, however, is not immanent essence, although it presents itself as such. We must therefore now look at the game itself – at precision, legality, and genius, not as absolute traits, but as rhetorical constructs in a global debate, different only in scale from the contests of honor that supposedly characterize Mediterranean peasant communities.

4 Difference as identity

The European ideology: diversity in unity

The European ideology developed in part from a reaction to Enlightenment universalism. Characteristically, it represented European identity as revealed through specific *national* identities; paradoxically, it meant thinking nationalistically. The European ideology portrayed the internal disunity of the European peoples as a transcendent unity, their political divisions as a sign of robust health, and their squabbles as the free expression of individuality refined through constant competition.

This stance was fundamental to the emergence of the European nation-state (Hazard 1935:30–1; Chabod 1964:85, 1967). Until well on in the sixteenth century, Europeans felt safe in assuming their own moral and cultural superiority. But this was always an uneasy conviction. Columbus showed moments of doubt at the very start of contact with the New World (Hodgen 1964:18); less than a century later, de Léry's (1578) comparison of cannibalism with usury (see Chabod 1964:68; Schwimmer 1983) reduced the gap between wild savages and urbane Europeans. Closer acquaintance with China, notably through the accounts of Giovanni Botero and Ludovico Guicciardini (Chabod 1964:79), made it still harder to insist on an unqualified European superiority, since Chinese culture appeared to satisfy the most ethnocentric occidental criteria of "civilization." In the century that followed these remarkable explorations, therefore, a new understanding of European distinctiveness emerged – based, it was claimed (Hazard 1935:30–1; Chabod 1964:85, 1967), not on superiority, but on *internal diversity*. Such abnegations of hierarchical difference seem ironic, however, in the light of Dumont's observation that difference inevitably implies some measure of hierarchy. By the mid nineteenth century, François Guizot had no qualms about expressing the view that diversity conferred "immense superiority" (1856:40) on European civilization, while Tylor (1871:37) was able to treat all "savages" as essentially alike.

These features of the European ideology lie at the very heart of anthropological exoticism. They also affect the representation of cultural differences internal to European societies, reducing everyday discourse and

77

local variation to epiphenomena of a transcendent sameness. Thus, for example, the divisiveness that at home Europeans regarded as beneficial individualism became, amongst exotic or peasant others, mere egotism, a definitive sign of depravity.

Then again, when local differences could be assimilated to encompassing similarities, they were treated as signs of an inventive genius.[1] This version of Eurocentrism, like modern cultural relativism in anthropology,[2] thus reproduced the very form of social knowledge that it sought to repress. For it could not tolerate *irreducible* cultural diversity within the single nation-state; in particular, it regarded all local-level quarrels and feuds as a usurpation of its policing powers. At the level of the state and above, cultural differences were "European" and therefore good; below, they were anathema, inasmuch as they challenged the authority of the state. This ideology proclaimed external distinctiveness as the historical destiny of the state, while reducing internal distinctiveness to the measure of that same common denominator.

Expropriated discourse:
Vico and the ideology of European identity

The ideas of Giambattista Vico are especially germane, both because of his prescient mix of universalism and particularism, and because of his realization that even the most formal discourse was rooted in everyday experience. For him, the pomposities of statesmen and scholars alike subverted their best intentions at every turn. He enunciated a laconic but telling critique of ethnocentrism, arguing that history is too easily distorted by being written by scholars on the exclusive basis of their familiar, narrow world (I,2,2 [1977:174] [B/F 122–4]).

In retrospect, it is something of a shock to perceive how readily these radical views could be turned into nationalistic credos during the subsequent heyday of romantic statism. In recent years, his celebrated credo of *verum factum* has gained recognition as anticipating modern phenomenology (Bergin and Fisch 1948:Introduction; Berlin 1977) and structuralism (Leach 1969a, 1976; Merquior 1970; Hawkes 1977:11–15; R. Joseph 1981) – both philosophies that attempt to dissolve cultural particularities in a transcendent relativism. But Vico's thought elsewhere became a symbol of national genius, expropriated by the discourse of romantic statism and ultimately also of mid twentieth century Fascism, and thus suffered the very expropriation against which it is directed. His "refraction"[3] through ideologies so different from his own sounds a clear warning as modern structuralism faces the temptations of theoretical closure.

The opacity of Vico's prose perhaps lent itself to the great variety of conflicting interpretations that it has engendered. Vico may even have been playing a duplicitous game, masking with conservative rhetoric a philosophical radicalism that could otherwise have caused him fatal trouble (Vaughan 1972). Moreover, his concern with etymology led both to his dismissal as a poor philologist (e.g. Berlin 1977) and to his glorification as a founder of modern nationalism and statism – ideologies that make generous use of etymology for the purposes of cultural legitimation. Vico's own view of history seems to have been critical rather than legitimative. Thus, he used etymology to challenge the seeming permanence of social institutions by highlighting the instability of meaning in their outwardly static nomenclature. This interpretation accords with Vico's treatment of social institutions as products of the same structuring propensities of the human mind that also created their history; permanence is itself constructed.

Proceeding from an imaginative etymological play on the terms *mythos* and *mutus*, Vico argued that mythology represented the prelinguistic "poetic knowledge" (*sapienza poetica*) that corresponded to the state of barbarism, and that separated humans from the purely bestial state of savagery whence they had originated. This progression becomes cyclical if, but only if, the users of rational or scientific language forget its historical origins as these are encapsulated in etymology; at that point they suffer a relapse (*ricorso*) into barbarism. Linguistic history thus corresponds sequentially to the history of political institutions and encapsulates the latter (see also White 1978:214); for while constitutional monarchy represents the most "civilized" state of political evolution, far above anarchy and tyranny, a monarch who suppresses all knowledge of his dependency on popular support will open the gates to a new anarchy – the "second barbarism" to which he thereby condemns his people. As political institutions retain knowledge of their own history, science must retain a knowledge of its own metaphorical basis; if it fails to do so, it collapses into solipsism and error.

Social life, then, defined by language and politics, is caught in the snares of history; and the hubristic attempt to gain perfection is a denial of history that can only lead back to ignorance. This is the force of Vico's emphasis on *gentile* history, the history of the nations (*gentes*) dispersed after Babel; for unlike the Jews (and their divinely ordained successors in Christendom), the gentiles are in a state of permanent otherness – the *goyim* (Hebrew/Yiddish for "nations"; cf. "ethnics") of a world made by Hebraic Deity. For this reason, they can only understand divine providence indirectly through their own constructions of fact; *these* gentiles are not Guizot's (1856:41) Europeans walking "in the plan of Providence [and] . . . the paths of God." In Vichian terms, then, anthropology must come to terms with the besetting otherness of ourselves – an *ethnos* as alienated as any it selects for study (on which, see MacCannell and MacCannell 1982:168–83; Drummond 1983:201; Pandian 1984:123).

The fate of Vico's ideas during the century after his death confirms his thesis with brilliant irony: they served to legitimize the ahistorical nationalisms that eventually degenerated into Fascist excess. Vico's writings, which included a disquisition (presumably critical[4]) on the etymology of the term "state," became a text for forms of statism that we would today regard as repressively conservative – though at the time their demands for national independence seemed wildly revolutionary, while even Vico's espousal of constitutional monarchy was easily adapted to revolutionary ends.[5] But this was apparently not enough for his self-appointed successors. Among these, the most notable was Vincenzo Cuoco, a political and educational writer who far surpassed Vico in his espousal of monarchism (e.g. Cuoco 1966). Cuoco turned the Neapolitan philosopher's openended spiral of historical development and relapse into a linear march, a straight progression from savage to barbaric pride and then on to the "irreversible" pride of nations (1924:339–5; Brancato n.d.:40). At the same time, Cuoco collapsed the tension that Vico had posited between poetic and scientific language into an equally irreversible flow toward the latter. The permanent establishment of bureaucratic statehood, supported by a wellplanned system of education (see Brancato n.d.:38) and maintained through the strict control of historical truth, thus coincided with scientific rationality. The Italian nationalists treated Vico as one of their own, seeing in his thought a philosophical sublimation of the Italian national character and genius (Cuoco 1924:63; selected writings in Beccari 1938; Gentile 1963:411). A very similar process appears in the misappropriation of Herder, for whom European cultures were not necessarily superior or more "humane" (Barnard 1965:100–1), both in the nationalism of his native Germany and in the aggressively Eurocentric nationalisms of geographically more peripheral countries (e.g. Finland; see Wilson 1976).

Cuoco's discursive expropriation of Vico affords us an exemplary insight into the relationship between romantic statism, scientism, and referential definition. While evidence for Vico's influence on Greek nationalist writers remains inconclusive (see Herzfeld 1982a:26–8, 47–9), Italian nationalism provides a more complete text of romantic semantics from which, *mutatis mutandis*, we can then extrapolate the relevant aspects of the Greek experience. For what is clear in the transmission of ideas from Vico to Cuoco and then on down to the pedagogues of the Fascist era, as it is not in the transition from the linguistic philosophers of pre-Revolutionary Greece (on whom, see Henderson 1970) to the later apologists of Greek national independence, is the extraordinary degree to which romantic conceptions of national identity relied on validation by an absolutist science clad in a correspondingly rigid semantics. A similar transformation of Herder's ideas appears in Hegel's apotheosis of the state as the ultimate reality. The revolutionary import of the new ideologies – constitutional monarchy, nationalism, fascism – is soon transmuted into the exaltation of the absolute and a consequent collapse of what Vico understood by (historical) knowledge. National pride is irreversible because, once achieved, it represses knowledge of its own historical contingency. The practical logic of this is exemplified by Huxley's *Brave New World* (1932), and by the Portuguese dictator Antonio Salazar's grimly perceptive remark that "happy countries have no history" (Gallagher 1983:vi).[6]

Romanticism did not simply turn away from universalism and toward particularism (see Nipperdey 1983:3), though this was its surface expression. It also universalized the particular, rendered it absolute through the abolition of historical time. The state, in large measure a historically contingent product of the romantic ideology itself, became the necessary form of civilized social organization. The consequently more obvious political fragmentation of Europe became the oxymoronic source of its fundamental unity, just as "individualism" became the equally paradoxical criterion of social conformity; and, in the most radical undermining of the universalist agenda, many a culture appointed itself the touchstone of European identity. The last of these processes, that of ecumenical ethnocentrism, reached its greatest heights in Greek attempts to reclaim the intellectual leadership of Europe; it reverses Vico's relativism and, more especially, Herder's refusal to nominate a *Favoritvolk* (Barnard 1965:101). An essential component of the conflation of nationalism with Eurocentrism, it is exemplified by Guizot's (1874:21 cf. also 1856:6–7) boast:

France thus has the honor, Gentlemen, that its civilization reproduces more faithfully than any other the general type, the fundamental concept, of civilization. It is, so to speak, the most complete, the truest, the most civilized. It is this which has gained her the first place in the good opinion of disinterested Europeans.

That this passage hardly shows a disinterested spirit of its own renders it conceptually, if not politically, at one with the rival claims of other European nationalists. Of these, Vincenzo Cuoco, with his belief in the Italianity of Vico's genius, was no less representative.

The European ideology, by seeming to unite all its disparate entities in a single transcendent unity, reifies such concepts as meaning, law, and culture. True to its roots in the European ideology, the state represents a complexity united in the hands of a single authority, and views the peasant culture as chaos founded in simplicity. Vico realized, however, as Cuoco and other romantic nationalists apparently did not, that the separation of power and knowledge from their roots in social experience would bring a "second barbarism" in its train.

Romantic statism, law, and modern anthropology: some implications

The rise of romantic statism displays a clear pattern. Relativity and universalism were progressively disguised and concealed behind a rhetoric of absoluteness – of absolution, as it were, from the weight of history. Statism progressively forgot its origins. Nationalist history is not ahistorical because it is wrong (as in Toynbee 1922:128), but because, like myth, it *suppresses time*.

It is a search for the secular Eden of national purity, for the *Urtext* of a collective but socially problematical identity – for, in a word, that "eternal verity" that allowed romantic historians to invest the nation-state with all the force of a scientific fact (a *fait accompli?*) and that allows an anthropologist today to seek aboriginal European culture in the name of structuralist theory, as in *Kypseli*. The paradoxical achievement of romantic historians was to describe history, not as an open cycle (as Vico had done), but as a finite linearity, a predestined and irreversible progression to Cuoco's "patriotic pride" and to the discovery of a historicist Europe out of time. Although Vico has been credited with anticipating structuralism, what we might more precisely attribute to his thesis is a concern with the *structuring* propensities (Giddens's "structuration" [1984]) that produce process out of form, *make* history as well as the institutions that it is history's task to document. In taking only the static dimension of his theory, nationalism, Eurocentrism, and "vulgar structuralism" all wryly confirm his prediction that losing sight of the "poetic" origins of fact ultimately leads to a new ignorance: historicism, scientism, and literalism repress knowledge of their ideological motivations, and so create new illusions of absolute fact.

Since language and institutional law (Vico's major themes) are both features of culture that the state attempts to regulate, it is perhaps not surprising that the philosophical relativism of prestatist thinkers undergoes a particularly respressive transformation in its applications by theorists of romantic statism. Cuoco, for example, wished to impose a "totalitarian" (Brancato n.d.:40) system of education on the populace so as to ensure that it would retain the antique virtues of peasant life – an ideology that continued to flourish even down to details like the wearing of homespun Roman tunics amidst the smoking ruins of Mussolini's Italy (Lewis 1978:59). The effects of this ideological reification on popular conceptions of law and language cannot easily be gauged, but official orthodoxy will have fitted everywhere to achronic notions of "custom." As Bourdieu (1977:17) puts it:

Talk of rules, a euphemized form of legalism, is never more fallacious than when applied to the most homogeneous societies (or the least codified areas of differentiated societies) where most practices, including those seemingly most ritualized, can be abandoned to the orchestrated improvisation of common disputation: the rule is never, in this case, more than a second-best intended to make good the occasional misfirings of the collective enterprise of inculcation tending to produce habits that are capable of generating practices regulated without express regulation or any institutionalized call to order.

By assuming that rules function as the primary point of reference in his own society, however, Bourdieu has unwittingly accepted a central premise of statist ideology, perhaps in a way consistently with his refusal to conjoin state and local community in his consideration of Kabyle ethnography. This ideology presents laws, the embodiment of the state's authority, as absolute, in denial of both their historical constitution (B. S. Jackson 1982) and the philosophical discourse expropriated by romantic statism itself (Barnard 1965:64); and it delimits law from custom in terms of the European model of internal differentiation.

In balancing our analyses between rules and strategies, we easily forget that they are not reified actualities; they are *qualities* rather than *things*.[7] Statist ideology generally represents laws as both absolute and state-constituted – as bedrock *statements*.[8] Yet just as Bourdieu himself recognizes that custom constitutes its own sense of orthodoxy, it would be naïve for us to assume that legal rules in our own societies are as fixed as their format implies. They, too, are the product of what he calls "officializing strategies" (1977:38–40). Here, therefore, Bourdieu has compounded Eurocentrism by allowing the false distinction between *societies with codified laws* and *societies with a customary morality that can only be invoked retrospectively* to stand as a gloss for the equally nebulous distinction between less and more "homogeneous" societies – in other words, between "us" and "them."

In suggesting that the "homogeneous" societies and the "least codified areas of differentiated societies" exhibit signs of a radically less rule-governed idiom of social life, Bourdieu has confused the ideology of his own cultural milieu with its practices. We have already inspected the antecedents of this essentially Eurocentric formulation in the writings of Guizot and Cuoco. A thinker like Maine, more frequently acknowledged as an ancestor by the current anthropological canon, had allowed his ideological preoccupations to suppress the significance of hierarchy in Indian village life; and this perspective filtered through to Durkheim and beyond to many of his successors (Dumont 1975:112, 140–1). Bourdieu, residually faithful to this tradition even as he initiates a critique of it, regards certain societies as more homogeneous because the differences that are important to their members do not constitute major social differentiations in accepted anthropological usage: the unit of comparison remains a somewhat hypo-statized *ethnos*.[9] "Heterogeneous" societies have to make formal and irrevocable laws, where "homogeneous" ones have strategies.[10]

The distinction between *law* and *custom* that Bourdieu thus preserves from early folklore studies[11] rests on a model that both in fact share. In this model, the force of prescription is generically known to be irrevocable, but the specific determination of its irrevocability can never be known until after the event. This, as we have seen, is precisely the image in which most alleged fatalists actually cast the authority of fate. Law-like descriptions of custom, so often perpetrated by anthropologists because – as Bourdieu (1977:36) observes – they arrive *post festum*, thus become a mark of an exotic passivity. Bourdieu himself discerns this "fatalism" in anthropological theories of structure, as does Said (1975:77) in the linguistic classifications whereby modern scholars meekly submit to a particular ordering of knowledge – but only, we should add, in regard to the affairs of *others* in both instances. This, *mutatis mutandis*, recalls the fatalism that we have already discerned in totalitarian and nationalistic ideologies. "It is the magic of nationalism to turn chance into destiny" (Anderson 1983:19), to recast the contingent as the eternal and inevitable; but the academy, buttressed like any nation-state bureaucracy by scriptism and "printism," can generalize that magic still further.

As chronocentric projections, these academic fatalisms especially resemble the stereotype of oriental submissiveness to law and fate. They habitually flatten the experienced, specific struggle for immediate understanding into a generalized ("rule-like") synchrony, a condemnation to eternal imperfection in a langu.age whose scriptist authori(ali)ty the Greek image of a writing fate evokes: "what fate writes, it does not unwrite." Bourdieu departs from this traditional stereotype in his recognition that strategies flourish in supposedly undifferentiated societies; instead of treating them as fatalistic, he actually absolves them of that trait and relocates it in the academic practice where it properly belongs.

Bourdieu's perspective, however, does not include theoretical originality in the quality of active social invention (1977:18–19). He assumes with categorical certainty that the members of homogeneous societies will not independently develop a theoretical understanding of their own actions, and will only generate a *"semi-theoretical* disposition, inevitably induced by any learned questioning" (1977:18). But this automatizes the responses of informants; "the expectations of the ... formalism to which his own situation inclines the observer" determine their intellectual activity in an almost behavioristic fashion, relegating them to the enforced passivity from which the concept of strategy has just released them.

Bourdieu's argument, moreover, overlooks the theory-like propensities of etiological myths in many societies (Winner 1977: Drummond 1981). Like the grand comparative schemata of social anthropology, these too are recognitions of significant difference. If we fail to recognize them as significant (or as theoretical), it is because we have arbitrarily set the level of comparison as that of the *ethnos*, and so ignored other levels and types of differentiation that may be significant *to the actual members of the society* – those actors, in fact, whose existence is presupposed by, and necessary to, Bourdieu's own key concept of strategy.

Unlike these circumstances, theory serves rhetorically (or strategically?) as a proxy abstraction for a constantly comparing observer able to recognize complex differentiations at home and abroad. It is thereby opposed to an intellectually passive and merely "comparative" *ethnos*, a group of vaguely defined extent that is not subject to internal differences and is therefore an ideal subject for comparativist analysis. As such, "theory" stands apart from "practice" – a common exclusion in anthropology (see also Fabian 1983:137) – and marks the internal differentiation that romantic statism had earlier accorded the European mind. The connection between romantic statism and anthropological theory becomes even stronger if we accept Bourdieu's (1977:9) just criticism of the latter as "detemporalized": theory, a practice both born of its object yet conceptually detached from it, resembles the "eternal verity" of state patriotism in the formulations variously devised by Guizot, Cuoco, and Hegel, and dubbed "unhistorical" (*sic*) by Toynbee (1922:118).

The construct "homogeneous societies" surfaces even in the writings of those whose goal is, admirably, to resist the literalization of cultural experience. Sahlins (1976), for example, regards the societies that anthropologists study as differing from the latter's own "only" in that they tend to be externally (intertribally?) differentiated. In a still more stark idiom, we learn:

In cultures like our own, which stress the deliberate articulation of conventional contexts, these collectivizing controls are re-created by acts of *differentiation*, deliberate invention. In tribal societies and others that emphasize the deliberate articulation of nonconventionalized contexts, the differentiating controls are re-created by acts of *collectivization*, deliberate conventionalizing.

(Wagner 1975:58–9)

The societies of the West sustain creativity based on difference, while "tribal societies and others" seek occasional moments of high organization, "bursts of hysterical conventionalizing" (Wagner 1975:*ibid*.), that nevertheless fail to transcend an ultimately vitiating and pervasive fragmentation – the anarchic unity of Banfield's "amoral familism" (1958), for example. European society thus stands in absolute conceptual contrast to "tribal, religious, and peasant peoples" (Wagner 1975:87). Societies "like our own" subordinate context to invention, take control of their own destinies; others *depend* upon context to make sense of the world.

All these writers are inadvertent heirs to the romantic view of western culture as released from the trammels of context, united in a diversity that attests to its transcendent inventiveness (Guizot), progressing irrevocably toward the realization of its ultimate destiny as a "patriotic pride" (Cuoco), and embodied in the perfection of the bureaucratic nation-state (Hegel). Only Dumont, arguing that the modern view of hierarchy, "however opposed to the traditional, is still located within it" (1982:237), seems more willing to recognize the inevitability of this entanglement, and so can hold it up for critical inspection. But his argument seems at times to accept the rhetoric of western individualism at face value; and this, too, may repress the social character, which is ethnographically well documented, of "self-regard" among a European population such as the Sarakatsani (see Campbell 1964:307).

Bourdieu (1977:18) directly associates "undifferentiated" societies with a relative lack of theoretical explicitness. In such societies, strategies and immediate understandings take the place of laws and theories respectively. In this, he exhibits a curious parallelism with Lévi-Strauss's distinction between conscious and unconscious models, despite his own objections (Bourdieu 1977:4–5, 27) to the latter. Greimas's (1976) position similarly reduces implicit meaning to an invariant *langue*: "common sense" (*sens commun*) is the connotative aspect of culture, while denotation renders meaning free of context and sets the stage for self-conscious individualism and differentiation – in short, for the play of original intellect over the undifferentiated mental capacity that Greimas intends us to understand by the term "common sense." This version of structuralism makes its claims to superior cultural identity explicit (e.g. Greimas 1970: 19–20), and thus explicitly translates Lévi-Strauss's argument into an internal symbolic opposition between ethnographic subjects and theoretical actors: the conscious (denotative) models of the investigator cannot be treated as impoverished versions of collective knowledge in the same way as are the (connotative) models of the observed.

Greimas's conception of the lawmaker shares in this essentially romantic view of the theorist. For him law is produced through its pronouncement as such by the officers of established political authority – in other words, through the validation of a historically contingent fiat by virtue of the timeless power of the state. Through this arrogation of legal normativity by "heroic" individuals (Greimas 1976:67–88, 112; cf. B. S. Jackson 1982:149), he suggests that only those who dwell in state-like societies determine their affairs through the independent exercise of intellect; others – lacking explicit (denotative) law and possessing only the "semi-theoretical disposition" of Bourdieu's account – would then be subject by default to the invariant and immanent structures of tradition. Not only, then, are stateless societies somehow "incomplete"; those who dwell in them are correspondingly diminished as well.

Such positions easily slip still further into equating "undifferentiated" with "preconscious" and hence with "passive." This allows an imperious condescension to cloak itself in the rhetoric of tolerance and concern. From Kenneth Pike's characterization of emic categories as "a control system blessed of God to preserve tribes from chaos" (Hvalkof and Aaby 1981:37) to a well-meaning bilingualism advocate's concern to activate through the teaching of Spanish "600,000 [Indian] brains [in Chiapas] that until now have remained inactive" (cited in Haviland 1982:164), the implication is clear.[12] Only the differentiating effects of Euroculture can activate the passive intelligence of hitherto unenlightened peoples – or, in the case of the Greek villagers of some accounts, of people who have been discursively "reorientalized."

Greek illustrations

In Greece, this argument does in fact have a long history. In the early eighteenth century, it is exemplified by the botanist de Tournefort's declaration (1718:68):

> I regard the Brain of these poor *Greeks*, as so many living Inscriptions, seeming to retain the names quoted by *Theophrastus* and *Dioscorides*; these, though subject to divers Alterations, will doubtless last much longer than the most solid Marble, because they are every day renew'd, whereas Marble wears off, or is destroy'd.
> Thus the Inscriptions I'm speaking of will, to Ages yet to come, preserve the Names of many and many a Plant, well known to those learned *Greeks*, who lived in more enlighten'd happier Times. . . .

In the period immediately before the achievement of national independence, some observers still thought Greeks incapable of understanding even *their own* language; it was, of course, these same outsiders who thought to determine what the real Greek language was, and on whose condescension all the gallicizing calques of neo-Classical purism fawned. The French traveller Count Forbin, even as he recognized that the frustrated Greeks' "generous tears bedewed the marble monuments, the ancient trophies of the *power* of Athens" (my emphasis), nonetheless found nothing incongruous in remarking (n.d.[1820]:108):

> In the same way as the Jews expect the Messiah, so do the Greeks look forward to independence: liberty would, however, alight in vain on these shores, once her noblest domain. This nation would no longer comprehend her divine language, which would be confined exclusively to ignorant caloyers [monks[13]].

If not utter fatalists, then, the Greeks of this account are at the very best deluded by a superstition that delays their ultimate redemption beyond any conceivable future; a cruel inversion of the distinction between Hellenes and *barbaroi* allows the northern nations to inflict their standards of linguistic Greekness on the hapless people. For Forbin, the Greeks did not even

have the latent capacity to activate their intellects, whose irreversible decay
had reduced Greek to a barbarous tongue. The true European genius had
long since fled to the West and North.

Forbin, like his counterpart the English mercantilist F. S. N. Douglas
(1813), wrote before the Greek state came into being. Both doubted the
wisdom of letting the Greeks run their own affairs, since both considered
that the things they most admired in the ancient Greeks were not to be
found in the modern land. After the Greeks succeeded in establishing an
independent national state, an event that confounded the self-confident
predictions of these and other foreign observers, prognostications of total
failure – fatalism at the expense of the other again! – were no longer possible, and a more sympathetic observer could pontificate:

> Indeed, it is pretty certain that a powerful cross in any human breed . . . leaves the
> intellect improved – *if not in the very highest qualities*, yet in mobility, activity, and
> pertinacity of attention. The Greek nation has shown itself morally improved.
> (De Quincey 1863:328; my emphasis)

But even moral improvement is conditional, the result of contact with superior western values. In "commercial morality," for instance, a still more
recent author explains that the Greeks closely resemble "the typical Oriental merchant" (Mears 1929:178):

> Combining a newly developed knowledge of the ways of the Occident with an
> Oriental psychology, the Greeks have proved themselves to be remarkably
> adaptable, and usually successful in commercial enterprises of every kind.

Self-assertion even of such a restricted order required the activating effect
of European intelligence; we may recall the expected effect of contact with
the "great British public" upon the advancement of the Cypriots.

In politics, such self-assertion was conditional upon the sufferance of the
European Powers. De Quincey (*ibid.*) thought that the Greeks had "no
great rallying principle but the banner of the Cross against the Crescent."
The earlier fashion of denying the Greeks active intellectual capacities is a
fairly obvious rationalization of political hierarchy; but even when Eurocentric observers do acknowledge the existence of mental capacities, their
rhetoric of tolerance founders on the assumption that these capacities are in
some sense latent (Bourdieu's "semi-theoretical") in an "ethnic" population – that they are given (*data*) to passive subjects by God, but stimulated
into active form by European culture and language alone. Those with European culture *know*, claim *recognition*, of other cultures, which is what apparently licences even so critical a writer as Said to acquiesce in identifying
"the 'concrete' existence of Australian and Brazilian aborigines whose ways
Lévis-Strauss has chronicled *so well*" (1975:327; my emphasis). How does
Said assess the quality of Lévi-Strauss's description? Is the only basis for

judgment the Eurocentric stereotype that renders all tribal peoples as alike?

Exogamous and incestuous translations: knowledge and social life

Lévi-Strauss appears to fear mass westernization mainly as a threat to *non-European* peoples. In practice, however, he creates textually the sense of homogeneous otherness that we meet in the more obviously Eurocentric writers: internal differentiation is essential to the generation of energy characteristic of what he has called "hot" societies. Here lies the likeliest explanation of his persistent failure to address the problem of structural transformation in a historically self-documenting society, or to carry out his own implicit program of analyzing the *analysts'* exegeses (1955; cf. Herzfeld 1985c). Because internal differentiation leads to the conscious articulation of whatever ideology underlies it, the logic of his distinction between conscious and unconscious models means that the richer the analytical *tools*, the worse they are as analytical *subjects*.

Lévi-Strauss's commitment to an essentially Eurocentric perspective becomes clearer through juxtaposition with what we may call the endo-European cultural prescriptions of Steiner's *After Babel* (1975:49–109 and *passim*). Steiner advocates a form of cultural relativism as well intentioned and as protective of fragile native cultures as that of Lévi-Strauss. Both writers, true to a shared Vichian heritage, recognize the embeddedness of knowledge in the practices whereby it is obtained (e.g. Steiner 1975:111), and both see in those practices the inevitability of imperfection. Still in the same relativistic tradition, Steiner sees in Whorf's evocation of a "Standard Average European" language type a useful defense against the "hubristic simplification" of reducing the world's languages to a single, Cartesian grammaticality (1975:92; Whorf 1956:138). Steiner's actual tactic, however, is to retreat rather than advance: while familiar diversity makes translation within the European historical community both difficult and potentially deep, "translation at great distance turns out to be the trivial case" (Steiner 1975:393).[14] For Steiner, as for the long line of his predecessors, European culture has always been an elaborately defended and stylishly complex unity, not a denominator both low and common. But he does not reject exotic cultures as inferior. Rather, from the unexceptionable vantage point of conceding that "every human utterance can be construed as 'political' and every reflex as 'ideological'" (1976:98), Steiner argues that translation from exotic languages is at best an "invention" and a simplification, whereas European literatures compel our attention to the complex minutiae of difference (1975:359–63). Corresponding to the necessary self-delusion entailed in our understanding of exotic literatures is the – to him – unnuanced English of non-European speakers; even his seemingly reluctant concession to the dispersed, postcolonial forms of English (1975:469) pales to shabbiness besides, for example, George Orwell's generous tribute to Indian English (Orwell 1956:250–4). He tempers his already qualified approval throughout with the same fear of monoculture that we have already observed in Lévi-Strauss and Le Lannou.

Lévi-Strauss and Steiner thus both show clear signs of their commitment to the European ideology. Lévi-Strauss tempers his Rousseauvian nostalgia with an awareness of the necessary imperfection of all ethnographic data; like an archaeologist who recognizes that "[a]ll excavation is destruction" (Woolley 1954:40), he understands that encounters with alterity undermine its absoluteness. Steiner agrees: knowledge is translation, and all translation is imperfect. Moreover, Steiner (1975:38–9), like Lévi-Strauss, plays on sexual analogies of linguistic intercourse. But whereas Lévi-Strauss's anthropological imagination is thoroughly exogamous, Steiner's, addressed to a more exclusively literary constituency, is an exclusive exogamy. One must marry out – this is erudition – but marrying *too far out* is miscegenation born of the sins of ignorance and infidelity.

If knowledge is translation, as Steiner avers, then the multiplicity of languages is one of the conditions of sin. Within this etiology of imperfection, only the European cultures possess a sufficient sense of their ultimate, transcendent unity to pursue grace; the others, however worthy they may be, are so beyond the pale that they might as well seek their own salvation. The European tradition reproduces its own supremacy internally in the elevation of the erudite "high culture," so that the directing "Mind" that Cuoco (1924:94–6) attributed to "cultivated" people can both participate in and yet also direct from outside the formation of a truly national or pan-European tradition. For example, the Greek folklorists Spyridon Zambelios and Michael Lelekos thought that while they had participants' rights to emend folk texts, they did so on the basis of a superior erudition.

This logic is an old familiar of anthropology: it suggests the oxymoronic structure of "observer participation," the mediation of nature (otherness) and culture (identity) that authorizes the modern ethnographer to serve simultaneously as a representative of the domestic mind and as someone who has experienced the savage mind directly. In the symbolic language of the discipline, such knowledge can only be attained by means of ritual passage through *fieldwork* – that moment of transformation from the natural (*sauvage?*) of which Roy Wagner's rather Vichian exhumation of the agrarian roots of *culture* (cf. Latin *colere*; Wagner 1975:21) puts us suggestively in mind.

Participant observation is only a fiction inasmuch as we treat it as an activity *significantly different from that of the people under observation*: we are participant observers only as far as we are also prepared to accept our informants' right to the same title. This could be taken to mean that the knowledge garnered by anthropologists is not social, merely "factual." That is the position that permits even the assertion that all the members of a given society "believe" in the same ways (see Needham 1972). Ideas of this sort lurk in the best intentioned studies: in Bourdieu's undifferentiated Kabyle, in Sahlins's emphasis on *external* differentiation amongst non-western groups, in Wagner's summative "tribal, religious, and peasant societies." In taking up such uniform images of the cultural other, anthropologists have done to Vico – with his contention that all truth is constructed out of social and personal experience – exactly what nationalist writers had done to his memory a mere century earlier.

The view from too near-at-hand: Greek ethnography, cultural marginality, and the margins of erudition

This embarrassing genealogy goes some way toward both explaining the marginality of Mediterranean (and especially Greek) ethnography to the development of anthropological theory, and suggesting that a politically more reflexive stance might reverse that state of affairs. Just as textual exoticism can now be read as an expression of concerns specific to the context of colonialism, so too we can the more sensitively decipher "Mediterraneanist" texts in the light of the international power relations in which they are embedded. This does not entail a rabid attack on their authors' imperialistic designs. On the contrary, they exemplify the constant struggle of anthropological writing to resist an unsympathetic historical context, and their failures – which are only failures in an anachronistic sense – are ideally instructive.

In particular, we must view these texts as attempts to come to terms with the aesthetic problem of making the societies in question *interesting*, while at the same time respecting the ideological desire at the national level to avoid the generalization of "typicality" – being treated as a culture of undifferentiated picturesqueness. The relationship of each study to these wider contexts is not a simple one, but in some respects the two major ethnographies that launched modern research in Greece – Ernestine Friedl's *Vasilika* (1962) and John Campbell's *Honour, Family, and Patronage* (1964) – anticipate the problem with exemplary prescience. The first general study of *the* Greek peasant (McNall 1974), though largely based on a single village, was written by a sociologist; most anthropologists have tried to avoid such broad formulations of typicality.[15]

This is important in that the published ethnographies do not themselves contribute to a general reification of "Greek culture," whatever the uses to which they are subsequently put by other authors. Nonetheless, emphasis on moral values (Campbell 1964) or on childhood training in aggressive self-projection (Friedl 1962:84–7) sometimes seems to conjure up the teleological fatalism of social structure and of "culture and personality," respectively. Such overdetermination of cultural traits (see critiques by Fabian [1983:45–52] and Bourdieu [1977:84–5]) risks suggesting an unintended resemblance to the characterology of early nationalistic folklore studies. Unlike the latter, however, the ethnographies in question generally avoid claims to having portrayed Greek values in general. Such statements do occur in secondary treatments; Doumanis (1983:111), for example, nostalgic for an era free of unreasonable expectations, and generalizing rural Greek culture from Campbell's ethnography alone, claimed that the urban Greeks' rural ancestors did not resent their poverty. But ethnographies actually seem more frequently to attract the reverse charge, that of a frivolous atypicality (e.g. McNall, Vlachos in Dimen and Friedl 1976), even though a concern with typicality is not, in fact, a major component of ethnographic practice.

By moving the techniques of ethnographic description into Greece, moreover, the scholars in question effectively laid the grounds for a more comprehensive resistance to exoticism and to the hitherto unquestioned division of the world into two clearly demarcated cultural opposites:

In the last two decades many cultural anthropologists have turned to the study of societies whose cultures are in the main line of Near Eastern tradition. They have done so because of a conviction that the techniques and insights developed through the study of primitive societies are useful for the description and analysis of all societies. (Friedl 1962:2)

The decision to work in Greece bravely challenged an established tradition. Friedl argued that what went for Africa or the Amazon applied to "all" societies, including those of Europe.

But the weight of traditional exoticism still required at least a rhetorical justification for this heresy. By identifying "folk" and "peasant" societies with the "Near East," Friedl evoked an orientalist rhetoric of legitimation that attached the Greeks to the ancestral European tradition, the "main line" from which Europe emerged, rather than to modern Europe itself.

The first ethnographic studies of Greece did nevertheless break with exoticism, whatever traces of it may have persisted. Campbell's (1964) "dovetailing" mode of exposition, inherited from Evans-Pritchard and bequeathed to Campbell's own students (see Campbell 1975), underscores his radical achievement in rendering the Sarakatsani distinctive amidst a host of African ethnographies. In the same way, Friedl's *Vasilika* must be read in historical context. Otherwise, her cautious allusion to the "Near East" might seriously obscure a substantive literary achievement in "defamiliarizing" a people with whom she recognized such close cultural affinity.[16]

Much the same applies to her view of the villagers' knowledge of their own history. Anthropologists were then used to dealing with "peoples without history." A population that possessed some degree of *recognizable* historical consciousness – in other words, a sense of history that bore some resemblance to academic western models – invited judgments based on criteria largely extrinsic to village tradition (Friedl 1962:106):

Although the classical Greeks are by no means in the forefront of the villagers' consciousness, and although their understanding of the details of the classical age is incomplete, the knowledge that "Greece brought light to the world" contributes to the villagers' faith in their own ability to develop themselves and their country.

There is, then, some knowledge of the Classical past; but it appears here as a feeble refraction of that Eurocentric erudition so aggressively displayed in Steiner's *After Babel*. It is not a triumphantly *different* kind of knowledge – as both the local logic of *eghoismos* and the intellectual ideology of European diversity would demand – but merely *incomplete, imperfect*. The Sarakatsani, Campbell's "people without history," represent a still earlier stage in the state-controlled re-education of the Greeks. The inhabitants of Vasilika have adopted the prevailing ideology to the point where, at least in interaction with outsiders, they do more explicitly struggle for admission to the European canon of history.[17] Without history, there is no erudite distinctiveness and therefore no admission to the encompassing unity of modern Europe.[18]

Two parallel symbolic oppositions, one indigenous to Greece, the other a product of anthropological theory, together provide a framework for understanding the discursive interplay between the local Greek experience of historical events and the scholarly reification of History writ large. The first, the Greek polarity, is the balance between two models of Greek identity that derive from the Classical and Byzantine-Turkish models, respectively. The second, a feature of recent theoretical debate within anthropology, is the polar distinction between rules and strategies. As will become apparent, this latter pair effectively glosses a contrast that Greeks express between a normative and idealized Hellenism – official history – on the one hand and a roguish *Romiossini* on the other. Our concern is with social discourse; and discourse encapsulates and exploits history for its own strategic ends.

To some extent, the conflict between the two Greek models of history is a special case of the theoretical distinction between rules and strategies. Hellenism stands for a rule-bound concept of the past, highly idealized and conformist, and in this respect it captures the essence of a tradition of anthropological and historical theory that has dehistoricized and universalized itself. When the model of Hellenism begins to acquire the sheen of a universal model, this is because official interpretations adopt the rhetoric of western historiography, which makes ancient Greece the fount and origin of all civilization worthy of inclusion, and exclude most local-level perceptions of the past from the canon of "real" history altogether.

Romiossini, by contrast, represents the internal, practical history of Greece. It, not Hellenism, is the *difference* that constitutes Greek identity. If the social discourse that interests anthropologists is that of the villages and towns, of social life rather than of printed books and nationalistic pronouncements, then differences, not systems and rules, are what concern them: *istories*, not History. In the next two chapters, we now critically juxtapose the two symbolic oppositions that this distinction evokes: Hellenism/*Romiossini* in the specific domain of Greek ethnography, rules/strategies in anthropological theory. The comparison, which complements that already suggested between folklore/anthropology and honor/shame, brings into critical focus the relationship between the symbolism of anthropological practice and the logic of cultural stereotypes.

5 The double-headed eagle: self-knowledge and self-display

The clothing of identity: regulation against intimacy

The rise of an explicit ideology of European identity could not but exercise a strong influence on Greece, a nation-state conceived in relation to the idea of European culture and treated as an inferior variant by its politically stronger champions. Under conditions of such ambivalence, the double-headed eagle of Byzantium aptly became one of the symbols shared by the folk tradition and the official ideology. The symbolic opposition between European and oriental brought into play a series of further contrasts, which at first seem amenable to the formal structuralist device of the two-column diagram.

This device acquired a certain popularity in the 1960s, mostly amongst Oxford structuralists. In its bare essentials, it is a paired list of symbolic oppositions (left/right, black/white, sin/blessing, female/male etc.), arranged in such a way as to suggest that each opposition "stood for" all the others in a transformational series (see especially Needham 1973). One such diagram did in fact appear in a major ethnography of a Greek community, as a means of ordering the values associated with male and female stereotypes (Christ/Devil, wisdom/gullibility, and so on [du Boulay 1974:104]). But this soon paled into unobtrusive modesty beside a two-column proclamation of "*the* Mediterranean code of honour" (Blok 1981:430–1; my italics).

As a device of ethnographic representation, such diagrams are undoubtedly both useful and dangerous: useful inasmuch as they summarize the stereotypes at a glance, dangerous in that they very easily become an excuse for ignoring the *uses* that people make of stereotypical attributes. The diagram reifies the stereotypes, and thereby permits the sort of circular argument about Mediterranean homogeneity that I have just noted. In studying virtually any western nationalism, this becomes a conceptual trap, since the hierarchical fixity of the oppositions thus arranged harmonizes all too well with nationalistic values (e.g. male domination). In the

95

Greek case, the problem comes to a head; for the two-column diagram is very much a product of Europe, itself the ideologically dominant pole in the fundamental opposition between Europe and the Orient, and can indeed be traced back through a normative genealogy to the philosophers of ancient Greece itself (G.E.R. Lloyd 1966:31–48). One of its most popular uses had been in the global exploration of gender through the dichotomy of public and private; but, as Sciama (1981:91–92) has pointed out, this works better for British university life than it does for rural Greeks (see also Hirschon 1981, 1983; Danforth 1983a; Dubisch 1983:195).

Moreover, the two-column diagram is above all a *literate* device (J. Goody 1977a, 1977b:52–73), and as such it *literalizes*. Its use embeds ethnographic description and analysis in a dominant European tradition that claims literacy as both the instrument and the symbol of its own power. Let us therefore begin by inverting normative procedure, as I did earlier with the binarisms of Lévi-Strauss's conscious–unconscious distinction, and apply that device to the theoretical matrix of the Eurocentric anthropology whence it came.

What would we put in such a diagram? The obvious pairs already mentioned – rule/strategy, competence/performance, *langue/parole*, structure/process – can be expanded to include many more (e.g. paradigmatic chain/syntagmatic chain, culture/history, and even – not inappropriately – Vico's divine/gentile distinction). It would also include the theory/ethnography distinction, and this in turn directs our attention to the hierarchical relationship within each pair; the more normative term always seems to regulate the more processual. If the reader at this point feels discomfited by the simplistic bracketing that I have offered, how much more must the two-column diagram violate and constrain the cosmology of people dragged into western history and literacy by ideological forces over which they have little control.

So let us pursue this exercise in doing to ourselves as we have done to others. Two further pairs that we might well add are the contrast between activity and passivity, and that between legal self-regulation and social incontinence. These pairs not only evoke the parallel European-oriental pair in western stereotypes, but also the male-female pair that conventional western attitudes seem to share with those of Greek villagers. They appear in a common attitude that dismisses ethnography as mere anecdote: here, the theory-ethnography distinction reappears relatively unchanged as the Greek (and general European) contrast between (male) rationality and (female) gossip.

This set of relationships has its roots in the prehistory of anthropological thought. An early embodiment of familiar, stereotypical values appears in

Table 1. *Linnaeus's anthropological taxonomy*

Subdivision	Skin color	Temperament	Physique	Clothing	Government
American	copper	choleric	erect	body paint	custom
European	fair	sanguine	brawny	close clothes	laws
Asiatic	sooty	melancholy	rigid	loose clothes	opinions
African	black	phlegmatic	relaxed	body grease	caprice

Linnaeus's taxonomy of human groups. Among *Homo sapiens*, in addition to admitting a mysterious class of four-footed humans, Linnaeus acknowledged the subdivisions shown in table 1 (adapted from Hodgen 1964:425). Hodgen (1964:426) is sharply critical of Linnaeus's schema:

He not only believed in the existence of human varieties or races, but he failed as a proponent of the hierarchical arrangement of things to preserve any discernible order in their listing. He subscribed to the reality of fabulous, monstrous men. He was subservient to unexamined medieval ideas.

But Hodgen herself is guilty in this passage of *chronocentrism* – the historicist version of ethnocentrism. Above all, she fails to emphasize how these categories reproduce stereotypes that still have a great deal of currency, and that particularly determine her own and still more recent perceptions of the distinction between theory and description in anthropology. While seeing in the Linnaean system some "import for ethnological thought and future race relations" (1964:425), Hodgen ignores the *symbolism* of his taxonomy and consequently fails to elicit its relationship both to romantic ethnocentrism and the Cartesian presupposition of an observing, theorizing, independent mind.[1] By slighting the long period between Herodotus and the Enlightenment, moreover, she reproduces the flattened historical perspective of the romantic era's self-genealogy. It is no coincidence that, as Chabod (1964) has pointed out, the medieval era also saw the categorical banishment of the Greeks to the conceptual nether regions of the Orient.

   In a fascinating recent debate, Frake (1985) and Gell (1985) have demonstrated that chronocentrism has damaged modern understanding of medieval navigational science as fully as ethnocentrism has dismissed that of non-western peoples.[2] One could say much the same, and with necessarily heavier irony, about the various "authoritative" histories of anthropology. This romantic elision of the time gap between Classical Greek and eighteenth-century thought had two effects, the one dependent on the other. First, it forged a relation of similarity between the *contemporary exotics* studied by anthropologists and the anthropologists' own *exotic ancestors*, by dismissing the scientific acuity of both. Second, by relegating the medieval and Renaissance periods to a sort of primitive intellectual age, it sealed off critical historical access to the symbolic underpinnings of scientism in modern anthropology. This is what Vico intended by the return to conceptual barbarism: as soon as scientific thought loses sight of its historical contingency, it ceases to be scientific.[3]

Between the vertical columns of the Linnaean schema, we find an arresting agreement. Traces of the old humoral associations, as well as of the association of blood with vigor, infuse the parallels between the second and third columns (*skin color* and *temperament*). Only the strongly implied dualism of mind and body prevents a total merging of *temperament* and *physique*. In the relationship between *physique* and *clothing*, the European particularly stands out: one can almost hear the stentorian echoes of the generations of schoolteachers admonishing their young charges, uniformed but unformed, with the old saw, *mens sana in corpore sano*.

But it is between the last pair of columns (*clothing* and *government*) that we find the most illuminating correspondence. For while *physique* embodies a particular mental set (and therefore, as we shall see, has a great deal to do with the frequency of bodily metaphors in conjunction with inner-directed stereotypes of culture), *clothing* represents the external persona that corresponds to the ideal type, so to speak, of the society as a whole. Thus, the American and the African appear to have made relatively little progress from a state of nature; they therefore passively accept government by abstract principles external to their individual selves (custom and caprice, respectively). If even people of cultured intelligence cannot discipline their physical selves into a controlled cultural appearance, then these people are clearly still in a symbolically unclean state. The loosely clad Asiatic thus forms opinions which do not have a sufficient coherence to merge into a legal system. But the European, whose self-control is symbolized by tight-fitting garments, is also socially and legally continent.

Note that this is specifically a description of male dress, and that laws are thought to be made by men; racial and cultural inequality are reproduced hypotactically *within* each subdivision. The symbolism persists: recall Campbell's account of Sarakatsan female dress as a disguise for women's stereotypical social and moral lack of self-control (1964:287): a young woman "who by artifice or accident allows her [head] scarf to become frequently undone gains an evil reputation." Exposure of the body is, concomitantly, exposure of the uncontrolled essence of Sarakatsan female sexuality. Even the "only concession to the display of the hair" consists in growing long pigtails; and these are clear enough expression of physical control. It is also no coincidence that in Greece, men, living more public lives than women, have generally been quicker to adopt European dress norms. Outer clothing conveys key messages about stereotypes of inner continence.

Clothing both embodies and disembodies; it represents the barrier between the intimate and the public that for many Europeans defines both culture and the cultured individual. This is not a hard-and-fast dichotomy of good versus bad. Only language has a trick of making it seem so. The close intimacy suggested by body metaphors, for example, has entirely positive connotations in the right place. The apparent contradiction between the diabolical and virginal aspects of a woman's sexuality in both Greek and Italian culture (du Boulay 1974:119; Hirschon 1978; Giovannini 1981), for example, is better seen as an expression of *tension* – that is, the tension between the sweetness of domestic intimacy and the fear men have of their wives' and daughters' defilement by other men. Dirt is indeed culturally defined as "matter out of place" (M. Douglas 1966). What changes is not the definition of "dirt" so much as the location of "place" – and it can change very rapidly indeed, as when an alleged rapist recoups his victim's good standing by marrying her, or when (notably on Crete) a young man whose suit has been rejected by the woman's father "steals" (abducts) her in order to prove his worth and simultaneously make it impossible for anyone else to marry her. In both these instances, an outsider successfully challenges the boundary that hitherto, so to speak, dis-placed him. Exclusion is always relative.

Dumont's contention that difference implies hierarchy provides a complementary perspective. Dumont adds that any inequality can appear inverted from the perspective of a broader (more inclusive) or narrower (more exclusive) comparison (1982; see also Sahlins 1985:103). An obvious case in point concerns male-female relations, stereotypically represented in many of the ethnographic accounts as a simple, one-way hierarchy – a perspective that ironically reinforces the androcentric tone of the public ideology by suppressing the alternative view, not simply *of the women*, but *of most villagers when discussing intimate situations with those whom they regard as intimate friends*. The aggressively male Cretan animal-thief who remarks on his mother's or his wife's distaste for his activities, for example, may well express sympathy with her attitude or even fear of her derision.

The point at issue here is that in speaking of *the* symbolism of a given community, we too easily play into the hands of the dominant groups, those who *define* propriety. What we are then discussing is an official praxis; we ignore interpretations that may reverse the system by redefining, not matter, but place (Galaty 1979). In the Greek context, the two-column diagram simply reproduces the males' point of view – one that the women play a major part in transmitting to succeeding generations, as

Handman (1983) has pointed out, but that does not necessarily embody the values that they may conceal behind their silence or their sexless clothing. They do not hide their values; they, the women, are themselves hidden. But what is true at the domestic level also applies at the national: official power suppresses ordinary social discourse. That is why so much of the work of recasting the learned classification of folklore by nationalist authors involves a recovery of the indigenous categories and interpretations that local and foreign scholars' neo-Classical aspirations have thoroughly suppressed.[4]

Clothing embodies in the sense that it defines the contours of a being; it disembodies in that it denies others access to a critical appraisal of that representation. It is a boundary between the intimate and the social; and inasmuch as the body provides primary metaphors for our pragmatic understanding of the world (M. Jackson 1983a, 1983b), clothing provides a fundamental metaphor for our representation of ourselves to that world. Our language is full of evidence for this: such terms as *garb, guise, clothed, clad,* and *dressed* shows how basic the metaphor of clothing is to our conception of rhetoric. I have *clad* this argument in a familiar *garb*.

The metaphor of a clothed body is particularly apposite for this investigation. It is part of the Greek imagery of culture; the writer E. Roidis, for example, ideologically a supporter of the vernacular but unfamiliar with it as a result of long residence abroad, spoke of language as "clothing" (see Dimiroulis 1985:268). This metaphor also conjures up the notion of embarrassment and secrecy that is so vital an aspect of the honor/shame literature, suggesting repeatedly that the national concern with symbolic inclusion and exclusion reproduces a vernacular idiom that it has coopted for its own ends. And it reminds us of the rapid westernization of Greek clothing in the literal sense: a public affirmation of the official and pragmatic dominance of the European aesthetic to which, as we have seen, anthropology is also a direct heir.

Rhetoric is thus not an exclusively linguistic concern, but consists in the aesthetic principles of persuasion in all semiotic domains. Clothing has served as a convenient path of entry into other, congruent rhetorics; later in this chapter, for example, we shall see that architectural form plays a (literally) powerful role in Greek social intercourse. Much social life – including most anthropologists' – entails compromises between opposing *social constructions of reality*. This formulation disposes of the Cartesian distinction between objective and subjective knowledge with a single, essentially Vichian stroke.[5] In its place, it opens an inquest into the power that authorizes these various constructions. For evidence, it does not confine its attentions to language. Instead, it asks why language should be given so much priority in many of the constructions in question, and demands examination of the many other codes that express the tensions between the body politic and the clothes it wears.

Inclusion and exclusion: the pragmatics of Greek identity

In the Greek context, these tensions are most obviously expressed in three domains. One is the contrast between the two largely literary stereotypes of Greekness, *Romiossini* and *Ellinismos*, that we have already briefly discussed. The second, the best known outside Greece, is the celebrated language question – the debate between neo-Classical purism and demoticism (advocacy of the vernacular). And the third is a symbolic reproduction of the same basic opposition: the double birth of a hero claimed as national by the dominant scholarly tradition.[6] This character, whose most commonly cited name (Digenes) alludes to his dual parentage (Greek mother, Arab father), reappears under a variety of other names and in quite different special roles in folksongs, and thereby enables us to begin examining the relationship between official discourse and the more familiar forms of everyday life in a larger historical context.

The language question is obviously central to any inquiry into the forms and development of modern Greek identity. But what is perhaps particularly revealing is that the very pre-eminence of language has rarely been made the object of critical scrutiny. The enormous importance of lexicography and grammar in European nationalism set a standard that the Greeks were in no position to resist. Their consequent concern with the niceties of what constitutes authentic Greek – the language spoken in everyday concourse, or the various degrees of neo-Classical restoration – has dominated education, politics, and literature from long before the inception of the bureaucratic nation-state (see Henderson 1970; Kedourie 1970:37–47).

But the tension between the purist and demotic language forms belongs to the larger distinction between origins rooted, respectively, in the Classical past and in more recent history. The double image of Greek cultural origins generates some wrenching paradoxes for Greek nationalism. On the one hand, the attempted recovery of the Classical past suggests the survival of paganism and therefore evokes, or evoked until comparatively recently, the ire of the church. On the other, the enthusiasm for things Byzantine and post-Byzantine includes at least a tacit recognition of the Islamic contribution, and especially that of the Turks, to present-day Greek culture. These ideal types have become known, respectively, as "Hellenism" and *Romiossini*. The first is named for Classical Hellas, the second for the *"New Rome"* that the Roman Emperor Constantine founded and that became the capital of the Eastern Roman – later, the Byzantine – Empire.

Greek life is marked by this intense conflict between the Romeic and Hellenic images and ideologies. There are other images and terms of Greekness, as a huge critical literature attests (see Mandouvalou 1983), and the symbolic opposition between the Romeic and Hellenic stereotypes should be understood as a flexible instrument of thought rather than as an absolute and deterministic model based on exact readings of history.[7] Nevertheless, these terms do give some historical weight to the suggestion of a fundamental tension between national images. These ostensibly historical images, the Hellenic and the Romeic, inform the respective ideals of *self-presentation* and *self-knowledge* (or *self-recognition*). This direct connection between historical models and social constructions of the self is clearly rooted in the political origins of the Greek nation-state. Because official cultural forms in Greece are largely predicated on the ideal of a Classically-derived European identity, Hellenism represented the dominant official version of national identity for most of the country's history. This is the version that can be presented to outsiders: it conforms to the ideals of a renascent Hellas. The traces of later cultural accretions are an embarrassment of foreign matter, even though they are both socially familiar and closely connected with the history of the orthodox church – the object of many tortuous attempts to prove that orthodoxy was a logical heir to Classical philosophy.

The nineteenth-century Greek citizen often did not know of such intellectual convolutions until suitably taught. He "knew he was a *Romios* . . . a Christian, not that he was a Hellene" – which it therefore became an urgent goal of the state to inform him (Mouzelis 1976b:445). The means adopted for this pedagogical conversion was systematic education, very much of the kind that Cuoco advocated for the Italians. In its most extreme forms, it refused the premise of a modern Greek culture altogether (see Valetas 1982:17). Greeks came to experience the curious situation of seeing whatever was most ordinary, intimate, and unexceptional in their daily lives treated as relics of an undesirably exotic past. Even those who defended the ordinary language against linguistic formalism found themselves branded as slavophiles or communists (see Petrounias 1978:199; Sotiropoulos 1982:27, n.52): this defined them as enemies of individualism and Hellenism, the twin virtues of Europe.[8] In Greece, the defensive boundary that the West erects against the incursions of the exotic has imploded.

But this would not have been the case had the official view prevailed and the traces of Arab, Turkish, and even Italian culture been eradicated for good. In practice, these elements of a disreputable past flourish as the very substance of a familiar and desirable present. For social life is a complex of *competing* codes; everyday interaction often contradicts official usage.[9] Since official discourse in Greece is symbolically cast as the very antithesis of the quotidian, there are times when the practical conduct of daily life inverts the official ideology altogether. This becomes clearest in popular attitudes to literacy, a quality that official ideology has often associated exclusively with Classical learning. The poor but hospitable villager tells the obviously literate ethnographer that the latter "has nothing" and so should accept the edible and potable marks of dependency; the illiterate Maniat village mayor boasts that he can still wield the official rubber stamp "better than scholars" (Meraklis 1984:73); the Cretan bonesetter who learned his trade on flock animals gloats over stories that tell how he forced the officially appointed doctors to recognize his skills even though the law forbade him to practice them. The very embarrassment of subordination makes its reversals so much sweeter.

These local instances of the inversion of official values are perhaps self-evident. It has always seemed harder, however, to specify the connections between such symbolic reversals on the one hand, and, on the other, the rather abstruse academic issues that seem to be involved in the language question, the historically appropriate terminology for Greekness, and the analysis of the manuscripts and folksong texts that tell the story of Digenes and his various epiphanies. Yet the academicism of these three grand historical themes is itself an important part of the story, since it has proved a potent factor in maintaining the domination of the official point of view. The high status of literacy lends force to the written forms and scriptist rules in each case, and gives authority to the highly educated few who pronounce one set as correct and all others as corruptions. Exemplified here is the close bond between scientistic scholarship and the demands of a bureaucratic ideology: literate reductions of culture inevitably emerge from the romantic use of science to formulate nation-state structures. They are as insensitive to local values as the two-column diagram, and for historically related reasons.

Although both the "language" question and the epic battles between the images of Hellenism and *Romiossini* cover a larger canvas, and are much better known to both Greeks and scholars of modern Greece, the poems and songs about Digenes of the dual ancestry help us to set the tensions current in modern Greek culture somewhat further back historically than the advent of nationalism as we now know it. They also touch on themes of everyday life, and so help us to connect the historical dimension with the social. The stories of these texts reflect a period of Byzantine history, as well as the local circumstances and values portrayed in subsequent reworkings. In many respects, they anticipate structural contradictions that are very much a part of social life today. The tensions in modern Greek culture did not arise with nationalism; rather, nationalism exacerbated them and gave them a form suited to the larger ideological context into which the emergent nation-state had been thrust.

I shall therefore begin the ethnographic discussion with the song texts and their multiple exegeses. This will provide a broadly historical introduction to the ways in which the dualism of Greek culture ramifies beyond language and into other codified areas of everyday life. In the next chapter, I shall then continue the same line of argument to examine the tensions that subsist between (official) definition and (daily) usage – yet another fight, like that between "Classical" and "folk" models of Greek culture, between eternal verities and transient pragmatics; and I shall extend this in Chapter Seven to an analysis of the radical divergence between official and popular understandings of the social and political world, thus paving the way for an etymologically based re-examination of the Greek-flavored formalism of the discipline in the concluding pages of the book.

Double images

Embarrassments of ambiguity occur at all levels of Greek social and cultural discourse: national, regional, village-level, familial. As a result, the characteristic cultural forms of one level can serve as metaphors for those of the others. In what follows, for example, it is essential to bear in mind that the scholars and politicians who have dealt with this material have often been motivated by concerns with covering and display that structurally resemble, at the national level, the smaller-scale interests of the dramatic characters we meet in the texts themselves. This will become clearer as we proceed.

It is not known when the epic poem about Digenes (S. Alexiou 1985), a baron of the Byzantine Empire's Mesopotamian borders in the eighth or ninth century, was first rendered into written form. The central character is known to us with certainty only from the poems and songs, despite serious attempts to identify him with historically attested personalities (e.g. Kalonaros 1941; Grégoire 1942). The versions of the epic vary in date (from the early fourteenth to the sixteenth century) and length, but they all recount in fairly exhaustive genealogical detail that the hero was the child of an Arab Emir; his mother was Greek. In the song versions, Digenes, after displaying remarkable precocity, goes to challenge the Arab enemy. His boasting, however, comes initially to naught, for he is captured and dragged off before the Arab leader, who, after an exchange of insults, recognizes the lad as his own son. This dénouement does not occur in the manuscript versions, which nonetheless make great play with the hero's precocious strength and wisdom, with his dual ancestry, and with his effective but independent-minded guardianship of the margins of the Byzantine territory; at one point, he is called to account by the emperor in terms broadly like those in which his Arab father upbraids him in the songs. He also engages in battle with rebellious warriors in his own domains; but his death, when it comes in the fullness of time, is peaceful.

In the course of the adventures recounted in the manuscript poems, several incidents occur that have also formed the nuclei of some of the songs. Prominent among these is his abduction of his bride-to-be; and the theme of his death, treated as the just end of a renowned chieftain, becomes in the song tradition a superhuman struggle with Death personified. On the other hand, his successful battle with the fearsome Amazon Maximo and his chivalrous treatment of her afterwards both appear to be among the motifs that are not represented in the folk tradition.

It is now unfortunately all but impossible to reconstruct the social milieu in which the folksongs in question were performed. They were most popular in the eastern and southern reaches of the Greek-speaking world, notably in Cappadocia, Pontos, Cyprus, the Dodecanese, and Crete. Today, with few exceptions, they are rarely heard in the villages. Although many are now available in printed form, few villagers sing them, and fewer have been heard to offer any kind of exegesis of them. Textually, however, it seems evident that for long periods the folksong tradition developed quite independently of the manuscript poems. Comparatively few of the folksongs mention Digenes by name, and the scholarly category of "Akritic songs" – for *Akritēs*, "borderer," the principal epithet of the manuscript Digenes – obliterates other important connections. To take just one example: many of these songs more closely resemble those sung about the guerrilla fighters of the War of Independence than they do the manuscript poems of Digenes Akritēs. The conventional scholarly label thus begs the question of historical development: it assigns all the relevant texts to a single period, and dismisses as corrupt those texts which admit other elements and allusions.

Nonetheless, there are a number of observable thematic connections between manuscripts and songs, and of course the efforts of nationalistic scholarship to exploit these links is itself of intrinsic interest in that it illustrates the uses of tradition in the construction of a national identity. For no less a luminary than N. G. Politis, the dominant figure of Greek folklore studies in the later nineteenth and first two decades of the twentieth centuries, pronounced the manuscript poem "the national epic of the modern Greeks," and proceeded, with great energy and meticulous scholarship, to detail its textual links with the folksong tradition.

Structural as well as thematic similarities abound. But the songs also depart from the manuscripts in matters of significant detail. The most relevant of these for present purposes concern the hero's birth. Instead of an Arab father, many of the song heroes have instead a *mother* of socially outsider status – usually a nun or a widow: marginality is now introduced, not by a warlike and respected foe (male), but by a socially humiliating flaw (female). Sometimes, the latter figure is complemented by the dramatic revelation that the hero's father is none other than Death personified:

having defeated the evil character Tsamadhos, the hero suddenly recognizes him as his long-dead father. The crushing of this unsavory revenant appears to signify the possibility of overcoming social marginality. Both widows and nuns are associated with the diversion of ordinary sexual and social intercourse, and the risk of sexual pollution that men attribute to sexual contact with any unmarried woman.[10] Moreover, a widow is often thought to "belong" to her late husband's family, so that any further sexual union is a betrayal; although nuns swear lifelong chastity, some are women who have borne illegitimate children and have retreated to the monastery as the sole acceptable solution to their shame.

But the marginality of these women is precisely what gives meaning to the victory of their son, the hero. Just as the extreme of *filotimo* (social worth) is furnished by the poor old woman who provides passers-by with a glass of water because that is all she owns, so these songs illustrate how a socially marginal person must always be thought capable of redeeming a persona tainted by his mother's evil sexuality. This character is something of a trickster, constantly on the alert for chances to reverse his lowly condition. As a symbol of social redemption, Digenes suggests a strong analogy with that embodiment of the Greek *rayas* (chattel) of the Ottoman Empire, the shadow theatre trickster Karagiozis, who constantly turns the tables on the Turks who gave him his name ("Black-Eye") and much of his stereotypical character.[11] Victory here is as much over one's own origins as it is over an external enemy. It is this, I suggest, that makes the entire gamut of texts so apt a metaphor for a nation struggling to obliterate a recent history that the tutelary West deemed degrading.

Structurally, it is tempting to draw an immediate parallel between this kind of *social* marginality and the *ethnically* ambiguous status of the "twyborn" Digenes. Within the ethnically heterogeneous character of the Byzantine Empire, the double birth of the manuscript hero seems to express ambiguities inherent in unstable borders and constant cultural borrowing (Karolidis 1906). Those scholars who wanted to turn the entire collection of manuscript poems and folksongs into a unified national monument, however, purified both the hero and the text at one and the same time. They treated the manuscript versions as an *Urtext*; the unseemlier variants then merely served as evidence of the decline of morality and good taste amongst the Turkish-dominated peasantry. The philological grounds for such an argument are purely speculative; the epic texts probably just represent a variation on the general theme of social and cultural ambiguity – the antithesis of the scientific ideals of romantic statism.

Digenes thus epitomizes the conquest of social or cultural disadvantage. This is a theme that leads us back to Dumont's point (1982) about the reversibility of value hierarchies. For in everyday life neither Turkishness nor femaleness is unambiguously bad. The image of women that we encounter in the published ethnographies is not purely negative;

every man is born of woman, and these stories exemplify the male/public/ heroic redemption of that essential weakness in the human condition (as the prevailing androcentric ideology presents it). Equally, Greeks often acknowledge the pleasant familiarity of traits that they attribute to Turkish influence, or that they at least see as points of commonality. Cretans who had returned from a period of work as *Gastarbeiter* in Germany assured me that they felt closer to their Turkish colleagues than to any other group. The "flaws" of descent from woman (often symbolically mitigated by likening a mother to the Virgin Mary)[12] and of cultural derivation from the Turkish invaders are part of the intimately experienced world, and, in that world, they carry positive meanings. The various songs and epics that I have summarily described express this marginality in *both* the ethnic and the social senses; and they celebrate the ability of the hero, no fatalist he, to transcend and glorify it.

The conquest of origins

The epic texts, the songs, and the various modes of exegesis all share a common goal. They are the attempts, by Greeks of widely varying background and ideological commitment, to assert what Said (1975:32) calls *beginnings* over mere *origins*, to *authorize* their own text. *Arkhi*, beginning, is that in which was the Word (*Loghos*, discourse), the unity to which all human activity ultimately must return (as some folk curing texts show[13]), and is synonymous with Authority (*Arkhi*) itself. In the biblical narrative of the Creation, as Leach (1969b) has argued, the fashioning of Adam and Eve overcomes the difficulty of deriving the human race from an aboriginal act of incest. Just as social laws regulate the sexuality that makes human existence possible, but fail to prevent the occurrence of incestuous unions or the procreation of sons by nuns and widows, so Hellenist statism represses the recurrent cultural otherness essential to its very being. The nationalists' Digenes emerged from an act of preordained miscegenation whose subsequent recurrences were to be regarded as corruptions of the Hellenic ideal, affronts to the national honor (*ethniko filotimo*).

This is the logic whereby some nationalists and philhellenes accepted the orientalizing influences at work in the pre-Classical era but contrasted their complete absorption into Greek culture with the tenacity of the latter, which was to survive the pressures exerted by the "foreign" (i.e. Romeic/ Roman) clergy and royalty of Byzantium as well as their Turkish successors (Zambelios 1859; d'Istria 1867; Paparrhegopoulos 1925–32). Oriental elements, subsumed in the national culture at the point of (time-less) *origin*, become polluting if persistent presences during the subsequent effort of creating a good (historical) *beginning*. In much the same way, we can see the Digenes songs and epics as attempts of individuals to overcome their disadvantages in order to create a new beginning – whether in the border struggles of the Byzantine Empire or in the critical social milieu of village communities under Byzantine, Frankish, or Turkish rule. That perspective then allows us to treat the nationalist historians and folklorists within the same frame of reference: they, too, are attempting to create a new timeless history, a perfect genealogy of the "race" (*i Fili*[14]).

The distinction between beginnings and origins is that of the active over the passive. For Said (1975:142), largely following Vico, "secular narrative ... is based on – *begins* in – the common and indisputable fact of natural human birth – or, using more severe terms, in the natal banishment of man from immortality and in his initiation in an afflicted family...." Origins thus precede the possibility of any kind of original sin; the latter, conversely, entails beginnings in the struggle for identity. For Western Europeans, the association of modern with ancient Greece is a discourse of sanctification, of *canonization* (but the canon is not that of the Greeks), and the ottomanization of Greece is the historical flaw against which it deploys its formalist tactics. In the terms of Mary Douglas's *Purity and Danger* (1966) again, the ancestral holiness of the Greeks and the current pollution of their Turkishness are mutually analogous in that both are western discourses that exclude Greece from the European structures of power. The *Greek* discourse of cultural imperfection, by contrast, is both a response to the negative opinions of outsiders – European ideologues or critical covillagers – and an assertion of the imperative quality of the fight for redemption and independence. It is a way of reclaiming history from those who have representationally repressed both that history and the active initiative needed to reclaim it.[15]

There are, predictably, significant differences between the different ideological traditions represented in the Greek material. Nationalist exegeses (e.g. those of N. G. Politis) vie with Marxist interpretations (e.g. Lambrinos 1947; Kordatos 1972), pitting ethnic identity against class solidarity. While the nationalists moved the marginal, ambiguous hero to the political center, claiming him as one of their own, the Marxists saw in him evidence of the arbitrary injustice of national borders. Moreover, the nationalists argued that the epics furnished the model for the folksongs; this enabled them to treat the absence of ethnic concerns therein as the result of the corruption of texts at once national and aristocratic; their opponents, by treating the songs as logically and chronologically prior, replaced the nationalists' concerns with *social* conflict on a truly *international* scale.

The epic versions, which in fact represent several changes of historical and ideological context, differ from the songs in what they consider to be the basis of social difference; the epics seem to posit ethnic origin, while the songs play with various more parochial contexts of birth. Nevertheless, these materials all display (various groups of) Greeks' desires to create active beginnings, to create a point of departure. In the nationalistic tradition, this comes to mean an active attempt to wrest control of their destiny from a dominant West: again, hardly the hallmark of either fatalism or inferiority complexes, but possibly an explanation of why some western scholars might pre-emptively wish these attributes upon the Greeks. Yet this could not be done straightforwardly: for while the literary commonplace of the West showed the dominant figure of the male Christian soldier-hero courting and converting the female oriental/effeminate Orient (Kabbani 1986:15), here the *father* of the hero is an Arab, whose Greek wife – like the nun or the widow of the oral variants – represents both a fallen condition and the indomitable recovery of a repressed tradition.

Living history

The control of origins lies at the heart of the implicit dispute between the philhellenes and the Greek nationalists. It was not an ephemeral matter that disappeared with the founding of the Greek state. On the contrary, it remains the source of a continuing disparity between patterns of self-presentation and self-knowledge. It is well illustrated by the following summary of attitudes in the Greek diaspora in Australia:

If people of British ancestry can take legitimate pride in British-derived institutions, such as the Westminster-style parliamentary democracy, it is also legitimate for Greek-Australians to remind their British counterparts of the *Greek origins* not only of our notion of democracy itself, but of our science, and of the Western ideal of the integrity, autonomy and freedom of the individual. This . . . represents a vital aspect of our civilisation. . . .
  If one recognizes the Greek origins of this common heritage, the English achievement would appear as its articulation within certain specific channels. From this perspective, the Australian type of parliamentary democracy is just a variant on the common European theme, with certain unique features of its own.
                                                                (Smolicz 1985:19)

From their own perspective, then, the Greeks' claims to have originated Australian democracy is not a passive acceptance of the ancestral role, but a symbolic demand for the right to active participation in the political system, based on the assumption of a common "Western ideal of the integrity, autonomy and freedom of the individual" – in other words, on the Eurocentric premise of ethnic distinctiveness within a shared ideological unity, metonymically symbolized by the distinctiveness of the individual within the ethnic or national entity.

Were the Greeks condemned to play the passive role of living ancestors, or would they be able to claim participation in modern Europe? The philhellenic strategy was to demand of the Greeks that they adopt the former course, and then to criticize them for their consequent inability to measure up to the latter. It was against this double bind that the ever sympathetic Houssaye demanded of his compatriots with deep indignation (1879:143; my italics):

Does this mean that for those who do not live in Athens in a virtual communion with the past, and who refuse to recognize in the modern Greeks the distinctive traits of Demosthenes, *Greece should be Paradise regained and the Hellenes a perfect people?*

Houssaye recognized the impossibility of the task that Greece had been set, that of a recaptured, Edenic past that would also be a Utopian present. The list of stereotypical failings that he cites – political instability, the horror of manual labor, inefficiency – is the pre-text whereby interventionist Europe decried the Greeks as flawed and corrupt, and whereby some of its self-avowedly Eurocentric representatives still condemn the same "un-European" traits in the modern Greeks. It reads, too, like part of a Greek catalogue of *romeika pramata*, Romeic things, at once the despair of occidentalist conservatives and the familiar blemishes of fond intro-spection. Houssaye, for whom (as a foreigner) such rhetoric could only be derogatory when applied to the Greeks, locates its roots in a widespread western reluctance to countenance anything exotic in the land of Europe's birth.

In his sympathetic clarity, Houssaye differed from those foreign com-mentators who preferred to represent the Greeks as the passive recipients of a cultural heritage that they did not understand very well. Unlike these condescending foreign observers, Greek peasants and academics alike have been far more inclined to affirm their active engagement in the definition of whatever identity they variously claimed. And when it came to nationalistic history, they did not accept foreign attributions of Classical origins fatalisti-cally – despite Toynbee's revealingly paternalistic remark that the Greeks had been "taught" (1922:128) to believe in their ancient heritage and could not now "learn" to shake free of it. It is Toynbee, with his presumption that the Greeks must follow the dictates of a "Near Eastern" identity he ascribes to them, who far surpasses the Greek nationalists as a (vicarious) fatalist.

To say, then, that the Greek nationalists merely imitated their western mentors plays into the ideology of tutelage.[16] Not only were the Greeks far from passive about their national independence; they actively resisted such charges of passivity. Even those who seemed to be the most subservient occidentalists among Greek intellectuals tried to refashion the dominant model into one of a beginning that they could genuinely claim as their own. Instead of claiming direct identity with the ancients, they constructed a text that made clear, as an authoritative text must (Said 1975:217), the rift between the idealized and model past that it represents and the experienced present for which it functions. Their premise was that of rebirth (*palin-genesis*) – a metaphor for *analogy*, not identity, between past and present.

Some of them (e.g. Zambelios 1859) recognized that even the supposedly aboriginal culture of Classical Greece had incorporated foreign elements of still greater age: the Greek genius for subordinating such oriental elements and bending them to the national will represents an *active* principle that contrasts with the philhellenic image of Greece as merely, in Byron's wistful archaeology, a "sad relic."

This gives a new significance to the Digenes story. At first blush, the ethnically ambiguous Digenes would seem an odd choice for a national epic figure. Similarly, one may wonder why the folksong versions enjoyed such wide currency in former years; adumbrating them to the category of "trickster myths," for example, is at best descriptive rather than explanatory, and perhaps misleading into the bargain (see Beidelman 1980). The salient point, however, applies equally to the nationalists' adoption of the manuscript poems and to the widespread popularity of the songs. It is that Digenes and his epiphanies all *struggle against the negative side of their origins*: the social disgrace of the widow or dishonored nun, the revenant-father Tsamadhos, ethnic otherness. In remodeling their origins, they create new beginnings; and this, too, is exactly what the nationalistic folklore tradition does with them in turn.

The nationalistic tradition glosses over the flaw in the Hellenic ideal; as for the folksong texts, they are "corruptions" in any case. But nationalistic scholarship does also tacitly acknowledge the presence of the ethnic and social ambiguities, and attempts to come to terms with them in a constructive way. Turning aside from passive *origins* that combine the pollution of the oriental with the sanctity of the ancient, the recreated hero creatively *begins* a new discourse which is itself an avid refashioning of identity out of humble beginnings. Social experience does not live up to the idealized perfection, which remains a goal to be sought but will be never more than provisionally attained. The heroic figure reconstructed by the nationalistic folklorists is, to use Said's (1975:142) Vichian imagery, born into an "afflicted family" that is secular rather than divine. That family is the chequered lineage of the modern Greek people, a history compounded of both Turk and European; and against both the former and present oppressor the reconstituted hero must struggle for the recognition and independence that they menace always.

Disemia: self-knowledge and self-display

The recognition of a chequered history is thus no barrier to attempts to remodel it. Although they presented an idealized neo-Hellenism to the outside world, even the most nationalistic Greek folklorists must have been well aware of the darker side. Greek identity is caught between two extreme poles, each derived from the image of a conquering Other. At one end stand law-abiding Europeans, imposing on themselves laws for which they can give objective reasons. On the other are the no less stereotypical orientals, loosely clad (as Linnaeus would have it) and as loosely organized, lacking in organization and self-control but rejoicing in their natural spontaneity as well as in their ability to fix events according to their needs. Koraes (the standard bearer for *katharevousa*) and Zorba vie for the Greek soul; but both proclaim its independence. The tension between them is everywhere. Perhaps its most expressive embodiment is the nineteenth-century urban house with a neo-Classical façade and simple, village-style interior: an architectonic trope of the tensions that subsist between self-display and self-knowledge (see Iakovidis 1975; 1982:31–3).

For despite the emphasis on the much discussed "language question" in Greece, the tension between external and internal images – between self-presentation and self-knowledge[17] – is not purely, or even primarily, a matter of language. The fact that the phenomenon was categorized in Greece as "the language question" (*to ghlossiko zitima*), and further glossed – so to speak – as *diglossia* in technical linguistics (Ferguson 1959), means only that it has become more *explicit* in language. But this in turn shows how easily scholarship accepts an élite point of view – a tendency further accentuated by the transference of evaluative language attitudes ("high" and "low" registers) into the technical vocabulary of diglossia. The highly literate elite, presiding over a peasantry of initially low literacy, paid special attention to language, not only because its neo-Classicism appeared to satisfy the wishes of the tutelary Powers, but also because linguistic specialization restricted access to the economic and political sources of power (see Sotiropoulos 1977, 1982). In short, the elite reproduced internally the pattern of domination that it both resisted and exploited externally; and this combination of circumstances reinforced the authority of linguistic purism and eventually made language the primary focus of all cultural debate, popular and academic alike.

Anthropology as a discipline is hardly free from these scriptist biases. Here, for example, is Bourdieu (1977:89):

In a social formation in which the absence of the symbolic-product-conserving techniques associated with literacy retards the objectification of symbolic and particularly cultural capital, inhabited space – and above all the house – is the principal locus for the objectification of the generative schemes . . .

The Kabyle inscribe their notions of the world on their physical space; but there is increasing evidence that western industrial societies are no less prone to imbue the built environment with relational meaning (Preziosi 1979; Lagopoulos 1980). Indeed, the very language of *structure* and of *inclusion* and *exclusion* in anthropology strongly suggests the architectonic basis of our own primary metaphors of self-presentation. Just as clothing encloses the individual self, so architecture clothes the collective identity, and demarcates it from the still more encompassing social bodies to which it belongs (Hirschon and Thakurdesai 1970; Hirschon and Gold 1982:69; Hirschon 1985). The house is an apt metaphor because of its close involvement with daily experience; Rhodian villagers described both the Turkish invasion of Cyprus in 1974 and the rape of a covillager's daughter by a resident *maepsari* (outsider[18]) as "entering a house." Given both the close symbolic association of the vulnerable female body with spatial closure, and the practical exercise of female power through the covering of domesticity and intimacy (Hirschon 1978, 1981, 1985:21; Danforth 1983a:206–9), we should expect to find architectonic tropes serving as a more or less pervasive idiom of differentiation between self-display and self-knowledge.

The generalization of diglossia to a model of ideological tension between these two poles allows us to bring together a number of issues that have hitherto been kept in separate academic compartments, and see them in relation to our central theme. The many domains in which this basic duality is reproduced – architecture, music, dress, gesture, moral values – provides us with the key to the essential homology that subsists between the readings of Digenes and the choices of style in everyday life. Indeed, the last of these codes, that of morality, enables us to go still further: it brings us full circle back to the analogy between sexually suspect origins and the symbolic condition of Greek culture, and so also to the direct entailment of anthropological discourse in the dialectic of honor and shame.

At the outset, it is important to establish that we are not well served by any analytical distinction between the real and the ideal. Appearances of "two-faced" hypocrisy in Greek culture have arisen from the necessity of responding to exterior probings, most recently represented by anthropological research but for much longer a direct product of the discourse of morality that had Greeks begging for inclusion in the European standards to which they had supposedly given birth. Thus, rather than posing a traditional real-ideal dichotomy, I would prefer to suggest a polarity between *two ideal types that are constantly and dialectically parlayed into virtually the entire range of social life*. Both are ideals in that both are stereotypes; but, by the same token, what gives both experiential reality is their *use* in the day-to-day rhetoric of morality. That rhetoric constitutes their reality.

It is fashionable, in this poststructuralist era, to attack any binary code as evidence of the imposition of a foreign system on indigenous values; and sometimes, as in the case of *Kypseli*, the complaint seems justifiable. But it does not automatically follow that oppositions such as those between male and female will not be salient for local actors. What must be resisted is the temptation to credit them with coercive power over those actors; for it is the *actors* who use *them*. When a Rhodian villager wanted to tell me how clever he was, he first told a story illustrating the diabolical cleverness of women: to win a wager with the Devil that she could not arrive home without getting wet in the rain, she took her clothes off until the very end of her journey – a significant inversion in light of the discussion earlier in this chapter. The narrator, however, then recalled how he, a male, had done the same thing.[19] One can multiply the examples easily enough. Here are a few: the variable use of the term "*katharevousa*" (in opposition to "demotic") to imply an impossible and absurdly pompous language and a standard of correctness; the association of goats in opposition to sheep to signify both uncontrolled sexuality and manly prowess (Campbell 1964:31; Herzfeld 1985a:17); and the use of the verb *vyeno* ("come out," often opposed to *beno*, "go in") both as a synonym for victory (e.g. in elections: "I come out [of it the victor]") and as a term for exposure to ridicule (e.g. *vyeno yelasmenos*, "I come out of it looking a fool"). In the latter situation, clothing may serve as the physical boundary of propriety: Sarakatsani laugh at a man whose self-display leads him to tear his shirts in shreds at weddings (Campbell 1964:45–6), while Rhodian villagers still recall – in verse – a man who habitually exposed himself at feasts as a sign of his high spirits (Herzfeld 1979). Actors must show themselves to be in control of these potent symbols; otherwise, meanings are inverted and other actors seize control.

Thus, too, the key images of Hellenism and *Romiossini*, or "outside" and "inside" views of Greek culture, are counters in a game that never ceases. The tension between these sides constitutes the dialectic of Greek identity, linguistically embodied in the model of *diglossia*. A conceptual expansion of that model, *disemia*, conveys the *multiplicity* of sign systems; it includes language, but does not necessarily accord it pride of place (Herzfeld 1982b).[20] Disemia is the expressive play of opposition that subsists in all the varied codes through which collective self-display and self-recognition can be balanced against each other.

This approach allows us to join up aspects of Greek culture (among others) that had hitherto been separated by the dictates of academic practice. Thus, for example, we can now perceive the close connection between the diglossia of sociolinguists and the moral value systems described by anthropologists. Language is either respectable or intimate; "shame" (*dropi*) is a covering of inward embarrassments in contrast to *timi* ("honor," better rendered as "social worth" [Campbell 1964:268]), the mark of outgoing self-respect. The advantage of this semiotic expansion is that it enables us to work beyond the self-sustaining ideology of a literate and highly language-aware élite, and – as in the *dropi/timi* example – it also permits us to include the symbolism of morality within our comparative scope.

The extension beyond language actually helps the analysis of the language question itself. The term *katharevousa* is directly associated with purity (*kathariotis*), and its proponents have invested true moral fervor in its propagation. But precisely *what* constitutes *katharevousa* has not always been entirely clear, despite all the attempts of grammarians to formulate rules for the categorical separation of the two major registers of Greek. Even leaving aside the variable degree of purism involved,[21] we find rural Greeks using the term in a variety of senses. For example, Rhodian villagers apparently thought of mainland speech as *katharevousa*, by which they meant "uncorrupted" (since they had endured the corrupting Turkish yoke longer than other Greeks – a common formula, of variable historical accuracy). But they also said that local speech was *katharevousa*, by which they presumably meant the archaizing features of which their relatively well-educated sons and daughters have made them aware. Even here, the standard is modern Europe rather than high antiquity: "they used to speak Greek by means of [printed] notes (*me tes notes*)," declared one Pefkiot, using the rather ambivalent gallicism by which rural people sometimes dismiss musicians who need to use anything as "European" as sheet music. Finally, we should note that the attribution of linguistic purism does not necessarily convey approval: it was certainly used to exclude me, the literate "scholar." Linguistic purism can index gaucherie, sarcasm, or sheer snobbery (see Kazazis 1966, 1982a:236; 1982b:116; Sotiropoulos 1977, 1982; Petrounias 1978). Purity, as we have already noted, is a function of the definition of place, and all we gain by privileging the formal definition(s) of *katharevousa* is an identification of the anthropologist's position with the statist control of literacy and aesthetics.

But if the state does not have a pragmatic monopoly over the definition or purity, the neo-Classical ideology has nevertheless exerted a pervasive influence. Diaspora Greeks, who tend to be linguistically conservative, react with moral outrage to newer importations, and may specifically dub the latter *akatharta* (literally, "unclean": Boston area; L. Papademetre, personal communication, 1985). Clearly, this is more than simply a split between two formal linguistic registers. Critics of the diglossia model have complained at great length about its simplistic implications, and have specifically charged that it fails to take account of intermediate forms. But Ferguson, who formulated the sociolinguistic model as we now generally know it (1959), had indeed acknowledged the importance of mixed forms in Greek and other languages, and even specified that the fundamental instability of the diglossic situation would eventually lead to the triumph of such linguistic compromises. The critics are quite right in seeing that symbolic opposition between "high" and "low" forms does not correspond perfectly to actual linguistic behavior, but their insistence on reading the diglossia model literalistically shows how far they are themselves subject to the imperatives of binarism (e.g. Shouby 1951; Fishman 1976; B. C. Johnson 1978). Here it should suffice to recall a point made earlier in this chapter – namely, that the real-ideal distinction of which social scientists are so fond is no less artificial and problematical. It, too, is a *disemic* pair, and it exhibits a concern with appearances ("neat analyses") not unlike that of Greek villagers in their official mode.

Linguistic pollution often models other kinds of pollution: both are a problem of disemia, and both are expressed in the architectonic terms of inclusion and exclusion. Thus, for example, Rhodian villagers paint a white line around the raised outer thresholds of their houses for reasons of *kathariotita* – a term we might pedantically translate here, not as "cleanliness" (its dictionary meaning) but "avoidance of categorical confusion," since the practice is clearly understood to have nothing to do with questions of biological hygiene.[22] Sometimes, speakers imply the outsider-like properties of their neighbors by allusion to cultural geography, and particularly to the cultural origins of particular epithets. In Rhodes again, the term *ghrousouzia* ("symbolic pollution" – another unavoidably pedantic rendition) is sometimes used for the evil eye when speaking with covillagers.[23] The members of the community know that the term is of Turkish derivation, and as such, unlike *vaskania*, an appropriate label for a communal flaw that outsiders should not be allowed to perceive.

In general, where such semantic "doubles" exist, the "Turkish" term is commonly the more derogatory of the two (see Kazazis 1981b, 1982b; B. Joseph 1983). But note that *ghrousouzia* can be admitted *within* the community, and that villages do not charge those who are guilty of it with *deliberate* evildoing. On the contrary, they insist on the involuntary nature of *ghrousouzia*; but its bearers are flawed and usually unpopular members of the local community. There are also usages in which a "Turkish" term carries a meaning that is less negative than intimate (as in the example of Macedonian villagers' use of *moukhabet*, "chat," mentioned earlier). The evaluation of a "Turkish" term can be positive or negative; as I have already pointed out, the usefulness of the binary code is lost when we attribute single values to each term. The entire system allows a constant manipulation of meanings through the use of a social architectonics of belonging and exclusion, and enables actors to acknowledge that "outsider-like" pollution can exist *within* the community – which never admits its presence to "real" outsiders.

Associations of language with purity are by no means unique to Greece. Tamil, a language spoken by people who are deeply concerned with purity and pollution even by the exacting standards of Indian ritual practice, seems to evince a comparable preoccupation with the preservation of the boundaries between its registers (Schiffman 1973, 1978). Greek culture is not marked by such careful prescriptions about hierarchy and pollution. On the other hand, its secular concern with the separation of official from ordinary social life does, as we have already noted, parallel concerns with a sexual definition of social integrity and defilement – the honor/shame opposition, which is given this form in anthropological discourse by the encompassing norms of bourgeois respectability. One sees this particularly in the close association middle-class Greeks assume between depraved sexuality on the one hand, and music and dance of recognizably Turkish origin and nomenclature on the other.[24] Sexuality is a common theme in both the Tamil and Greek discriminations between the public and the intimate.

This calls for a further clarification. The stereotype of the rural Greek woman, somewhat supported by most ethnographic accounts so far, makes her chaste and modest in her demeanor as well as in her actions. What this stereotype overlooks, however, is the *context* in which such modesty becomes mandatory. In Crete, in fact, women joke about how they keep a nightly tally, so that their husbands will have to make up any missed nights to them. These jokes, which may be bandied across the street in friendly company, disappear completely when strangers show up. Clark (1982), too, notes how the women of Methana engage in ribald joking in mixed company, provided that all present are relatives (see also Campbell 1964:275). Sexual humor is a mark of intimacy. While there may be considerable regional variation in the degree and forms of licence, it seems increasingly likely that female bawdiness pollutes in a strictly *social* sense – that is, when it acts to expose a family or village to outside disapproval. It, too, obeys the architectonic relativity of disemia.

Sexual and other ideas about pollution and purity thus link rural values with the bourgeois concerns of nationalism, and especially with that concern with the covering of all intimacy that characterizes both individual respectability and national pride. At the same time, they are cloaked with the absolute rhetoric of religious prescription, and religious texts are often quoted to justify both female modesty and the subordination of women to their husbands and fathers. Nationalism, too, often adopts a religious vocabulary, and this highlights the persistent analogy between family respectability and national pride. Patriotism is a *holy duty*, and the national language a *sacred charge* from ancient times. Much as in Tamilnadu the local Brahman tradition preserves sacred texts with rare precision, and uses them as the standard of all religious discourse, so – if the comparison is not too extreme – the earlier Greek nationalists attempted to rescue the Hellenic language from the defilement of centuries. It had, after all, been *thelima Theou i Poli na tourkepsi* – "the Will of God that the City should turn Turk [=Muslim]." Pollution still flows from the divine ordinance that brought Greek Christendom to its fall before the definitive enemies of the Cross.

The architectonics of Greek identity

The constant recurrence of the theme of inner- and outer-directed ideologies[25] conveys the strong spatiality of this discourse. Even a relatively humble nineteenth-century neo-Classical façade allowed the bourgeois household head, once he stepped outside, to exclaim proudly, "I am a Hellene!" (Iakovidis 1975). His house presented an ideally respectable outer face to the world, a celebration of *embourgeoisement* in progress. What went on inside was the family's business. Rural Greek house construction, too, has traditionally aimed at preventing penetration as far as possible (Friedl 1962:13–14). Since the interior is the wife's domain, it is significant that here a wife's "mask of expressionless humility" may give way to active participation in the discussion of household affairs (Campbell 1964:152). The façade, maleness, and Hellenism are symbols of self-display; domestic interiors, women's work, and the familiar world of the *Romios*, of introspection.

This link between physical interiority and social intimacy is reflected in domestic architecture in a variety of ways, and seems to outlast historical style shifts. In Cyprus, for example, the change from traditional to imported architectural models did not erase the functional distinction between the (more and more expensively appointed) room where those defined as outsiders could be received, and the humble domestic interior; as outsiders become more familiar, they may more comfortably be brought into this everyday zone, thereby symbolically affirming the newly created intimacy (Markides, Nikita, Rangou 1978:80). In Crete, in the hierarchical *saloni*, decorated with women's handicrafts that celebrate the official face of the island's culture, the women themselves may help to entertain, but they almost never sit down with the guests, as they sometimes do in the kitchen. On the island of Mytilini, a more or less severely Classical niche framed the (Byzantine) family icons (see Pavlides and Hesser 1986:77–81). As we have seen, the house is a potent symbol of the moral community at all other levels as well.

Throughout Greece, even the most sonorously neo-Classical exterior might mask the comfortingly village-style interior over which the women of the house preside; and the formality of the receiving-room (*saloni* – a revealing gallicism!) masks a more homely atmosphere elsewhere in the house. Such architectonic distinctions between formal/male and familiar/ female have clearly existed in Greece for centuries, as travellers' accounts attest, and are equally common to Turkish domestic architecture (see Stirling 1965:238). But the advent of national independence seems to have colored them with the ambiguities of Greece's role in Europe, and particularly with the anxieties of neo-Classicism. In the critical period following the departure of the Bavarian monarchy and the first Greek attempts to make new *beginnings*, we repeatedly meet the same enigmatic architecture: traditional features – many of them with "Turkish" names – constituting a "distillation of the experience of generations of craftsmanly tradition" hidden behind neo-Classical façades (Iakovidis 1982:31–2). Social space reproduces history and presses it into the service of daily life.

Such architectural and decorative expressions of social duality are no more exclusively Greek than is the association of language with ideas about purity and pollution. Pocius (1981), for example, has noted the way in which the designs of Newfoundland wall-rugs fall into two categories, one hierarchical and the other neutral, that respectively correspond to the distinction between receiving areas and private family space. Closer to the Greek case are the so-called "Brazilian" houses of Yoruba townspeople in Nigeria. Here, the adoption of a "western" (but supposedly non-colonialist) façade is paired with a stylized "African" disposal of interior space (Vlach 1984:19). Not only is the example more directly comparable to the Greek pattern in its exploitation of the façade/interior opposition, but it similarly alludes in direct and obvious ways to the contrast between two idealized historical pasts, associating one with intimacy and familiarity and the other with essentially Eurocentric criteria of cultural excellence. The sense of removal from the realities of everyday life that the Hellenic label can convey ironically echoes the pattern of pre-independence Greek usage: the Hellenes were then that mythical race of giants who had built all those mysterious temples; but that once popular understanding of the term has not survived eras of nationalistic education and mass tourism.[26]

Note, too, that the architectonic idiom of Greek cultural ambiguity is concomitantly a *visual* one, reflecting the visual basis of western discrimination between European and exotic. Fabian (1983:105–41) and J. Goody (1977a:219) have both commented on the visualist bias in anthropology, a bias that certainly received much support from racial and cultural stereotyping. Significantly, in this context, Mosse describes racism as "a visually centered ideology" and one that "projected its stereotype upon any who failed to conform to the proper manners and morals" (1985:134). The primary concern of respectability is always that things should "look right."[27] Architecture, the covering of the social body that corresponds to the clothing of the individual, is in Greece one of the most obvious loci of that concern; but the language, too, harps on the physical division between interior and façade. In the Cretan dialect, social "exposure" is tellingly conveyed by a word – *kseyevendisma* – that "conceals" a Turkish root between a Greek prefix (*kse-* < *eks-*, "out") and a Greek grammatical suffix: the Turkishness within is ex-posed, as it were, to the critical eye of a Hellenic public morality. At the same time as the visualist mantle of western-inspired bourgeois respectability began to cloak all of Greece, rigid cultural boundaries – themselves a visualist metaphor – were the mainstay of both European nationalisms and social theory. And as Greece itself interiorized the exotic-familiar distinction, these boundaries became entangled in confusion.

As we have seen, the two pasts-in-the-present in question are the Helle-nic (*Ellinismos*) and the combined Byzantine-Turkish (*Romiossini*). These are not the only pasts available to Greeks in search of an ideological ident-ity. They do nevertheless seem to form a pair: at the very least, we can say that many Greek writers formulate the choices in terms of this pair. Like the linguistic pair of *katharevousa* and demotic, they are a *symbolic* oppo-sition; it is not always clear what the specific content of each is supposed to be, and they often seem interchangeable. To take a germane example: when Greeks criticize themselves as a society, they often talk about "us *Romii*," but may substitute the term *Ellines* ("Hellenes") here since the comparison is with outside cultures (or perhaps because *Ellines* has become very general as the officially sanctioned designator). Conceptually, however, the sense of a fundamental distinction persists to this day, even when it is not articulated as an explicit terminological opposition. One can still justify an absent-minded oversight, for example, by saying, "[I have but] one mind, and that Romeic" (Anon. 1986). Social reality is the anti-thesis of a perfectly ordered human condition. But note again: as with appeals to fate, such invocations of imperfection always occur after the event, never as an excuse for prospective passivity.

Kostas Kazazis, a Greek-born linguist, has suggested that the term *Romios* varies in the degree to which it is semantically *marked*. When opposed to *Ellinas*, it tends to acquire a pejorative meaning that is not necessarily present at other times (1981a:54–5). Kazazis recounts an inci-dent in which a Greek-American visitor to the homeland told off his daugh-ter, who was pushing her way to the front of a queue, by telling her they should behave "like human beings, not like *Romii*!" This created a furore, until one grumbler gave him the opening he needed by complaining that he should not have said "that Greeks [literally 'Hellenes'] are not human beings!" The Greek-American grasped his opportunity, insisting that he had *not* said "Hellenes" but "*Romii*" – and everyone was placated. It is in order to criticize *Romii*, for this is what Greeks themselves do (as, for example, in their fulminations against the "Romeic bureaucracy" – sup-posedly a legacy of Greek opportunism living off Turkish inefficiency): but one is not then criticizing the idealized essence of Greekness implied by the term "Hellenes."

Language encodes such tensions in ways that the conventional model of diglossia cannot capture. Take, for instance, the ironic description of the *Romios* as *Homo katafertzikos*, from *katafer(n)o* ("come out on top, manage") (Likiardopoulos 1983:15). A linguistic analysis of this term could show that the *-ertzikos* adjectival suffix is a quasi-foreign (and there-fore Romeic) marker (cf. B. Joseph 1983), and that the verb *katafero* carries a strong sense of conniving, underhand, but ultimately genial behavior (again the diagnostic traits of the *Romios*); and one could add that the verb's

Romeic character is further evidenced by the fact that, unlike verbs for official matters or scientific practice, it never takes the archaizing aorist internal augment (**katefera* for *katafera*, "I fixed, set up"; see also Kazazis 1982b). But none of these intrinsically interesting points means very much unless we are also aware of the ideological implications of *Romiossini* in everyday life.

The current status of *Romiossini* seems to have had a long history. In the nineteenth century, demotic Greek was called *romeika*, clearly a pejorative term for many educated people, and contrasted to the *ellinika* ("Hellenic language") of both the ancients and the purists. But those who mocked the official order, and did so for internal consumption, inverted this hierarchy much as Dumont's argument (1982) would lead us to expect: one critic, Souris, made the *Romios* the title and irreverent hero of his satirical weekly journal, as well as the desired reader. (In recent years, usage has swung around yet again: *Romiossini* has become the butt of sour satirists who deplore the anti-intellectualism they associate with the term – and it is hardly irrelevant to our theme that the attack on this formalized version of *Romiossini* likens it, not Hellenism, to Cartesian positivism [Likiardopoulos 1983:12]![28]) Finally, there are senses in which *Romios* is opposed to those categories of outsiders who are thought morally *inferior*, and the Romeic language affords a rich and impenetrable interiority. The structure as well as the actual words of this satirical rhyming couplet make the point (Rhodes; recorded 1974):

Ta torina ta ghlendia sas miazousi san ovreka,
san ton Alin to somaran pou lei ta romeika.

Your parties are now like Jewish ones (i.e. stingy),
Like Ali the saddle-maker [a Turk] speaking *Greek (romeika)* (i.e. poorly)!

Clearly the very notion of Romeic identity is not only context-dependent, but *includes context-dependency as one of its diagnostic traits*. It resists authoritative definition: at least one recent writer on *Romiossini* declined the privilege of defining it, preferring instead to provide a "tactile picture of it" – the phrase is his – through the texts of folksongs (Dizikirikis 1983:9). The same applies to grammaticality: while largely successful attempts have been made to formalize demotic Greek, this language is *ideologically* free from the burden of rigid rules. As Sobré (1983:56) has remarked for Catalan: "Any language aspiring to a grammar is a politicized language, whether it is necessary to claim it explicitly or not." And we can recall the other side of this coin – Houssaye's deprecating remark, already quoted, that the grammarian would be upset by the folksongs of modern Greece. These various examples support the development of a model of disemia, rather than merely of diglossia (which is also a highly ambiguous term in the Greek context[29]). Not only is it a false academicism to separate the language question from the encompassing play of the self-knowledge/self-presentation antinomy, but the question of grammaticality underscores the character of the values involved: the very ambiguity and context-dependency of the terms *Romios* (f. -*a*) and *Romiossini* reproduce the trick-sterish traits that they suggest in people and their actions.

The ease with which Greek speakers switch between more and less marked uses of the term *Romios*, as they do (for example) between critical and amiable uses of terms of abuse,[30] shows that *Romiossini* is the domain of social experience – a domain characterized by shifting meanings and relative values. In this, it is the antithesis of the Hellenic, which the state upholds as an absolute value enshrining the bureaucratic ideology itself – and which only changes its meaning when an upstart Romeic point of view takes center stage. From the official perspective as it has existed since the inception of the Greek state, Hellenic values are eternal verities; the "foreign" Romeic elements take their meaning from a context of opposition in which the Hellenic is always politically dominant. True to its romantic heritage, nationalistic discourse dehistoricizes its own past and decontextualizes the present. In the next chapter, when we consider the tension between definition and usage in Greek speech, we shall see that context-dependency is one of the characteristic markers of what the official ideology chooses to regard as alien and inferior. This is the tragic oxymoron of Greek life: official discourse treats ordinary social experience as the mark of an evil otherness that delays the return to Eden.

6   Strict definitions and bad habits

Disemia and the politics of morality: individualism versus self-interest

The dualities of disemia represent the play of cultural form and social knowledge and action in political context. In the last chapter, we looked at the uses of such pairs as demotic and purist Greek, and the Hellenic and Romeic stereotypes. Clearly, these pairs are not simply lists of symbols with fixed meanings. On the contrary, they are flexible representations of the dilemma, common to all societies, of balancing social knowledge against the exigencies of collective self-representation to more powerful outsiders. Disemia is the play of cultural contradictions produced by conditional independence – an independence, cultural or political, that is paradoxically enjoyed only on the sufferance of some more powerful entity. Greece, whose War of Independence brought a Bavarian monarchy and foreign-dominated political parties, raised this paradox to exquisitely refined heights of irony. The new state could not afford to allow much questioning of what or who the present-day Greeks were. In such circumstances, legalism flourishes, not only in the passport office, but in all areas of discourse. Lexicography becomes an instrument of national revival and thereafter develops into a state activity. As it does so, its revolutionary activities ossify into prescriptive forms (see Anderson 1983:70–1; Mouzelis 1978:146). In short, meaning becomes an object of official control. Only through meticulous attention to this regulation of discourse can we avoid being seduced by it ourselves. This chapter sets out some exemplary cases from the official/anthropological encounter with ordinary language use in Greece.

The seeming ethnographic minutiae that we are about to examine could all too easily be dismissed as the merest linguistic pedantry. In fact, however, they are possibly the best warning we can have against the smug conviction that we have "understood these people." They also provide evidence for the still continuing tussle between local elite and tutelary foreign powers over the definition of the nation's role – that is, over the contest between ascribed origins and locally created beginnings. The legal and academic establishment tries to reify meaning as far as law and formal education will stretch; the supposedly absolute character of official discourse reproduces the attempt of the state to create independent beginnings, to escape from the albatross of ascribed origins, when the game is still in practice defined by external powers. The government tries to fix meaning; context-dependence becomes the symbol of political dependence. When tutelary outsiders define the criteria of local culture, insiders find it necessary to disguise those aspects of ordinary social life that conflict with the imposed models. They do so by invoking a rule-like exterior. This not only matches the tutelary powers' demands for regimented predictability in the nation as a whole, but buttresses the (sometimes rather desperate) official insistence on a genuinely independent and unified national destiny, represented by the institutions and functionaries of state.

Greece exemplifies this pattern, which is international in its implications. Since official ideology seeks the criteria of Greekness outside Greece, the most familiar aspects of daily life are, as we have seen, those that official discourse labels as the most foreign. Turkishness, in particular, serves as a metaphor for insubordination. Cultural flaws are blamed for political disobedience, and "Turkish" elements in speech are taken as evidence of not knowing how to conduct oneself properly in approaching functionaries of the state bureaucracy. Yet *past* insubordination appears as that most Hellenic, and European, of virtues – individualism – for then it was (or can be represented as having been) directed *against* the Turks.

Such semantic slippage reflects a historical shift in the symbolic alignment of identities: if the nuances of language use are essential to an understanding of social relations, one equally cannot derive much benefit from an examination of language issues outside the broader framework provided by the imagery and ideology of the cultural fall. This framework explains a Greekness that has adopted much of the coloration of "Turkishness." Under Ottoman rule, the survival of the Greek Christians as a cultural and religious entity depended on their ability to resist the Turks' more onerous importunities; then, it was Greekness – not Turkishness, as today – that served as the metaphor for insubordination. This was especially the case in the towns, where contact was more direct. The British historian George Finlay, whom many Greeks thought unsympathetic to their cause,[1] nonetheless had some understanding of the problems they faced (1861, I:14):

The servile position of the Christian subjects of the sultan, and the corruption of the Othoman administration, rendered deceit the best defence against extortion. Truth and honesty were impediments to the acquisition of wealth; and consequently the prosperous Greek trader was very rarely a better man than his poorer countrymen. Falsehood and fraud became habitual, and were considered by strangers as national qualities rather than individual characteristics.

Greekness, Finlay goes on to remark, was better preserved among the rural population, who were less subject to direct pressure by their Turkish masters. And we see that what the Greeks supposedly learned from the Turks became very much their own distinctive strategy for dealing with oppression (although Finlay cautiously notes that in many areas the Greeks were able to take advantage of their literacy and run segments of the bureaucracy). But it was to meet with official disapproval and repression as *Turkish* behavior as soon as it persisted beyond the establishment of an independent Greek state.

Even the acidulous Finlay, who was neither impressed by the Greek guerrillas nor charmed by the European-trained Greek politicians and intellectuals, accepted the survivalist thesis that pure Hellenism survived best in remote places. He could thus fortify his very considerable detestation of the metropolitan Greek leaders without sacrificing his loyalty to the philhellenic ideal. But he was clearly not alone in thinking that the cunning and guile to which the passage just quoted alludes, and which a later observer cheerfully associates with levantine mercantilism at large (Mears 1929:178), were essential to the Greeks' survival under Ottoman rule. Essentially the same negative stereotype still features prominently in the collective self-view – the *Romiossini* – of Greeks of all kinds, rural as well as urban. In the same way, Greek observers follow their foreign exemplars in blaming bureaucratic inefficiency and corruption on the Turkish precedent (e.g. Argyriades 1968; see also Herzfeld 1982c). Finlay (1861, I:16) observes, with characteristically even-handed nastiness:

The effects of this system of taxation on the condition of Greek agriculture may still be studied in the dominions of Sultan Abdul-meshid, or of King Otho, for they rival one another in the disastrous effects of their fiscal administration (A.D. 1859).

It may then be that Turkishness stands for inefficiency, graft, corruption, and insubordination in the conventional self-portrait of modern Greek culture. But the official explanation for this, and the one most likely (in the logic of disemia) to be offered to foreigners, is that the Turks had corrupted the Greeks by forcing them to fight Turkish guile with Turkish guile. While the Greeks saw this corruption as reversible, however, many of the disillusioned foreigners who had flocked to the Greek cause decided that it was evidence of the ultimately oriental character of the modern Greeks.

In short, the fatalism associated with Greek bureaucratic and political habits is a foreign concoction – a realization of the same *attributed* fatalism that Bourdieu and Said recognize in much anthropological and literary theory, and that Cassirer and Innis discern in totalitarian ideologies. According to this viewpoint, behavior is racially inherited, and its consequences are unavoidable (see also Anderson 1983:108). For Cassirer (1946:225), for example, Gobineau's work – the direct ancestor of Anglo-

Saxon immigration laws that restricted the entry of "Mediterranean" peoples on the grounds that they were mentally sluggish (see, e.g., Gould 1981:232–3) – was "filled with a strong *amor fati*," a "fatalistic" recasting of history in the language of a determinate racial "science." Race, in this acceptation, is destiny; and the widespread popularity of ideas about *ratsa* in Greece (cf. also Campbell 1964:185 and n.) even provides a domestic idiom for the scientistic self-deprecation of "national character." When a Rhodian villager justified the 1967 military coup on the grounds that "we Greeks need a strong government," he evoked the racial scientism, not merely of the western-supported regime, but of the tutelary West itself.

The development of a bureaucratic state system does not alter those popular theories and concepts. It does, however, recast the symbolic language that they activate, so that they now support the *realia* of the new regime. Instead of the several *yenies* (patrilines) of each guerrilla-infested mountain range, the nationalist rhetoric promotes the unique lineage (*yenos*) of all Greeks united behind their new state. Ideological events such as the founding of a new nation-state can radically change the disposition of symbolic elements. Greece provides innumerable examples of the process. One dramatic illustration is the re-evaluation of the marginal figure of Digenes: as the various local refractions of Digenes converged in the highly respectable hero of the "national epic," and as the cultural and moral margins that these represented now similarly converged in a protective dome around the administrative center, the Turkish-derived shadow theater trickster Karagiozis fulfilled the demands of a Romeic trickster's role.[2]

At Independence, many of the guerrilla heroes of the still recent struggle submitted, more or less grudgingly, to the rule of the "pen-pushers" (the power of literacy again!) – the scholar-politicans who dictated events in Athens and who now, in the name of national unity, rewrote the guerrillas' often rather self-interested exploits as national heroism. Those of the erstwhile freedom fighters who were unwilling to submit fought against the central government as they had once fought the Turks and were recategorized as "brigands" for their obduracy.[3] What had passed for the Greekness of pre-Independence rebellion became the definitively "foreign" phenomenon of insubordination in the context of a Greek-governed national state.

The heroism of the pre-Independence guerrillas became, in retrospect, a mark of Greek individualism, a purported characteristic of Europeans that came to be contrasted with both oriental fatalism and Slavic "communism."[4] But what is this individualism? Is it the same as the self-interest that has been the despair of western observers, from the soldier-philhellenes of the 1821–33 War of Independence to the agricultural experts of post World War II economic reconstruction (McNeill 1957;

Thompson 1963)? Is it the characteristic that leads Greeks to complain of chronic political atomization – recall the proverb "twelve Greeks [make] thirteen captains" – and to deplore the personality cult (*prosopolatria*) of present-day electoral politics? Is it the driving force that Greeks supposedly bring to their intense business activity, or is it the conventionally attributed levantine attachment to self-interest? Is it what Greeks bring to their collective self-emancipation from the domination of East and West alike – Papandreou's now celebrated retort that "we don't belong to anyone"[5] – or is it the morally dubious remnant of what has meanwhile flourished elsewhere as European and American "individualism"? Is it the means of the nation's political and cultural revival, of a new beginning; or is it merely the dual symbol of Greece's present marginality and dependence – the desecrated relic of an ancient and holy origin?

Morality as insubordination: ambiguity versus the state

These questions realize a basic symbolic opposition: self-reliant agency versus enervating disunity; or, once again, vibrant beginnings versus tarnished origins. The ethnographic literature presents the phenomenon as *eghoismos*, self-regard, in both guises. In some places, *eghoismos* appears to be positively valued (e.g. Campbell 1964:312; Herzfeld 1985a:36), at least as a social stance to be adopted in this hostile and imperfect world; elsewhere, it is a threat to social harmony (e.g. du Boulay 1974: 75–6). Glendiots indeed assured me that *eghoismos* could have two values: a positive one that leads through competition to ever greater achievements (in Glendi, most dramatically in the form of a proliferating supply of competing coffee-shops!), and a negative, vengeful one that seeks violence and sudden death. It is always egocentric in reference (< *egho*, "I"), and this too easily deflects attention from the *social* character of its deployment, nicely captured by Campbell (1964:307):

Fundamentally, self-regard is the inner necessity and obligation to achieve identity with the image of the ideal self. This image, of course, is a stereotype presented by society, there is little room for individual speculation, nor would it occur to most Sarakatsani to question its traditional content.

But I must emphasize here that it engages with an enormous range of social identities, expressing numerous concentric identities: family, kin-group, village, even – on occasion – nation.

Walcot (1970:45, 87–92) notes the duality of positive and negative interpretations of competitiveness, and compares it directly to a similar duality in the Classical Greek concept of *eris*, "conflict." But one could extend the analysis far beyond Greek parallels, or even pan-Mediterranean ones; the search for an ancient peasant morality merely begs the question of

Mediterranean homogeneity in a historical rather than strictly ethno-graphic idiom. *Eghoismos*, by its very name, simply invites Eurocentric charges like those of "amoral familism" (Banfield 1958) – discursive stranglings of sub-national social identities: only a Eurocentric, statist defi-nition of virtue could define family allegiance as "amoral."

In every case where an egocentric definition of the social comes into play, the evaluation of an individual's pride will always depend on whose interests are affected by it. The concept of *eghoismos* is a relativity, a *shifter*, in that its meaning depends on both the actor and the audience. As such, it conflicts directly with the official elevation of certain virtues – notably those of patriotism and individualism – to the status of absolute good. Patriotism represents the subservience of the individual to the state; indi-vidualism, the stereotyping of national heroism. *Eghoismos* is neither. Like good luck and bad character, it is always negative in others, positive in members of one's own social group. But because the Greeks feel forced to contend with the otherness within themselves, they often express profound moral ambivalence about *eghoismos* while acknowledging its pervasion of social life. Does it more closely resemble European individualism or orien-tal divisiveness (the dependence on "opinion" that Linnaeus attributed to the eastern peoples)? For the Greeks, *Romii* and Hellenes at one and the same time, it partakes of both. As a product of the fall of Adam, replicated in the evil habits and social pollution (*ghrousouzia*) derived from the later fall to the Turks, attributed by foreign observers to the corruption of the East, it is the antithesis of what Greek nationalists and enthusiastic philhel-lenes claimed to discern in the prototypical heroes of the struggle for national independence. As a flaw, it is the mark of fatalism; as a virtue, it is the claim to struggle for a new beginning. That struggle permits *active* identification with heroes as *eghoistes* as any latter-day member of their own rural communities. Far from being the fossil of some prototypical Euro-pean individualism, for example, the *eghoismos* that Campbell describes represents an *active* claim on history (1964:307; my emphasis):

A boy learns from songs and stories (*and later at school*) to identify himself with the values of the idealized heroes of the Revolution. He comes to believe in the superhuman deeds of Katsandonis and Kolokotronis, and in the ability of men to repeat them where the cause has sanctity and men possess honour.

Campbell here accords a strongly personal sense of history to the Sarakat-sani. This, like the identification of the Sarakatsan nuclear family with the Holy Family (Campbell 1964:354), belongs to the history that official discourse either ignores or coopts: in its turn, it is an expropriation, a disemic reworking, of that discourse. Idealized individualism in the service of the nation belongs with official History, while personal self-regard and family concerns are a matter of intimate *istories*.

Eghoismos is the result of original sin in a cultural as well as the more obviously religious sense. Not only is it a consequence of the sin of pride; it is also, and consequently, the source of "differences" – boasting (which may be cultural, artistic, intellectual, or merely personal), quarrels (often *called* "differences" in Greek as in English), social estrangement. For rural Greeks, therefore, *eghoismos* in its negative refractions is responsible for sundry "bad habits," including blasphemy, ill temper, jealousy, boasting, excessive competitiveness. But this negative evaluation always issues from those who have been cursed, envied, or knocked out of the contest. From the point of view of those ranged on the side of the *eghoistis* by kinship or some other association, the habits in question are only bad in the comfortingly generic sense afforded by original sin: socially, like successful cunning, they are entirely positive. It is not merely the self-interestedness of *eghoismos* that places it in this category; its very lability places it on the side of actual social knowledge and experience, and contrasts it with the arid idealizations preferred by statist ideology. Relativity of social values undermines the scientific absoluteness of state control.

The same horror of the relative informs the statist view of law, which categorically excludes "custom" as inimical to its Eurocentric interests (see also Tsoukalas 1983:27). As we have seen, survivalist anthropology not only saw the rule of law as one of the great achievements of civilization, but bequeathed this persistent credo to subsequent anthropologies – to Malinowski's utilitarian functionalism ("myth as charter"), to Radcliffe-Brown's nomothetic structural-functionalism, and to Lévi-Strauss's "functionalist" structuralism (on which, see Said 1975), with its formal binarism that *Kypseli* instructively travesties. Indeed, the anthropology of the nineteenth century, by placing scholarship at a higher evolutionary level of reason, paved the way for the anthropological proclivity for generalization; Malinowski in particular, while acknowledging the significance of observer error, appears paradoxically to have confirmed the Frazerian schema whereby science represents a higher order of analysis than the indigenous reasoning it observes (see Thornton 1985:9–10).

These successive anthropologies have paid court to the importance of context; today, for example, Malinowski's work on language in *Coral Gardens and their Magic* (1935) is often lauded for anticipating this cornerstone of sociolinguistics, while transformational series of joking relationships (Radcliffe-Brown 1952:90–116) and mythological structures (e.g. Lévi-Strauss 1955) depend on the prior assumption of a contrasted set of social contexts. Always implicit in these formulations, however, was the assumption that anthropology had discovered the Archimedean square foot of solid earth – that the culture of the observer was, for all practical purposes, context-free. From this, it appeared to follow that the analytical ("etic") categories and definitions of anthropology possessed the fixity that the emic categories lacked. The very lability of a term like *eghoismos* was a mark of its emic character. It conveys "the inner necessity and obligation to achieve identity with the image of the ideal self" (Campbell 1964:307); but the social level at which this occurs is always somewhat ambiguous. Such values, like the sexual morality that they accompany, lend themselves to expansion to the widest possible level of identity as a pan-Mediterranean symbol. This becomes immediately apparent in nineteenth-century novels and operas.[6] *Eghoismos* can be an individual value in relation to constantly shifting social worlds; but, for that very reason, it cannot be the basis of an independent political morality.

Without government there can be no civic sense of responsibility according to the bourgeois patrons of the Sarakatsani – the lawyers, officials, and merchants on whom they depend, and who contemptuously dismiss them as mere "tent-dwellers" (another sign of their "shiftiness"). The context-dependence of *eghoismos*, its situational semantics, brings it into contrast with an essentially bourgeois political culture, in which nationalists associate "egotism" – a besetting lack of self-sacrifice and self-control – with ethnic outsiders, women, and effeminate men (Mosse 1985:79). The official representation of self-regard as a political liability foists outsiderhood upon the Greeks in their own land.

Campbell's distinction between the amorality of *eghoismos* and the morality of honor and shame captures these assumptions of official discourse. In a sense, it is precisely his sensitive articulation of Sarakatsan ideas about social worth and obligation with national electoral politics that backgrounds – although it certainly does not deny – the close association between respectability and nationalist statism. Both have little tolerance for either the politics or the semantics of labile social boundaries.

For *eghoismos* stands for the very instability that statism seeks to deny. In the Mediterraneanist literature, morality appears largely apolitical; like the local folksongs, excluded as parochial by nationalist scholars, the atomized values of *eghoismos* and the like did not suit the finitudes and fixities of a regulated world order. The study of indigenous morality has been more than commonly well documented in the Mediterranean area. This derives from the area's peculiar ambiguity between the familiar and the exotic. Here were state-dominated societies, in which the self-control and good manners of the powerful West and North appeared to be late in arriving; the imperfect integration of the local community into the state structure represented an earlier stage on the evolutionary scale, permitting an exploration of the Mediterranean as a liminal zone between the situational ethics of exotic peoples and the ordered morality of European culture. The analysis of *the* values of "Mediterranean society" (Peristiany 1965), while an important step in that it at least got Mediterranean ethnographies into the literature, reproduces this evolutionist argument to a marked degree.

The reasons for this had much to do with the particular point at which the Mediterranean entered the anthropological consciousness, at least in England. The "Middle Sea," now a liminal no man's land separating the Orient from a Europe that had migrated elsewhere, could no longer claim to be the "Sea in the [absolute] Middle [of the World]" of the ancient acceptation; studied by the heavily Africanist-derived and largely Oxford-trained social anthropologists, its peoples now exhibited a relativistic morality that came midway between the completely segmentary system of Nilotes and the ordered ethic of a state-controlled society. They had values, but they did not obey; their own self-view as imperfect children of the aboriginal fall debarred them from the secular emancipation, embodied in the nation-state, of a rationality defined by European criteria. And some of those who have attacked anthropology for focussing only on marginal communities were simply expressing the corollary of this Eurocentric survivalism: *if* Greece was indeed a modern state, one would understand nothing of it by studying its remote rural populations, whose bucolic values – the very stuff of nationalistic historiography – were incompatible with modern visions of economic and political progress.

Sociological and urban studies make only rare mention of the rural anthropologists' concern with moral values (important exceptions in Greece are Hirschon 1978, 1981; Safilios-Rothschild 1969). Embarrassment with local-level morality reproduces yet again the Eurocentric split between the primitive and the complex that we also find embodied in statist conceptions of morality. Terms like *eghoismos* are not merely the expression of an insubordinate ideology. Their lability also makes them a threat to the ordered *discourse* of state legality. With the language of local morality, this does not constitute a problem; rural ethnographers simply illustrate the semantic range of each term, and describe the nexus of ideas to which it relates, with anecdotal materials from their fieldwork. Unless one is a social critic, *eghoismos* is not something that one would normally attribute to the organs of state; in the local and rural context no conflict arises between ethnographic precision and the dictionary. The usual emphasis of rural ethnography has served, however inadvertently, to perpetuate the image of a rural morality sundered by its capricious small-mindedness from the eternal verities of the state, rather than one conjoined to national identity by a shared concern with the tension between collective concealment and collective introspection.

Ethnic terms represent a still more extreme version of the same logic. Unlike *eghoismos*, whose lability is palpable and whose moral basis had therefore to be explicitly denied, ethnic labels seemed to possess an easily identifiable referentiality. There were clearly bounded ethnic groups, and these were their names. For this reason, although ethnic labels might possess meanings as much moral as "simply" social at the local level, they are of vital concern to the state in its drive to national homogeneity. Since the state claims to control the identity of its citizens through the usual bureaucratic tools of census and registry, it has a major investment in preserving the official definitions. Thus, for example, official discourse uses the term *Vlakhos* to mean a Koutsovlach-speaking, transhumant shepherd, whose identity may not disappear with the onset of sedentarization but whose primary mark of difference is language (see also Schein 1975). In everyday parlance, however, the term becomes one of moral exclusion; from the point of view of an Epirot villager, for example, all transhumant shepherds can be so characterized, while for a Rhodian islander virtually all rural mainlanders are *Vlakhi*. This kind of social relativism has no place in official language.

In some domains, moreover, sheer materiality conceals the moral ambiguity of key terms. The language of economics, in particular, seems subject to hidden semantic shifts that the formal apparatus of economic anthropology is ill equipped to anticipate. Although the local ethnographic analyses showed that rural Greeks do not necessarily make a sharp categorical distinction between material wealth and moral worth (e.g. Campbell 1964:268), most discussions of rural economics ignore the semantic slippage that this feature permits, and separate moral from economic issues as irrelevant to each other or reduce the moral to an epiphenomenon of the material (e.g. Davis 1977:75–101). Such perspectives give as short shrift to the moral basis of economic practices as they do to the essentially moral character of ethnic designations, apparently because, in both cases, the notorious lability of moral concepts threatens the positivistic program. This obviously raises serious practical problems for fieldwork; how, for example, could one collect data about such institutions as dowry and bridewealth if indigenous categories proved to be as uncooperatively slithery as something more obviously labile like the terminology of moral values? The risk lies in calibrating material categories to a reified language, the official "standard," when usage may defy lexicographical definition, and when a common vocabulary may gloss over radical semantic divergences that are themselves of deep significance to the communities in question.

The problem here is not that a set of "Greek" terms is opposed to a set of "Turkish" ones; that formulation would simply reproduce the old formalism. Nor is it a clash between divergent interpretations of a superficially common concept, as in the tension between occidental individualism and oriental self-interest as alternative readings of *eghoismos*. Such tensions are, it is true, refractions of the same fundamental disemia. But the issue here is, rather, that definition and usage themselves represent opposing aspects of disemia. Behind a single term there may lurk, not simply two definitions of a word or expression, but two different concepts of meaning in which definition and usage come into direct and mutual opposition to each other.

Emblematic of this is the divergence beneath the bureaucratic definition of meaning itself. The Greek term *simasia* appears in official discourse as a strictly lexicographical phenomenon; daily usages, corresponding to the "bad habits" of informal discourse, often represent it as residing only in the contingent, the socially extraordinary, or even (in rare cases) the illegal, and depart from the official acceptation also in that *simasia* is often a far wider category than the purely linguistic concept of the pen-pushers (see Herzfeld 1981b, 1985a; cf. also Rosaldo 1982). Here, it is not the *eghoistis*, but daily usage itself, that threatens to subvert the ordered morality of officialdom and bureaucracy. In both cases, it is ambiguity that most threatens the ideal order of the state.

The outer face of disemia: language as control

As a conceptual conflict, disemia consists in this contest between ambiguity and order. It is thus not a static cultural condition, nor yet a simple listing of alternative codes, but a pragmatic contest between radically different ways of understanding social life. While its two poles are those of official discourse and daily usage, this does not mean that it simply organizes all cultural forms in two discrete registers, an upper and a lower. The two discourses do borrow symbols, lexical forms, and even entire images from each other, but they *deploy* these *realia* to quite different ends. It is our task to examine these contrasted deployments and thereby to unravel the mutually opposed conceptions of meaning that they serve. In so doing, we must not lose sight of the relationship between disemia in this ethnographic sense, and the historical tensions between scientific order and the mysteries of the exotic that continue to pervade anthropology.

Ethnographically, at least, the fundamental contrast can be stated in explicit terms. Official discourse creates a rhetoric of definitional fixity and absolute morality, and depicts the populace as falling far short of the abstract ideal. Conversely, everyday usage – the semiotic or hermeneutic common sense of people trying to make sense of an oppressive bureaucracy – constantly erodes these fixities, and critically rejects official idealizations as a poor substitute for social experience. The language of law and morality, seemingly a representation of eternal verities in the image of the state itself, now appears to be fundamentally problematical (see also Meeker 1979:30). Everyday usage continually subverts the official code, by deploying its constituent elements in order to achieve meanings that are local and immediate, rather than national and eternal. Its mask is the ubiquitous expression of respect for the learned scholar, the Greeks' *epistimon*; its flexible voice may express an equally pervasive contempt for the pen-pusher, the Greeks' *kalamaras*.[7]

Local usage here reveals the hidden underside of Bourdieu's (1977:40) "officializing strategies," which lend the appearance of systematicity to quotidian, commonsensical forms of knowledge (see also Crick 1976:142; Geertz 1983:78–84). Local usage (like state discourse) is not systematic; it *uses systematicity* – that is, it deploys it rhetorically, much as it selects pre-suppositions as well as more tangible *realia* of "high culture" in order to interact with the latter.[8] Actual practice, however, entails a constant sub-version of that systematicity. As practice, and in defiance of its own as well as official and (as Bourdieu recognizes) anthropological rhetoric, local usage denies the very possibility of systematic consistency, and therefore creates a far more radical challenge to official norms than the latter, with their orthodoxy, their categorization of all utterances as right or wrong, are capable of acknowledging. It breaks – "transgresses" – established bound-aries of meaning, secure from doubt or criticism in the unconsciousness of its doing so.

That it is unconscious (or at least not deliberate) follows necessarily from its denial of systematicity; informality itself can become a sort of *rule of cat-egorical informality* that reproduces itself in countless ironies, each of which can be subverted in turn. Take, for example, the purism of Greek demoti-cists who have codified "correct" usage and thereby deny the social reality of *katharevousa* usage in everyday speech (and see also Dimiroulis 1985; Tziovas 1985). They also reduce the demotic language to another legalistic formula, a purism merely alternative in form – but not in usage or ideology – to the neo-Classical version. In consequence, they remove it from the experiences of everyday life, and reduce it to an epiphenomenon of abstract political aesthetics (see also Mouzelis 1978:134, 136, on "formalism").

The consequences of this pedantic precision can be entirely antithetical to what the best-intentioned reformers intend. The Rhodian villager who tells me that my carefully demotic Greek is *katharevousa*, for example, recognizes not only that I am speaking an urban language, but that I am submitting too fully to the dictates of this emergent purism – a purism that would exclude some of the *katharevousa*-like, archaizing elements in the vil-lager's own local vernacular! (It also shows the villager's awareness of this irony quite a long time before the restoration of democratic government in Greece brought the new purism any official status, by making demotic Greek the official language in 1975.) More important, then, than the par-ticular forms of *katharevousa* and demotic is the tension between obvious normativity and socially familiar usage. It is the impossibility of ever sub-jecting this kind of observation to a predictive rule, even that of a home-spun demoticism, that marks the interior face of disemia. The exterior face is made up entirely of officializing strategies, from those of the individual to those of the state. The interior face, on the other hand, is a private denial of the relevance of *any* formalization to social experience, and a recognition of its role as a means of repressing individual or local individuality. As Eagleton (1984) has pointed out, it is the oppressed who make the best interpreters of signs; for it is they who must decode the idiom of oppression in order to objectify their goals of emancipation (and, we might add, insubordination).

The ideational poles of disemia are formalism and social experience, or self-presentation and self-knowledge. They are *not* the paired alternatives posited by the formalist debate itself, that is, particular cultural forms – *katharevousa* or demotic, neo-Classicism or rusticity, Turkish or European mannerisms. All supposedly recognizable forms, on both sides of each symbolic opposition, are demonstrably less stable "on the ground" than official formalism – or than radical critiques, including that of Mouzelis (1978) – would suggest. Although there is a historically embedded tendency for some forms to appear more consistently in one or the other case, the meaning of all the terms, symbols, and models is always negotiable. As soon as this essential lability is denied or forgotten, rigidity clamps down anew. Anthropologists, with their love of finding systematicity in local forms of knowledge, would do better to unearth the inconsistencies in the official forms instead: the common ground of both is not regularity, but the *rhetoric* of regularity, balanced against a critical social experience that denies it. Everyday usage does not contrast with the normativity of official discourse, but, both by its accessibility and by its richness in examples, directs us to the social character of *all* usage, from informal interaction to even the most tiresomely formal official rhetoric.

Official discourse blocks that understanding through the characteristic strategy of denying its own rhetoricity. Language is merely one arena for this tussle, although an important one in that the verbocentric discourse of officialdom thereby situates the contest on its own preferred ground. In moving from diglossia to disemia, however, we have already taken a major step away from the reification of linguistic registers, and toward the recognition instead that the symbolism of social and cultural identity evolves through a more general dialectic of form and interpretation. The primacy hitherto accorded to language – especially when language is conceived as a grammatically predictable system – is itself a "high register" phenomenon, the intellectual ideology known as verbocentrism (and, in a more extreme form, scriptism). In Greece, the representation of the main dispute as *the language question* – the representation of one code as the entire issue – shows how the mutual interest of competing, educated elites orchestrates the perceptions of ordinary people. Official ideology treats language as uniquely context-free and therefore as the only exact means of fixing the truth for all eternity. What it fears is not just demotic Greek, which can after all be tamed with grammatical orthodoxies of its own, but a subversively unruly demotic reunited with equally critical understandings in other domains of everyday life.

Anthropology, as an academic discipline, has absorbed a predilection for verbality very similar to that of romantic Greek nationalism. This reinforces the discipline's tendency to excessive formalism (its officializing strategy, in Bourdieu's terminology), as well as to the representation of all meaning as linguistic.[9] Such verbocentrism is in practice a specialized variety of the more general proclivity for formalism. Especially in its official guises, verbocentrism is itself a repression of intimacy. The preeminence of language as a cultural shibboleth in Greece illustrates this finely: language is outer form, Roidis's "clothing," disguise of the self and of the embodiment of meaning. As such, it often disguises the intimate dimensions of sociability, much as a Sarakatsan woman's shapeless costume disguises her embodied sexual identity, or as a neo-Classical façade masks the inhabitants' raucously Romeic domesticity. The tension between more and less controlled selves reproduces, in the inhabited theory that we call modern Greece, the nineteenth-century anthropological survivalists' model of a progression, still embodied in the theories of Elias and Blok, from exotic savagery to the post-courtly courtesies of Victorian Europe.

Between the faces of disemia: gesture as cultural incontinence

The parallels between power, clothing, and language do in fact have a long history in anthropology. To the tight clothing of Linnaeus's seventeenth-century northern Europeans, the nineteenth century added the whalebone corsetry of scriptism, severely curtailing the spontaneous bodily elaboration of speech. What could not be written did not belong in polite intercourse. The upper-class Victorian English regarded gesticulation as a "natural" act, and therefore as "rude" (cf. Latin *rudis*, "raw, unformed"). As a feature of the savage stage in human evolution, and indeed as the only expressive recourse of true savages, it could be treated as both universal and fundamentally invariant; and in this regard it contrasted diametrically with the precise language of educated people – especially of the Europeans, whose linguistic diversity was but one mark of their transcendant unity.

The use of gesticulation was thus a categorical anomaly, a breach of etiquette, and an absence of culture at its most rarefied (Bernstein's "elaborated" [1971]) stage. The Victorians' early childhood training, by corsetting the expressive incontinence of gesture, provided an ontogeny of good manners. It now became, like so many other childhood ontogenies, part of the survivalist phylogeny (Tylor 1964:37; my italics):

We English are perhaps poorer in the gesture-language than any other people in the world. We use a form of words to denote what a gesture or a tone would express. Perhaps it is because we read and write so much, and have come to think and talk as we should write, and so *let fall those aids to speech which cannot be carried into the written language.*

The courteous modesty that concedes the English to be "perhaps poorer" in gesture than otherwise less well endowed peoples should not mislead us. In a few polite words, Tylor subtly but firmly argues that the English have *voluntarily* left behind ("let fall") the crudities of gesture, as being appropriate only for those who still remain in an infantile stage of cultural development. His very politeness reproaches those who do not know how to behave.

Survivalist anthropology thus locates gesture, thought to be closer to pure bodiliness than language, at an early point on the evolutionary scale. Tylor, a true heir to the European ideology of differentiation, argued that the uniformity encountered in a museum of ethnology and archaeology would support the thesis of aboriginal uniformity. Gesture, being less precise in meaning and yet cross-culturally more uniform (as he evidently believed), must be less European than language on both counts (Tylor, *ibid.*; my italics):

Gesticulation goes along with speech, to explain and emphasize it, among all mankind. *Savage and half-civilized races accompany their talk with expressive pantomime much more than nations of higher culture.* The continual gesticulation of *Hindoos, Arabs, Greeks, as contrasted with the more northern nations of Europe*, strikes every traveller who sees them; and the colloquial pantomime of Naples is the subject of a special treatise. But we cannot lay down a rule that gesticulation decreases as civilization advances, and say, for instance, that a Southern Frenchman, because his talk is illustrated with gestures, *as a book with pictures*, is less civilized than a German or an Englishman.

Europeans are literate; but some, in the Orwellian logic of the European ideology, are more literate (or less dependent on "pictures") than others; and Tylor, while perforce accepting the French as colleagues in civilization, nevertheless manages to suggest that their hold on it is more tenuous than that of the English.

The French use gesture like pictures in a book: they are at least literate, although Tylor hints that they need practical aids to reading. But the Greeks are not so privileged. They belong to that large category of peoples, the "half-civilized" whose cultures are ancient but who have remained in a state of arrested development. Amongst these peoples, gesture may be classified as "pantomime." Once again, as in his treatment of the French, we see Tylor's penchant for malicious ambiguity: pantomime was a Hellenistic dramatic genre, and thus appropriate as a metaphor for Greek and Italian conversation; but it had also been reduced by Tylor's own day to a children's entertainment, and thus no less appropriately served to convey the survivalist phylogeny.[10] Pantomime is only *half*-civilized; antiquity is equated with comparative simplicity; and the descendants of the Classical Greeks and Romans serve as the living ancestors of the northern Europeans. Moreover, English reactions to the expressive incontinence of such peoples match their stiff-lipped horror at revelations of intimacy in general.

For Greek nationalists and Victorian survivalists alike assumed that cultural intimacy represented the object of control – self-control where the cultural level permitted, control by a superior and imperial rationality otherwise. Whatever the differences in their respective aims, both groups operated on the oxymoronic grounds of their own participation in *and* superiority to the dominated culture. One's membership in the nation is natural, a matter of birth (*natio*); but it is culture that bestows superiority over one's fellows. Nature and culture thus conspire to legitimize the oxymoronic structure of cultural science. Tylor thought it natural for humans to gesticulate; but, as members of a culture that boasted a high degree of social self-control, he and his contemporaries also felt justified in looking down on cultures that supposedly lacked the ability to control this spontaneous inner nature. The persistence of this idea is amazing; and its success in Greece may be judged from the fact that Greeks themselves still allude to their supposed lack of self-control and to their "warm-blooded," "Mediterranean" impulsiveness.

But in so-called Mediterranean societies as much as anywhere, the *control* of violence is a greatly admired virtue: retaliation should not be immediate (Kabylia [Bourdieu 1977:15]), peacemakers show strength over the immoderately angry (Crete [Herzfeld 1985a:82]). Just as locally people deny the quality of restraint in those they despise, the stereotypes of the gesticulating, improvident, shiftless Mediterranean peasant represent similarly imperious contempt in a much broader context. As I have already pointed out, the game of honor is not an exclusively Mediterranean preoccupation: the anthropologists who write about Mediterranean values are themselves powerful players.

The official discourse of countries like Greece, beholden as they were to the western Powers, responded to the disdain of the latter by developing a verbal discourse that both *expressed* an individual's self-control as part of the larger ideal, and could also be used for the purpose of *maintaining* control – especially economic and political – over the entire citizenry (Sotiropoulos 1977, 1982). The obvious normativity of *katharevousa* would have represented each individual Greek as the token of the idealized type of the Hellene – the quintessential European. This explains why Greeks were so anxious to speak *katharevousa* in front of foreigners, even (or especially!) when the latter could not understand what was said: it clothes the more intimate aspects of Greek identity in an impenetrable linguistic disguise.

Language is not merely a form of cultural clothing; it is at times a virtual straitjacket. The lexical and syntactical homogeneity of official *kathare-vousa* gave some confidence that the language would also be semantically predictable – in other words, controllable. This pattern, moreover, set the model for all other domains of culture, so that the upper register of each disemic arena would provide an outward model of harmony that suppressed the clamor of differences within. The desexualized Classical aesthetic of Winckelmann, for example, still informed the theory and practice of architecture, and in Greece, for some years after the War of Independence, the Bavarian presence maintained its visibility in the neo-Classical design of public buildings. Order and uniformity, orders and uniforms: the discipline of Eurocentric Hellenism, like the discipline of anthropology, suppressed or ignored the everyday subversion of normativity by the living inhabitants of the land.

The inner face of disemia: usage as subversion

Official discourse necessarily places great stress on both homogeneity and predictability, and uses language as both symbol and instrument of these goals. Official ideology views strategy and subversion as alien, and this leads to the association of Turkishness with unruliness. Officialdom could hardly afford, however, to represent folk culture as subversive in this sense. On the contrary, it assigns to "values and customs" (Greek *ithi k' ethima*) the regulatory function of unquestioned law – an inferior version of law, to be sure, since it lacks written codification as well as its subjects' conscious consent (Vazouras 1974), but one that is nevertheless a pure distillation of Greek antiquity. The rural population is thus doubly passive: as a repository of ancient legal wisdom, and as the unresisting partner to the state's hierarchical differentiation between two kinds of legal discourse.

Custom, then, is the supposed locus of the alleged fatalism of rural Greek society, and nowhere more so than in those domains, notably the distribution of property, where fate is explicitly called upon to arbitrate in place of a human lawcourt. The play of fate (*mira, riziko*) and character (*fisiko*; cf. *fisi*, "nature" [Classical Greek *physis*]) in everyday Greek discourse resembles attributions of rule and strategy in the anthropological literature. *My* successes are the result of my character (*fisiko*) and my failures simply the effect of malign fate (*riziko*), while *your* (i.e. *another's*) successes are attributable to a benevolent fate and your failures to ineradicable flaws in your character – recall the similar relativity according to which the *eghoismos* of others is bad, one's own morally justifiable and good. In the same socio-logic, *their* rules are passively and unthinkingly accepted, while *our* strategies represent the quintessentially European virtue of individualism. Pragmatically, then, the rural Greeks' use of fate is far from being fatalistic, and their appeals to custom have a similarly strategic ring to them. As we shall see in the next section of this chapter, fate and custom together play a vital role in Greek social rhetoric; and rhetoric, the art of persuasion, is hardly the expression of resignation to the inevitable. On the contrary, the uses of this rhetoric are subversive of the very interpretations that official and foreign interests wish upon it.

A common logic thus informs all hierarchical distinctions between self and other, from the interpersonal to the international. Both sets of generalizations deny the *other* the capacity for successful, individual, *differentiated* action, while insisting that the *self* possesses that capacity. Differentiation is indeed crucial here. The European ideology treated differentiation as its own prerogative; discord among savages and peasants was uniformly attributed to a Hobbesian brutishness that justified the intervention of state or imperial law. In other words, like the paired categories of strategy/rule and character/fate, that of differentiation/homogeneity is a rhetorical construct, jointly constituting a moral shifter: the evaluation of each term depends on who is defining the specifics of self and other, and whether in cultural or political terms. As we saw in Chapter Three, such masked semantic contingency is what links the theoretical discourse of anthropology to more obvious examples of the rhetoric of identity.[11]

Given this logic, differentiation, the proud boast of pan-European identity, is an embarrassment when it appears instead at a more local level. On the one hand, it belies the ideological and political unity of the nation-state; on the other, it provides a subversive commentary on that unity, in that it reveals an intimately concealed otherness at the very heart of the supposed unity. The nationalist ideology, which happily accepted the swashbuckling exploits of Digenes and the pre-Independence klefts as evidence of ideologically Hellenic and European "individualism" in the national character, reacted fiercely and repressively against their contemporary embodiments in an "egotism" directed against the bureaucratic state itself. To some extent, of course, gross practicality dictated the official response: the government had to prove itself master of its own house. The onus of proof, however, shows very clearly that the greater power lay in the hands of the tutelary Powers. Thus, when in 1865 a group of English travellers was attacked by brigands (the famous "Dilessi affair"), certain apologists for the official government line insisted that such activities – lauded as the very essence of Greek patriotism when directed against the occupying Turks – were "foreign" to the Greek character and tradition when directed against the central government, which was in turn answerable to the self-appointed protectors of the new state (see especially Soteropoulos 1868). Internal unity was required for external consumption; but local-level actions and interpretations constantly threatened it from within.

On the surface, then, Greek identity suppresses differences of all sorts: they are the signs of alien identity. But the differences, both of opinion and of culture, subsist nonetheless. Moreover, this conceptual economy recurs at every level of social interaction. Everyday usage breaks the uniformity of official definition; *istories* and *dhiafores*, quarrels and differences – the contentious matter of actual events – challenge the unified history of a politically, religiously, and culturally homogeneous nation-state. At each level, however, people take care to ward off the curiosity of outsiders. One Rhodian villager warned two others quarreling in a coffee-house in front of people from a neighboring community, *"Koumbare*,[12] there are *kseni* (here, "non-villagers") here!" People from mutually antagonistic villages in Crete may elsewhere agree to be known under the general rubric of the more powerful community.[13] People from a particular island or region are acutely alive to the importance of displaying a united front to those from elsewhere. And, at the level of national identity, this premise of transcendent unity becomes reified to the point where the state refuses all recognition to the lower levels of differentiation.

The pattern I have just described is the conceptual matrix of social relativity, or segmentation, and we shall turn to it in greater detail in the next chapter. It brings into sharp focus the differences between statist and local-level ideologies, and on that basis offers a useful vantage point for our examination of the relation between anthropological theory and social practice. For the moment, however, I propose to concentrate specifically on the tension between state formalism and village usage. To date, most anthropological studies of rural Greece have a village focus, but the linguistic, historical, and political knowledge that authors generally bring to their research is predominantly formulated at the national level of generalization. This makes it extremely difficult to discern the many ways in which daily usage subverts, mocks, and subtly modifies the values of the bureaucratic state and its foreign supporters. History is "national" (or at best regional); language is mostly "standard demotic Greek"; and political activity follows rather than leads a national system. In the following sections, I hope to suggest some of the ways in which this too ready privileging of reified national culture undermines anthropological claims of ideological independence from modern as well as romantic statism.

Values and usage: history, morality, language

The national focus of pre-fieldwork training particularly applies to language. Although anthropologists' primary concern with local communities disinclines them to embrace *katharevousa*, they have nonetheless proved willing to accept in practice a scarcely less standardized demotic, and to attribute to it a high degree of semantic consistency in all areas of social life. Yet this seems uncharacteristically trustful. Statist ideology expropriated Digenes, Tsamadhos, the klefts, the *rebetika*, even the demoticist movement in language itself (as the *conservative* government's dismantling of *katharevousa* from 1975 on demonstrates [see Mackridge 1985:10]). The complete identification of official with bourgeois values can be seen in the widespread adoption of folk themes in children's literature as well as *décor rustique* (Greek *dekor roustik*!) in architecture, the middle class affectation of ultra-demotic speech, the taming of the cheeky shadow theater antihero Karagiozis (Danforth 1976), and the progressive prettification of the *rebetika* songs; the bourgeoisie had formerly rejected these songs as Turkish, linked to drug addiction, and immoral. Is it not likely, on the face of it, that the same also happened to the semantics of everyday speech? And, if so, in what sense could anthropologists, who generally learn the principled demotic of the bourgeoisie, claim to be speaking – and, more to the point, understanding – *the* language of the communities they studied?

Although many anthropologists working in Greece speak the standard language with reasonable fluency, they have generally not made language itself a major or critical object of study. This is a striking omission, given the enormous prominence that the Greeks themselves accord to language. One result has been a submersion of the ideological origins and present consequence of the anthropologists' own attitudes to the Greek language. Even without in the least supporting *katharevousa*, for example, some investigators have blithely acquiesced in the transliteration of modern Greek on the basis of the Classical language, and a few continue to do so (but see Friedl 1962:107 – a rare exception; Campbell and du Boulay, with equal respect, give Greek terms in the Greek alphabet). Other systems of transliteration, based on literary and journalistic models, and often internally inconsistent in themselves, show scant respect for local phonologies. Dialect, sometimes perhaps well understood in the field (although it would be valuable to have the assurance of such competencies), thus tends to disappear in analysis, and fails in consequence to achieve the prominence as a social marker that we should expect it to have in the ethnographic record of Greece. Such uncritical acceptance of the standard dialect by foreign scholars represents a triumph for the nationalistic point of view: one of the enabling conditions of European nationalism was the reduction of multifarious dialects to whichever of them proved most printable (Anderson 1983:48).[14]

This is a matter for general concern. Anthropologists rarely comment on the relationship between local and standard usage, but tend to adopt the phonology and semantics of one or the other for specific purposes. The question of variation is rarely raised. Campbell, for example, gives most Sarakatsan technical terms (except those that are strictly local in meaning) in standard demotic form, in contrast to Garoufas's perhaps more stylized vocabulary. Ethnographers working in bilingual communities have generally demonstrated little interest or competence in the "other" language (except when their primary focus was linguistic [e.g. Tsitsipis 1983a, 1983b]). Legal and economic terminology usually appears with a standard set of meanings throughout the country, determined by the provisions of the Greek Civil Code.

The consequence of such neglect is that anthropologists usually speak the Greek of the state, which is not necessarily the Greek (or, indeed, the local language) of the community under study. This can only encourage a more general failure to place sufficient distance between the state's professions of national homogeneity and the practice of anthropological research. Anthropologists do not willingly support that ideology; on the contrary, as we have seen, Friedl's exemplary refusal to assign typicality to any one community speaks for the profession as a whole. But the separation of anthropological research into discrete zones of relevance, and particularly the long-standing anthropological suspicion of both philology and folklore, has masked the ideological implications of the role of language in modern Greek life. This is at best dangerous for a discipline that collects data through the medium of language, in a country where the criteria of linguistic excellence and purity are a subject for everyday conversation.

But a further trap, and one that offers far more of a threat to accuracy, lies in superficial resemblances between local-level usage and official language. Lexical homogeneity can camouflage a wide range of semantic variation. Too uncritical an acceptance of the ideal of a standard language can disguise these vagaries, which are of some intrinsic interest in their own right, and may at the same time produce serious misunderstandings of local ideologies and practices. Anthropologists may have graduated beyond such crude linguistic abstractions as Whorf's Standard Average European; but it is important not to repeat the same mistake at the national level. One must always ask *who* defines the "standard" in Standard Demotic Greek.

This is an area, in fact, where our errors of interpretation can be especially helpful in redressing the façade of linguistic homogeneity. It becomes particularly helpful in those areas – notably the rhetorical contest between *custom* and *law* – where the state must rely on linguistic precision to achieve its goals, and where the vagaries of usage make control of local practice especially difficult. Questions of law – those surrounding the interpretation of inheritance terminology are perhaps the liveliest arena of conflict between official and local modes of interpretation – pit rules against practices.

Both the official discourse of law and the officializing strategies of custom ("that's how we found it" [e.g. du Boulay 1974:49]) suppress time through claims of eternal validity. Yet, as critics of legal positivism have pointed out, the law has antecedent sources and law-*givers* (e.g. B. S. Jackson 1982:159–60); in this, it resembles *data* ("things given") in the extent to which its authority rests on a naturalization of contingency. Western law, moreover, opposes uncontrolled *initiative* – taking the law into one's own hands – but instead represents itself as the guardian of *originality* (as in copyright legislation) or *individualism* (as in the laws of property and inheritance). Put in terms of Greek ethnography: it does rot tolerate the exercise of *eghoismos* but sanctions personal heroism in defense of the state's interests, much as folklore scholarship often rejects individual "authorship" but admires a conventionalized skill at "improvization." This is another version of the reduction of *istories* to History.

Romantic ideologies, political and academic alike, adopt a pose of historicity that ignores what Culler (1981:103) rightly recognizes as the ineluctable interdependence of human agency and convention:

Discursive conventions can only originate in discourse; everything in *la langue* . . . must have first been in *parole*. But *parole* is made possible by *la langue*, and if one attempts to identify any utterance or text as a *moment of origin* one finds that they depend upon prior codes.

Originality and individualism are Eurocentric, romantic notions that, as Valesio (1980:33) rightly observes, suppress a clear understanding of the rôle of convention in ordinary discourse – the dependence of the commonplace on "common places" (*koinoi topoi*), which themselves, as we have already noted, are culturally specific. Statist discourse, by attributing its conventions to a single class of heroes and authors, suppresses the possibility of new beginnings, and replaces it with a galaxy of prehistoric and ahistorical origins. These are the arbitrary originary principles that suppress the recurrence of agency in the experienced social world; they are the tenets of romanticism and statism, of the linguists' recursive *langue*, and of the structuralist reduction of the world "as a closed set of what J. L. Austin called 'performative statements [*sic*]'" (Said 1975:331). Only the determined particularism of ethnography can rescue anthropology from this taxonomic imperative.

Usage against institutions: inheritance, marriage

That imperative accepts the author(ial)ity of a strictly referential legal and moral discourse. While anthropologists would presumably agree that the moral terminology does not exhaust the full range of meanings that a local ethic can encompass, and while most ethnographic descriptions are sufficiently particularistic and detailed to give some sense of the range of usage for each term, the relationship between those usages and the indigenous understanding of meaning is often much less clear. Most ethnographers, while careful not to request definitions outright, tend to set definition as the final goal of their indirect questioning. But definition is also, as we have seen, the goal of official discourse, which seeks thereby to *naturalize* the socially contingent meanings that suit its particular aims, and to render all other usages invalid.

Anthropologists rarely make explicit their need for some level of indigenous definition. One unusual exception is provided by Boehm (1980), perhaps significantly also an advocate of sociobiology, who has essayed the elicitation of "natural [*sic*] definitions" of Montenegrin moral value terms. By assuming that definition is the goal of an anthropological semantics, rather than the imposition of a socially arid theory of meaning where local concepts may be far more responsive to deal with local usage (see Rosaldo 1980, 1982), Boehm explicitly does what many scholars in this area have left implicit: he reduces the morality of a partially segmentary, feuding local society to an impoverished version of romantic discourse – a medley of folk concepts, dependent on a folk view of meaning that can only be elicited by an active outside observer.

In the general subject area of moral values, this procedure at least had the virtue of making explicit the presuppositions of comparative research to date. Where ethnic and economic terms are concerned – to take two domains where officialdom may be said to have a more pragmatic interest – such procedures have rarely been applied. The referential basis of definition appears to be self-evident, being respectively applied to ethnic groups rather than ethnicity, and to economic institutions rather than morally ambiguous concepts of value. And yet it is precisely in these areas that the anthropological problem becomes particularly interesting; for it is here that the most serious challenge to a concept of pure referentiality can be mounted. In dealing with economic and social institutions, one is dealing with the immediate concerns of the state bureaucracy; in addressing ethnicity, one may be challenging the very *raison d'être* of the nation-state. It is here, then, that usage challenges official acceptations; and it is here that anthropology has to work hardest to escape the identification of its goals and methods with those of the bureaucratic state ideology.

A brief description of two cases must suffice to make the point here. In the first, I describe the mistakes I made in the Rhodian village of Pefko when, armed with the ethnographic vocabulary of inheritance norms, I began trying to elicit the content of Pefkiot women's dowries at marriage. One product of this revelation was that economic terms, which anthropologists would presumably prefer to interpret *as* strictly economic terms, convey a moral evaluation as semantically slippery as any in the established code-book of honor and shame. A curious consequence of this is that the economic and social implications of the terms come to mean the diametrical opposite of their formal definition in civil law.

The second case, drawn from my fieldwork in Glendi (western Crete), addresses ambiguities in the terminology of engagement and marriage. This time, I start from the lesson learned in Pefko – that what ordinarily pass for institutional terms may function as moral indexes – but discover that, in Glendi, institutional terms may also serve as indexes of moral *licence*; this hardly represents the official view. In both cases, I found usage to be serendipitously subversive of accepted meanings, and to have serious consequences for the picture of traditional Greek values that emerges from the ethnographic record.

In the first case, I began with the usual assumptions that economic categories would be more or less standard throughout Greece, varying only in their material content and mode of transmission but not in their fundamental legal definitions. In this, I did not diverge essentially from the compendium put together by Baron von Maurer, and later translated into Greek (Khrisanthopoulos 1853). A member of the triumvirate that essentially governed Greece on behalf of the young King Otho in the early years of independence, von Maurer treated local law as "customs" of great antiquity but little economic significance; and since his interpretation harmonized with the statist equation of definition with meaning, with the court's *laissez-faire* policy, and with the growing use of rural folklore as proof of the Greeks' racial antiquity, it strengthened the assumption that one could take fixed local definitions for *prika* ("dowry") and *klironomia* ("inheritance") for granted. Since these terms corresponded lexically to the formal legal nomenclature, moreover, von Maurer – whose survey is by any standards a remarkable ethnographic document – simply calibrated local practices to the definitions of state law, putting all local divergences down to the vagaries of custom and tradition.

My own initial tactic sprang from very similar (and hardly more conscious) presuppositions. I requested definitions, not in the belief that they were "natural" (Boehm 1980), but because this was what I felt to be the real point of my immediate investigation. By hindsight, to have asked what *prika* meant now seems both a silly question and one dictated by a statist understanding of law. Fortunately so; for it was the apparent inconsistency of the answers I received that eventually led me to focus on usage rather than on definition. This in turn produced a reading of the inheritance terminology that, to my surprise given that this was an ostensibly law-abiding and conservative community, revealed not only a pervasive distrust of bureaucratic law, but a set of usages that almost invariably contradicted the principles on which the law was based.

In Pefko, all offspring receive approximately equal parts of the major property of both parents, and in this respect local practice follows the Napoleonic principle of equal partible inheritance common throughout much of Europe. Today, the significant item of property is land, and all real estate holdings are divided amongst all the children. Each child's portion is known as *meridhio*, and this may include cash as well as the endowment of land that accrues to a daughter at marriage. The house that each daughter receives at marriage is not regarded as *prika*; it is, rather, "her own" (*dhikon dis*) – a categorical exclusion.

Now this is a curious distinction in the light of the pre-1983 Civil Code provision that all property bestowed on a woman at marriage was hers to possess if not control (Articles 1416–17; Friedl 1962:55). Certainly, the term *prika* has long carried a negative connotation even in the most traditional parts of rural Greece. In early nineteenth-century Epirus, there were severe limits on the size of the dowry, the growth of which was regarded as an abuse (Campbell 1976:24); while, both among the Sarakatsani (Campbell 1964:302) and on Rhodes (Herzfeld 1980d) the cash dowry, at least, is seen as a recent and destructive innovation. It is quite conceivable that the concept of dowry has had this negative significance for a long time, and that it has always been regarded as an externally derived social evil. Even today, feminist objections to the traditional form of dowering, leading to the recent abolition of *prika* as a legal category, seem to have derived in part from a perceptive understanding of the way in which the law masked inequitable practices (see also Skouteri-Didaskalou 1984:246).

That money can be squandered by an irresponsible husband is obvious enough, as is the relative difficulty of disposing of a woman's house. There still remains the question of her land: how could that be taken from her? In Pefko, *all* land is technically inalienable; and this means that sons' as well as daughters' *meridhia* are considered to be their own. But a wastrel husband might contrive to sell it to pay off drinking or gambling debts, or again he might lose it through neglect; the encroachment of pine forests after a statutory ten-year lapse from use would allow the government forestry agency to make such land available to another local purchaser. Since a wife does not actually control the family finances, there is very little that she can do in practice to prevent such abuses.

Land itself is almost never given as a *definiens* of *prika*; it is only so described in those rare cases when a husband's actual or potential lack of worth enters into the discussion. It is, however, a major component of the *prikosimfona* (marriage agreements) of which one extant Pefkiot specimen dates back to 1713. This is less of an exception than it might seem: the signing of the marriage agreement is the one moment when even the most approving prospective father-in-law may suspect the groom's intentions, and may therefore want to insure legally against any possible abuse. In short, when land is described as a *meridhio*, it is an unproblematical item of property, transferable according to strict norms. When, however, it is described as *prika*, this alludes to the discomfiting doubt about its viability as a woman's independent means of support that, in the larger arena, has finally led to the legal abolition of the *prika* as a legal category altogether. Usage, which proved locally subversive of legally fixed meanings, has wrought a much more radical revolution on the national stage.

The basis for this becomes clearer when we consider the status of money in such communities. Rhodian villagers sometimes define *prika* as money, also known as *ta refsta* ("fluid matter" – a revealing name in this context). Certainly, there is a general perception among Pefkiots that money is an un-reliable form of property; one song, referring to the obverse design of the old five-drachma pieces, relates that 'five-drachma pieces have eagles on them, and they go and fly away!" Thus, money is a fundamentally unstable *prika* component. Finally, the pre World War II allocation of *prika* usually consisted of pack-animals, then known as *khtimata*; that term is now ex-clusively given its "standard" meaning of "landholdings," but it is clear that pack-animals represented a more disposable form of property. *Prika*, then, does not have a fixed material referent. The term is *used*, however, with great consistency, of a wife's material inheritance in any context where her legal ownership could be undermined by her husband's irresponsibility or greed.

In the course of my inquiries about *prika*, I frequently used the term *kli-ronomia*, a straightforward gloss (as I ingenuously believed) for the hoary anthropological and legal category of "inheritance." Here again, I found a radically different local reading. Villagers denied absolutely that it was possible for a child to receive *klironomia* from a parent. Literally translated according to the standard gloss, this would have meant that children could not inherit from their parents – a manifest untruth, given the principle of the *meridhio*! Further queries revealed, however, that villagers only used *klironomia* of the legal process proper: if one were to "write the property" upon someone other than the traditionally designated group of heirs – one's own offspring – one would get a lawyer to draw up the necessary documen-tation; and this – only this – qualified as *klironomia*.[15] But the irony did not stop there. In its Classical Greek derivation, *klironomia* means "[property acquired as a result of] distribution by lots [*kleroi*]." In Pefko, however, the practice of dividing up the parental estate by casting lots was usual for ordi-nary purposes; in other words, *klironomia* meant the only kind of land transfer that did *not* entail this ancient practice – the persistence of which has been used to identify one strand of continuity with the ancient world (see Levy 1956; see also Herzfeld 1985b). In other words, the official discourse rejected mere "customs" as being unworthy of an emergent European state, even though their antiquity *in the countryside* provided evi-dential support for claims of an ancient heritage (but also, of course, for the persistence of "fatalism" if one wanted to read it that way instead). Official discourse adopted the *language* of Classical jurisprudence, but the *practices* of the modern European nations – a tactic parallel to the promotion of *katharevousa* as the national tongue.

Clearly, then, even the best acquaintance with Standard Demotic Greek will not insure the ethnographer against misunderstandings of a fairly radical kind. But this practical issue is merely the tip of an epistemological iceberg, that of disciplinary compartmentalization – in this case, the artificial separation of linguistic from economic anthropology. I have even been told, at a professional gathering, that the difficulties of determining the semantic range of inheritance terminology were irrelevant to an investigation of local-level economics, being a matter for the separate competence of "linguistic anthropology." While one would hope that such views are increasingly rare, they represent an anthropological variant of what we may call *linguistic fatalism* (or *determinism*) (see also Anderson 1983:46–7[16]). Either we are condemned, as anthropologists, to misread every use of language that diverges from the scriptist standard; or we are guilty of deliberately conducting our analyses on the grounds that the linguistic hegemony of the state is right and proper. In either case, we have allowed the perspective of anthropology to become identified with that of ideological statism.

My second example illustrates the point in another arena. Here we return to a more restrictedly *social* institution, namely that of marriage. In the Cretan village of Glendi, a morally conservative place on the surface, I was startled to hear people talking about the "wedding" (*ghamos*) of a couple I knew to be merely about to get engaged. I asked whether perhaps they meant the engagement ceremony (Cretan *arravoniasi*). Yes, I was told, that was right; that's what they had said!

I recount this moment of linguistic bewilderment in an anecdotal fashion because I want to suggest its evanescence – something that even the most evocative ethnographies convey with difficulty. In a profession that seeks hard data, how much reliance can we place on the fleeting impression of a passing remark, dismissed as soon as it was called to the speaker's attention as a slip of the tongue? But slips of the tongue are one of the few means whereby the wary ethnographer may hope to penetrate the disemic screen. Young Glendiot couples, contrary to the standard sexual ideology so familiar from the published ethnographies, sleep together *from the day of their formal betrothal*. Sexual intercourse is denoted by the verb *ghamo*, an etymological cognate of *ghamos*. While, then, the official values of church and state alike required them to desist until marriage, Glendiots simply separated the social institution of marriage – often called *stefanosi* ("crowning") in reference to the church ceremony – from the term marking the beginning of sexual intimacy.

Because *ghamos* means the *social* event, it also attaches more firmly to the secular celebration than to the church service. An extreme case will illustrate the point. After the consecration of one marriage between members of two rival Glendiot patrigroups (note the emphasis on agnatic kinship at a time of crisis), the party split into two *ghami* – in this instance, "marriage celebrations." In this context, a term for the *uniting* of different *families* became instead a symbol of communal *discord* between *patrigroups* – a double divergence from official ideology, marked by disregard for the new affinal connections and for the creation (to which every marriage looks forward in principle) of a brood of children with a cognatic kindred including people from both sides. As in its use to mark the beginning of sexual licence, here too the term *ghamos* not only departs from official usage, but actually *signifies* that departure, which is itself reproduced in the disemic deployment of two kinds of kinship idiom. As also on Corfu (Couroucli 1985:47–73), agnatic kinship articulates an alternative to official reckoning for precisely those purposes and occasions that official discourse would regard as inimical to local unity and hence as a threat both to state control and to the homogeneity of the national culture. As we shall see in the next chapter, sexual relations not only replace previous hostilities between kingroups; they also express those tensions, and so implicitly belie the encompassing unity preached by both the church and the state.

A practical difficulty that such evanescent usages present is the instantaneous denials that almost every attempt to check them will elicit. Here we encounter the suspicion that any attempt to verbalize the rejection of official values may have unpleasant consequences. The very desire for definitional clarity, the threat of a hidden but authoritative pen writing down the linguistic (as well as legal and moral) indiscretions of ignorant villagers, the anthropologist's ill concealed anxiety to "get it right" – all these reactions make the villager properly suspicious and defensive, and the chances are high that an officializing strategy will result: the offending usage simply vanishes as though it had never been. We shall see more examples of this, especially in the virtual impossibility of getting people to discuss the peculiar features of blasphemy when blasphemy itself is a proscribed form of speech, a "bad habit" the analysis of which can only mean trouble. By unconsciously echoing official attitudes – remember that questioning is itself a posture of authority, the formalism that it serves a technique of *reduction* – the ethnographer risks driving these usages still further underground.

Disemia opposes both context-dependency and fuzziness to definition. Authoritative discourse requires a rhetoric of precision, whether in anthropology (see Zonabend 1985:36) or in political life in the narrow sense. But disemia is necessarily a condition of ambiguity: just as animal-theft, amiable abuse, or blasphemy become marks of an affective sociality from within, so the "inconsistency" of unofficial speech can appear as "flexibility" from within the ranks of the relatively powerless (see Lederman 1980:492). This is the corollary of the logic whereby officialdom expropriates "egotism" in order to represent it as "individualism."

The brief illustrations from Greek ethnography that we have examined here all illustrate the power of usage to subvert formal definition through the evocation of social experience. Usage springs from the everyday actuality of events, *istories*, and as such differs radically from the definition-bound fixity of official history. Usage is an unself-conscious form of creativity, the latter being "a license exercised within a socially-constituted frame of reference" (M. Jackson 1983a:131). While particular oppressions may evoke more self-conscious attempts at reading the codes of the powerful, the everyday subversion of official doctrine continues unabated. Only when it is made explicit does it become an active threat to official discourse in general, rather than a gentle undermining of specific and local forms of control. But that gradual erosion is the interior world of the local community, the world the ethnographer seeks to know. Any representation of it in the terms of the official discourse is mere reductionism, a contribution to the statist argument and to the larger European ideology that engendered it.

The moments of suddenly aware rebellion reveal the radical nature of the disemic gap. Official discourse is symbolically and pragmatically opposed to social experience. Angered by a disrespectful policeman's refusal to accept the customary local escort when tracking a village miscreant, a Glendiot reportedly fumed, "You may represent the law (*nomos*), but we have two laws (*dhio nomous*; cf. *n-omos*, "shoulder") here!" The message is clear: *our* customs make us carry our social responsibilities on our backs; our laws are not those of the official body politic, but of the body humane – the sweated, twisted, familiar, sinful body of everyday experience. By punning on the homonymy of "law" and "shoulder," the speaker expressed his understanding that there were essentially two ways of encountering the world, though encompassed within a single symbolic (and even lexical) idiom of representation. There is the perspective of the state, which Glendiots regard as intrusive and repressive; and there is their own, which they regard as natural and good. In their own world, ridden as it is with the imposed burdens of cultural and ethical sin, the sheer unpredictability of *eghoismos* and the vagaries of linguistic usage make nonsense of fixity and definition. On this side of disemia, the finitudes of official discourse are sterile, meaningless artificialities.[17]

7 The practice of relativity

Disemia and segmentation:
the relativity of social knowledge

Disemia operates between official discourse and social knowledge. We can put this in another way: that it pits the fixity of official rules and regulations against the shifting implications of anything people say or do in actual social life. So far, we have considered the tension between these two poles mainly as it occurs at the level of national stereotypes, examining the ways in which national culture and nationalist scholarship contend with insubordinate corrosion by daily social experience.

But the fixing of orthodoxy at the national level is itself an orthodoxy, formed in response to the dominant ideology of European nationalism. In practice, even people who talk as though they fully endorsed and agreed upon the ideals of national unity do not necessarily mean the same things by it. Rhetorically, national values are the yardstick to which all more localized orthodoxies must be calibrated, and they provide a rich source of metaphors – invariably represented as literal truths – whereby strategies officialize themselves. But this does not mean that the speakers are good statists, even if they so present themselves. "Every man is a state," a Pefkiot villager told me, articulating in that simple proposition both the legitimizing power of the state as a metaphor for all subordinate entities from the region down to the single actor and, by a paradoxical converse, the independently minded individual's disdain for either state or social control. The state can fight for its national self-aggrandizement (*eghoismos*); true men of self-regard (*eghoistes*) can gird themselves with all the accoutrements of official rhetoric. But the ultimate power of the state is revealed in the actor's rhetorical dependence on the state as a model of legitimacy. The actor can only recover that power symbolically, by metaphorically posing *as* a state.

The fact is, however, that many individuals do just that. By inverting the official formula in this way, they challenge the very logic of statehood. They carve beneath the skin of national unity; they suggest the possibility of fragmentation, of conflict between individuals and small groups without

152

regard to official policing, and they do so by masquerading as state-like entities in their own right. Real social knowledge emphasizes the differences and self-interest typical of the fallen human condition: even the states themselves quarrel in the same illogical way as ordinary men and women.

This fits the logic that we have been exploring. It was the fall of Adam and Eve that divided human society and gave free rein to the play of self-interest. At the most localized level of refraction, this history informs the tension between the unity of brothers and the insidious corruption of that unity that their wives, the lineal and ethical descendants of Eve, introduce through their gossip and backbiting (see Campbell 1964:336, 354; du Boulay 1974:102). Other rivalries – those between villages or regions, for example – also reflect the fundamentally corrupt nature of human society. From the state's idealizing perspective, all lower-level social cleavages are by definition subversive; they are the political and legal equivalent of the condition that the doctrine of original sin attributes to everyday life. For these western-defined weaknesses of Greek culture, extreme (and mostly militaristic) nationalism offers sundry surgical cures (e.g. the 1967–74 régime; see Clogg 1972). In practice, however, everyone knows that even – or especially – the state is subject to human frailty. A Khalkiot islander on Rhodes, who had been much snubbed in his adoptive endogamous village, and perhaps therefore unusually sensitive to the relationship between personal pride and collective identity, insisted that the hostility between Greece and Turkey resulted entirely from "the *eghoismos* of the prime ministers."

This understanding contradicts the bland unanimity presented by the official doctrine. Greek statist writers sometimes object to what they represent as an immature local habit of personifying political relations between countries, and contrast it to the sensible European abstractions (for such they fondly imagine them to be) of politics for politics' sake. What they really seem to be doing, then, is attacking the whole socially aware, culturally insubordinate phenomenon of *Romiossini*, here embodied in the orientalized image of a nation that can do nothing except by means of personal influence and graft, and comparing it to the no less stereotypical image of a "European" polity and morality.

Yet social knowledge, which springs from the sinful knowledge of difference and pride, does not readily incorporate the grandiose unities of state ideology or the lofty and impersonal pretensions of historical destiny, any more than it obeys the fatalistic structures of deterministic anthropologies: "'Absolute knowledge,' however, is no knowledge, an insight we have to thank Eve for, who reached out for the fruit" (Duerr 1985:133). Statism tries to banish the knowledge of a past fall behind the present perfections of a created order: an inversion of biblical history. Ordinary people, however, know better: they understand the social character of self-interest, and they know that it affects the highest levels of political activity. The insidious weakness of Banfield's "amoral familism" thesis (1958) lies in its support for the statist view of bureaucracy and civic institutions as above human agency both politically and morally.

Disemia is thus not merely a symbolic opposition between interior and external perspectives. It is also, and much more significantly, a battle between intimate social knowledge and official cultural form. As such, it occurs at all levels at which people recognize certain social alignments as relevant to their lives. This is significant in itself: it makes nonsense of the state's self-proclaimed right to generalize cultural orthodoxy as "national character" (on which, see Caro Baroja 1970). There are many levels at which people reject outsiders and acknowledge insiders, and the criteria of admission fluctuate both between levels and between particular situations.

This pervasive relativity is expressed linguistically in the common use of *group shifters*. Shifters, which for present purposes may be exemplified by the English-language terms "outsider" and "one of us," are signs whose meaning depends both on the perspective of the speaker and on that of the people whose actions are described. There is no fixed social definition of *outsider*; the meaning of this term depends on the character of the reference-group, which is in turn determined by the speaker's intentions and social identity (see Galaty 1982). Even ethnic labels, which commonly seem to refer to absolutely defined cultural entities, often possess this semantic slipperiness; we have already seen how the meaning of *Vlakhos* ranges through several degrees of specificity from "Koutsovlach-speaking transhumant shepherd" to "rural Mainlander in general." The exact meaning, as with all shifters, depends on who is speaking, to whom, about what, and in what context.[1]

In the sclerotic grip of official discourse, group shifters tend to lose their semantic lability. *Vlakhi*, to continue with this example, are narrowly defined by language and community origin. English-language speakers generally forget that the label "foreign," now routinely associated with the rigid boundaries of national identity, was once itself a relativity, originating in the Latin shifter *foranus, -a* ("one who comes from outside") and continuing through medieval derivatives of similarly relativistic significance. Until the state finally succeeded in stabilizing its meaning at the single level of national identity, this word retained its sense of social relativity. Those who were defined as outsiders were the people "we know less well" – a clear statement of the relationship between social distance and knowledge; but who "we are," and therefore who it is "we know better" (and by how much), were decisions based largely on circumstances. Social knowledge, always relative to actors and their interests, is something for *negotiation*.

Official statist discourse takes the opposite tack. It treats all social boundaries as absolute: foreigners are foreigners, and the immigration authorities apply a set of rules and definitions that allow of no ambiguity. That, at least, is the theory; practice is likely to be very different. Whatever the actual state of affairs, however, official discourse has certainly succeeded in making nationality *look* absolute. English usage is illuminating here. The rustic-sounding variant *furriner* – meaning, among other things, someone from the next county or village – serves most commonly as a cruel quip by urban sophisticates: the generically bucolic dialect form marks the sub-state levels of discrimination. A relativistic view of social relations becomes the sign of a bumpkin otherness, an "Anglo-Saxon" antidote to the highfalutin' Latinity of formal language, much as Romeic scurrilities oppose Hellenic pieties. These disemic distinctions operate to distinguish between a definition fixed referentially at the state level, and a supposedly rural usage that allows any number of levels provided they have something to do with social experience. It is a long-term effect of state control that leads people to laugh at parochial antipathy to "furriners" while accepting the political submersion of foreigners into their adopted *culture* as *naturalization* – a particularly brazen case of rhetoric denying its own rhetoricity in the best romantic tradition.[2]

In Greece, a common terminology disguises the distinction between absolute and relative social boundaries: one of several official terms for *foreigner* still possesses the lability of *foranus* in everyday usage. It is in fact the "outsider" member of a pair of social-group shifters: *kseni* (outsiders) and *dhiki (mas)* ([our] own [people]), can operate at virtually any level of social inclusion or exclusion. The moral terms in which Greeks enunciate the discrimination are roughly the same at all levels: *kseni* are contextually inferior, untrustworthy, dependent (for hospitality), and suspect. This holds true at every level of identity – religion, nation, region, province, district or island, village, neighborhood, patriline, kin-group, household, or even individual. For the state, however, the only members of the category of *kseni* are non-citizens, although there is some official awareness of ambiguities in everyday usage: when the military junta tried to improve police recruitment in 1974, they were at pains to stress that *Ellines* ("Greeks, Hellenes") included the Muslim minority – that the latter were, in other words, "Greek *citizens*" (*Ellines ipiköi*).

Anything that conflicts with official values, however, and especially any diagnostic traits of local, class, or ideological difference, is un-Greek: beards (under the junta), communism (sometimes called a "Slavic dogma" even after the collapse of the right-wing military dictatorship in 1974), Turkish elements in the language, brigandage, sexual immorality, local separatism. To use the distinction between *kseni* and *dhiki mas* in any but the national sense is equally "foreign" to official dogma. Official ideology not only privileges its own emphasis on language as the definiens of national purity, but also dismisses local differences as themselves on the wrong side of the disemic divide: in other words, it not only condemns the "non-Hellenic" side of a highly institutionalized two-column diagram, but also, and above all, rejects any attempt to read that diagram in any but the official way. If local distinctiveness belies Greek homogeneity, then, conversely, folksiness is next to Turkishness.

This picture of shifting relationships fits a model initially devised for the analysis of political life in certain exotic societies: that of *segmentation*. Segmentation is the relative deployment of political alliances according to genealogical or other criteria of social distance between the parties to a dispute. Anthropologists most commonly treat it in conceptual contrast to state-like formations, and hence as irrelevant to the study of occidental political life.

The classic studies of segmentary political systems are those conducted by E. E. Evans-Pritchard and his students, mostly in Nilotic and West African societies and later amongst Muslim nomads (especially Fortes and Evans-Pritchard 1940; Evans-Pritchard 1949; Middleton and Tait 1958; Peters 1967; cf. Barth 1959). Evans-Pritchard's own study of the Nilotic Nuer people (1940) established a framework that numerous revisionist studies have modified but not displaced (see Karp and Maynard 1983). In demanding respect for Nilotic societies on the grounds that they did have a *political life*, which did not of itself necessarily entail a bureaucratic or military system of *government* (Fortes and Evans-Pritchard 1940), anthropologists inadvertently made these societies seem deficient in comparison with their own. As an exotic form of political life – what Middleton and Tait revealingly described as "indigenous systems, unaffected by European contact" (1958:1) – segmentation is an incomplete political mode, an institutional poverty perhaps most honestly glossed by the jacket description of Evans-Pritchard's *The Nuer* as a society that "*lacks* government and *is without* legal institutions" (my italics).

Such comments seem to represent non-statist political systems – and especially segmentary ones – as incomplete (see also Clastres 1974; Kuklick 1984). It thus places "acephalous political systems" in the same class of deficient culture as "folk poetry" and "ethnoscience." Segmentation works through a system of shifters; Nuer *cieng* ("community") works in a relativistic sense much like that of the English "insider." It thus closely resembles folk categories and popular history alike in its lack of any claim to absolute referentiality.

Whatever the descriptive adequacy of approaches that oppose segmentary to statist *ideologies*, it is clear that social life in statist societies is not free of segmentary proclivities. That the official *language* of political life, its lexical camouflage, admits of no internal contradictions does not mean, as we have seen in the previous chapter, that these do not exist: "We may speak the same language, but we have a different discourse" (Dimiroulis 1985:59). Greece, as a nation-state, can hardly be called a "segmentary society." But a segmentary perception of social relations vies with the absolute centralization of the bureaucratic Greek state. Its existence, the inner face of Greek political experience, subverts – and is denied by – the state ideology. In the statist perspective, an *outsider (ksenos)* is always a *foreign citizen*; the only way to exclude Greeks is to deny their citizenship by bureaucratic means, as the military junta of 1967–74 did to many of its exiled opponents. But in fact European statism itself, paradoxically, rests on a segmentary basis: nation-state vies with nation-state to be more European than all the others; and Greek province vies with Greek province to appear as the most perfect representative of those ancient Hellenic traditions from which European identity is distilled. By denying certain citizens their Greekness, the junta revealed the segmentary basis of their absolutist rhetoric: Greekness became a relative attribute simply because it was now seen to be something that factions could confer or take away, rather than the eternal immanence of a timeless people. It was left to one of their victims, Melina Mercouri, to point up the sheer contradictoriness of their action by declaring that no one *could* take away another's national birthright: what false nationalists were these?

Refractions of identity: disemia and hierarchy

We shall return in a moment to the status of segmentation in Greek society. It would be useful, however, to begin with a brief comment on the significance of this phenomenon in anthropological theory generally. Segmentation gained rapid acceptance in the political analysis of rural descent systems, most dramatically in the study of Nilotic societies; later work elaborated and confirmed this Africanist bias, and also extended the analytical construct to the Islamic world (see Peters 1967).

More than a quarter of a century earlier, however, Durkheim had already articulated the concept in a Mediterranean context – an irony that Davis (1977:2), who uses this fact to deplore the lack of subsequent Mediterraneanist theorizing, fails to appreciate (but cf. Black-Michaud 1975). Although segmentation returned to Mediterraneanist anthropology through the study of various Arab political systems, its appearance in the European section of the area has been largely confined to three surveys, all in the context of allegedly lineage-like systems of political interaction, and all largely unknown outside Greece (Kavadias 1965; Alexakis 1980; Meraklis 1984:59–69).[3] In general, however, I suggest that it has not gained popularity in the European Mediterranean because it would subvert the *cordon sanitaire* provided by that area between the familiar and the exotic. As a counter-illustration, Nicholas's (1966) rather successful application of the segmentary model to factional politics in India could have provided illuminating insights into Greek, Italian, and Spanish politics; but in fact segmentation has only appeared in the analysis of Greek politics in atypical cases where factions follow a unilineal descent pattern – most fully in highland western Crete (Herzfeld 1985a), where *edhiči mas* (= *dhiki mas*) are exclusively agnates for some purposes.

The problem with segmentation is that, uncombined with such exotic phenomena as unilineal descent, it is one of the most self-evident truths of social experience: people ally with those whom they consider relatively "close" against those whom they regard as more distant. When it is not exotic, it must be trite. Imagine trying to write an *interesting* account of soccer team allegiances in these terms! One is again reminded of Linton's doomed attempt to get American readers interested in the "totemism" of the U.S. military. Occasionally, it is true, segmentation does appear in a familiar cultural context, where it may index some heavily overlaid exotic past; for example, one study identifies it in Black Power politics as a trace – a survivalist shade? – of African culture (Gerlach and Hines 1970). But as an aspect of everyday life in western societies, segmentation seems little more than a wilted platitude – one perhaps most happily refreshed by a novelist (Greene 1943:68): "That is what people are saying all the time everywhere; the two great popular statements of faith are: 'What a small place the world is' and 'I'm a stranger here myself.'" Despite one major attempt to deprive segmentation of its exotic associations and to recognize its presence in all complex systems of political life (Smith 1956), it was until recently treated as an exotic *type* rather than as a universal *aspect* of political life.[4] In it, the older strain of survivalism continued to lurk.

Recent research has at last begun to reverse that reading. The first step came with the rejection of the view that if events did not reproduce the segmentary model literally, the latter did not really work. Galaty (1981, 1982) demonstrated that conflicts at one level might well *stand for* more inclusive levels of opposition, while Meeker suggested that the segmentary model could best be read as a metaphor for the uncertainty of political relations rather than as a literal description of specific events (1979:100). Karp and Maynard (1983) rediscovered in Evans-Pritchard's Nuer research the fundamental principle that segmentation as such is not necessarily entailed in a particular mode of descent reckoning (see also Herzfeld 1984b; Dresch 1986), and indeed that it extends to the social organization of academe itself as what outsiders see as "schools of thought" in contrast to the more fractured view from within (Karp and Maynard 1983:482). In their concluding response to the *Current Anthropology* commentators, these authors again briefly commented upon this covert dimension of academic knowledge (1983:497). Such insights into the social constitution of knowledge paved the way for Kingsbury's (1984) remarkable analysis of the recognizably segmentary way in which attributions of the supposedly absolute and innate value of "talent" operated in a New England conservatory: these depended on the variously defined but always relative social distance between students, their families, and their teachers.

Segmentary action can also include speech. This is not simply because, as in "segmentary societies" of the conventional canon, the terminology of social group classification is relative (e.g. Evans-Pritchard 1940:135); nor is it simply a metaphorical extension, as in the recognition that segmentation constitutes an "idiom" of social relations (Bohannan 1958:39–40). Even in societies not normally recognized as possessing a segmentary political life, people organize social experience in relativistic ways, and this is sometimes reflected in speech. By "screwing *your* Virgin Mary," a blasphemous Greek can divide up the holy image of the Virgin between rival factions or regions. Other semiotic systems, including silence, follow this pattern also. Good examples of non-linguistic embodiments of the principle are portraits of some revered political figure from the past emblematically placed in the coffee-houses of bitterly opposed political groups, each of which claims the hero as its spiritual ancestor; and even the deliberate *avoidance* of violence that allows the stronger side in a quarrel to demonstrate its moral superiority.[5]

Indeed, this last example again shows that stereotypes of Mediterranean people as socially incontinent are ethnographically unsound; the treatment of segmentation as the moral economy of violence associates otherness-in-general (societies "unaffected by European contact") with lack of individual self-control. But this perspective depends on being able to unravel the concept of segmentation from its association with a particular social form, unilineal descent. The only general treatment of segmentation by a Greek scholar (Meraklis 1984) compares Sarakatsan and Maniate "lineages" with the segmentary lineage systems of the classic social anthropological literature, thereby conceding – significantly, for a Greek readership – the presence of "internal exotics" and placing the latter at an early stage in the evolution of modern Greek society. Local scholarship seems here to reproduce the survivalist strain in the dominant idiom of Mediterraneanist anthropology.

The question is not whether a given society *is* segmentary or not (see also Salzman 1978a:62). All societies must be segmentary inasmuch as they recognize more than one level of social differentiation. It would be more useful to inquire instead whether the prevailing ideology makes the presence of segmentary relations explicit or attempts to suppress it. Nuer, for example, are quite specific about the segmentary proclivities of their society, as Evans-Pritchard's account clearly shows; in Greece, I found the Glendiots – with their contempt for law and bureaucracy – far more explicit about the semantic relativity of terms like *kseni* and *dhiki mas* than were the firmly law-abiding lowlanders I encountered on Rhodes. The latter seemed to have gone much further in internalizing the ideals of the state, whose ideology of national unity reproduces the still more encompassing and transcendent unity of European identity.

But European unity, like that of the nation, is anything but unitary: some European countries are more European than others. European identity is both a unity and a mask for what Anderson (1983:123) calls "modular" nationalisms – the "sublineages," so to speak, of the European tribe. The resulting concealment of an essentially segmentary concept within a rhetoric of unanimity is the same kind of romantic sleight of thought that animates "European individualism," or, in a more specialized variant of the same idea, the differentiated "talent" of Kingsbury's (1984) conservatory students.

The parallel deserves a moment's attention, since it brings together two quite different levels of the same way of thinking. Even though one addresses (European) collective identity and the other that of the (talented) individual, they are closely linked: the ideal European hero is the individualist or, more cerebrally, the genius. The two cases thus represent the extreme poles of a segmentary value system concealed behind, but necessary to, the rhetoric of European unity. In both instances, a supposedly absolute quality is refracted through the relative social or cultural distinctions of immediate experience. European identity, which each European culture claims to embody most fully, becomes the object of competition. Individualism, similarly represented as an infrangible unity, is again a mask for the multiple levels of social identity. The concept of talent is a special instance of this romantic preoccupation with individual genius, a quality that could attach to any individual (usually male), any country, or the entire European world. Indeed, the segmentary realizations of talent, so well documented in Kingsbury's study, are historically and ideologically much closer to those of Greek *eghoismos* than the relegation of the latter to "Mediterranean" and "peasant" value systems might suggest.

The concept of *eghoismos* is part of a disemic pair, the outer face of which is the absolute, abstract principle of individualism. As self-interest or *amour propre* (Vico's *amor proprio*), refracted from within through the fractured social relations of common experience, it is only noble when it is performed by one's own side; it becomes mere selfishness in others. Recall again the operation of ideas about fate and character: as moral attributes shift from self to other, they also change from positive to negative (or vice versa). This is a characteristically disemic phenomenon, and one that reflects the Greeks' dependence on external models of political and civic virtue.

Eghoismos is, recognizably, an etymological cognate of the English term "ego[t]ism." It also carries some of the same pejorative implications. Western nationalism, at least until the collapse of its extreme embodiment in Nazism, often treated egotism as a correlate of sexual degeneracy, "lack of shame" (*sic*), and cultural otherness (Mosse 1985:79). For west European nationalists, therefore, the Greeks' love of self-interest was the very hallmark of their otherness, in contrast (most dramatically) to the patriotic self-sacrifice of European philhellenes; the philhellenes themselves, of course, as well as many of their admirers down to the present (see especially St. Clair 1972:75–7), were outraged by the contrast. As Mouzelis (1978:137–8) has noted, the roots of what passes for Greek political self-centeredness lie in the larger institutional framework within which Greek politicians are able to operate, not in some putative national character; the very ideology that condemns them for their un-European behavior creates the conditions under which they are most likely to go on exhibiting it. For the Greeks, forced to judge themselves by these largely extrinsic standards and thus to interiorize their own otherness, the disemic tension between an aggressive "Hellenic love of independence" and passive resignation to an internalized "Romeic quarrelsomeness" reflects the political conditions constraining cultural identity.

In Greece, moreover, the same opposition appears as a contrast between centralized, unified government (the sublimation of the individual) on the one hand, and segmentary social relations (the relativization of self-interest) on the other. These are the disemic poles: a rigidly centralized and "European" bureaucratic system of law and government on the one side, a pervasively exotic segmentary idiom for the expression of social relations on the other. Each level of this segmentary system reveals a further disemic tension between the unities of self-display to those one does not "know" (*kseni*) on the one hand, and the knowledge of further internal subdivision that one shares with insiders (*dhiki* [*mas*]) on the other.

The very demands of self-interest at any given level require that it display itself as noble individualism on behalf of the social group. This transformation of "egotism" into "legitimacy" comprises the essence of Bourdieu's "officializing strategies" (1977:40). Bourdieu is constrained here by his interest in those societies that he considers to be "less differentiated" (e.g. Kabylia, rather than Algeria). But his point applies all the way up to the institutionalization of state values: all that has changed is the *degree* to which contingent self-interest is converted into timeless truths about *the* social order. As we also saw in the last chapter, open "egotism" is a mark of otherness in Eurocentric ideologies. By contrast, exemplary individualism marks devotion to a common ideal: the hero embodies the social whole. At each level, unity is the mark of the officializing strategy (including official discourse itself), disunity the familiar problem to which only insiders have the privilege of access. In order to see that the change is one of mere scale, and not one of basic principle, recall again the Pefkiot's warning: "*Koumbare*, there are outsiders [i.e. non-villagers] here!"

In the final analysis, segmentation is disemia in a hierarchical framework – a mode of organizing social knowledge in terms of self-presentation and self-knowledge within a hierarchical framework ordered from the top.[6] The state encapsulates, but cannot internally suppress, the social world of segmentary relations over which it rules. This helps to understand changes in the meaning of the war fought by the guerrillas who provided the back-bone of the Greeks' struggle for independence. Their own goals were patently personal and parochial, and would almost certainly have been dismissed as mere egotism had they been directed *against* the legitimizing authority. Indeed, this is apparently what happened to the few who were foolhardy enough to carry on their activities once a bureaucratic and military régime was firmly ensconced in Athens. Those who laid down their arms in time, on the other hand, were invested with the absolute qualities of romantic "individualism" and "heroism," terms that both tied them to the self-authenticating, neo-Classical ideology of European identity and suppressed their strongly anti-authoritarian proclivities.

All social entities and concepts are subject to the same fundamental tension. This is very noticeable in discussions of cultural quality. For instance, when Pefkiots called their own dialect *katharevousa* they were simply expressing a corollary of the relativistic principle entailed in their using the same term about my urban style of talking. The principle is one of mutual exclusion – you can't understand us, we can't understand you – as is clear from the joke, heard all over Greece, about a foreigner who thought he had learned to speak Greek well until he tried to find out about boats to the islands; to his questions about where the boats berthed, when the last one had left, and when there would be another one, he was treated to a series of expressive whistles and gestures but no words at all. In this way, he learned how hard Greek really was!

That story has been the bane of many a foreigner's visit to Greece, so frequently is it repeated and with such triumphant chortles. It expresses a view of the Greek language from the underside, as it were, of disemia. Language is a defense against any kind of cultural or social penetration. Like European intellectualism – of which, as *the* ancient language of Europe, Greek is a segmentary refraction – it is thought to be too difficult to admit of mastery by outsiders. In the anecdote, however, it is not the stilted official language that we meet. There, instead, a thoroughly Romeic, "restricted code" contrasts dramatically with official discourse, and especially with the gestural self-restraint that Tylor and the Victorians generally considered to be appropriate behavior among "civilized" people.

Everyday language – or, more accurately, communication – emerges as a means of depicting the outsider as incomprehensible to insiders, while at the same time it protects insiders' intimacies – symbolized by the physicality of gesture – from the inquisitiveness of outsiders. Precisely because a foreigner might well turn out to know grammatical, formal Greek, and because the European-dominated social aesthetic of officialdom demanded a discourse of pure language, the tale can represent everyday intercourse as an impenetrable barrier, just like that entailed in dismissing a foreigner's Greek as *katharevousa*. One version of the tale about the whistles and gestures, in which the opposition is not between Greek and foreigner but between the inhabitants of different regions (du Boulay 1974:48), shows how even such lighthearted anecdotes can be *segmentarily deployed* in the exploration of cultural difference. The joke has a flexibility hardly known in official pronouncements, and is all the more piquant in this case as the butt is an Athenian who cannot cope with village dialect!

Anderson (1983:122) argues that "[l]anguage is not an instrument of exclusion. . . . On the contrary, it is fundamentally inclusive, limited only by the fatality of Babel; no one lives long enough to learn *all* languages." For the Greeks, however, the supposed difficulty of their language provides them with a rare joke at the expense of their tormentors. The consequences of the cultural fall, of that refraction of Babel that makes their spoken language so *un*-European, feed European contempt for their culture as well as local élite contempt for the peasantry; yet it is precisely this oriental obscurity that leaves the pompous oppressor helpless. As Anderson recognizes, mortality is what makes it impossible to learn all the languages of the world, and this fact assures what he rightly calls "the vast privacy of the language of the oppressed" (1983:135).[7] From a segmentary point of view, the privacy of Greek combines the holiness and the pollution that together define the modern Greek condition as politically and culturally marginal, and with sweetly ironic revenge turns these features back against their inventors in the West. The logic is again pure disemia: as *katharevousa*, Greek is the quintessence of the European intellect, and that is why Greek-as-rules is difficult; as demotic, Greek is too exotic and too undisciplined ("so many words for one thing!" [Handman 1983:15]), and that is why no outsider has a chance of understanding Greek-as-usage.

The insubordinate logic is clear: you too are mortal, and so you will not be able to master my language before you, like me, must die. This secular rendering of original sin repeatedly calls the bluff of statism and of the oppressive ideologies that support it. Yet the converse is also recognized, as the logic of segmentation demands. A villager, sighing portentously, yearns for the return of unity and Eden: "The whole world should speak one language!" In a segmentary view of the world, this is the idealizing corollary of the anecdote just discussed. It corresponds to the Sarakatsan representation of bread as the symbol of social unity (Campbell 1964:117), and of the lover's rhyming plaint from Rhodes in which we hear the inverse sentiment of the idiom of blasphemy:

My girl, even if we did quarrel, we kiss a single [icon of the] Virgin,
and at one set of plate we go and take communion.

Similarly, holy icons are the object of veneration at all levels, from the family to the entire spiritual community of orthodoxy; all are refractions of the Holy Spirit through the social order, and the largest refraction is the national or religious community of all Greeks (see Dubisch 1985; Kenna 1985:364–8). Social life is riddled with relativities.

Strategies of the kind entailed in telling the anecdote about the hapless foreigner/Athenian's attempt to use Greek pose a contrast between the official logic of a universal language of pure wisdom and grammatical exactitude, and a socially practiced language requiring deep, intimate knowledge to negotiate its inevitable ambiguities. Such strategies do not only officialize; they also keep official people (and values) on the outside. They are the disemic interior of social ideology. Like the demotic tongue that they use, they possess a "vast privacy," one that reproduces the state's attempt to legitimize a unique national language as a local strategy of exclusion. Now it is the state, rather than the imperial power, that has become the conservative and oppressive enemy. Local usage permits a degree of impenetrability that no protestations of national unity can ever overcome; individual strategies furnish the kind of baffling front that colonial masters dismiss as native laziness and the western Powers regard in the Greeks as inexplicable cheek. This *reproductive relativity* is what segmentation is all about.

Bourdieu, in seeking to explain Kabyle segmentation as a negotiation of rules, seems to overlook this crucial relationship between the theory and what is observed: the model of segmentation is a model of the relative differentiation between rules (how you face outsiders) and strategies (how you describe your activities to insiders). It is not just complementary opposition (*pace* Salzman 1978a), but the relativization of an opposition between two radically contrasted forms of social knowledge. This is what the Greek distinction between *kseni* and *dhiki mas* conveys: *dhiki mas* are defined as those we (relatively speaking) "know," and the distinction encapsulates an indigenous theory of social knowledge that official discourse necessarily ignores. At each level, provisional solidarity is expressed through rule-like formulations, and these culminate in that bureaucratic reification of collective identity that we call the nation-state – the product of a sort of officializing super-strategy.

In the traditional anthropological literature, moreover, the symbolic opposition that ranges segmentation against state centralization is itself a rhetorical device of the kind that works by denying its own rhetoricity. The romantic European ideology viewed the state as both embodying and eternalizing all significant social relations. Segmentary perspectives persisted as "folk models," whence they may have influenced the development of anthropological theories of the segmentary polity (see Kuklick 1984; but cf. Kuper 1985). Their attributed currency among ordinary people, as in the well-worn jokes about yokels and "furriners" in English, made them an apt metaphor of the otherness that came to be associated with acephalous political systems. By thus separating the segmentary from the state-like – much as similar arguments separated the rhetorical from the factual, the poetic from the scientific, and the ideological from the material – the romantic ideology backgrounded its own necessary conditions of existence.

For the European ideology, as I have already briefly noted, encapsulated a segmentary system of its own – perhaps most ironically captured in Guizot's proclamation that represented the European diversity in its greatest richness. Eurocentric rhetoric, similarly, may acknowledge only one principle of European identity, but that did not stop each member state from claiming to embody it the most perfectly. In this – its *Animal Farm* quality again (Orwell 1945) – European statism strikingly recaptures the segmentary sense of the Greek proverb, "Not all the fingers are equal [in length]."

It also resembles intellectual debate, and here we return to a point raised earlier in this chapter (Karp and Maynard 1983:497):

We do recognize . . . that intellectual debate tends to be a segmentary process, that reading can never be neutral, that interpretation is relative to both the theory and the interests of the reader. We continue to believe, however, that interpretation is underdetermined both by theory and by the interest situation of the interpreter. . . . While all interpretations are provisional, they are not all equal.

Segmentation therefore organizes interpretation, but *within* the confines of a particular level of seeming consensus (discipline/school/working-group) interpretations can be qualitatively ranked. Interpretations, again like the fingers of the proverbial hand, are not equal; their very provisionality and historicity make the question of absolute excellence meaningless and sterile. Some interpretations exercise a more lasting effect on subsequent understandings, it is true, but this is in part because they, in turn, determine the kind of questions people continue to ask. Political pragmatics demands no less.

Disemia is a conflict between interpretations. The symbols of social group membership slither about on very slippery ground. The Greek proverb about the inequality of fingers can be used at virtually any level of social or cultural differentiation to express the conceptual tensions of disemia; but the fact that it can be *used* at any level – kin-group, village, regional, or national – explains how at each level people appeal to a higher one in order to legitimize their actions as conformity. Conformity, the external face, is a matter of definition: internal differences, the very essence of ambiguity and hence of a usage-based understanding of meaning, define excellence *only from the inside*. In the Eurocentrism of Guizot and Cuoco, cultural difference writ large (all over the map of Europe, in fact) defined excellence because the audience for this ideology was itself European.

We may formulate the principle quite clearly, and its close resemblance to village rhetoric stands out at once. *Others'* homogeneity marks their fundamental inferiority, *our* internal differentiation a familiar and complex excellence. Again, the differences that *others* display mark their inevitable quarrelsomeness, a defect of collective character; *our* internal unity is the sign of our maturity. Recall again the charge that the Greeks are "politically immature": failing to unite, they blame the Great Powers for "their" failures; "therefore," they are immature. Yet, in saying this, does one not again fall into the same rhetoric oneself? *Their* failures are defects of character; *ours* are not even mentioned. The similarity of this mode of argument to the rural Greek dialectic of fate and character – to what, indeed, is so often dismissed in Greece and elsewhere as mere fatalism! – constitutes one of the great ironies of Great Power ideology and scholarship.

Refractions of holiness, tropes of pollution

Unity is the secular expression of the ritual perfection in this secular European cosmology. Conversely, "differences" are the pollutant that makes social experience real. As I have suggested, Greece conflates holiness with pollution: national unity takes its substance from the ancient heritage, while internal diversity and dissension derive, in the official view, from the pollution of oriental weakness.

A religious parallel with this unhappy blend appears in the segmentary idiom of Greek blasphemy already mentioned. Blasphemy is proscribed by the church, and can provoke quite severe sanctions. By threatening a wide range of holy figures with sexual violation, it expresses the tension between idealized holiness and the defiling effects of human fractiousness. It refracts, so to speak, some of the holiest figures of the Orthodox hagiology through the experienced divisions of social life (". . . your Virgin Mary," "your Faith," "your Christ," and so on). If religion expresses identity (Mol 1978), then the fragmentation of holy figures is an apt metaphor for the silent, non-violent, but nonetheless *experienced* hostilities of social existence (see also Meeker 1979:100), and especially of the rejection of shared identity with one's enemies of the moment.

In this way, Greek blasphemy evinces a startling resemblance to the practices of the Nuer, who similarly "refract" the divine spirit of Kwoth through the segmentary divisions of their lineage system (Evans-Pritchard 1956:196). Unlike the Nuer, however, Greeks regard the nation-state in which they live as representing an identity concentric with local ones, whatever they may think of its functionaries and formal institutions. In response to both the secular restriction of blasphemy in public and the religious injunction against it at any time, Greek villagers hastily respond to questions about it with the usual self-deprecating remarks about "bad habits." These denials, however, do not address the *form* of the blasphemous utterances: in retreating to the official level, at which it is wrong to impugn *the* Virgin Mary, they cover up the political implications of talking about individuated *refractions* of the Virgin altogether. Official discourse can combat blasphemy only in terms compatible with official political values; the effects of segmentation pass it by altogether.

The idiom is quite clearly political, and it does challenge the official unities. In this, it recalls the black American ghetto boy's disquisition on the existence of God, in which Labov (1972:214–15) "discovered" abstract reasoning. The boy expressed deep doubt about the existence of God-in-general, arguing that a Deity favouring Blacks would probably not be represented as white; therefore, there was no reason for a Black to respect God. Rather than abstract thought, however, which is a Eurocentric standard in itself, we might more usefully see in the refraction of Deity a *pragmatic evaluation* of color discrimination. This in turn constitutes a subversion of the official norm of unity: it mocks the proud motto *e pluribus unum* – so like Greek villagers' plaints that humankind should make peace, worship one God, and *speak one language*. Segmentary usage expresses the experience of an uncertain social world, in which those who wield power may fail to carry conviction when they preach the transcendant unity of the nation; the ghetto child who prefers a black God because the white God has turned away from him actively resists the homogenization of the melting pot. Today, when Hvalkof and Aaby (1981) ask, "*Is God an American?*," we share their recognition in missionary activity of the same logic of cultural domination through the idiom of religion and education. Deity, like talent and European nationalism, has become a piece of *bricolage* in the grim tussle between identity-as-process and identity-as-defined-by-the-state – the political essence, in short, of disemia.

Unlike Nuer when they talk about the specific epiphanies of Kwoth, but more like the black ghetto child, Greek villagers who blaspheme are actively (if unselfconsciously) contravening an official norm. To outsiders, they call this activity a "bad habit," attributing it to the state of original sin in which ordinary mortals must live. Internally, however, it is a mark of sociability, very much like that of amiably calling one's best friend "cuckold" or "bastard." By impugning the Virgin Mary of *others* in an idiom that everyone knows to be illegal, they express solidarity even with their foes in terms of a shared and familiar imperfection that unites them all in opposition to official values. Religion here serves as the basis of identity

– not as objective membership in a religious organization, but as an immanent property capable of refraction through the many levels and degrees of
differentiation. Once again, unity is the face an internally divided entity
presents to the outside; and, in this regard, the blaspheming villager
sounds curiously like the state ideologues, or indeed like the eloquent
Guizot. The symbolic opposition between state unity and social disharmony is a figment of the Eurocentric, statist ideology; the latter could not
exist in opposition to the undifferentiated hordes of the Orient were it not
for the segmentary logic that permits internal diversity.

In the eighteenth century Vico had already perceived this, a fact that
makes his subsequent assumption into the romantic pantheon all the more
ironical. Not only had he observed that all conquering nations tended to
regard their own deities as refracted through diffusion to other societies
(I,1,1 [1977:136] [B/F 53], I,1,12 [1977:144] [B/F 68]), but he had noted
the proclivity of established powers to present themselves as having come
into being by divinely ordained, spontaneous generation – "like a frog after
a summer rain" (I,1,3 [1977:138] [B/F 56]). This false synchronicity suc-
ceeds the gradual development of each power to the status of state, and
Vico notes the progression for both Assyria and Egypt (I,1,7 [1977:140] [B/
F 60]; I,1,12 [1977:144] [B/F 68]). The stage of full statehood thus entails
the suppression of historical experience and relative social distance, which
are mutually convertible in a segmentary model (cf. Evans-Pritchard
1940:108). It would be interesting to know whether Evans-Pritchard, who
was strongly indebted to the Vichian scholar and philosopher of history R.
G. Collingwood, thereby found Vico's ideas a direct inspiration for his penetration of the segmentary form of Nuer political life (see also the closely
related suggestion made by Karp and Maynard 1983:485).

Certainly, Vico's historiography illuminates the cryptic relationship
between statism and segmentation. As a critic of social institutions, he was
thoroughly sensitive to the absolutist recasting of history for official ends.
Moreover, he realized that the beast within us never sleeps: again like
Evans-Pritchard, he wrestled with this fundamental issue as Hobbes had
formulated it. He understood that the imposition of a more comprehensive
political system may simply have translated the "tyranny of self-love," the
consequence of humanity's "corrupted nature," into ever larger domains
of evil (Vico I,4 [1977:240–1] [B/F 341]) through, as it were, all the steps of
the segmentary pyramid:

Thus we establish that man in his bestial state loves his own welfare alone; when he
has taken a wife and sired sons, he loves his own welfare along with the welfare of
families; once arrived at the level of civil life, he loves his welfare along with the
welfare of cities; as state power spreads over ever more people, he loves his own
welfare along with the welfare of nations; when nations unite in wars, peace,
alliances, and trade, he loves his welfare along with that of all humankind: man in

all these circumstances [i.e. at all these levels] is mainly concerned with what is
useful to himself.

It would be hard to better this as a description of the relationship
beween self-love (Vico's *amor proprio* seems to mean much the same as the
Greek *eghoismos*) and segmentation. Vico had perceived in the eighteenth
century what is for the most part only implicit in Evans-Pritchard and
Bourdieu in the twentieth: that the state, far from representing a radical
break with segmentation, depends on endowing the historically contingent
facts of segmentation with the authority of timelessness. It represents the
triumph of an officializing strategy, a performative utterance, whose major
distinction is its huge and repressive generality. Here there is no distinction
between societies with and without government, or between more and less
differentiated societies, but a continuum of societies ranged according to
the degree to which they manage to generalize their self-aggrandizement
and make it stick.

Despite his penetrating critique, however, Vico's ultimate goal was cautiously Utopian. He wished above all else to produce "a reasoned civil theology of Divine Providence" (I,4[1977:240–1] [B/F 341] and *Spiegazione*
[1977:87] [B/F 2]). This turns out to be a theory of political reflexivity, in
parallel with his theory of knowledge: those wisely governed states that
maintained a conscious memory of their more fractious past would have
a better chance of maintaining unity into the future, just as those scholars
who remembered the humble and poetic origins of abstract reason would
be less prone to slip back into the ultimate folly of self-delusion.

For Vico, this eminently practical philosophy was a means of redemption from original sin [I,2:5 [1977:175] [B/F 129]). The foolish and sin-
begotten vainglory that had led so many peoples to claim themselves as the
originators of sacred and secular knowledge (I,1:1 [1977:136] [B/F 53];
1,2:3 [1977:174–5] [B/F 125–7]) does not lessen as its social scope grows
wider; on the contrary, it becomes the very essence of state self-
aggrandizement. Vico saw that greater removal from events in time or
space made for correspondingly greater risk of distortion or falsehood
(I,2:1 [1977:173–4] [B/F 121], etc.), and that in consequence the claims of
the mighty to have emancipated themselves from the taint of original sin
were baseless and stupid. It is only by tracing the history of institutions –
or, more specifically, by digging the segmentary worm out of the statist
apple – that we can begin to appreciate these ideological contradictions for
what they are, and to confront the grandiose civil structures of power with
the historical and social experience on which they are based.

Similarly, Vico's history of language, which is superficially like Tylor's
in that Vico derives the mute communication of gesture from the "natural"
association between gestural form and signified idea (II:2,1 [1977:280]

[B/F 401]), suggests an understanding of the relationship between knowledge and intimacy of scale that we do not find in Tylor's writings. Vico associates the stage of gestural communication with a societal phase whose major unit was the family, whereas poetry came with the age of heroic rule, and conventional language only with republics and monarchical states (*Spiegazione* [1977:112–13] [B/F 30–1]). Nature thus remains associated with the most intimate level of social life; the abstractions of convention are the prerogative of organized power, while nature marks intimacy. Such intimacy does not imply a lack of real knowledge – quite the reverse – but its conversion into abstract, linguistic form will be vitiated from the start unless the scholar takes the trouble to keep its origins in mind at all times. Arguing that "in all languages the majority of expressions for inanimate things are made by means of allusions to the human body and its parts and to human sensations and human passions" (II:2,2,2 [1977:284] [B/F 405]), a remnant of the stage of general ignorance in which men measured the universe only in terms of themselves, Vico suggests that we need to remember these crude origins of abstract reason if we are not to sink back into a "second barbarism" as degrading as the ignorance of those far-off days: the conviction that our thought exists above and beyond our corporeal, historical selves.

While there is an evolutionary argument of sorts in all this, it is far less contemptuous of the early stages than are its various nineteenth-century successors. The idea of "natural" gesture was around for a long time before Tylor converted its splendidly mythological crudeness (Vico's "poetic wisdom") into the mere rudeness of Victorian etiquette manuals, and thereby in a single stroke cut gesture off from the "higher" *forms* that it supposedly *in-formed* in some fundamental way. Most nineteenth-century evolutionists tried either to suppress human corruption altogether, or always to locate it in *other* societies. They thus ignored Vico's basic lesson: that to forget the fall is to recreate it.

Penetrations: sin and diversity

Popular Greek cosmology has it that, without the sin of Eve, there would be no human community. The social relativity that, as Evans-Pritchard noted, converts social space into historical time, requires *differentiation*: once again, the theologically sinful state of disharmony and disjuncture is socially necessary and desirable. Woman is the instrument of the *social* creation, the births (*yennimata*) of new *genea*logies as well as genealogies (*yenies*[8]) – beginnings, certainly, not origins; such is the basis of *gentile* histories of the births and deaths that constitute the tragedy of human existence. Vico wrote about the ancient pagans, about *tutto lo scibile gentilesco* ("everything knowable about the gentiles"; I:1 [1977:134] [B/F 51]). The leaders of these ancient peoples were men; their suppression of dissent was an imposition of male power – a rejection, that is, of social and historical knowledge in a world where division, like birth itself, is made by women.

Greek ethnography confirms this comparatively. The explicit and unambivalent expression of segmentary relations appears almost exclusively in those exceptional communities that have an unashamedly agnatic ideology, with segmentary patrigroups (*yenies*): the condition of social gentility/ generation, made possible by the procreative powers of women.[9] And indeed woman, in the androcentric ideology reported in varying degrees by all ethnographers of rural Greece, reproduces the sinful condition of Eve as though it were a blessing – a segmentary reproduction, as the Pefkiot distich expresses it:

I wish that you might branch forth as the mint bush does
as Eve branched forth so that the world was filled.

Carnal knowledge creates the entire world, the only justification for its presence on earth as well as the source of all discord and difference.

The sin of Eve is not only the source of sexual experience. It is also, and concomitantly, the source of the "differences" that the fact of procreation inevitably creates in a *segmentarily conceived* social universe. It is the enabling moment for intercourse both social and sexual. Vico (*Spiegazione* [1977:87] [B/F 2]; my italics) wrote of

men, whose nature has this main characteristic: *to be social*. To this, God in His Providence has so ordained and arranged human affairs that men – fallen from total justice through *Original Sin*, [and] trying at all times to do things *differently or, even more often, in a way that [deliberately ran] contrary [to each other]*, and so having no practical recourse but to live in solitude like wild beasts – would be induced for the same practical reasons to live in justice and in society, and so to enjoy their social nature.

The tension between individual and totality that constitutes the segmentary quality of society has never been better expressed. In each social unity, the desire to "do things differently" threatens communal harmony, producing the reality of social life as we know it. If we lived in complete isolation, we would be beasts; if in perfect accord, divine. As it is, we live in a world where, for example, the rules of incest recognize the necessity of making social distinctions within the encompassing totality. Vico recognized this quite clearly (*Spiegazione* [1977:98] [B/F 17]). So do Greek villagers, commenting on the inevitable presence of *eghoismos* in their lives: "we are human (*anthropi*)," they shrug, with a wry (and perhaps not altogether regretful) acceptance of the consequences of original sin.

Discord is in practice so much a part of ordinary experience that it *increases* with proximity. On Rhodes and Crete, for example, brothers supposedly feel greater love for each other but also – since inheritance practices give them many common and potentially disputable land boundaries – greater anger than non-kin could ever arouse. Love and hatred alike, expressed in the flaring intensity of specific encounters, are said to arise from the boiling of the blood – a metaphor that also partially absolves those concerned of personal responsibility for the violence that may ensue. This is the logic of segmentation: as Evans-Pritchard (1940:150) observed for the Nuer, conflict increases with proximity.

But love and hatred are also metaphors for the disemic poles of self-display and self-awareness; the public unity of brothers is, in this respect, not significantly different from ideals of national harmony. Friedl, in a characteristically unobtrusive but incisive choice of ethnographic illustration, reports a Vasilika farmer's comment on the reasons why brothers will often delay splitting their parents' property up between them (1962:60; my italics):

before brothers divide the patrimony, it seems as if they have a lot of land and are earning a good living, but once the property is divided, each brother has little and then *one sees that* the family was not so wealthy after all. *Appearances are important to the villagers*, and a group of brothers may be reluctant to reveal the details of their economic condition.

As a result, considerations of self-sufficiency may delay the division of the patrimony. A higher order of *eghoismos*, that of the fraternal group, temporarily prevails. Segmentation and disemia are the intersecting axes of a common social process.

This is true at the broadest levels. One need think only briefly of the major European international rivalries of the last 200 years in order to realize how closely the European ideology of transcendant unity approaches the segmentary logic as an encapsulation of social and cultural contradictions. If that unity symbolizes an impracticable perfection in political terms, the divisions that it masks represent the consequences of an ancient fall from grace.

In the Greek tradition, the metaphor of a cultural and political fall, or of a social Babel, attributes imperfection to the weak and sinful condition of woman. The most misogynous of the Church Fathers maintained that amongst all women only the Virgin Mary deserved eternal life; the others, as agents of the Devil, were to be denied any hope of redemption. But it is important to recognize that this, at least in the terms in which today's Greeks understand it, is a categorical rather than a specific statement: men do not condemn their wives and daughters to eternal perdition, any more than they accept for themselves their ironic portrait of "all" Greeks as hopelessly ineducable drudges of the West. It is always *other* brothers' wives who cause the split that leads to the division of the patrimony; *other* women whose families fail to raise them as exemplary representatives of the community; the women of *other* regions and nations whose looseness betrays the ancient virtues – a constant theme, this last, in the grumbling that the influence of tourism sometimes evokes from the traditionally minded. What appears to be a contradiction between general stereotypes and individual domestic loyalties becomes understandable as a disemic tension that shifts between the levels of segmentary social space.

In the idiom of Greek blasphemy, already mentioned, not only does wickedness flow from carnality, but carnality in turn expresses the transcendence of that wickedness – the perpetual fission, the rampant *eghoismos*, of social life. To screw one's enemies' kinswomen, still more the female or feminized images of *their* Virgin, Christ, and Cross, is to couple couplings – sexual rivalry with social difference. It seems impossible here to think of women without also contemplating social division, most strongly felt amongst brothers divided by their quarreling wives (Campbell 1964:71–2; Friedl 1962:60); and it is equally difficult to imagine social distinctiveness in any but the most sexual terms.

Men's dependence on women for the procreation of their line is not merely a sore open to every kind of symbolic pollution. It is also, and this is the socially significant factor, an opening through which exteriority – *ksena* things, *kseni* people – can peer and pollute. Again, in its interiority and inevitability, the symbolic weakness of women makes men vulnerable to attack from both their affines and unrelated individuals: from the male point of view, women represent the vulnerability of the domestic hearth. Because the rules of incest debar men from marrying close kinswomen, every marriage must admit the blood of potential foes; and if a man marries beneath himself, observers unrelated to him will hasten to take malicious advantage.

All sexual relations represent an invasion of something that belongs to *kseni*. This is the logic of the rapist who "entered the house" of his victim and then married her, as well as the more general logic of bride-theft.[10] The corollary is provided once again by the Pefkiot man who deliberately avoided sex with his new wife because he wanted to avoid "spoiling" her virginal perfection for as long as possible. This man's unusual attitude was of a piece with all the peculiar vices – hobnobbing with foreign tourists, taking too much interest in other people's business, admiring property that was no concern of his, scrounging free beers from non-local visitors while disdaining the more usual reciprocities of the coffee-house – that gained him his reputation as an antisocial person and a caster of the evil eye. His sexual abstinence, while it lasted, was an abdication from the amiably sinful company of real people.

His case, in fact, provides us with a useful insight into the nature of "spoiling" (verb *khal(n)ao*) as a metaphor for *social* intercourse in Greek communities. It is a man's duty to spoil whatever of his own possessions will generate sociality; conversely, he may not "spoil" existing social reciprocities. One may, for example, "spoil" a large banknote in order to treat the assembled company in a coffee-house; one may not "spoil a favor" (that is, refuse to respond when a tried and trusted friend or patron requests help). Since spoiling is also a euphemism for sexual spoliation, the idiom of blasphemy indexes friendships and enmities: to attack another's Virgin Mary means a declaration of ineradicable difference, of the other's otherness.

A Rhodian couplet shows how the act of "spoiling" may be acceptable if its object can be represented as an "unnatural" (i.e. non-social) rule-governedness. One of the leading men of Pefko some fifty years ago, a certain Diamandis, broke the rule of village endogamy by marrying a woman from the nearby island of Khalki. The rather approving comment was:

Diamandis has "spoiled" [*ekhalasen*, i.e. broken] the law in the City,
and [now] all who love Khalki women will marry them!

Not only does this verse recognize the moral congruence between the authority of the village and that of the City – which is Constantinople, former seat of Byzantine and then Ottoman power – but it also shows that the "law" (*nomos*) is something to "spoil" if one is to prove oneself a good fellow. Recall the Cretan villager who derided the law by saying that the villagers had two "shoulders" [*n-omous*] – an apt metaphor for local-level disemia, putting "our bodies" against "the (disembodied) state's law." The couplet about Diamandis's "offense" spells out local disemia as an analogue of national or even imperial disemia – a truly segmentary view, in which Diamandis reproduces the defiance of Digenes. Indeed, the image of the timeless, authoritative City appears (in this ironic discourse) to belie the fall that reduced the City, and all the Greeks, to political servitude and cultural corruption. In this corruption of authority, the irrepressible Diamandis, like the good fellow he is, glories with all the impish glee of a Digenes, a kleft, or a Karagiozis.

In the segmentary idiom of blasphemy, the tension between levels is obvious: in affirming one's identity, one must destroy a more broadly inclusive one. The act of blasphemy makes *kseni* out of those who might, until that moment, have considered themselves *dhiki mas*. The same logic applies, though less directly, to marriage. From a man's point of view, his new wife's position is ambiguous: to whom does she "belong"? At the very least, two domestic groups now have some interest in her (cf. Campbell 1964:137). In more explicitly patrilineal communities, she is thought to have transferred her allegiance from the patrigroup of her father to that of her husband. If the husband of a Glendiot woman should die, for example, she accepts (at least as far as the public is allowed to see) the social and jural control of his brothers. Yet she always retains a link with her natal family, and this makes her an object of occasional suspicion to her in-laws. She is both *kseni* and *dhiki mas* (see also Mandel 1983:180–2), as this Cretan wedding distich makes clear:

What's this now – the stranger with the stranger-woman,
becoming patrikin and trusting friends?   (Lambithianaki-Papadaki 1972:39)

They become patrikin;[11] but they also become "friends," a term that generally excludes kin and implies a highly contingent basis for affection ("trust").[12] In "spoiling" her, is her husband doing the right thing socially by creating children who will continue the community (but also its divisions)? Or is he attacking a *kseni* woman, the daughter of an unrelated family as the incest rules demand?

He is doing both. This is a disemic dilemma: his wife must be pure socially, but her "impurity" – her sexuality – is domestically vital to the husband. Thus, the dual image of woman as Devil and Virgin Mary is not necessarily contradictory. Rather, like the quality of the woman's role in tending the most hallowed objects in her husband's house or in mediating social space as she moves between the domestic interior and the neighborhood street (Hirschon 1981:87), it reflects the more general tension – the conflict between different kinds of interest – that subsists between levels of social intercourse.

Indeed, there is some evidence that the Devil metaphor is not wholly disapproving. Recall the man who used in real life the tactic of the woman who won her wager with the Devil by removing her clothes until the rain stopped – an image that, in a woman, might be taken to suggest depravity and lack of control. The man who told me this story would presumably have acted differently had he thought it truly shameful to adopt "female" wit (Herzfeld 1986a). In the same village, a priest, upon learning that I was going to marry an educated woman, informed me that women were generally weak but became "diabolical" with education. Again, this was not entirely disapproving. Such sentiments have the status of those amiable cries of "cuckold" that one hurls at a dear friend. They also utilize something of the formulaic hyperbole that indicates irony in such remarks as – to a foreigner – "You speak Greek better than we do!"[13]

Inasmuch as women belong to *our* community or have married *our* friends, the wickedness that they represent is familiar and even desirable. And inasmuch as a specific woman is *kseni* to her husband, she has the potential of being truly diabolical; but in that she is "his," her devilries (which may include the clever concealment – a female specialty – of *his* crimes[14]) are a source of pleasure and comfort. A man who rejected his wife's sexuality would be a monk, an antisocial oddity, or quite simply mad. The *categorical* ritual pollution of women (which the film *Kypseli* literalizes) may elicit sententious disapproval in public; but none of these men who wag their heads so sternly then is likely to take the same attitude in the privacy of his marital bed. Nor do I think that Cretan men avoid sleeping with their wives for fear that they might lose at cards the next day (a well-known consequence of sex); on the contrary, the teasing that their losses provoke confirms their masculinity.

The pollution of women is thus relative, and is associated with their contingent status as "outsiders" (*ksenes*); it evaporates when they are "our own." This shifting internalization of otherness culminates in the dilemma of the Greeks as a nation. Pollution and cunning are the attributes that women find themselves saddled with; violence is the mark of the oppressor and the means of imposing these stereotypical traits (Handman 1983). As women are caught between the disadvantages of devilry and virgin(al)ity, both metaphors of subordination but in the opposing quadrants of pollution and holiness, so Greece is caught between *Romiossini* and Hellenism, which are distributed in relation to each other in the same way. Once again, it is what is most familiar in social life that the dominant ideology marks as "foreign" (*kseno*). And this basic characteristic of disemia operates in a segmentary framework that also represents what is most characteristic of women as those traits by which they, as representatives of "other" (*ksenes*) families within the families of their husbands, are supposed to be most embarrassed.

A historical example:
pollution and war in nineteenth-century Crete

A historical example will lend ethnographic specificity to these points. When the Greek War of Independence erupted in 1821, the Cretans responded by taking up arms in various mountainous areas. They were not to achieve their own, highly conditional independence until 1898, and it was only in 1913 that Crete was finally taken under full Greek sovereignty. This was not for want of dedication. The Cretan rebels kept up the struggle throughout the first few years of the Mainlanders' war in the hope that they, too, would be emancipated; and they maintained the pressure on the Turks throughout the remaining decades of occupation. Kazantzakis's novel *Freedom and Death* gives a graphic account of one of the most violent periods of conflict, the 1866 revolt, which culminated in the mass suicide at Arkadi Monastery: the defenders – monks and refugees from the neighboring villages – blew themselves up by exploding the powder magazine just as the Turks breached an entry.

The local conflicts triggered in Crete by the 1821 uprising on the Mainland were no less ferocious than the later ones. The English traveller Robert Pashley, who covered much of the island and left us a stunningly evocative two-volume account of his experiences (*Travels in Crete*, 1837), was appalled at the cruelty and destruction still indelibly stamped on the memories of the inhabitants and on the ruins dotting the countryside. Pashley, whose principal aim was the usual antiquarian one of discovering as many ancient sites as possible and relating whatever he could of modern life and manners to the testimony of the ancient authors, showed the usual occidental superciliousness in talking about the local women (1837, I:183). In particular, he compared the oriental seclusion of both Greek and Turkish women on Crete to similar practices (as he conceived them to be) amongst the women of Classical antiquity. In this, he clearly subscribed to current philhellenic doctrine, which looked down on the modern Greeks as both unenlightenedly hallowed and orientally polluted – because they reproduced the more repressive practices of their Classical forebears but had meanwhile absorbed too much from the anticulture of their Turkish rulers. His stance reproduces that of Lord Charlemont some eighty-five years earlier (1984[1749]:126): "At Athens ... whether from an imitation of the Turks or, as I am rather inclined to believe, from a more perfect retention of the ancient manners, the women are very reserved."[15]

It is in this light that we should interpret Pashley's reports on the treatment of women in war and peace. He was outraged to learn that an unmarried Cretan woman from the Sfakia district, if caught in a compromising situation with some daring suitor, would be killed by her father without hesitation (1837, II:250). But this was as nothing to his horror at learning that, in war, the Cretans did not spare the wives and daughters of their enemies. He was told (1837, I:66–7) that this was "so that no Christian should be polluted (*na mi molinthi*) [by sleeping] with a Turkish woman." Pashley was at pains to point out that this was not a general Greek practice, but suggested that it formed part of an altogether more intense religious fervor among the Cretans.

This fervor, he thought, also explained another (to him) extraordinary abstention (1837, II:175):

[They] were thus raised to so exalted a pitch of religious fervour and enthusiasm, that, in their zeal for God's honour and service, they could, one and all, subdue even their dearest affections, when they believed that, by indulging them, they would be rendered unworthy champions of the holy cause which they had espoused.[16]

And he amplifies this observation (*ibid.*, note 32):

The Christian husbands of Crete, on thus becoming soldiers of the Cross, shrunk from the caresses of their wives, as from a pollution, which would most probably be punished by their failing in the next engagement. This singular piece of religious self-denial lasted, with most of them, for the greater part of the first year.

The idea that sexual pollution exhausts the martial properties is found in many societies, and is often reinforced by symbolic play on the relationship between sex and war. But if in fact sex and war are symbols of each other, then the repression of sexuality is not just a matter of conserving some masculine elixir.

The attitudes to women that so excited Pashley's curiosity are perhaps best understood in terms of the symbolism of spoliation. To sleep with one's wife is to "spoil" her in both the senses discussed above. When war threatens the community, she is no longer a possible *kseni*; on the contrary, the principle of segmentation demands that she *and the members of her natal family* be treated, not as *kseni*, but simply as members of the total community. To enjoy sexual relations with her means metonymically breaking the unity of the village, and of the larger Christian community of which it is a microcosm. In the same sense that stealing sheep from one's own kin or covillagers is "polluting" (*oghoursouza* or *magharisa*), and in the sense that east Cretan lowlanders (who seem to have a more official view of legality) extend this to *all* theft, sleeping with one's wife – despoiling the daughter of another village family – is a betrayal of village solidarity, and as such is analogous to what a man is said to have done to himself when, after making love to his wife, he loses at cards to an unrelated opponent.[17]

It is also inversely analogous to the behavior of the Rhodian who would not sleep with his newly acquired bride for several weeks, and who was similarly regarded as a socially polluting individual. In time of peace, one should reiterate the conquest of the *kseni* woman as often as possible, to raise sons to the name of one's own patriline and thereby to outdo her father's. (Recall the folksong Digenes's conquest of his embarrassing maternal origins.) But even then a tension persists between violation and possession, expressed among the Sarakatsani through a deployment of visualist logic according to which it is "shameful for a husband to gaze on his wife's body" during sexual intercourse (Campbell 1964:277). To do so is to gaze on *the body of her kin*; she should instead remain forever a *kseni* in her husband's *sight*.

While this prohibition may express a more general male distaste for female sexuality, it also implies that even here, in the most intimate of all relationships, the wife remains a *kseni*, the physical child of another family. Visual penetration is thus a violation of that family's most intimate image, its physicality reproduced in a particular female form. In a segmentary social universe, moreover, there is no contradiction between the two levels of interpretation: shame at the visual penetration of one's wife's family constitutes a *refraction*, in the classic segmentary sense, of categorical revulsion from the female interior of the entire social world. It is the inverse of the no less categorical insistence that women should wear sexually neutral clothes. Furthermore, as visual avoidance, it is also a refraction of the still larger association of visualism with spoliation that, as we have seen, sexual and ethnic stereotypes as well as anthropology seem – shamelessly – to exploit. To look upon the Other is to define its otherness as irrevocable. In an affinal relationship, that constitutes a horrendous insult: in ethnic prejudice, or in an exoticizing scholarly activity, it would seem merely necessary.

The tension between membership and outsiderhood also informs the logic of the Cretan and Sarakatsan practice of bride-theft. Here, contest is between families, and the man who "steals" his bride initially opens himself to charges of ill-conduct by the bride's family, charges that threaten his social standing if he fails to marry the abducted woman. By accepting the marriage that was in fact his goal, on the other hand, he instead accepts a *commonality* of social worth: as affines, henceforth he and his bride's family stand or fall together. This, too, is segmentary social logic. In the same way again, in time of war, when the entire community became in essence one family or one patrigroup, sex with one's wife might temporarily acquire the character of (relative) incest, translated for a brief while to a broader level of segmentary inclusion. Captain Mikhalis, the hero of Kazantzakis's *Freedom and Death*, blames his failure on having slept with a Turkish woman – but it is significant that he did not thereby "violate" *Greek* solidarity. The Turks had long been the definitive enemies of Christendom eastern and western. When Cretan Christians fought them in the historic struggle that initiated Greek independence, abstention from sex became a first, halting step on the road to redemption – and, one might add, to the eventual secularization of this imagery by the forces of state nationalism and respectability.

I do not wish to suggest that this brief analysis holds true, in the form in which I have presented it, for all of Greece. Pashley himself contrasts the Cretans' self-denial with the more relaxed attitudes he encountered on the Mainland. Nonetheless, many elements of this symbolism – the forms of blasphemy, the perception of women as *ksenes* to their families of marriage, the prohibitions against sexual relations during religious festivals that stress communal unity (especially Easter) – are found throughout Greece. Some, notably the progression from hostility to alliance entailed in bride-theft, are found elsewhere (see Lockwood 1974). But the major point would also seem to apply fairly generally in Greece at least: that sexual pollution, the church Fathers notwithstanding, is not absolute. It is a relativity, refracted through the segmentary cleavages of a corrupted social fabric; and it reflects the disemic tension between inclusion and exclusion that characterizes the actual conditions of social life.

Relativities of pollution

Perhaps this is why the image of woman seems such an apt metaphor for the bivalence of Greek culture. The externally directed puppet dictators of the 1967–74 regime appear in jokes as "screwing mother Greece" (Orso 1979:3–4). These express the incest with which segmentation ever threatens social unity, and give special emphasis to Meeker's (1979:100) treatment of segmentation as a model of social uncertainty. Every sexual act is a spoliation of a group of others *who become one's "own" at the next most inclusive plane of the segmentary model*. The persistent contradictoriness of a moral universe in which each level is ethically congruent with all the others informs the peculiar agonies of disemia at each one of these levels. Sexuality provides the metaphor of choice: it has always been a rich source for the tropes of nationalism (see Mosse 1985). In that nationalism represents the control of intimacy pushed almost as far as it can go, Vico had accurately predicted this relationship when he argued that one of the earliest benefits that Heaven conferred on the human race was the fear that made people conduct their sexual coupling in private (2,3 [1977:353] [B/F 504]; my italics):

> They enjoyed human sex with them [their women] under cover, in concealment, that is to say, with a sense of shame (*pudicizia*); and so they began to feel shame, which Socrates used to call the "coloring of virtue." This, after religion, is the other bond *that keeps nations united*, whereas boldness and impiety are what ruin them.

For Vico, the gradual increase in the human capacity for abstract thought enabled the creation of ever larger political entities. Sexuality represents intimacy; control over that intimacy is not only the basis of political control, but it also becomes the means whereby nations protect their inner flaws from outside intruders. By extension: representing Mediterranean societies as governed by the principles of (sexual) honor and shame is a penetration of disunities that nationalism constantly tries to counteract.

This inverse relationship between sexuality and nationalism colors the power relations between nascent Mediterranean nations and their foreign "protectors." It explains, for example, the persistent reproduction of the formula:

male:female::Hellene:*Romios*::"European":"Mediterranean"

Again, the measure of Greekness lies outside Greece. The ritual pollution of the man who has slept with his own wife is that of a sacred Hellenic past suffused with the taint of Turkishness. As the church determines the role of a man in the image of a flawed male Christ constantly vitiated by the sin of Eve, so too the philhellenic ideology has cast modern Greece in the role of a Periclean past always and inescapably corrupted by its barbaric *Romiossini*. Official ideology attempted to overcome the tension between the two levels – Christianity is a basic component of *Romiossini* – in the military dictator George Papadopoulos's notorious slogan, "Hellas of the Hellenic Christians." This phrase, with its discomfiting evocation of that structurally similar oxymoron ("participant observation") whereby anthropologists try to coopt otherness for their own ends, reproduces a long established formula that thinly veiled the historical tension between the church (suspicious of a pagan revival) and the neo-Hellenists (contemptuous of the "oriental" or "Romeic" church). It, too, was an expropriation of otherness – in this case, the "foreignness" of *Romiossini* – for ends that were often quite unsympathetic to the entire range of Romeic culture.

These historical contradictions inform the segmentary deployment of disemia. What is Hellenic at the level of international relations conceals an internally Romeic social reality in which the Greek Orthodox Church continues to play a directing role, itself further split between the image of an officially incorruptible hierarchy and deep popular resentment and mockery of the priesthood.[18] The state could not have sustained its unitary, Hellenic ideology without the flexibility that an internally segmentary ideology of social relations gave it. Such is the radical irony of the triumph of Eurocentric statism in Greece.

The relativity of innocence

The penetration of village interiority goes to the heart of what the nation is all about. As long as anthropologists were content to track ancient parallels with modern practices, they were doing what the local folklorists had done before them; and they were demonstrating the effectiveness of the façade presented to the philhellenic outside world. Anthropological concerns, however, have mostly been more synchronic, while at the same time attending more carefully to the inner than to the outer face of disemia. They thus become a significant element in the tension that I have been describing, their penetrations of interiority a potential violation at every turn.

There is rich irony in this. People construct and negotiate cultural boundaries, and disemia – unless we are to reify it – belongs to a range of labile phenomena generated by this character of contingency (see also Drummond 1980). To this process, anthropologists come with a decided innocence of their own. They often write as though they were describing a virtually immutable society or culture, rather than a rhetoric of cultural difference in which they are themselves actively engaged. In so doing, they inadvertently endorse the diagnostic feature of nationalism: the suppression of relativities in favor of a reified and bounded set of semantically and politically "defined" entities. From this absoluteness comes a more general concern with the control of language and other discourses: the intellectual background to Greek independence is studded with lexicographers and linguistic philosophers.

Anthropological discourse picks up many of these absolutes, and projects them on to still larger stages. I have already discussed the peculiar status of "*the* values of 'honor' and 'shame'" in "Mediterranean society." The era of romantic nationalism doubtless generated a strong sense of these unities; the literature and especially the operatic repertoire is full of these themes. But to whom are they addressed? What anthropologist would argue that Bellini's or Verdi's rustics were convincing as ethnographic representations? While the values expressed in these works are clearly recognizable from the semitheoretical ethnographic literature about honor and shame, even the more bucolic characters rarely have much to do with direct ethnographic experience. As for the romantic aspects, they would seem more closely related to the great Veneto-Cretan verse romance *Erotokritos* (Kornaros [1980]) than to attitudes that one encounters in the Cretan mountain villages of today. Anthropology as a body of theory is committed to the rejection of stereotypes; but anthropologists are people themselves, and their practices are acts of engagement with other people.

The idealized values of honor and shame are the façade of innocence, which anthropological penetration irrevocably breaches. The sexual eschatology that Vico and the Greek villagers share also incorporates the anthropologist's presence. The anthropologist's dilemma is that such an insight would not be possible without first having been there: violation must precede the shock of self-awareness, of the realization that one is in some sense the representative of an intrusive power and that one's scholarly activity is enabled by that discomfiting fact. The anthropological condition mirrors what anthropologists study; and this seems to be the strongest argument for including the theoretical capital of the discipline in a wider comparative framework, as I have tried to suggest throughout this essay. Yet without such penetration, we lose all sense of our historical entailment. Knowledge, in this eschatology, is the very opposite of innocence.

The rhetoric of sexuality models and represents this social logic. Carnality is a consequence of the aboriginal fall; recall that the distinction between *kseni* and *dhiki mas* is a distinction between those one does not know and those one does, so that it reiterates the theme of *(social) knowledge*; a fallen condition admits, so to speak, the knowledge of otherness. One cannot create children without sexuality; one cannot, as Lévi-Strauss realized in *Tristes Tropiques* (1974), practice anthropology without irrevocably altering the unknown culture one had sought. "To know is to deform" (Buttitta 1971:10): deformation is a necessary condition of love, intimacy, nostalgia for times gone by. Perfection is for outsiders, synchrony, and the abstractions of pure structure. Social perfection, then, is not absolute but relative; the rhetoric of absolute perfection is a ploy for power. This is the rhetoric of definition, grammar, precision, legal control, formal clothing, sexual chastity. And conversely, in the logic of disemia, imperfection is the mark of a shared sociability: tacit understanding, good fellowship, daring exploits, casual wear and behavior, procreation.

I mention the sexual dimension last in each of these two lists, not because it is unimportant, but – on the contrary – to give it the emphasis it deserves. Anthropological treatment of sexual mores has certainly not been lacking in the ethnography of Mediterranean countries; indeed, it has been a – perhaps the – defining theme. But Mediterranean sexuality has largely been treated in the literalistic fashion that ignores its rhetorical status in the play of reputation. True, as many authors have pointed out (sometimes citing the Greek proverb, "[It's] better to lose your eye than your good name"), an undeservedly spoiled reputation can do more harm than many undetected sins. The further consequences of this, however, appear to have received little attention. Chastity, as a variety of social worth, is somewhat like literacy: it is relative, that of *kseni* being held both in cheaper regard and yet, because unknown, harder to puncture effectively. In a word, it follows the segmentary conceptual organization of literacy, ethnicity, hospitality (see Friedl 1962:105), and all the other forms of identity discussed in the previous several chapters. The ironic use of *Frangopanaya* ("European Virgin Mary"), contemptuously bracketed with a *katharevousa* phrase meaning "Madame Do-not-touch-me" by a villainous character in one of Yannis Maris's bourgeois detective novels (n.d.: 129), nicely captures the conjunction of sexuality, purity/impurity, and inequality in Greek disemia: the speaker resentfully mocks the lady's finesse as "European" because, although she will not so much as look at him, she does appear to be committing adultery with someone of higher social status than himself. Such is the moral economy[19] of purity.

What anthropologists have frequently omitted to mention, following the prudishness of folklorists, is that sexuality is not always, or necessarily, an embarrassing subject for Greek village women, even in relatively public contexts. While the Glendiot women's sexual tallies may be unusually frank, the virginal/ashamed image of Greek womanhood is surely as much a function of all ethnographers' outsider status as it is of a single, monolithic reality, a response to an essentially romantic ideal that anthropology historically shares with Greek official values. It is not that women are less chaste, or less modest, than they appear to be; it is not even that appearances are more significant than reality; it is rather that two different rhetorical formations compete with each other, the intimate and the formal, and reproduce each other at opposite ends of the spectrum of social possibilities. Bawdiness conflicts with the romantic image of Hellenism, and this ideological tension is reproduced at the village level.

Virtue, like sin, is socially relative. Glendiots, who would surely defend the sexual purity of the Cretans against all comers, were shocked when a technically incestuous union occurred in their own community, a first-cousin relationship that eventually produced several children without benefit of clergy or registrar; but they were then also at pains to point out that it had only happened because of the influence of the more powerful village up the road, where such things had reportedly happened several times before. This is the same logic whereby Pefkiots, as we noted in another connection, attribute *ghrousouzia* to *insiders to their own community* but treat it as *evidence of Turkish influence* on linguistic as well as on moral grounds. The logic is this: since, from an external perspective, the community defines perfection, all flaws must be of external inspiration; but since the community is only aware of its own identity by contrast with that of others, the intrusion of such imperfections must internally represent otherness-within-the-self. This, again, corresponds closely with the contrasts we have noted earlier between the formal models of Hellenism and *Romiossini*, and ultimately those between anthropological models of order and ethnographic accounts of action.

In this chapter, I have brought three models of social relativity into juxtaposition: segmentation, honor and shame, and disemia. This may look as though I were concerned to argue an evolutionary progression from tribal to peasant (or feudal) and thence to statist political systems. But note: the progression is not an evolutionary one as such. Rather, it organizes historical changes in the thematic scope of anthropology itself, and particularly the concurrence of theoretical developments and ethnographic area interests. In this way, the three models represent the symbolic character of anthropology as an unfolding exploration and negotiation of otherness. What looks like a feature of the object of study – a differentiation between the tribal, the peasant, and the modern – instead more accurately characterizes the history of the discipline. To the extent that anthropology falls into the trap of representing these models as mutually exclusive in some objective sense, it will remain tied to statist rhetoric and perspectives, and to the survivalist reductionism that treats European statist ideology as the supreme achievement of political evolution. But a critical juxtaposition shows how this very illusion supports the boundary-making properties of anthropological discourse.

The three models only seem mutually exclusive if they are taken as typological criteria. Disemia is not exclusively a feature of conditions in a statist system, while segmentation (as I have insisted in this chapter) may well exist there. The values glossed as honor and shame are not simply the ideology of a political phase intermediate between tribalism and the state; they represent a concern with concealment and intimacy as active at the level of the nation-state or of regional pride as it is amongst Nuer kin-groups and Greek village households. This is not to deny ethnographic differences; but these should not be reduced to a survivalist typology of political evolution, culminating in the Eurocentric perfection of the state. Nor do I want for a moment to suggest that the earlier models have become redundant or irrelevant. On the contrary, in the spirit of Vico's intellectual etymologies, I want to suggest that *no* anthropological formulation has much value if it is taken out of its historical context. And that context consists of both the related models that preceded it and the usages and concepts that it glosses in our own as well as "other" societies.

We have thus fully returned to the theme with which I began: the treatment of anthropology as a practice, comparable as a symbolic activity to what it observes, and historically derived in part from some of the same sources. For once the rigid differentiation between tribal, peasant/feudal, and modern types of society collapses, the privileging of anthropological discourse must logically also disintegrate: it becomes just another mode of expressing identity, which trivializes its own significance by ignoring this condition of its existence. A truly comparativist anthropology must include within its scope its authors' own symbolic elaborations of cultural identity, made accessible to analysis by precisely such a denial of their privileged status. The Vichian epigram at the head of the next and final chapter embodies in exemplary fashion the practical justification of this entire exercise.

8 Etymologies of a discipline

> . . . in every language the words that are needed in the cultivated arts and arcane sciences are of peasant origin.
>
> Vico 2,2,2,1 (1977:284) (B/F 404)

Etymology and discipline

In this book, I have attempted the exploratory etymology of an academic discourse. But I have not done so by considering in much detail the origins of anthropological thought as such: that has been the task of the discipline's numerous historians. Instead, I have explored the ethnography of a particular place, modern Greece, whose relative absence from the disciplinary canon ought in my judgment to occasion some considerable but ultimately critical bewilderment.

The object of this pursuit has by stages turned out to be a mocking shadow of the etymology of the discipline, a parallel outer form with an opaque interior, a theory inhabited by unruly practitioners. The modern Greek nation-state is a creation of the same Eurocentric lust for self-definition that also generated anthropology during roughly the same period. Unlike anthropology, however, which at first could easily afford to pontificate about radically exotic others and only haltingly came to realize that this was not consistent with ethnographic experience, the Greeks from the beginning have found it necessary to come to terms with an official discourse and ideology that rejected many of the most familiar aspects of indigenous culture as foreign, exotic, and flawed. The Greeks' social life, which generates so many of their self-stereotypes as rebellious and uncontrollable lovers of independence, constantly conflicted with the official forms and norms. Their dependence on the West made the Greeks strangers in their own land at a time when the task of anthropologists was merely to represent strangers *to* their own compatriots.

The etymological trail has accordingly followed the comparativist characterization of the discipline set out in the first chapter. It has been to compare the etymologies of modern Greek identity with some of the most prominent amongst those of current anthropology. Whether this is a theoretical or a practical undertaking, it is certainly not inconsequential.[1] It places a significant anthropological silence in relationship to the more general development of the discipline, and so illuminates some of the avoidance that anthropology has systematically practiced. It argues for a more serious consideration of modern Greek ethnography both for its intrinsic interest and for a reconsideration of anthropological exoticism. It indicates that Greek agonizing over the "lost center" of the national culture (see Lorenzatos 1983) is as much a problem for the dominant cultures of the West as it is for the Greeks themselves. Finally, and in an altogether more immediate sense, it directs an urgent political critique at Greek debates about whether the nation "belongs to the West/Third World/no one" as well as at western journalistic representations of Greece as a wayward and politically/militarily irresponsible child of the cultural world to which it is supposed (read: "the West supposes it") to have given birth. But these debates, again, serve to locate the practice of anthropology – and especially its active role in the creation and legitimation of categories and concepts of cultural identity – in a global political context.

I am not, however, recommending the usual panacea, which seems to be to move the study of identity out of the wilds altogether, to forget about anthropology and do more topical-seeming studies instead. If anthropologists occasionally feel that their researches in out-of-the-way places expose the discipline to ridicule as a useless luxury – this seems to be a common complaint in the Third World (see also Owusu 1978), and it is certainly present in some sociologists' irritation with current anthropological work in Greece, as well as in some internal criticism – they should not therefore immediately run to the "relevant" areas. The complaint that only a relatively small proportion of the Greek population is still rural (Wallace 1984:40), for example, does not of itself bring the charge of exoticism home to Danforth's (1982) symbolic study of rural death rituals. On the contrary, this type of argument merely privileges the "predominant [sic], urban Greece"[7] whose rural roots it represses, while condemning the peasant remnant to an even more terminal obscurity than that to which the urban centers have already subjected it. In short, it completes the very process of cultural homogenization that its rhetoric claims to oppose on the grounds of a prima facie case against anthropological exoticism in general.

The remote places are no less relevant than the accessible. Their relevance materializes, however, when we place our studies of them in a larger intellectual context, which we shall not do if we reject the practice of rural ethnography altogether. *Why* did the earliest ethnographers think it advisable to work in Africa, Australia, the Trobriands? Why did the Victorian traveller-folklorists only discover the "pure Greek race" in remote islands and mountain villages? *How* do modern ethnographies shed light on national self-images? Avoiding the study of remote communities simply displaces the problem itself, and still further trivializes the voice of the already much neglected rural population. The more honestly self-critical approach seems instead to entail inserting our studies in a historically sensitive contemplation of the ways in which stereotypes embroil observers and observed in a common symbolic negotiation of their respective identities. By revealing the commonalities of anthropology with the exotic and the remote, an etymological approach to the discipline may help to break down the neat categorical quarantining of exotic peoples from "ourselves."

(Ab)original sin: the political etymology of otherness

In comparing theoretical anthropology and Greek ethnography, one factor that draws these two strands into juxtaposition is the common theme of original sin. While it does not feature very explicitly in recent anthropological theory, biblical images have certainly played a creative role in forming anthropological discourse; obvious parallels subsist, for example, between theological symbolism and early evolutionism, which in turn partly derives from assumptions about the postlapsarian condition of the human race (see Hodgen 1964). Survivalist concepts have proved surprisingly persistent in the ethnographic analysis of modern Greece, not only in explicit demonstrations (e.g. Blum and Blum 1970; Walcot 1970), but also in approaches that emphasize the synchronic aspects of Greek culture.

At this point, it would be useful to recapitulate some of the reasons for bringing the writings of Giambattista Vico, a controversial (some would say, marginal) ancestor-figure in anthropology, into such close juxtaposition with the equally peripheral topic of Greek ethnography. Is this not a formula for disaster, for ensuring that *both* will be ignored? On the contrary, I submit, the parallel is a very striking one, and may serve to bring the message home. Vico's marginality to the history of social science springs from the same positivistic embarrassments as the marginality of Greece. Both raise discomfiting questions about the political sources of otherness. Vico's writings give us a source of critical insight into the relationship between political ideology and scholarship. They thus challenge romantic positivism, of which statism is the political doctrine *par excellence*, just as the rigid privileging of scientific over everyday discourse is its intellectual form. They provide a strong justification for the comparison of anthropology with one of its own humbler ethnographic domains, a culture in which the contest between the formal and the experiential reproduces many of the features of the tension between theory and ethnography. The neglect of these issues belongs to the same agenda as the neglect, until very recently, of Vico's critical thought.

It is from Vico's interest in original sin that I have tried to draw the key lesson he has to offer us here: that the sources of theoretical insight are never totally removed from the phenomena to which we apply them. They share with these phenomena an imperfect state that is as universally human as is the plastic human mind that both acts out the events of history and writes them down as part of the ennobling struggle for enlightenment. If Vico had studied Greek villagers, original sin would have been a part of his theoretical stock in trade; but it would also very probably have been a major object of ethnographic interest to him, as it was to be for Campbell and his students in our own day.

In fact, Vico seems to have had little time for the modern Greeks.[2] All the same, the resemblance between his and their respective understandings of original sin unmasks the historical artificiality of separating our own theoretical tradition from its object of study. Survivalism both recent and Victorian has a strong flavor of postlapsarianism, so that at least something *analogous* to the concept of original sin lurks in anthropological thinking, and buttresses its more persistent strains of exoticism. This brings anthropology into direct comparison with politically motivated Greek and western survivalist theses about Greek culture; for these stereotypical constructions share a common political etymology in the image of washing off the stains of collective, evil otherness.

There is another and closely related reason for turning back to Vico at this point. His *New Science* is an ambitious attempt to attack the pretensions of both nations and science at the same time. His critical understanding of how and why people construct history not only challenges the self-aggrandizement of states and empires; it also directs our attention to the embedding of scholarly pretensions in national and international politics. As Said (1981:127–31) points out in a deliberate evocation of Vico, scholars adopt a rhetoric of intellectual disinterestedness that itself serves political ends, but at the same time they tend to assume that the people they have studied lack a comparable measure of intellectual curiosity.

Moreover, he argues, such charges of intellectual passivity – which correspond to the correlation of *lack* or *absence* with inferior otherness that we have already noted – eventually come to perfuse media rhetoric; and in this way, scholarship is directly involved in political actuality. In western coverage of Greek affairs, the media attribute political and cultural immaturity to the Greeks, a psychological generalization also characteristic of the inferiority complex explanation of nationalistic "fakelore." But the Greek media, too, in a typically disemic internalization of otherness, castigate Greek social and political attitudes with the Eurocentric rhetoric of oriental inefficiency, fatalism, and ignorance. Clearly, scholarship – and Said (1981:131–2) generously acknowledges anthropology's rôle in generating this kind of criticism – is far from irrelevant to broad national and international issues. This is because of, not despite, its exoticism; for it is exoticism that sends anthropologists to far distant places to begin with. The conflict between ideological exoticism and ethnographic experience may then generate a much needed crisis of conscience. Meanwhile, in Greece, that crisis has already long been objectified internally as a crisis of *identity*.

Vico anticipated the connection between abstract scholarship and practical politics, and particularly the relationship between state and scholarly authority. He insisted that the social world was "made by men," so that historical truth must always be constructed by human agency also (1,3 [1977:232] [B/F 332]). Unlike so many of those who claimed to be his successors, he thus refused to privilege the discourse of scholarship over its object: historical science, too, is a social institution, embedded in the practical needs (Vico's *utilità*) of the nation and the state, just as myth had been embedded in the needs of heroic society and gesture in those of the family.

For Vico, then, the imperfections of historical science are of a piece with the imperfections to which all humanity is heir; they all stem from the condition of original sin. Even the nation does not escape from these consequences of its ultimately human and therefore social character. At each level, the theory of social relations becomes a description and a code for actual relations at a more intimate level. The balance between theory and practice is never absolute, because (in Vico's schema) perfection would represent the achievement of the final ends to which the Divine Providence works. Like the Greeks whose everyday norms and practices have preoccupied ethnographers, Vico understood that the relationship between theory and practice was always embedded in a still higher order; only the state, usurping the role of Vico's Divine Providence, declares its *ne plus ultra*, and turns fate into *fatalism* – the key reification that generates all the others (folklore into the bureaucratic shows and festivals of *Folklorismus*, history into historicism, language into a dictionary). From a pragmatic perspective, the relationship between theory and practice, like that between context and text, is social. It is therefore always relative, always segmentary, and always disemic. Theory seeks perfection; it does not represent it. "Theory always places itself at the beginning or the end of thought . . . It is unhappy with the middle realm of history, practical conduct, and business as usual and so tends to seek a final solution, a Utopian perspective, which *presents itself as a point of origin*" (Mitchell 1985b:7; my italics). Although it remains the prisoner of the unsatisfactory realities, like statist discourse it often tries to elevate itself above them by claiming originary status.

Vico's understanding of the relationship between human imperfection and social knowledge closely resembles that of the Greeks, whose culture I have been using as my main ethnographic illustration. For this reason, I have in several places found it convenient to make the comparison explicit. Structuralist anthropology, which is as guilty as any "school" of excessive formalization, does after all claim Vico as an ancestor. Moreover, we have seen (especially in the discussion of the film *Kypseli*) that structuralism can easily become a search for ultimate origins as absolute and as removed from social experience as any that are mandated by statist ideologies.

Are we then in danger of repeating the romantic statists' expropriation of Vico as a proponent of rule-governed society, of – ironically – what he himself recognized as the close relationship between discursive expropriation and power (2,1,2,2 [1977:270–2] [B/F 386–8])?[3] Or may we deploy another of his insights, the parallel between scholarly and social fallibility, against that temptation? It is certainly a temptation to be resisted with all the means at our disposal. It would seduce us into what Vico saw as the "second barbarism" of scientism and literalism – the loss of historical memory, the creation of false regularities, the oxymoronic delusion of a timeless Eden regained within our own historically circumscribed lifetimes.

The recovery of etymology

Resistance to this temptation would indeed seem to be the strongest argument for recovering the Vichian use of etymology along the lines sketched by Struever (1976, 1983) and briefly discussed in the first chapter of this book. What etymology can legitimize, it can also subvert. If etymologies have been incorrectly used in support of an established order, Vico – himself a shamefully slapdash philologist at times – showed that incorrect etymologies can at least also disturb our complacency.[4]

One of his more general points, for example, does not stand up well to critical inspection in its specific details but nonetheless anticipates much modern thinking on the subject. This is his argument that abstract thought began from the experience of the body, through which it worked through various kinds of trope before becoming disembodied altogether. Here, Vico anticipates current interest in the embodiment of social knowledge, as also in the derivation of scientific as well as everyday language from metaphor.[5] He also points in a direction much clarified by Fernandez's (1974) treatment of metaphor as a glossing of the imponderables of selfhood with tangible images, "the predication of a sign upon an inchoate subject." In these terms, anthropological exoticism is a sign predicated upon a dimly perceived, shifting cultural "we"; and Greek ethnography can become a disclosive metaphor for the ambiguities of our own professional perplexities.

Vico long ago saw that the embodied character of discourse constituted the most fundamental objection to Cartesianism; it certainly undermined the positivistic kind of comparative study soon to be proposed by Victorian anthropology (1,3 [1977:232] [B/F 331]). The mind, argued Vico,

immured and buried in the body, is naturally inclined to pay attention to the things of the body and must use so much effort and exhaustion in order to understand itself, like the corporeal eye, which sees all objects outside itself but needs a mirror in order to see itself.

Under such circumstances, how could the acutest observer be certain of the inner self, except – conditionally – by likening it to palpably different others? A shifting relationship of likeness/otherness moves uncomfortably from metaphor to metonymy and back. As a subject of study, Greek ethnography is a *part* of anthropology, a metonym of it; but as an object of study, it is, rather, a metaphor of the discipline's concerns. The terminological distinction between anthropology and ethnography has not solved the problems that we observed in the conflation of practice and object in the term "folklore." On the contrary, it suggests that what needs assessing is not some supposedly objective difference between the two dimensions of our scholarly activity, but the cultural and social import of the *rhetorical* separation of the two terms.

Like any pair of terms that are historically linked, and so share a contiguous history but have separate and therefore directly comparable identities, Greek ethnography and theoretical anthropology are united both metonymically and metaphorically: Greek ethnography is both a part of the total enterprise, and a dramatic image of how that enterprise is constituted. Together, these two poles provide the general framework for the present comparativist essay. All historical connections – what I have here called etymologies in the wider sense that goes beyond mere linguistic form – are tropological; they are diachronic puns that play on both metonymical and metaphorical connections. They can teach us a great deal about the flux of ideas. Etymologies can show us the common derivation of disciplinary confusion and cultural ambiguity; but also, and far more importantly, they can show us where these common concerns with identity have diverged from each other, and where anthropological theory has lost sight of its own cultural genesis.

But they must not be interpreted as literal history. It is probably because romantic nationalism treated etymological connections (resemblances, or contingent metaphorical links) as precise equivalences (continuities, or metonymic cause-effect links) that anthropology refused to credit them with much usefulness. By saying that the modern Greeks *were* [descended from] the ancient Hellenes, Greek nationalists and foreign philhellenes alike could authorize a confusion of *identity* ("who the Greeks are," a historically contingent question) with *identicality* ("whom the Greeks are the same as," which is ahistorical).[6] Anthropology, despite its own forays into scientism, usually resists such self-authorizing etymologies, in part because the discipline has had a pervasively antihistorical trajectory of its own. Aside from its own legitimative devices, however, the discipline may inadvertently have helped establish some other, quite localized identicalities. The Mbororo of Cameroon, lighter skinned than their vassal serfs, justify their supremacy (and their skin color) on the grounds of a fictitious link with the virtually homonymous South American Bororo (of Lévi-Straussian and parrot fame;[7] Barley 1983:151). One cannot be sure that anthropology itself – perhaps indirectly Lévi-Strauss's work – spread the name of the Bororo to Africa; but the suspicion remains. "If it is not true, it is well invented." How scornfully this legitimative use of etymology-as-equivalence mocks Lévi-Strauss's own cultural gloom in *Tristes Tropiques*!

Legitimative etymology, then, is a variety of metaphor. It allows "us" to determine who we are by reference to a significant other, removed in time or place but rendered conditionally "the same as" ourselves. It also conforms to "discipline" in Weber's (1968:16) sense of "'habituation' characteristic of uncritical and unresisting mass obedience." Weber, of course, was writing about discipline in the more everyday sense of military or political discipline. But once we accept the position that academic scholarship is political, the argument that this characterization of discipline has nothing to do with *academic disciplines* becomes meaningless.[8] Sheer habit protects some of the most basic ideas and concepts of anthropology from critical penetration. Once the metaphors/etymologies are duly institutionalized, our task is to recover the *differences of identity* lost in their emphasis on totalizing *identicality*.

This is, in fine, what the present essay has been all about, in its exploration of the relationship between formal and social kinds of knowledge. So far, I have tried to stress the etymologies of ideas rather than of specific words, pointing mostly to numerous similarities between anthropological and rural Greek experiences of the tension between formalism and actual experience, and suggesting that these derive from some common roots in Eurocentric ideologies. In order to clarify the process of comparison through which we have moved, however, I now briefly return to an area with which etymology is more conventionally associated: that of (lexical) terminology. Some important divergences have occurred in the semantics of social terminology as Greek words have moved along the disparate paths of abstract theory and modern rural Greek life. These provide a historical and linguistic capstone for the comparativist framework sketched here, and within which we have been deliberately pursuing connections between the discipline and one of its most marginal objects.

Modern Greek is full of terms whose etymological cognates have become part of the stock-in-trade of anthropological discourse. Even in their own languages, anthropologists have found, time and again, that the very *ordinariness* of much of their technical vocabulary provokes the reaction that anthropology is simply a matter of common sense, and therefore does not deserve the status of a scientific discipline. I do not propose to enter the lists on either side, since it is clear that the definition of "science" is a highly arbitrary factor in such debates. Nor, concomitantly, do I want to suggest that this discussion legitimizes the claims for a Greek (and specifically Herodotean) origin for the discipline. On the contrary, in what I take to be a Vichian spirit, I would like instead to suggest that, by examining the Greek etymological cognates of current jargon, we can deflate some of the more rarefied pretensions of technical usage. This dethronement of theory, from an absolute priority conventionally accorded it over ethnography, can help to restore a sense of proportion, while at the same time exemplarily re-emphasizing the importance of anthropological theory as an intellectually and politically productive form of social practice in our world.

The gossip of the centuries:
anthropology and exoticism revisited

In twentieth-century anthropology, despite Benveniste's (1973) alluring linguistic excavations of Indo–European social concepts, there has been only slight practical interest in etymology, which has usually served as little more than a conventional adornment. When Max Gluckman (1963:314) observed that the Classical *anthropologos* meant "scandalmonger," for example, he meant merely to reinforce in an amusing way his insistence that gossip constituted a valid field for anthropological study. This was a legitimizing strategy, which subsequent research – including an important ethnographic contribution from Greece (du Boulay 1974:201–29) – has confirmed. But Gluckman really only used the etymology to legitimize professional interest on what might otherwise have seemed to be a rather trivial phenomenon, rather than to valorize the subject as in some sense *equivalent* to the discipline. Folklore, at least, still ostensibly studies folklore; anthropology, in partial contrast, appears to have privileged itself over the *anthropoi*.

Gluckman quite clearly did not intend his etymological sally into the 'origins of "anthropology" to be critical of the discipline itself. On the contrary, he cast it in the classic/Classical design: there is no *modern* Greek in it, nor any suggestion that the ancient Greeks would make a good field for ethnographic exploration. Gluckman was simply interested in showing that gossip would provide a legitimate field for serious investigation; he wanted to remove it from the domain of the faintly funny to that of the scientifically respectable. He did so in terms that recall the heyday of romantic etymologizing. The term *anthropologos* has not survived into modern Greek with its Classical meaning, and its academic usage has been largely restricted, at least until recently, to physical anthropology. Thus, Gluckman's academic witticism, gently persuasive though it may have been for some classically educated readers in the Britain of the 1960s, did not entail bringing anthropology itself into the comparativism that it advocated for other cultures.

I am advocating a more critical application of etymology here than Gluckman apparently intended: the use of etymological comparisons between anthropological theory (or at least a part of it) and a specific body of ethnographic material. If bureaucratic nationalism and social science suffer from parallel and inflated pretensions, as Vico intimated over two centuries ago, then an etymological puncturing of our pomposities may bring us back to our senses and to a more becoming modesty towards our "ethnographic subjects."

What, then, happens if we turn to the modern rather than the ancient language, and with critical rather than consensual goals? The term *anthropos* continues in general use in modern Greek, not only in its dictionary sense of "human being," but, in a semantically more marked embodiment, as "sociable and attractive personality." One can treat the term adjectivally – that is, as the expression of a personal quality – so that an individual whose decency and sociability one admires is *poli* ("very [much of an]") *anthropos*. But while these are all excellent features, to be an *anthropos* is a statement of involvement in the hereditary fall. The condition of being *anthropos* is not an idealization of perfect *Humanität*. On the contrary, like *Khristianos* – a "Christian" mainly in the sense of being *socially* good, a *Romios* in faith, word, and deed – so too an *anthropos* must continually strive for redemption from the travails of segmentary sociality. An anthropology that concerns itself with *anthropos* in this sense must then be a discourse (*loghos*) about that struggle.

Eksotika as visitations: an ethnographic glimpse of otherness

The antithesis of *anthropi* are *eksotika* – a marvellous pair of cognates, this, for contemplation by an anthropology struggling to escape its pervasive exoticism. In many parts of rural Greece, *eksotika* are evil spirits, defined as being "outside" the boundaries of both the inhabited area of the village and the moral community that it represents (see Blum and Blum 1970:12, 95; Herzfeld 1983a; Stewart 1985:249). These spirits are "devils," thus like the medieval imaginings of early anthropology, deformed or formless, inhuman (cf. Hodgen 1964:29–33; see also White 1978:150–82).

And yet, today, they are also human at the same time. In the golden age of "our fathers," Pefkiot villagers say, when people believed in their religion, such spirits undoubtedly existed; but modern wickedness has conflated unbelievers with the spirits whose existence they have rejected. (There is some irony in the fact that the formula of attributing the lack of modern miracles to the decline of belief has been transferred to a cosmology of largely non-Christian origin.) It is the mortal evildoers who are now the true *eksotika*. This, again, is the metaphor of the fall: wickedness has entered the human (and, more specifically, the local) community, and there, where once people were "more loving" toward one another (cf. also du Boulay 1974:249), it has created bitter differences of moral standing. Note, too, that these acknowledgments of an internally admissible state of sin also reproduce the segmentary form of social relations. The local community encounters *eksotika*, its own rejects, as metonyms for the general exclusion of deliberate sinners from the world of true *anthropi*, or Christians.

The Pefkiot symbolism is highly expressive in this respect. *Eksotika* were conceptualized as ghostly apparitions, white and formless, who swept through the village at night. Pefkiots say that nighttime is when evil abounds; no decent villager would be up and about, and those who are must be after illicit sex or theft. They recall instances when local inhabitants, usually women and often resident non-villagers (a visiting teacher, for example), would shroud themselves in a white sheet and flit about the village streets after dark in order to scare the inquisitive away, thereupon to repair to the cemetery for their assignations. Note all the marks of outsiderhood and marginality that mark these human *eksotika*: non-residence (in a normatively endogamous village), femaleness, prohibited sexual encounters after dark and in the place *outside* the village in which only the dead have any business. In a community where guards were once set over a newly wed couple to ensure that they did not consummate the marriage until after both the church ceremony and the wedding sponsor's banquet the next day, illicit sex represented the culmination of depravity.

But these beings were still human in some sense – people, however, who had denied their essential *anthropia*. By saying that it is "people" (*anthropi*) who are today's *eksotika*, Pefkiots acknowledge the relativity – the segmentariness, as it were – of sin. This becomes even more apparent when we perceive that the comparison of today's "human *eksotika*" with yesterday's golden age of innocence is rhetorical and ahistorical. Exactly a century before my own fieldwork in Pefko, a Cypriot folklorist had noted similar attributions of innocence to the past, linked to similar attributions of scare tactics to "witches" who were actually disguised women meeting their lovers in cemeteries (Herzfeld 1983a; cf. Loukas 1874)! Clearly, the Pefkiots (and rural Greeks generally) regard the relativitity of sin as a definitive confirmation that the social world *in general* is permeated with wickedness.

The Cypriot antecedent makes it very likely that those of my Pefkiot friends who could say that they had checked up on the supposed apparitions and found them to be real people were not, in fact, the first such skeptics. From social experience, they *know* – and knowledge is social – that the allegedly *formless* ghosts are likely to be *specific people*, and people whom (again) they *know*, at that. Although such people are "outside the community," "devils," they are also "our own" (*dhiki mas*) in some larger sense. This is why villagers are able to accept amongst themselves the proposition that members of the community may be depraved, tainted, and thoroughly polluting (*ghrousouzidhes*). What they do not accept, however, following the (always relative) logic of disemia, is that such internal flaws might be anyone else's business. (Perhaps the Turks actually have such people, they observe; after all, *ghrousouzia* is a Turkish word!) But this does not mean that they have not collectively internalized the otherness that is associated with a ritually flawed condition, that of humankind, just as politically they have come to believe that – with the possible exception of the local community! – they have also internalized the foreign ("Turkish") culture that alienates them from their culturally ideal selves.

External differentiation is thus the mark of a state of innocence, of the European ideology's noble savage dwelling in an undifferentiated society, but clearly marked off from *us*. "They" are the exotics of anthropological discourse. In the Edenic past, perhaps, they were not quite human. Now that they have become the object of our sympathetic interest, however, they enter into a common state of postlapsarian humanity with us. Similarly, for Greek villagers contrasting the present with an idealized past, social experience has become one of *internal* differentiation: the *eksotika* have entered in. The villagers are now their own exotics. The Greek villagers' etiology of social experience stresses internal differentiation and individual action both within and against the social order. As such, it recognizes what anthropology often does not – the pragmatic character of *both* theoretical generalization *and* people and events that simply do not fit in.

The gritty historicity that characterizes being an *anthropos* – what we call social experience – is not uniquely the lot of a homogeneous crowd of "informants." We, too, inhabit institutions – including that of anthropology. This provides an important modification of Crick's (1976) view that all informants *are* anthropologists.[9] They are not, certainly, practitioners of the historically grounded profession of academic anthropology, but their concern with *anthropia* renders their situation directly analogous to the latter.[10] Inasmuch as their cosmology is, or at least includes, a way of making sense of the relativity of social life, it tries to do some of the same things that anthropology has historically always tended to do – especially, as their treatment of *eksotika* as *anthropi* shows, to "exoticize" flawed beings while insisting on their common humanity. This is not doing anthropology, perhaps; but it is doing something that has long characterized the practice of theoretical anthropology.

**Ethnic and historical:
anthropology and the confrontation of official truths**

There are other terms for social bounding that support this analogy. In particular, the history of the term *ethnos* – which reappears in anthropology as the ubiquitous and often misleading *ethno*-prefix – recommends caution in believing the seductive relativism that the anthropological prefix usually connotes. Fabian (1983) has devastated the claims of tolerance and equality that ethnosemanticists and ethnoscientists have put forward, and especially their claims – also critically reviewed by Geertz (1976) – to be representing the "native point of view." (One is reminded of "ethnic food," perhaps, with all its implied class distinctions between the representatives of cultures more or less like "us.") Similar charges have been made against ethnopsychiatry, which appears to regard western scientific categories as the definitive touchstone of psychiatric illness in other cultures (Duerr 1985:89–90). Finally, it is worth mentioning that some postcolonial responses have generated generalized non-western cultures and conceptual systems that suspiciously resemble their predecessors. Houtondji (1983) criticizes various models of "African philosophy" on these grounds.[11] The literary formalization of *Romiossini*, with its rigid demoticism, offers a comparable illustration. The good intentions of ethno-anthropologists can hardly be a sufficient means of escaping from ethnocentrism, when those who are emerging from their oppression themselves find no adequate way to be rid of such discursive habits.

But in practice not all the ethno-anthropologies are equally guilty of insensitivity. There is nothing intrinsically wrong with the prefix, any more than there is with attempts to break down old stereotypes by erecting alternative models. In a sense, the argument that I am putting forward here is an extension of the ethno-anthropologists' original intentions, although framed in a postcolonial context of knowledge. The danger from the "ethno-" prefix comes only with the rhetorical abuse of its authenticating stamp of cultural tolerance. There are many studies, of which I can only name a few by way of illustration, that not only avoid this self-delusion but exploit the ever present risk of it to good effect. In the Greek context, Danforth (1976, 1979) has given us a telling, "ethnopsychiatric" account of how the Anastenaridhes ("fire-walkers"), Thracian refugees now living in Macedonia, explain a disturbed sense of self in relation to social and religious experience. There are splendid investigations, some (but not all) ethno-prefixed, of indigenous history (e.g. Basso 1979; DeMallie 1982:389–90; n.d.; Hanson 1983), indigenous concepts of meaning (notably Rosaldo 1980, 1982), indigenous poetics (Hymes 1979), and, in ethnomusicology, indigenous theories of musical production (e.g. Feld 1982; Seeger 1986). This last category includes studies of western traditions (Kingsbury 1984, already cited). As some writers (notably Drummond 1981; MacCannell and MacCannell 1982) have pointed out, this is the acid test: how truthfully can we include our own perceptions under the "ethno-" rubric? For if we cannot do so, then ethnofolk are nothing more than unredeemed others; and we should stop pretending otherwise.

Appropriately enough, the domain in which the issue seems to be most accessible is that of ethnosemiotics. This term has had a rather variable fortune. It has been used as a descriptor for the investigation of indigenous systems of meaning (Herzfeld 1981b; Drummond 1981; MacCannell and MacCannell 1982).[12] But it has also been used as a term for the decoding of indigenous systems – for example, those of Hungarian peasant customs (Hoppál 1979). In such cases, especially where the precision of the method seems to depend mainly on a sufficiency of case studies, it is hard to see where ethnosemiotics differs from the traditional approach. It is not really enough even to say that the study must be capable of incorporating ourselves; it must also be able to reflect on the problematic of who "we" are – as members of a culture, but also as scholars – and that dimension is not apparent in the more positivistic readings of semiotics. Lurking behind every terminology, as certainly those who claim a semiotic tradition should know, is the risk of neo-Cratylism – the confusion of terminology with some objectified reality. The "ethno-" prefix may index an *intention* to include "us" in the analysis; but, as Vico would have understood immediately, it is the conviction that one has completely escaped the ethnocentrism of earlier formulations that undermines the project and sends us tumbling back into a second barbarism.

Once again, etymology may help to clarify rather than to confuse. The romanticized term *ethnos* has had a surprising history in Greek, where it has both included and excluded the *Romii* – the Greeks-as-they-know-themselves. (The etymological pair romantic/*Romios* invites dis-closure here: for etymological roads also lead *away from* Rome, and from the originary, unifying legitimation that it bestows.) The modern sense of *ethnos* is that of the entire Greek nation, a spiritual unity that opposes it to the merely bureaucratic fact of the state (*kratos*). Because, as we have seen, the logic of disemia entails treating national identity as concentric with the Greeks' more localized allegiances, the *ethnos* is a loyally accepted unity to which only a few scattered regional separatists have ever – and then only sporadically – objected. It is easily assimilated to people's segmentary perception of the social world, as the outermost ring (surpassed only by the vastness of Orthodoxy and ecumenical Christianity).

The vicissitudes of the term are closely tied to those of "Hellenism." Note that the latter concept, applied to the post-Classical pretensions of hellen*izing* non-Greeks, had by the Byzantine period become synonymous with preserving the pagan religions; the characterization of individuals as either *Hellenes* or *ethnikoi* carried entirely negative meanings for the church-dominated authorities. At that time, the term meant that one had preserved the ritual practices of religious systems now rigorously proscribed by law. It was not an official term of inclusion at all. But when it reappeared in nineteenth-century romantic discourse, it was as a reified nationality, and indeed as a physical population. Diaspora Greeks are still often collectively called "expatriate *Hellenism*" (*apodhimos ellinismos*). In the age of historic*ism*, legal*ism*, national*ism*, and scient*ism*, why not a triumphantly reified Hellenism too? A mere suffix has little power to maintain its critical challenge to authenticity against expropriation by so dominant and all-embracing a discourse as that of the romantic nation-state.

In that same broad sweep, too, *ethnos* completely lost its negative association with paganism. But the pejorative phase of this Classical term in Byzantine times reminds us that *national* labels – or even labels implying ethnic self-reference – may have little to do with internally developed self-perceptions or historical consciousness. Indeed, not only did "Hellenes" probably mean mythical giants of a long-lost era to most rural Greeks (*Romii*) of the pre-Independence period, but an *ethnos* that commanded people's primary loyalty also seems to have been quite novel to them (see also Mouzelis 1976b:445). What brought the *ethnos* into everyday Greek discourse was precisely the ideology that treated all the familiar aspects of Greek life as foreign. Thus, even though ordinary discourse has by now long since assimilated the concept of the *ethnos* to the experienced social order, the term remains as a constant reminder of the imploded otherness that Eurocentric nationalism brought to Greece.

This parallels the manner in which the "ethno-" prefix preserves something of the exotic focus of traditional anthropology. But the other element of the term "ethnosemiotics" deserves a passing mention as well. This is the -*sēm*- morpheme. In official modern Greek, meaning – *simasia* – is the referential meaning of romantic lexicography. But this is not what the term invariably signifies in everyday speech. In Pefko, it clearly is applied to the shifting relationship between utterance and context, in a sense that anthropologists would find entirely familiar. Perhaps we should not be surprised to find that concepts of meaning do not obey our lexicographical traditions in societies where those traditions have not permeated historically (see especially Rosaldo 1982). But the divergence of meaning in a country like Greece, disemically masked (like the inheritance terminology discussed in Chapter Six) by identical words, certainly adds grist to our etymological mill.

In Glendi, *simasia* seems to obtain *especially* in situations where individuals pit their wits and their actions against authority. A daring sheep theft that deserves elaborate narration, a cutting rhyme, a joke at the expense of some self-important but influential politician, a song that takes old words and piquantly applies them to a novel situation – these are the sources of *simasia*. Note, too, that meaning is no longer verbocentric, although it certainly does not *exclude* the verbal. Anything that is repeated, hackneyed, or too obviously sticking to the literal letter of the conventions rather than their high spirits, will be rejected as lacking in meaning. Here, perhaps more dramatically than elsewhere in Greece, it is possible to find alternative readings of a discourse that officialdom insists is semantically uniform throughout the land. This is truly the other side of disemia; and as one follows Glendiots pitting their wits against people from the nearest villages, or joining forces with them against the Cretan townsfolk, or allying even with these corrupt beings to show Athens that Cretans manage best, one encounters directly the relativity of social knowledge that a romantic anthropology must always repress.

Witty worstings of the bureaucratic tyrant are the very stuff of "stories" (*istories*, Cretan *athivoles*). By the same token, they are the inverse of what officialdom is pleased to regard as "History" (*i Istoria*). In the nineteenth century, when folklorists collected songs as evidence of the indomitably Hellenic spirit of the people, prose narratives were evidently much harder to elicit (Tozer 1869, II:261–2): these *istories* appear, unlike (for example) the grand swashbuckling of the "kleftic" songs (i.e. those claimed by nationalist folklorists to represent the guerrilla lifestyle of the War of Independence), to have been just too intimate and suggestive to share with strangers.

But they existed nonetheless: we do know that much, although the judgment as to which were fittest to survive has limited our purview. Just as local-level meaning is a subversion of official lexicography, local tales – which include the recognition that the *eksotika* are now living people, accounts of bloody feuds and silly quarrels, scatological and sexual gossip, and jokes at the expense of bureaucrats, doctors, and the learned and wealthy in general – subvert the doctrines of unity that the state promotes. They do not do this by means of a literal separatism; on the contrary, they belie the statist argument by demonstrating that it is not necessary to be a separatist in order to be a social critic, or in order to perceive and play upon the delicious ambiguities of social segmentation. They provide an*other* kind of history.

We need not further belabor the moral for anthropology. The contrast between official and socially embedded discourse – what I have been calling disemia throughout this discussion – is a central part of the discipline's problematic. The choice between rules and strategies is not merely a matter of ethnographic description; it is also a question of ideological persuasion and preference. Disemia is a condition of anthropology; the ethnographer, a Digenes of ambiguous descent (from Herodotus? or Vico?), is caught in the same tensions, and the same irreducible relativities, as any social being.

For a practice of theory

This brief sniffing at the etymological traces allows us to return now to the central symbolic opposition between ethnography and theory. Traditional usage makes ethnography the *raw data* that theory *processes*, rejecting the rotten parts (or deriving special satisfaction from being able to do something with them) and processing (cooking?) field material of variable meatiness into entities fit for the etiquette of tabulation. This is a process of cultural conversion, inviting culinary triangulation (on which, see Lévi-Strauss 1968:403–10). It is not so much that our data are mythical, as that the alimentary metaphors we use for our handling of them betray a submerged but vital recognition that our own thinking, too, is embodied. To dismiss this as "mere" metaphor, or as a joke in poor taste (*sic*), affirms the Cartesian separation of mind from body and literal from tropological as refractions of the political separation of "ethnic" from "real" people. It thus undercuts the anthropological commitment against prejudice.

Drummond (1983) has pinpointed the characteristically cultural activity of ethnography: "graphing the *ethnos*" as a practice of inscribing a passive entity in a discourse.[13] I have already noted the hegemonic implications of writing and literacy in the discursive interaction between ethnographer and informant. In fact, Drummond's etymological insight (for that is of course what it is) subverts the apparent modesty of the claims made for ethnography. It now appears instead as the procrustean fiat, the grand performative utterance, that constitutes raw data so that they already, *post festum* as Bourdieu would say, seem "given" indeed, laid out on the festive tabulation. Above all, it is the presupposition of *rawness* upon which every subsequent theoretical move rests. We may accept theory as a second-order activity, but then we must do so in a sequential rather than in a timeless hierarchy. Theory and practice, poles of an intellectual disemia, constitute a shifting relativity.

Ironically, Classical Greek *theoria* meant "observation." The visualist bias of anthropology belongs to a wider tradition of privileging the visual over virtually all the other sensual channels (Mitchell 1985b:6; cf. Fabian 1983). It appears most fully developed in the discipline's determined comparativism, and in the metaphorical iconicities of "structural" relationships. (What is a structural relationship, if not iconic?[14]) The verb *thoro* still means "see" in Cretan and several other dialects; and in Cretan, at least, it conveys a sense of visual contact that is primarily social in its implications.[15]

These etymologies would make *ethnography* rather than theory the second-order activity. But if we take the more ancient etymological claim, now technically discarded, that makes theory the *divine* basis of perception (< *theos*, "god"; see Stamatakos 1972:450), we discover theory in its privileged position of intellectual *originality*, usurped by humans from the divine order of things. Vico has bequeathed to us a telling critique of what this implies.

Vico derived the abstraction of theories and theorems from the practice of divination, the inspection of the sky and other mantic sources (*theōrēmata*: 2,1,2,3 [1977:273–4] [B/F 391]; 2,8 [1977:501] [B/F 711]; 2,10,2 [1977:522] [B/F 739]). But divination, in Vico's view, was a usurpation of divine knowledge and an index of humanity's corrupted state; it was thus something from which the human intelligence gradually moved away. (In fact, the Roman emperors had gradually arrogated to themselves the right to conduct all divination as divine beings in their own right, and with the advent of the Christian religion the act itself became sinful [Grodzynski 1976].) In Vico's scheme of things, theory gradually escapes its sinful origins by moving towards the perfection of abstract knowledge; at the point when the learned think they have reached that goal, however, and have left wrongheaded superstition behind them, they slip back into the barbarism of folly: human knowledge is not, in a pragmatic reading, perfectible. It is always the "inchoate subject" of our troping, groping efforts. Anthropology is always "shifty" (Boon 1982:42; Fernandez 1983a:324).

We do not have to accept Vico's historical reconstructions literally in order to appreciate their critical value. The point that he makes about divination, that it is emergent theoretical knowledge and should be respected as such, can be matched in modern ethnographic accounts of divination, as I have argued elsewhere (Herzfeld 1985a:257). It is, moreover, *pragmatic* theoretical knowledge: the view that divination is somehow a *failed* form of science, rather than an attempt to explore the imponderables and indeterminacies of social life as scientists explore the imponderables and indeterminacies of the physical universe, belongs to an assumption that we have attained the level of perfect(ible) knowledge and of a thoroughly un-Vichian contempt for the achievements of cultural others.

Vico's etymology strips theory of its pretensions to having sprung fully formed from the minds of brilliant scholars, to an originary creativity born uniquely of their intellects (cf. also Said 1975:360–2, 379–80). In this, as our opening epigram shows, Vico saw scholarship as distressingly similar to the pretensions of nations. In fact, it is theory that is etymologically exotic (in the sense of "outside"). Again and again, in the recent literary debate about the status of theory, it has been described as an attempt to get "outside" practice (see especially Fish 1985; Knapp and Michaels 1985; Mitchell 1985a). This is a visualist trope in itself, of course; but it is also explicitly architectonic, and it immediately recalls the defensive walls of disemia. Theory, argue Knapp and Michaels (1985:30; my italics), "is the name for all the ways people have tried to stand *outside practice* in order to *govern* practice from without." Now it must be apparent that I do not share these authors' commitment "against theory," and I am equally reluctant to regress to a Steinerian separation of the literary from the anthropological. It seems socially improbable that one could ever escape theory, any more than one can ever escape practice. Effective social theory must be "ethnographic in intent" (Karp and Maynard 1983:497). But its formalizations may serve as a protective wall against scientistic criticism, while ethnographic experience does constantly call anthropologists back to the realization that, in the final analysis (*sic*), they are dealing with *anthropi*.

In following Vico's etymological strategy, we reiterate his reinsertion of theory into history; or in his own terms divine history casts the intellect out of Eden, *recasts* it as "gentile" or postlapsarian, condemns it to a sisyphean struggle for intellectual control over its own products. From this perspective, Evans-Pritchard's surely Vichian view of the "impossibility" of anthropological comparison becomes, not just an elegant paradox, but a recognition of the discipline's radically oxymoronic condition. Evans-Pritchard never advocated sacrificing ethnographic quality to a pose of theoretical elegance. To have done so would have slighted a key etymology – the Classical Greek root *empeiria*, "experience," now too often reified into the crude *empiricism* that bedevils ethnographers' attempts to be conscientiously *empirical*.[16]

The theory-practice conundrum in anthropology is a problem drawn from everyday life. The comparativist program with which we began this exploration has now come full circle. For, like modern Greeks confronting the complexities of their identity, anthropologists – as well as historians, literary scholars, and philosophers – do not have to choose between theory and practice in any irrevocably ultimate sense. The choice is a rhetorical one, and reflects the characteristic professional perplexity of disciplines whose subject matter is on the same intimate scale as themselves. If what anthropologists study is either exotic or trite – the discussion of segmentation seems an apt metonym for the whole discipline here – then theory serves as an officializing strategy in the social pragmatics in which anthropology is embedded. One cannot say that there is no such thing as theory; but it is a culturally contingent and pragmatically evanescent phenomenon. In this regard, it is not essentially different from the official discourses of other formal systems, including that of the state. Every Greek, caught in the disemic dilemmas of modern Greek life, experiences the same undismissible choices at every moment of every day. Why should anthropologists expect to *resolve* in their own practices the very problem that constitutes the object of their study of "others"?

A Greek is never *just* a Hellene or *just* a *Romios*. A scholar is never just a theoretician or a pragmatist. Greek and scholar alike oscillate between contrasted rhetorical poses for which they can deploy a rich store of symbolic flags and stakes. There is nothing deprecatory about calling both aspects of both parallel situations rhetorical, unless one starts pre-emptively from an absolute distinction between the tropological and the literal, or between the ideal and the real (and in that case there is nothing to argue about). The Greek materials examined here show that in social life, despite the antirhetorical rhetoric of the deifiers and reifiers (Vico's bombastic statesmen and scholars, respectively), rhetoric is as real as the elements that it deploys *as* realities.[17] And although one might be excused for occasionally doubting it – for such is professional rhetoric – anthropologists are social beings too.

Notes

1 Romanticism and Hellensism: burdens of otherness

1 An exception is Mouzelis 1978. Even here, however, the general applicability of the models has yet to be developed in other cultural contexts, and the author's dimissive neglect of the "standard" ethnographies, as well as his complete exclusion of the national folklore tradition, undercut the usefulness of his study as an approach to the analysis of national cultures. But now see also Dubisch 1986.

2 Handler (1984:56) has made a closely related point with regard to French Canadian nationalism, arguing that "a nationalist ideology is a product of the Western tradition, closely allied to another product of that tradition: social-science theory." See also Handler 1985a and 1985b for further exploration of his position; and cf. MacCannell and MacCannell 1982:69.

3 See Fernandez 1983b, for the initial criticism of Quigley. I have discussed "residual patriliny" elsewhere (Herzfeld 1983c) in more detailed connection with the variation of Greek kinship usage.

4 On Vico's attitude to scientism, it is worth recalling that he dismissed "clear and distinct knowledge" as a spurious claim to difference from ordinary social knowledge (Giuliani 1976:33, n.11). In the modern context, consider Clifford's (1986:24) timely warnings against the likely reaction to analyses of ethnographic writerliness.

5 Vico thought that class differences had originated as differences between pairs of cities, in each of which the loser was the one that lacked the marriage institutions governing correct interfamilial relations (e.g. 2,6,1,3[II] [1977: 485] [B/F 683]). This account, again, acknowledged a kind of social otherness-as-imperfection-as-fuzziness, as part of a larger recognition that social and cultural difference necessarily also meant hierarchy.

6 Cf. Goldschläger's (1982) concept of "authoritarian discourse."

7 For a positivistic comparative account of ethnocentrism, see LeVine and Campbell 1970.

8 The paternalistic image evoked here is one that a conservative, pro-western Greek politician may sometimes use.

9 Even Elgin's contemporaries were not entirely convinced of the virtue of his claims (see St. Clair 1967). This is apparent from contemporary accounts both descriptive and fictional.

10 See also Ridgway and Ridgway 1979:240 and Fagan 1975:304, on Wallis Budge's similar (and equally specious) argument that the Egyptian Pharaohs could sleep more easily in the British Museum than anywhere else.

11 The use of the shorter, *katharevousa* (i.e. neo-Classical formal register, corresponding to Ferguson's [1959] "H") form is a further index of respect, because

it alludes to a hierarchical code. In ordinary ("demotic," Greek *dhimotiki*, Ferguson's "L" diglossic register) speech, commonly available *katharevousa* forms are almost always semantically marked in this way.

12 This exemplifies the process described by Ardener (1975:25) as "englobing" – i.e., when the oppressed conceptually "englobe" their oppressors.

13 R. Harris (1980) sees an affinity between his view of "scriptism," the literate modelling of language in linguistics, and Derrida's (1976) rejection of logocentrism. I use the term "writing" here in Harris's more restricted sense, since it appears thus in the discourse under consideration as an active symbol of domination.

14 See especially J. Goody 1977a, 1977b; Ong 1982.

15 For the debate on this question, see especially Just 1973; Herzfeld 1981a, 1984a, 1985c; Galt 1982, 1985; Gilmore 1982; Fernandez 1983b. A key issue concerns how far people locally use such terms as "Mediterranean" or "Balkan" of themselves.

16 I use "reproduction" here to mean, broadly, the modelling of one level of inequality on another. As Needham (1971) has pointed out, the automatic privileging of the social over the symbolic is logically indefensible. Equally, there is no reason to privilege one *level* of the social over another; thus, a given collective representation (e.g. anthropology-as-a-discipline) can symbolize more than one level of social identity (e.g. European, Greek, and individual) at the same time, and this congruence is reinforced by parallel inequalities linking the several levels (here, Europe:Greece::state:peasantry).

17 "Tracking" is the root meaning of Herodotus's term *historiē* (see Hodgen 1964:22).

2 A secular cosmology

1 This distinction should be differentiated from the real-ideal dichotomy of more literalistic approaches. Experience is constru(ct)ed to the same extent, if not in the same way, as the idealizations of official discourse. In the Greek case, *both* stereotypes of national identity are constructed; the claims of each to be more "real" than the other testify to the rhetorical character of both.

2 "Greek," in its semantically marked sense, means "ancient Greek" – a fair indication of western Europe's relative indifference to the modern Greeks and their culture. Cf. Kazazis's (1981a) discussion of degrees of marking in the term *Romios*.

3 In semiotics, this corresponds precisely to the distinction made by MacCannell and MacCannell (1982) between the "semiotics of unity" and the "semiotics of difference." In their view, a semiotics of difference must resist its own potential transformation into a mere decoding activity. Critics of sociolinguistic models have similarly objected to the tendency to reduce the vagaries of speech to statistical regularities (e.g. Webber 1973; Kendall 1981; Karp and Kendall 1982).

4 These generalizations may have more impact in the Romance languages and in Greek, where the definite article makes explicit its generalizing significance; cf. French *la mentalité africaine*, etc. One of the major postcolonial responses to the suppression of separate African identity, Léopold Senghor's concept of *Africanité*, emerged in francophone Africa; so, too, did the negative responses of African scholars concerned that the tendency to overgeneralization did not disappear with colonialism, but merely adopted its rhetorical forms (see especially Houtondji 1983; Mudimbe forthcoming).

In Greek, the definite article is also used with proper names, as it is in Italian for the names of famous individuals: it thus serves as a useful device for reifying identities in the manner required by the romantic preoccupation with both individual genius and collective "national character."

5 Vico made a very explicit connection between theory and folk conceptions of the divine: as part of his larger thesis that knowledge among the gentile peoples began from the prohibited art of *divination*, he recalled that the sections of the sky that haruspicers recognized "were called *templa coeli* ['temples of the sky'], whence the Greeks must have obtained their first *theōrēmata mathēmata*, 'divine or sublime things for contemplation,' which finally ended up as metaphysical and mathematical abstractions" (2,1,2,3 [1977:273–4] [B/F 391]). As divination evolved into science, according to Vico, the "observation of things divine" became instead the purely abstract contemplation that we now call "theory."

6 Mainly Gypsies, *Arvanitovlakhi* (Albanian-speaking), and *Koutsovlakhi* (Romanian-speaking); there are also sedentary Slavophone communities further to the east, as well as Slavophone Muslims (Pomaks). Greek contempt for all those groups is traditionally considerable; they only become an object of interest when they can be portrayed as lapsed Hellenes (e.g. Daskalakis 1965; Papazisis 1976; cf. also Campbell 1964:3–6). The Gypsies never seem to benefit even from this degree of acceptance.

7 In some communities, acceptance of domination by others is contemptuously attributed to the *pous[h]tis*, the passive homosexual – an interesting point, in light of the concern with sexual respectability that I discuss at greater length below. See, e.g., Loizos 1975:255, 286 [n.10]. See also the more extended discussion in du Boulay 1974:105, n.1.

8 The parallels between the Italian chapbooks and Greek demotic poetry of this period are striking. See especially the collection in Lambros 1908.

9 These issues are taken up again below in the discussion of fatalism and especially in the comments on Handman's (1983) use of it.

10 Ideological Hellenism did not of course provide the theoretical basis of anthropology. On the contrary, that argument is the "ecumenical ethnocentrism" of the nationalistic Greek ethnologist-folklorists of the nineteenth century, as also, *mutatis mutandis*, of Greek literary studies until still more recently (see critiques by Jusdanis 1985; Lambropoulos 1985; Tziovas 1985), but antithetical to the stated ecumenicalism of anthropology. Anthropology is implicated in the creation of Eurocentric conceptual boundaries (cf. also Pandian 1984:62–9).

11 The resemblance is strengthened by the use of the verb *mirazo* for "divide up," as also for the bureaucrat's "distribution of favors" (*mirazo rousfetia*); it is transparently cognate with *mira*, "fate." I have elsewhere discussed the links between these various images at some length (Herzfeld 1982c).

12 This is perhaps why some spells against the evil eye, for example, achieve textual closure through the evocation of the oneness of the Word. See Herzfeld 1986b.

13 Shifters are linguistic (or other semiotic) features whose interpretation depends on the relationship between the context of utterance and the context of action (e.g. personal pronouns, verb tenses, etc.). On shifters used especially in the context of ethnic and other terms for identity, see especially Galaty 1982. For a more general discussion, see Silverstein 1976. In terms of the present discussion, see also Chapter Six.

14 See my fuller account of this (Herzfeld 1983b) for the relevant details. Cf. also Campbell 1964:vii.

15 See Campbell 1964; Peristiany 1965; Pitt-Rivers 1971; Gilmore 1982; Wikan 1984.

16 Re–course: cf. Vico's notion of the *ricorso*, a slip back into an earlier phase that results from forgetting the historical dependence of the present upon the past, and, more specifically, from ignoring the figurative basis of all scientific and historical discourse.

17 See my specific discussion of this in Herzfeld 1981b; 1985a:xii–xiv and *passim*. The problem of indigenous aesthetics is also addressed by Caraveli in a series of enlightening ethnographic case studies of song performance (1980, 1982, 1985).

18 As well, perhaps, as what the literati who originated the style had recognized (Beaton 1980:174–8); but this simply means that the thread of a dominant discourse passes from one group of literati (medieval and Renaissance poets) to another (nineteenth- and twentieth-century scholars), once again bypassing the people who actually performed the songs in the villages. We should not ignore the literary sources, if such they be, but by the same token we should also not privilege them over their epiphanies in village discourse and performance.

19 *Ghrousouzia*, < Tk. *ugur*, "fortune" + *sız*, privative enclitic, "without."

20 The verb *khal(n)ao* means "spoil," often in the sexual sense; it is also used to mean "change" (i.e. money). It thus implies earthly benefits to be reaped from spoiling something ideal. See the further discussion of this in Chapter Seven.

21 See Herzfeld 1983b:163. The weakness of the translation metaphor lies in its failure, curious in the authors who use it, to insist on foregrounding the ethnographer's presence in the text – something that conventional literary translators usually try to avoid. Geertz (1976) attempted a comprehensive inspection of the translation metaphor and its implications, which he has since traced back to "Evans-Pritchard, at least" (Geertz 1983:9). For a very different perspective again, see Duerr (1985:129), who criticizes the equation of translation with understanding as this occurs in anthropology.

3 Aboriginal Europeans

1 Bibliographical sources for these are given in Lambros 1908, and discussed in full by M. Alexiou (1974:85–90).

2 Georges (1978, 1984:214–15) addresses some trenchant remarks to the stereotyping of Greeks by foreigners, especially with regard to such alleged characteristics as fatalism and self-interest. His critique of excessive generalization is apposite, and provides further documentation of the tendency of social science to homogenize its object. His argument also shows that the distinctive elements that Greeks adopt as badges of ethnicity cannot be interpreted referentially; they are *used* to encode different messages and evaluations at different times. He does not, however, examine the extent to which the Greeks' own apparent acceptance of the ways in which foreigners stereotype them indexes a strong sense of political inequality.

3 This of course conflicts with the American ideology of the self, that of "rugged individualism." One could regard Le Lannou's comments and opposing American statements as discourses in contest over the recognition of America's adherence to a truly European identity.

4 For another example of this racial mode of argument, consider the following passage, signed "J.B.," from the *Journal of the Royal Anthropological Institute* (28[1898]:343): "Professor Sergi has just published in the *Nuova Antologia*, a

very interesting paper, entitled 'Inglesi e Romani.' Therein he justifies his adhesion to the opinion that of all modern nations the English most nearly reproduce the moral type of the conquering, colonizing, organizing Roman. And he proceeds partially to account for this similitude, by pointing out that the Romans were in the main southern or Mediterranean dolichokephali, and that the British are in the main northern dolichokephali; and that these are after all at bottom one race, though divided ages ago by the intrusion of the eastern or Alpine brachykephali, whom he considers to be the true Aryans." This is another attempt to correlate physical traits with moral characteristics, in this case by linking together the long-headed imperial genii of two distinct epochs and places.

   A precise century before the publication of Davis's attempt to systematize Mediterraneanist anthropology, Bell (1877) attacked the genetically based category of Mediterranean races, arguing instead that linguistic indicators would make the term "Aryo-Semitic" more appropriate. As the notice about Sergi's researches shows, however, genetic explanations of national character died hard; their resemblance to the widespread symbolism of blood and descent may well have contributed to the popular success of their embodiment in Fascist discourse.

5 The definition of *whose* history is at stake illustrates the problem well: "Nothing very important had happened in Australia. At school Australians learnt a lot of English history, and when they did learn Australian history at secondary school it was called British history anyway" (Watson 1984, cited in McQueen 1984–5:10).

6 From discussions with Greek scholars, I am aware that folksongs that allude to local events are systematically excluded from anthologies unless the events in question have been canonized by official history.

7 Evans-Pritchard was not a supporter of colonialism as such, and sometimes criticized the heavy-handedness of the British occupiers of the Sudan (e.g., 1940:187–8). Nor should it be thought that Campbell was a pale imitator of Evans-Pritchard. On the contrary, the very similarity of textual strategies between *The Nuer* and *Honour, Family, and Patronage* – the ecological setting, the use of spatio-temporal principles to link that setting to the symbolic life of the community, the heavy emphasis on moral concepts, and the image of sanctity "refracted" through the social divisions of the community – all serve to emphasize Campbell's originality in other ways. Of these, I would particularly single out his brief but diagnostic introduction to the historical battle over Sarakatsan origins, and the thorough documentation in support of his argument for the (most un-Nuerlike) cognatic character of Sarakatsan kinship.

   Note that J. G. Peristiany, whose editorship of the volume on Mediterranean social values (1965) did so much to advance interest in the ethnography of the area, and who was one of the teachers of Campbell, cut his ethnographic teeth on Africanist research with a well-known study of the Kipsigis of Kenya (1964).

8 Cf. Muecke's (1983:88,100) comments on the literalism of "romantic discourse."

9 I insist on the sincerity of anthropological attempts to resist all discernible exoticism and ethnocentrism. The key word here is, of course, "discernible": the discursive formation of a particular phase in the development of the discipline imposes limitations on what it is possible to achieve. But nothing is to be gained by excoriating all anthropologists as colonialists or worse. If anything redeems the discipline, it is the commitment to resist exoticism while recognizing its

roots in an exoticizing past; at the moment we fail to do so, to adopt a position taken directly from Vico, we lose the very basis of insight.

10 Visual (photographic and film) images, far from being neutral, may exoticize their subjects by creating "distinct semiotic boundaries" (Seremetakis 1984:69) between photographer and community member. Seremetakis's remarks deal with A. Tsiaras's contribution to Danforth 1982, in which she sees a radical conflict between the photographer's obtrusiveness and Danforth's "structuralist" universalism. Contrastively, this illustrates what parochial meaning is given to the concept of structure in *Kypseli*.

11 See Herzfeld 1985a:157–9; 211–20; 1986b. On the various uses of male and female *personified* symbols of national identity in Europe, see Mosse 1985:23. The masculine suffix *-ismos* is associated with reified, precise *definition* (cf. Chapter Eight); the feminine suffix *-sini* indexes an inherent *quality* (e.g. *kalosini*, "goodness").

These two terms are perhaps not strictly comparable, since, unlike *Ellinismos*, *Romiossini* is a literary neologism of relatively recent coinage. Nonetheless, those authors who have developed its use are themselves Greek; to deny its relevance to the present debates about the character of modern Greek identity would exclude an important intellectual tradition. Nor should we doubt that literati are as liable to the symbolism of grammar as those who are illiterate.

12 Aguilar's argument is all the more useful here in that, although it is psychological in orientation, it still provides some confirmation of the *political* dynamic in which broad psychological generalizations of the genre I criticize here are enmeshed. Whether the Indians in question have genuinely internalized *feelings* of shame seems unclear, despite Aguilar's claims. On the other hand, his assertion that they "have no hesitation in asserting their moral superiority over Ladinos ... but they also admit to inferiority in terms of political-economic power and 'civilization' (a form of power as it pertains to the utility of literacy)" (1982:163) seems much more persuasive. Ardener's (1965) "englobing" model begs fewer questions about internal psychological states, which have long been a stock-in-trade of the more exoticist anthropological traditions. Chapman (1978:197–8) applies this model to scholars rather than to local-level populations alone.

13 I have argued this point especially on the basis of the performance of improvised rhyming couplets, but it seems to be generalizable to other areas of social performances (Herzfeld 1981b, 1985a).

14 The evidence for change is impressive. See especially Kiriakidou-Nestoros 1978, 1985; Danforth 1982; Meraklis 1984.

4 Difference as identity

1 See Chapter Seven for a fuller discussion of the formal relationship between segmentation and the European ideology of common identity through diversity.

2 See Hanson 1979; Hvalkof and Aaby 1981; Fabian 1983.

3 The metaphor of *refraction* for the division of a spiritual concept through the categories of social differentiation is taken from Evans-Pritchard (1956:52), whence Campbell (1964:344) also borrowed it. In Campbell's study, it is also suggested by the inverse phenomenon of the shared Communion bread, symbol of a transient but transcendent unity (1964:345). See also Chapter Seven for a further exploration of the relation of refraction to other formal properties of segmentation. I have used it elsewhere in discussions of the refraction of secular

images, especially that of a prominent figure of political history, through local divisions of political interest (Herzfeld 1985a:99, 149), as well as in the analysis of blasphemy (Herzfeld 1984b).

4 I have elsewhere essayed a reconstruction of Vico's likely attitude to the status of the term *stato* as a *perfect participle* (i.e. of the verb *stare*, "to stand, to be in a state of being," hence also used for *essere*, "to be," with consequent intimations of eternal [i.e. dehistoricized] verity) (Herzfeld 1986c).

5 We can get some idea of the fervor with which the prospect of a pan-Italian monarchy was received while Italy was still under foreign domination from the scenes of pandemonium that broke out in La Scala opera theatre in Milan after the first performance of Verdi's *Nabucco*. This play about the redemption of the Jews from their Babylonian exile under Nebuchadnezzar served as an allegory of Italian aspirations, marked by the enthusiastic cries of *Viva Verdi!* and the acknowledgment that the composer's name was a suitably cryptic acronym – while the Austrians were still in charge – of *Vittorio Emmanuele, re d'Italia*. Note also that the famous peal of choral enthusiasm of Verdi's next opera (*Ernani*), *A Carlo Magno sia gloria e onor!* was rephrased by the public: *A Pio Nono sia gloria e onor!* Thus the papacy, too, was largely viewed as a key element in Italian national redemption; secular imagination had adumbrated it to its own political ends. See Toye 1962:38.

6 I am indebted to Robert R. Reed for this lapidary citation.

7 This is the same issue that in semiotics, for example, requires discussion of iconicity/indexicality/symbolicity rather than of icon/index/symbol; see Eco 1976:49, 216.

8 Austin (1975:47) contrasts *statements* or *constative utterances* with his model of *performative utterances*, the former being a concept that ignores social context. While we might agree that *statements* are therefore ethnographically improbable or even impossible, they are *rhetorically* the equivalent of the decontextualized eternal verities (including Bernstein's [1977] "elaborated code") that suppress their own dependence on context. The relationship between statism and the authority of context-free utterances is nicely captured in the etymologies of both *statement* and *constative*.

9 This complements the force of Hymes's (1979:xii–xiii) comment that Bourdieu "appears to think of ... the practical life of most peoples known to anthropology, as in principle in a state of *doxa*, of unquestioning acceptance of the social order as an order of nature ... Yet imaginative analysis of worlds alternative to the accepted is uncovered among Native Americans." And, we should add, the unquestioning acceptance of the social order as natural is exactly what the state demands of its citizens in European society.

10 Strategies, as devices for representing "egotistical" aims as the general good (Bourdieu 1977:40), may not be as far removed from state laws *in practice* as Bourdieu seems to imply. The notion of societal differentiation to which he appeals, moreover, is heavily dependent on the hypostatization of key terms (e.g. "rule"). It thus fails to move away from the very similar generalizations that make "art," for example, a general rather than a specialized activity in so-called undifferentiated (for which, read "primitive") societies. Beattie (1964:205) claims that "expressive" practices replace "scientific" ones in such societies, as a means of coping with illness and other disasters. But this is simply a functionalist justification for the stereotype of "natives" as both unspecialized and uniformly artistic and expressive (cf. "musical" stereotypes of Blacks). These ideas seem to have wide currency in anthropological texts (e.g. Nanda 1984:328).

11 For a discussion of this conceptual opposition and its history in the Greek context, see Herzfeld 1985b.

12 Regimented bilingualism is the linguistic equivalent of other, more obviously repressive policies, whose ultimate aim is to destroy the otherness represented by the indigenous population. Compare, for example, the nineteenth-century Colombian liberal Pedro Fermín de Vargas's proposal to induce "miscegenation" with whites among the native population as a means of "hispanicizing" them, and of reversing their "idleness, stupidity, and *indifference towards normal human endeavours*" (Anderson 1983:21, citing Lynch 1973:260; my italics). Note again the use of fatalism and passivity ("indifference") as discursive indices of otherness.

13 From Greek *kaloyeros*, "good old man" – actually a somewhat derisive term in modern usage; the formal term is *[iero]monakhos*, "[holy] monk" (cf. *monakhos*, "alone," i.e. having taken a vow of ascetic self-sufficiency).

14 This would be a curious eventuality: Whorf conflated European languages thus partly as a means of *contrasting* them with more exotic ones. To that extent, he seems to have shared the literary view that European languages were at least intertranslatable to a much greater degree than would be the case between a European language and, for example, a North American one. But he also thereby intended, as Handler (1985a:176–7) correctly points out, to defamiliarize European linguistic habits. What is less clear is whether he recognized any non-standard subversive usage that defied the grammaticality of official European discourse; or whether he seriously doubted the ontological unity of "Standard Average European."

15 In one notable exception, Doumanis (1983) generalizes the rural Greek family almost entirely from Campbell 1964. See also the brief discussion of typicality in the previous chapter.

16 The aesthetic concept of *defamiliarization* is taken from Shklovskij (see Stacy 1977). For a contrary view, see Duerr 1985:126. The problem of overcoming ethnographic dullness becomes increasingly acute the closer one comes to home, and must be seen in aesthetic terms. Another useful concept from the semiotics of art is Mukařovský's concept of "backgrounding" (see, e.g. Hawkes 1977:80); cf. also Roman Jakobson's (1960:356) "poetic function," and, from a more strictly anthropological tradition, Ardener's (1971b:xvii) "critical lack of fit of (at least) two entire world-views, one to another" (specifically and productively applied to Mediterranean cultures by Just [1973]).

17 The premise that non-European, illiterate peoples possess their own concepts of history is a relatively new one, even in anthropology where one might expect it to have emerged far sooner. Among recent contributions, which have done a great deal to make up for lost time, see especially Meeker 1979; DeMallie 1982, n.d.; Hanson 1983; Sahlins 1985.

18 Wolf's (1982:4) ironic allusion to "people 'without history'" initiates an important critique of anthropological reification, and one that – in a Marxist idiom – interestingly parallels the semiotic analyses of Boon (1982) and Drummond (1980, 1981). Equally perceptive and relevant is Wolf's (1982:5) observation that the western habit of reifying cultural boundaries derives from a tradition that places ancient Greece genealogically at the head of "an entity called the West." This then generates a sense of categorical alienation from a Greekless non-European world. Modern Greece, however, is neither "tribal" nor fully European. For this reason, it differs from the more obviously colonial peoples discussed by Wolf, in that it has a history, though this is not its own but an

ancient history expropriated by the West. There is a (surely unintended) irony in the fact that Wolf only makes a single reference to modern Greece as such (1982:292), and then merely to a country that economic observers treated as one of the failures of western finance. But being subject to a distant history that was not its own, Greece has fared worse in the anthropological literature than have most cultures thought to have no history at all.

5   The double-headed eagle: self-knowledge and self-display

1 For a symbolic analysis of Linnaeus's classification of nature in its historical and epistemological context, see now van den Broek 1986.
2 The debate reveals something of the difficulty with the ethnosemantic approach, to which Frake originally contributed substantially. Gell objects to Frake's emphasis on the singularity of those whose medieval achievements parallel the ingenuity of modern science; but his position could in turn fall prey to the criticism that *both* sides of the debate are conducted within a criterial system defined by the modern culture of science.
3 This is essentially the critique that Crick (1976: ch. 5) and Eco (1976) level at scientism (or "literalism").
4 See my discussion in Herzfeld 1982a; A. Politis 1973; Kiriakidou-Nestoros 1978; M. Alexiou 1985.
5 On the importance of this for anthropological knowledge, especially in the study of indigenous models, see Galaty 1981.
6 For a fuller exposition of the relationship between the epic, song, and exegetical texts, see Herzfeld 1985a; problems of taxonomy and marginality are discussed in Herzfeld 1980b.
7 This is a historical incarnation of the tension between rules and strategies.
8 This bracketing of the official Greek and philhellenic stereotypes of slavophile and communist is not as anachronistic as it may sound. Long before the establishment of Marxism as a state doctrine in several Balkan countries, some observers (e.g. d'Istria 1867:590) thought they detected a Slavic proclivity to communistic attitudes, a view that may have resulted from oversimplification of the *zadruga* form of social organization (a patrilineally organized extended family with communal living space and facilities).
9 See Lotman 1985; also Bakhtin 1981 on heteroglossia and official discourse. See also note 19, below.
10 See especially du Boulay 1974:122–3.
11 The name is derived from Turkish *Karagöz*, "Black-Eye." Attempts to rename the character by the formal Greek equivalent *Mavromatis* failed; this is not surprising, given Karagiozis's almost emblematically Romeic character. On the relationship between Karagiozis, *poniria* (cunning), and status reversal, see Danforth's (1979) thorough analysis; on versions in which Karagiozis embarrasses the Nazis, Mussolini, and American tourists, see Danforth 1983b.
12 For a textual illustration from a Nisirian funerary dirge, see Baud-Bovy (1935,II:165). For ethnographic parallels of the "paradoxical" ideology of womanhood, see Giovannini 1981.
13 E.g. the one discussed in Herzfeld 1986b.
14 *I Fili*, "*the* Race," glosses such terms as *ethnos* and *yenos*, all of which imply common descent. It also glosses the popular *ratsa*, from Italian *razza*. *Ratsa* is often encountered in its plural form (*ratses*) but used of a single nation (e.g. the

Turks as *atimes ratses*, "worthless races") – an indication of the internal *dhia-fores*, or differences, that index imperfection of all social entities. The seamless singularity of *i Fili* is thus the representation of a perfect national identity, one that does not admit such flaws from the East.

15 Handler (1985b:211) shows how the British administrators' conviction that the French Canadians lacked both a history and a literature of their own sparked off an intense revival, and notes that this reactive pattern resembles the conditions under which nationalistic folklore emerged and flourished in Greece "at exactly the same time."

16 This, I think, represents a substantive departure from my position in *Ours Once More* (Herzfeld 1982a), where I focussed on the western origins of much of the discourse without, as I now believe, sufficiently attending to the significant differences in *interpretation* that divided the Greek leaders from their foreign supporters. This is an implicit consequence of the criticism levelled by Caraveli (1983); her critique compelled me to rethink the explanatory framework in more international political terms.

17 The Greek terms that I have used here in presentations to Greek-speaking audiences (initially at the University of Thessaloniki in the summer of 1984) are *aftoparousiasi* and *aftoghnosia*. I have been particularly encouraged in the adoption of this pairing by Professor Alki Kiriakidou-Nestoros at the University of Thessaloniki; she has verbally expressed to me the opinion that it makes a more fundamental and therefore more satisfactory opposition than that of *Romiossini–Ellinismos* on which to project a general model of Greek disemia. The symbolic binarism of Greek identity is still forcefully expressed, as in an article appropriately entitled The Two Greeces, which appeared in the critical journal *Andi* (263, June 15, 1984, pp. 32–8).

18 *Maepsari* (or *maepsimi*) (from *maevome* "I gather myself, impose myself"), in-marrying man or woman in the prescriptively endogamous villages of western Rhodes; cf. *anemazoksaris* in western Crete, where there is a preferential norm of village endogamy.

19 This story, and the exegesis, are given in more detail in Herzfeld 1986a.

20 The concept of disemia evolved directly from the need for a semiotic expansion of Ferguson's (1959) diglossia model, itself in part a formalization of earlier research that possibly originated with Greek material (see Petrounias 1978:193). Some partially parallel concepts may also be noted in the Russian semiotic tradition and its offshoots. In particular, Bakhtin's concepts of "official discourse," "polyglossia," and "heteroglossia" (1981:61, 288–300, etc.) may suggest ways of further strengthening intercultural comparisons, as may Lotman and Uspenskii's (1985) pursuit of the binarisms of Russian culture. A notably challenging and useful approach that has particular relevance to problems of nationalism and everyday discourse has been developed by Even-Zohar (1979, 1981).

21 Details of the range of variation are given in the excellent survey of modern Greek recently compiled by Mackridge (1985), and with useful anecdotal support in Kazazis 1981a and 1982b.

22 Nevertheless, the connection between cleanliness and ritual purity may also be stressed in a more literal way. To take a specific case, this time from Italy, Frankenberg (1985:9) reports a family's distress when the doctor, called to attend their sick son, showed up too quickly for them to clear away the dirty towels and crumpled bedsheets. This was considered deeply embarrassing, a source of *vergogna* ("shame"): dirt here was *both* the Douglasian "matter out of

place" *and* physical pollution. It also occasioned some resentment toward the doctor, who nominally should be the object of respect alone: respect, however, does not necessarily mean affection or acceptance, an important point to bear in mind as we consider the dynamics of disemia. On the equation of "low" register culture with dirt, see the discussion of language, below.

23 This is only one of the meanings of *ghrousouzia*, which is more generally used to convey a sense of ritual or social pollution, as well as of physical dirt.

24 Recent unpublished research by Dorn (1985) has brought a further cultural irony into play. Among the Jews of İstanbul, two kinds of music are recognized, called by the Romance terms *a la turka* and *a la franka*. The *a la franka* category is considered culturally superior, at least amongst this rather cosmopolitan, Ladino-speaking community with extensive ties to western European culture (see Şaul 1983).

25 I take this formulation of the essential contrast from the excellent discussion of the social and ideological context of Greek diglossia by Sotiropoulos (1977).

26 See Herzfeld 1982a:124–8; cf. Pashley 1837, II:267–9; N. G. Politis 1874:503–4.

27 The "table manners" of anthropological formalism should probably be included in this discussion. Both Fabian (1983:116) and J. Goody (1977a:219) discuss the philosophical origins of diagrammatical visualism in the writings of Peter Ramus. The constraining character of the logic represented by the two-column diagram suggests a close analogy to Linnaeus's idealized and self-controlled European as well as to some current western codes of etiquette.

28 But see Tziovas 1985 for a thorough critique of demotic "nationism" (i.e. the "demotic" or "L" response to *nationalism*) that manages to avoid the judgmentalism of Likiardopoulos.

29 *Dhighlossia* can mean what English-speaking linguists more commonly indicate by "bilingualism" (cf. Greek *ghlossa*, "language").

30 For ethnographic parallels from Caribbean societies, see Reisman 1970; Abrahams and Bauman 1971.

6 Strict definitions and bad habits

1 St. Clair (1972) makes great play with Finlay's hostile reception in Greece, but puts it down to the Greeks' inability to accept foreign criticism of their cause. This, like Holden's (1972) essentially similar argument, as well as Dimou's (n.d.) fulminations from within Greece, misses the point of disemia, which permits a good deal of quite rancorous *internal* social and cultural criticism. It also overlooks Finlay's even-handedness; although the disillusioned philhellenes who had come to Greece to fight for the great cause might have found some support for their bitterness in his criticism of Greek politicians, bureaucrats, and military leaders, they could only do so by ignoring – as St. Clair appears to have done – Finlay's sympathetic assessment of the disadvantages that the Greeks had to contend with, not only from their Ottoman administrative heritage, but also from the ill informed Bavarian court.

2 Danforth (1976) has an excellent discussion of the Karagiozis part of this phenomenon. Although the line connecting these two figures can only be posited as an analogy, not as a direct influence, a structural analysis would reveal some of the same features of humor and status reversal that Danforth has identified in Karagiozis.

3 On the terminological changes that marked this new alignment, see A. Politis

1973:xii–xviii; Herzfeld 1982a:67–8. Jenkins's (1961;99–117) sneering account of "ethnic truth" should be set against the defenses of national integrity called forth by the international outcry that followed the murder of a party of foreign travellers at Dilessi in 1865 by brigands (*liste* to the government, doubtless *kleftes* to themselves!). Jenkins, like later writers of the same ilk, simply failed to see that the Greeks were not distorting some ultimate truth; they were constructing a history of imported cloth because that is what "international public opinion" demanded.

4 See especially d'Istria 1867, for an explicit discussion of the contrast between European individualism, supposedly derived from the model of the Classical heroes and maintained by the guerrillas of the modern Greek struggle, and the "somehow communistic influence of the Slavs" which conceptually excluded them from full participation in European civilization. The Slavs were regarded in many countries as not fully Europeanized; see, for example, Wilson 1976, on Finnish attitudes, remarkably similar to those of the Greeks.

5 In response to the conservative Prime Minister (as he then was) Karamanlis's slogan "We belong to the West." The two slogans were also couched in clearly recognizable demotic and *katharevousa* respectively.

Compare also the stance of a Greek scholar who has offered useful critiques of the language question (Sotiropoulos 1982:23): "Let us ... hope that modern Greece will cease to be 'a caricature of the West' and will finally find its own identity."

6 Many of Verdi's operas, for example, represent the social contradictions engendered by a repressive code of *onore* and *vergogna*. Usually, these are taken to represent the common values of Mediterranean society; and nothing could more effectively evoke the ethnocentric bias that this view entailed than the still common observations that such sentiments would not have seemed persuasive or realistic to an Anglo-Saxon audience – often invoked as an "explanation" of the failure of particular works (e.g. Toye 1962). Both *La Forza del Destino* and the earlier *Ernani* blend Italian music, Spanish history, and French backgrounds.

7 The term still preferred in Crete and Cyprus for *all* the Mainlanders – despised for their tendency to take refuge in the arcane writerliness of bureaucracy while the heroes of the Greek margins have to fight in the hills and mountains.

8 Lotman (1985) argues that the poetics of everyday social interaction required the existence of a "high culture" set of models, to which it would then allude by means of various tropological devices.

9 On this, see M. Jackson 1983a and especially 1983b.

10 Tylor thought children's games to be a major repository of ancient ritual and belief.

11 Its presence both in village discourse about personal responsibility and in anthropological explorations of identity lends corroboration to Drummond's (1981) thesis that anthropology is one elaboration – not necessarily a privileged one – of the search for difference-as-identity.

12 The speaker used this address form (*koumbaros*: ritual kinsman) to emphasize a solidarity within the larger solidarity, as a way of encouraging one of the others to consider the collective interests of the village as a whole.

13 For example, the neighboring Cretan villages of Glendi and Psila are at daggers drawn over a feud between two leading patrigroups, one from each. In Athens, they tend to express their solidarity as Cretans or as Milopotamites (i.e. a district identity that separates them from the "effete" townspeople and lowlanders). But Glendiots recognize the numerical and political superiority of the

Psiliots, a famous community with several past and present parliamentary
Deputies to their credit; and in Australia I heard the patrigroup of the major
Glendiot party to the feud mentioned as "Psiliots" by a Cretan from a different
area, apparently without any sense of incongruity. In Crete, of course, such a
remark would have meant bad trouble!

14 Had the philhellenes, and more specifically the English Benthamites, not insisted on providing Greece with extensive printing facilities (see St. Clair
1972:159), it is interesting to speculate on what alphabet and dialect would have
triumphed. In Renaissance Crete, for example, Italian orthography was almost
always the medium of record for works of literature in the Cretan dialect, to
which it proved highly amenable. The inadequacy of the Classical Greek alphabet for the modern standard language is far more pronounced in the case of
Cretan as well as of the Heptanesian dialects from which one of the major traditions of nineteenth-century demotic literature grew (e.g. the "national" poet
Dionisios Solomos). This makes even the use of the Greek alphabet problematical in anthropological accounts of regional cultures. Anthropological indifference to such matters represents yet another disturbing link between the
practice of anthropology and nationalistic rhetoric.

15 The *katharevousa* and formal demotic form is *klironomía*, as opposed to village
klironomiá. This stress shift is quite common as a marker of distinctions
between formal and informal or *katharevousa* and demotic, and the use of the
informal variant here suggests, less that its semantic content is viewed as a
"natural" part of village morality, than that it has been fully incorporated into
the range of symbolic possibilities.

16 Anderson recognizes two distinct varieties of linguistic "fatality," as he calls it:
the *diversity* of languages, and the destiny that *particular* languages impose on
their users. The biblical imagery of the successive falls plays a significant role in
this concept of linguistic fatality (1983:122): "Language is not an instrument of
exclusion: in principle, anyone can learn any language. On the contrary, it is
fundamentally inclusive, limited only by the fatality of Babel: no one lives long
enough to learn *all* languages. Print-language is what invents nationalism, not *a*
particular language per se." Elsewhere (1983:135), Anderson links this linguistic fatality to oppressed peoples' use of language to exclude the oppressor.

17 Cf. Basso (1979:64) on the manner in which Western Apache reverse the
Anglo–American self-stereotype as a socially and morally superior being, using
highly specialized codified forms of the *English* language and *English-speakers'*
manners to do so: "'The Whiteman' is a symbol of what 'the Apache' is not."
Otherness is always reversible. In the Greek context, see the mocking use of
katharevousa in jokes (e.g. Orso 1979:19). See also Dumont's remarks, already
cited (1982), about the reversibility of hierarchy at "lower" levels. Compare
also the instructive case of Catalan diglossia, where a local elite managed to
produce a "reversed diglossia" (Sobré 1980:52) in which the Andalusian
Spanish of the partially immigrant working-class takes an inferior position to
Catalan, elsewhere itself regarded as a regional (and therefore, in statist logic,
inferior) tongue.

7 The practice of relativity

1 In addition to Galaty's crucial study of ethnic shifters (1982), already cited,
James has published a major ethnographic study (1977) of the lability of ethnic
labels, demonstrating the importance of this phenomenon for historical recon-

structions that do not follow the historicist mode. Wallman (1978) has usefully documented the contextual variability of "racial" categories in Britain. Kuter (1985:23) convincingly stresses the plurality of factors affecting shifts from one meaning of "Breton" to another. Grillo (1980:9–11) gives an interesting structuralist account of the process of categorical reification in national ideologies. On the shifting definition of *Vlakhos*, see my earlier study of Greek ethnic terms (Herzfeld 1980b). In general, the anthropological study of ethnicity has moved from the analysis of bounded groups to a focus on constitutive process; examples of this trend are too numerous to list here.

2 Naturalization as a discursive strategy is a major theme in Foucault's works. For a comparable allusion to its role in the legitimation of citizenship in the U.S. context, see Schneider 1976:216.

3 Such agnatic systems exist also in the Mani. An unpublished doctoral thesis by M. Lineton is partially summarized by Davis (1977) and extensively discussed by Black-Michaud (1975). See also Alexakis 1980; Allen 1976.

Campbell (1976:20) has explicitly stated his preference for avoiding the use of a segmentary model to describe Greek concepts of opposition between insiders and outsiders. His position is clearly consistent with that of others among Evans-Pritchard's students, in that it treats true segmentation as entailed in unilineal descent *systems*. It must therefore be assessed in the context of (a) his representation of Sarakatsan kinship as primarily though not exclusively cognatic, and (b) the concept of segmentation prevalent at the time of his own research. Nevertheless, it is noteworthy that he does not express his opposition to the use of the model as forcefully here as do other Mediterraneanists working in areas where it might more conventionally be applied (e.g. Peters 1967; cf. now Dresch 1986:322, n. 1).

4 "One must avoid simplistic characterizations that seize upon one feature and make it the core of the system being studied" (Salzman 1978a:63). By asking whether "complementary opposition exists," however, Salzman both conflates hierarchical segmentation with the more general conceptual phenomenon of complementary opposition (on which see, e.g., Needham 1973), and implies that the abstract principle of complementary opposition only acquires ontological certainty when it is embodied in specific political action. For Salzman, segmentation is an alternative strategy, a "social structure in reserve" (1978a:69; 1978b:62), rather than a necessary feature of the logic of social relations everywhere; on this, see also Galaty 1981.

The typological isolation of "segmentary societies" is quite surprising (but see P. C. Lloyd 1965). Evans-Pritchard (1940:136) had clearly noted that segmentary opposition as such was to be found amongst the English as much as amongst the Nuer; the difference, as Karp and Maynard (1983:484) point out, is that the Nuer also had lineages. In the light of Evans-Pritchard's comment, one would seem to be more fully justified in cautiously suspecting the ideological reasons for the "repression" of segmentation in western society, and especially the possible links to the ideology of European identity.

5 In Crete, for example, restraint can often score more respect for one's own side than does violence. On blasphemy, see Herzfeld 1984b.

It is perhaps worth noting that the convergence of new ideas represented in this and the preceding two paragraphs represents, in part, discussions that took place between the authors mentioned. In particular, my 1984b paper (originally presented in a study that also included 1983c, at the 1979 meeting of the American Anthropological Association [AAA]) and Karp and Maynard 1983 (originally presented at the 1980 AAA meeting) represent an exciting convergence of interests and ideas, then mostly at Indiana University (where Kingsbury also made major contributions through his work on "talent" [1984]); the present discussion strongly reflects those interchanges. In addition, I should also mention Robert E. MacAulay, who as early as 1979–80 (when we were colleagues at Vassar College) was suggesting to me the relevance of the segmentation concept for a new view of the history of ideas. Among other authors mentioned in this chapter, I also benefited greatly from contact with John G. Galaty, Michael E. Meeker, and Philip C. Salzman during roughly the same overall period.

6 Dresch (1986:311) defines honor, which represents self-presentation in the model of disemia offered here, as "the quality par excellence that can only exist in opposition" at any segmentary level.

7 Cf. also Steiner's (1975:33) apposite observations on working class "seeming inarticulateness," which he identifies as "calculated to guard some coherence of inner life while wounding outward." The resentment of powerful outsiders' intrusion into linguistic privacy is not exclusively the product of colonial or tutelary political relations in the ordinary sense. During Pope John Paul II's 1985 visit to the Netherlands, his well intentioned use of Dutch caused serious trouble: "it was the Pope's pronouncements in Dutch which did most to harm his image . . . The Pope's Dutch was simply incomprehensible, because as all native speakers of Dutch know . . . no foreigner can ever master Dutch . . . [It] was an intrusion on Dutch privacy . . ." (Crump 1985:6). Crump, himself a foreigner living in Holland, seems surprised that the Dutch should "take such an extreme position with regard to the status of their own language" (*ibid.*). But he really makes the reasons quite clear: Dutch is the language of a small, independent country many of whose Catholic citizens saw the Pope's visit as a threat to their religious autonomy and *therefore* regarded his use of Dutch as symbolizing intrusion.

8 A term that also means "generations" (usually as *yenees*).

9 This appears to be locally recognized; see Herzfeld 1983c.

10 See, for example, Campbell 1964:129–31; Herzfeld 1985a. For a comparable ethnographic case from a neighboring culture, see Lockwood 1974, and the other essays in the special issue of *Anthropological Quarterly* devoted to bride-theft.

11 The term *dhikoloya* is somewhat ambiguous. In the west Cretan context, however, it usually appears to mean Ego's patrikin; *sinjenoloi* then signifies the cognatic kindred.

12 In Pefko, I was explicitly told that "friends" (*fili* or, more specifically, *yarenidhes*) are not only non-kin; they are usually not covillagers either. The obligations of reciprocal hospitality held between *yarenidhes*, who were from different villages; and, since most Rhodian villages are endogamous, this (at least in theory) precluded "friendship" between both kin and affines. On the relationship between self-interest and friendship in Cyprus, see Loizos 1975:89–92.

13 On this form of irony, see also Chock n.d.

14 E.g. in the concealment of meat from stolen animals during police searches, by women who would ordinarily oppose their husbands' involvement in animal-theft on principle.

15 There is a difference, however, in the two accounts; for Charlemont clearly believed the Mainland women to be more modest than those of the islands,

whereas Pashley explicitly says that men treated women with much more rigid ferocity on Crete than on the Mainland. It is possible that the powerful religious revival on Crete in the early years of the nineteenth century, which had reached its apogee shortly before Pashley's visit, partly accounted for the difference between these visitors' respective impressions. But Charlemont does not appear to have visited Crete; and his apparently more overtly amorous behavior may have given him a very different insight than that vouchsafed to the antiquarian Pashley.

16 He attributes this zeal to the Cretans' deep respect for the priesthood, which Llewellyn Smith (1965:91) suggests was greater than elsewhere in Greece (but cf. my observations on Cretan anticlericalism today, Herzfeld 1985a).

17 See my discussion of Glendiot cardgames (Herzfeld 1985a:152–62).

18 The local priesthood played an active role in the Greek Revolution of 1821–33, while a significant part of the upper hierarchy initially opposed it.

19 See Machin 1983, on the symbolic expression of moral economy in a Cretan community.

8 Etymologies of a discipline

1 I allude here to the debates, mostly conducted in literary philosophy, about whether theory can have consequences. See especially Fish 1980; Rorty 1982; Mitchell 1985a.

2 Vico thought little of the medieval Greeks, who, he thought, had allowed the achievements of Roman law to decay in their midst (4,3,12 [1977:640] [B/F 1002]). By contrast, he seems much more sympathetic to the indigenous peoples of the Americas, arguing that they would have reached a higher stage of civilization had it not been for European interference (5,3 [1977:695] [B/F 1095]). This is not an inconsistency, but arises from his concern to demonstrate the continual cultural resurgence (*ricorsi*) and relapse ("second barbarism") in human history.

3 "And authority began first as something divine, with which the deities appropriated to themselves the few giants that we have talked about, by properly burying them in the depths and by concealing them in caverns under the mountains..." (2,2,2 [1977:270–1] [B/F 386–7]). Vico has just suggested, in the same passage, etymological links between *autos* ("self," "own"), "author," and "authority."

4 I do not intend to imply by this that accuracy "does not matter"; but since Vico's sometimes rather wild reconstructions were meant to suggest the impermanence of social institutions, they threaten his argument far less than they would some attempt to provide a definitive history for some social institution. See also Battistini 1975:101–5.

5 On the embodiment of social knowledge, see especially Bourdieu 1977; Williams 1977; M. Jackson 1983a, 1983b. On the derivation of scientific and commonplace language from metaphor, see especially Black 1962; Ardener 1971b; Reddy 1979; Lakoff and Johnson 1980. I have drawn on the ideas of several of these authors earlier on in this study.

6 A horrible neologism, no doubt; but its meaning is not *identical* to that of "identity" – and the difference is crucial.

7 The issue is that of whether, when a Bororo man says, "I am a parrot," he should be taken literally; and what it would mean so to interpret his words. See especially Crocker 1977.

8 Or we might say "academic," which appears to be meaningless but is in fact political!

9 The argument has been made much more elaborately by Pandian (1984). The problem, which Pandian recognizes, lies in attributing intentions to native informants that have no social meaning precisely because these informants do not share in some of the more reificatory presuppositions to which we are heirs. Similar problems beset attempts to free local anthropologies from their colonialist past (cf. Jain 1977a; Owusu 1978).

10 Crick's mistake is to represent a tropological observation as a literal one – a curious slip for a writer so concerned with the evils of literalism.

11 Especially Senghor's *Africanité*, a model that Maquet did much to popularize amongst anthropologists. Maquet seems to acknowledge the problem, albeit in a very cautious and qualified way: "since it [Negritude] is a response to white racism, it must inevitably include certain racial overtones" (1972:14).

12 I am not persuaded that this requires the retention of the term "ethnosemiotics," although their use of it is certainly unexceptionable according to the criteria advanced here.

13 See also Boon 1982, for an extensive discussion of the writerliness of both the ethnographer and the informant, and the extraordinary reciprocity that binds a literate discipline with non-literate cultures.

14 Iconicity, of course, is not necessarily visual (see Sebeok 1978:117–18); but anthropologists' frequent use of diagrams to reify conceptual structures justifies my convenient ellipsis here.

15 As in the Cretan exchange of toasts, "I see (*thoro*) you!"/"I love you!"

16 Mouzelis (1978:72) offers a trenchant and substantially persuasive critique of empiricism from a neo-Marxist perspective. Its one weakness is a tendency, common among those who advocate a general systems approach, to equate empiricism in anthropology with ethnographic particularism. "Additive" analyses of the sort that Mouzelis rightly criticizes are certainly not *empirical*; whether they qualify as *empiricist*, however, depends on whether they reify their conclusions in the manner Mouzelis describes. That local-level studies *could* be misused is of course incontestable. But to ignore them is to suppress voices of the rural population and their interpretation of events – a common failing of rigidly large-scale perspectives.

17 Rhetoric *is* political. From a literary perspective Mailloux (1985:70–1; italics in original), after commenting on the "appropriations of Said's discourse" (i.e. of 1978 and 1981), remarks in a fashion that parallels my argument:

In fact, theory is a kind of practice, a peculiar kind because it claims to escape practice. But the impossibility of achieving this goal does not prevent theory from continuing, nor does it negate the effects it has *as persuasion*.

Note that theory "claims" to escape practice: it is a rhetoric that backgrounds its rhetoricity. Theory is itself "a form of social practice" (Eco 1976:29) – that is, a sub*set* of what it tries to sub*sume*. Mailloux's concept of "impossibility" seems to spell out once again the intended sense of impossibility in Evans-Pritchard's celebrated aphorism about social anthropology as a comparative discipline (on which, see Beidelman 1980).

Bibliography

Abrahams, Roger D., and Richard Bauman. 1971. Sense and nonsense in St. Vincent. *American Anthropologist* 73:762–72.

Abu-Lughod, Lila, 1985. Honor and the sentiments of loss in a Bedouin society. *American Ethnologist* 12:245–61.

Aguilar, John L. 1982. Shame, acculturation and ethnic relations: A psychological "process of domination" in southern Mexico. *The Journal of Psychological Anthropology* 5:155–71.

Alexakis, Elefth. P. 1980. *Ta yeni ke i ikoyenia stin paradhosiaki kinonia tis Manis*. Athens: privately published (doctoral dissertation).

Alexiou, Margaret. 1974. *The Ritual Lament in Greek Tradition*. Cambridge: Cambridge University Press.

1985. Ti ine i elliniki laoghrafia? In Sokr. L. Skartsis, ed., *Praktika Tetartou Simbosiou Piisis*. (Athens: Gnosis), pp. 43–60.

Alexiou, Stylianos, 1980. *Erotokritos – kritiki ekdhosi*. Athens: Ermis.

1985. *Vasilios Dhiyenis Akritis ke to asma tou Armouri*. Athens: Ermis.

Allen, Peter S. 1976. Aspida: A depopulated Maniat community. In Dimen and Friedl 1976:168–98.

Allen, P. S., Barbara Perry, Constantina Safilios-Rothschild, June Starr, Susannah Hoffman, Richard Cowan. 1978. Five views of *Kypseli*. *Reviews in Anthropology* 5:129–42.

Anderson, Benedict. 1983. *Imagined Communities: Reflections on the Origin and Spread of Nationalism*. London: Verso.

Anon. 1986. I mikri mou stili. *Rethemniotika Nea*, issue no. 4115 (26 July), p. 2.

Apostolakis, Yanis M. 1929. *Ta dhimotika traghoudhia: i silloyes*. Athens: Kondomaris.

Appadurai, Arjun. 1981. The past as a scarce resource. *Man* (n.s.) 16:201–19.

Ardener, Edwin. 1971a. The new anthropology and its critics. *Man* (n.s.) 6:449–67.

1971b. Introductory essay: Social anthropology and language. In Edwin Ardener, ed., *Social Anthropology and Language* (A.S.A. Monographs, 10) (London: Tavistock), pp. ix–cii.

1971c. Social anthropology and the historicity of historical linguistics. In Edwin Ardener, ed., *Social Anthropology and Language* (A.S.A. Monographs, 10) (London: Tavistock), pp. 209–41.

1975. The "problem" revisited. In Shirley Ardener, ed., *Perceiving Women* (London: J. M. Dent), pp. 19–27.

Argyriades, D. 1968. The ecology of Greek administration: Some factors affecting the development of the Greek civil service. In J. G. Peristiany, ed., *Contributions to Mediterranean Sociology* (The Hague: Mouton), pp. 339–49.

223

Asahi, The. 1932. *Annual English Supplement,* Present-Day Japan, Manchurian number, no. 8, p. 148: The Honest and Lovable Mongolians.
Austin, J. L. 1971[1956–7]. A plea for excuses. In Colin Lyas, ed., *Philosophy and Linguistics* (London: Macmillan), pp. 79–101.
    1975[1962]. *How to Do Things with Words.* Eds. J. O. Urmson and Marina Sbisà. Cambridge, Mass.: Harvard University Press.

"B., J." 1898. Englishmen and Romans. *Journal of the Royal Anthropological Institute* 28:343.
Babiniotis, G. 1979. A linguistic approach to the "language question" in Greece. *Byzantine and Modern Greek Studies* 5:1–16.
Bakhtin, Mikhail. 1981. *The Dialogic Imagination.* Trans. Carol Emerson and J. Michael Holquist, with an introduction by Holquist. Austin: University of Texas Press.
Banfield, Edward C. 1958. *The Moral Basis of a Backward Society.* Glencoe: Free Press.
Banton, Michael, ed. 1966. *The Anthropology of Complex Societies* (A.S.A. Monographs, 4) London: Tavistock.
Barley, Nigel. 1983. *The Innocent Anthropologist: Notes from a Mud Hut.* London: British Museum Publications.
Barnard, Frederick. 1965. *Herder: Social and Political Thought, from Enlightenment to Nationalism.* Oxford: Clarendon Press.
Barth, Fredrick. 1959. *Political Leadership among Swat Pathans.* London: Athlone Press.
Basso, Keith H. 1979. *Portraits of "The Whiteman": Linguistic Play and Cultural Symbols among the Western Apache.* Cambridge: Cambridge University Press.
Battistini, Andrea. 1975. *La degnità della retorica: Studi su G. B. Vico.* Pisa: Pacini.
Baud-Bovy, Samuel. 1935. *Chansons du Dodécanèse.* Vol. 2. Athens: Sidéris.
Beaton, Roderick. 1980. *Folk Poetry of Modern Greece.* Cambridge: Cambridge University Press.
Beattie, John. 1966[1964]. *Other Cultures: Aims, Methods and Achievements in Social Anthropology.* London: Routledge & Kegan Paul.
Beccari, Arturo, ed. 1938. *Vicenzo Cuoco: Educazione nazionale.* With editor's introduction and notes. Torino: Società Editrice Universale.
Beidelman, Thomas O., ed. 1971. *The Translation of Culture: Essays presented to E. E. Evans-Pritchard.* London: Tavistock.
    1980. The moral imagination of the Kaguru: Some thoughts on tricksters, translation and comparative analysis. *American Ethnologist* 7:27–42.
Bell, F. Jeffrey. 1877. Note on the name "Mediterranean," as applied to part of the human race, together with the proposal of a new term in its place. *Journal of the Royal Anthropological Institute* 6:271–8.
Bent, J. Theodore. 1886. On insular Greek customs. *Journal of the Royal Anthropological Institute* 15:391–403.
Benveniste, Emile. 1973. *Indo–European Language and Society.* Trans. Elizabeth Palmer. London: Faber & Faber.
Bergin, Thomas G., and Max H. Fisch, trans. 1948. *The New Science of Giambattista Vico.* Ithaca: Cornell University Press.
Berlin, Isaiah. 1977. *Vico and Herder: Two Studies in the History of Ideas.* New York: Vintage.
Bernstein, Basil B. 1971. *Class, Codes and Control.* 2 vols. London: Routledge & Kegan Paul.

Black, Max, 1962. *Models and Metaphors*. Ithaca: Cornell University Press.

Black-Michaud, Jacob. 1975. *Cohesive Force: Feud in the Mediterranean and the Middle East*. Oxford: Basil Blackwell.

Blok, Anton. 1981. Rams and billy-goats: A key to the Mediterranean code of honor. *Man* (n.s.) 16:427–40.

Blum, Richard, and Eva Blum. 1970. *The Dangerous Hour: The Lore of Crisis and Mystery in Rural Greece*. London: Chatto & Windus.

Boehm, Christopher. 1980. Exposing the moral self in Montenegro: The use of natural definitions to keep ethnography descriptive. *American Ethnologist* 7:1–26.

Bohannan, Laura. 1958. Political aspects of Tiv social organization. In Middleton and Tait 1958:33–66.

Bolinger, Dwight. 1975. *Aspects of Language*. 2nd edn. New York: Harcourt Brace Jovanovich.

Bona, Emma. 1940. Arti popolari e artigianato. *Lares* 11:475–7.

Boon, James A. 1982. *Other Tribes, Other Scribes: Symbolic Anthropology in the Comparative Study of Cultures, Histories, Religions, and Texts*. Cambridge: Cambridge University Press.

Bourdieu, Pierre. 1962. *The Algerians*. Trans. Alan C. M. Ross. Boston: Beacon.

1977. *Outline of a Theory of Practice*. Trans. Richard Nice. Cambridge: Cambridge University Press.

1979. *Algeria 1960*. Trans. Richard Nice. Cambridge: Cambridge University Press.

1982. *Ce que parler veut dire: l'économie des échanges linguistiques*. Paris: Fayard.

1984. *Distinction: A Social Critique of the Judgement of Taste*. Trans. Richard Nice. Cambridge, Mass.: Harvard University Press.

Brancato, Francesco. n.d. [=1969]. *Vico nel Risorgimento*. Palermo: Flaccovio.

Bucher, Bernadette. 1981. *Icon and Conquest: A Structural Analysis of de Bry's Great Voyages*. Trans. Basia Miller Gulati. Chicago: University of Chicago Press.

Burn, A. R. 1944. *The Modern Greeks*. London: Thomas Nelson.

Buttitta, Antonino. 1971. *Ideologie e folklore*. Palermo: Flaccovio.

Campbell, J. K. 1964. *Honour, Family, and Patronage: A Study of Institutions and Moral Values in a Greek Mountain Community*. Oxford: Clarendon Press.

1975. The honour of the Greeks. *Times Literary Supplement*, Nov. 14, p. 1355.

1976. Regionalism and local community. In Dimen and Friedl 1976:18–27.

Canapa, M.-P., F. B. Chary, S. Damianakos, C. Durandin, A. Gokalp, N. Gürsel, Cl. Karnoouh, A. Kyriakidou-Nestoros, D. Masson, M. McArthur, S. Papadopoulos, M. Rezvan, P. Shapiro, Z. Siaflekis, J.-Ch. Szurek, Z. Tordai, V. Voigt, and Z. T. Wierzbicki. 1985. *Paysans et nations d'Europe centrale et balkanique: la réinvention du paysan par l'état en Europe centrale et balkanique aux XIXe et XXe siècles*. Paris: Maisonneuve et Larose.

Caraveli, Anna. 1980. Bridge between worlds: The Greek women's lament as communicative event. *Journal of American Folklore* 93:129–57.

1982. The song beyond the song: Aesthetics and social interaction in Greek folksong. *Journal of American Folklore* 95:129–58.

1983. Review of Herzfeld 1982a. *Journal of American Folklore* 96:476–8.

1985. The symbolic village: Community born in performance. *Journal of American Folklore* 98:259–86.

Caro, Baroja Julio, 1970. *El Mito del caractér nacional: Meditaciones a contrapelo*. Madrid: Seminarios y Ediciones.

226   *Bibliography*

Cassirer, Ernst. 1946. *The Myth of the State*. New Haven: Yale University Press.
Casson, Stanley. 1921. *Rupert Brooke and Skyros*. London: E. Mathews.
Chabod, Federico. 1964 [1961]. *Storia dell'idea d'Europa*, eds. Ernesto Sestan and
    Armando Saitta. Bari: Laterza. In "Biblioteca di cultura moderna"; "Univer-
    sale" edn.
    1967. *Storia dell'idea dello stato*. Bari: Laterza.
Chapman, Malcolm. 1978. *The Gaelic Vision in Scottish Culture*. London: Croom
    Helm.
Charbonnier, G. 1969. *Conversations with Claude Lévi-Strauss*. Trans. John and
    Doreen Weightman. London: Jonathan Cape.
Charlemont, James Caulfeild, Viscount. 1984[1749]. *The Travels of Lord Charle-
    mont in Greece and Turkey, 1749*, from his own unpublished journals. Eds. W.
    B. Stanford and E. J. Finopoulos. London: Trigraph (for the A. G. Leventis
    Foundation).
Chock, Phyllis P. n.d. The Irony of Stereotypes: Toward an Anthropology of Eth-
    nicity. *Cultural Anthropology*. Forthcoming.
Clark, Mari H. 1982. Variations on themes of male and female (reflections on
    gender bias in fieldwork in rural Greece). *Women's Studies* 10:117–33.
Clarke, David L. 1968. *Analytical Archaeology*. London: Methuen.
Clastres, Pierre. 1974. *La société contre l'état*. Paris: Minuit.
Clifford, James. 1983. On ethnographic authority. *Representations* 2 (Spring,
    1983):118–46.
    1986. Introduction: Partial truths. In James Clifford and George Marcus, eds.,
    Writing Culture: The Poetics and Politics of Ethnography (Berkeley: University
    of California Press), pp. 1–26.
Clogg, Richard. 1972. The ideology of the "Revolution of 21 April 1967." In
    Richard Clogg and George Yannopoulos, eds., *Greece Under Military Rule*
    (London: Secker & Warburg), pp. 36–58.
    1985. Sense of the past in pre-independence Greece. In Roland Sussex and J. C.
    Eade, eds., *Culture and Nationalism in Nineteenth-Century Eastern Europe* (Col-
    umbus, Ohio: Slavica), pp. 7–30.
Cocchiara, Giuseppe. 1952. *Storia del folklore in Europe*. Turin: Einaudi.
Cole, John. 1977. Anthropology comes part-way home: Community studies in
    Europe. *Annual Review of Anthropology* 6:349–78.
Collingwood, R. G. 1939. *An Autobiography*. London: Oxford University Press.
Comte, Auguste. 1852. *Catéchisme positiviste, ou Sommaire Exposition de la religion
    universelle, en onze entretiens systematiques entre une femme et un prêtre de l'huma-
    nité*. Paris: privately published (2nd edn. 1874, E. Leroux).
Constantine, David. 1984. *Early Greek Travellers and the Hellenic Ideal*. Cam-
    bridge: Cambridge University Press.
Coufoudakis, Evangelos. 1985. Greek–Turkish relations, 1973–83: The View from
    Athens. *International Security* 9:185–217.
Couloumbis, T. A., John A. Petropulos, and H. J. Psomiades. 1976. *Foreign Inter-
    ference in Greek Politics: An Historical Perspective*. New York: Pella.
Couroucli, Maria. 1985. *Les oliviers du lignage*. Paris: Maisonneuve et Larose.
Crick, Malcolm. 1976. *Explorations in Language and Meaning: Towards a Semantic
    Anthropology*. New York: John Wiley/Halsted.
Crocker, J. Christopher. 1977. My brother the parrot. In J. David Sapir and J.
    Christopher Crocker, eds., *The Social Use of Metaphor: Essays on the Anthro-
    pology of Rhetoric* (Philadelphia: University of Pennsylvania Press), pp. 164–
    92.

Crump, Thomas. 1985. Problems in the local kitchen: *Or* why the Pope can't speak Dutch. *Anthropology Today* 1(6):5–6.

Culler, Jonathan. 1981. *The Pursuit of Signs: Semiotics, Post-structuralism, Literature.* Ithaca, New York: Cornell University Press.

Cuoco, Vincenzo. 1924. *Scritti vari.* Vol. 1. Eds. Nino Cortese and Fausto Nicolini. Bari: Laterza.

1966. *Saggio storico sulla Rivoluzione di Napoli.* Ed. Alberto Valles Poli. Milano: Rizzoli.

Damianakos, Stathis. 1976. *Kinonioloyia tou "rebetikou."* Athens: Ermia.

1985. Représentations de la paysannerie grecque (un cas exemplaire: la fiction clephtique). In Canapa *et al.* 1985:71–86.

Danforth, Loring M. 1976. Humour and status reversal in Greek shadow theatre. *Byzantine and Modern Greek Studies* 2:99–111.

1978. *The Anastenaria: A Study in Ritual Therapy.* Princeton University, Ph.D. dissertation.

1979. The role of dance in the ritual therapy of the Anastenaria. *Byzantine and Modern Greek Studies* 5:141–63.

1982. *The Death Rituals of Modern Greece.* Princeton: Princeton University Press.

1983a. Power through submission in the Anastenaria. *Journal of Modern Greek Studies* 1:203–23.

1983b. Tradition and change in Greek shadow theater. *Journal of American Folklore* 96:281–309.

1984. The ideological context of the search for continuities in Greek culture. *Journal of Modern Greek Studies* 2:53–87.

Daskalakis, Apostolos V. 1965. *The Hellenism of the Ancient Macedonians.* Thessaloniki: Institute for Balkan Studies.

Davis, John. 1977. *The People of the Mediterranean: An Essay in Comparative Social Anthropology.* London: Routledge & Kegan Paul.

1980. Social anthropology and the consumption of history. *Theory and Society* 9:519–37.

de Léry, Jean. 1578. *Histoire d'un voyage fait en la terre du Brésil, autrement dit Amérique.* [Geneva:] A. Chuppin.

DeMallie, Raymond. 1982. The Lakota ghost dance: An ethnohistorical account. *Pacific Historical Review* 51:385–405.

n.d. Art, Tradition and History in Lakota Culture. Ms.

De Mauro, Tullio. 1979. *L'Italia delle Italie: l'Italia, le regioni, le culture locali e le culture di base: le molteplicità locali nella tradizione italianna.* Florence: Nuova Guaraldi.

De Quincey, Thomas. 1863. *Modern Greece. Works,* vol. 13. Edinburgh: Adam and Charles Black.

de Tournefort, Joseph Pitton. 1718. *A Voyage to the Levant.* Trans. John Ozell. London: D. Browne.

Derrida, Jacques. 1976. *Of Grammatology.* Trans. Gayatri Chakravorti Spivak. Baltimore: The Johns Hopkins Press.

Dimaras, C. Th. 1972. *A History of Modern Greek Literature.* Trans. Mary P. Gianos. Albany: State University of New York Press.

Dimen, Muriel, and Ernestine Friedl, eds. 1976. *Regional variation in modern Greece and Cyprus: Toward a perspective on the ethnography of Greece.* Annals of the New York Academy of Sciences 268:1–465.

228   *Bibliography*

Dimiroulis, Dimitris. 1985. O Emmanouil Roidhis ke i tekhni tis polemikis. *Khartis* 3(15):266–90.

Dimou, Nikos. n.d. *I dhistikhia tou na ise Ellinas*. 5th edn. Athens: Ikaria.

d'Istria, Dora. 1867. La nationalité hellénique d'après les chants populaires. *Revue des deux mondes* 70:584–627.

Dizikirikis, Yorgos. 1983. *I esthitiki tis Romiosinis: To dhimotiko traghoudhi kato apo to fos tis palis ton sinkhronon idheon*. Athens: Filippoti.

Dodds, E. R. 1951. *The Greeks and the Irrational*. Berkeley: University of California Press.

Dorn, Paméla. 1985. A la turka/a la franka: Cultural ideologies and musical change. Paper presented at 19th annual meeting of the Middle East Studies Association, New Orleans.

Dorson, Richard M. 1968. *The British Folklorists: A History*. Chicago: University of Chicago Press.

Douglas, F. S. N. 1813. *An Essay on Certain Points of Resemblance between the Ancient and Modern Greeks*. 3rd edn. London: John Murray.

Douglas, Mary. 1966. *Purity and Danger: An Analysis of Concepts of Pollution and Taboo*. London: Routledge & Kegan Paul.

Doumanis, Mariella. 1983. *Mothering in Greece: From Collectivism to Individualism*. London: Academic Press.

Dresch, Paul. 1986. The significance of the course events take in segmentary systems. *American Ethnologist* 13:309–24.

Drummond, Lee. 1980. The cultural continuum: A theory of intersystems. *Man* (n.s.) 15:352–74.

1981. The serpent's children: Semiotics of ethnogenesis in Arawak and Trobriand myth. *American Ethnologist* 8:633–60.

1983. Jonestown: A study in ethnographic discourse. *Semiotica* 46:167–209.

Dubisch, Jill. 1983. Greek women: Sacred or profane. *Journal of Modern Greek Studies* 1:185–202.

1985. Golden Oranges and Silver Ships: Symbol and Myth in a Greek Holy Shrine. Paper given at the annual meeting of the American Anthropological Association, Washington, D.C.

1986. Introduction. In Jill Dubisch, ed., *Gender and Power in Rural Greece* (Princeton: Princeton University Press), pp. 3–41.

du Boulay, Juliet. 1974. *Portrait of a Greek Mountain Village*. Oxford: Clarendon Press.

Duerr, Hans Peter. 1985. *Dreamtime: Concerning the Boundary between Wilderness and Civilization*. Trans. Felicitas Goodman. Oxford: Basil Blackwell.

Dumont, Louis. 1965. The modern conception of the individual: Notes on its genesis and that of concomitant institutions. *Contributions to Indian Sociology* 8:13–61.

1966. The "village community" from Munro to Maine. *Contributions to Indian Sociology* 9:67–89.

1970. *Homo Hierarchicus: The Caste System and its Implications*. Trans. Mark Sainsbury. London: Weidenfeld & Nicolson.

1971. Religion, politics and society in the individualistic universe. *Proceedings of the Royal Anthropological Institute* for 1970:31–41.

1975. *La civilisation indienne et nous*. Paris: Armand Colin.

1977. *From Mandeville to Marx: The Genesis and Triumph of Economic Ideology*. Chicago: University of Chicago Press.

1982. *On Value*. London: Oxford University Press/British Academy.

Dundes, Alan. 1985. Nationalistic inferiority complexes and the fabrication of fakelore: A reconsideration of Ossian, the *Kinder- und Hausmärchen*, the *Kalevala*, and Paul Bunyan. *Journal of Folklore Research* 22:5–18.

Eagleton, Terry. 1984. Review of H. L. Gates, *Black Literature and Literary Theory*. *New York Times Review of Books*, December, p. 45.

Eco, Umberto. 1976. *A Theory of Semiotics*. Bloomington: Indiana University Press.

Eisenstein, Elizabeth L. 1983. *The Printing Revolution in Early Modern Europe*. Cambridge: Cambridge University Press.

Elias, Norbert. 1978. *The History of Manners*. Trans. Edmund Jephcott. Oxford: Basil Blackwell.

Ellverson, Anna-Stina. 1981. *The Dual Nature of Man: A Study in the Theological Anthropology of Gregory of Nazianzus*. Uppsala: Acta Universitatis Upsaliensis, Studia Doctrinae Christianae Upsaliensia, 21.

Evans-Pritchard, E. E. 1950. *The Nuer: A Description of the Modes of Livelihood and Political Institutions of a Nilotic People*. Oxford: Clarendon Press.

1949. *The Sanusi of Cyrenaica*. Oxford: Clarendon Press.

1956. *Nuer Religion*. Oxford: Clarendon Press.

Even-Zohar, Itamar. 1979. Polysystem theory. *Poetics Today* 1:287–310.

1981. The emergence of a native Hebrew culture in Palestine: 1882–1948. *Studies in Zionism* 4:167–84.

Fabian, Johannes. 1983. *Time and the Other: How Anthropology Makes its Object*. New York: Columbia University Press.

Fagan, Brian. 1975. *The Rape of the Nile: Tomb Robbers, Tourists, and Archaeologists in Egypt*. New York: Scribner.

Feld, Steven. 1982. *Sound and Sentiment: Birds, Weeping, Poetics, and Song in Kaluli Expression*. Philadelphia: University of Pennsylvania Press.

Ferguson, Charles A. 1959. Diglossia. *Word* 15:325–40.

Fernandez, James W. 1974. The mission of metaphor in expressive culture. *Current Anthropology* 15:119–45.

1983a. Afterword: At the center of the human condition. *Semiotica* 46:323–30.

1983b. Consciousness and class in Southern Spain. *American Ethnologist* 10:165–73.

Finlay, George. 1861. *History of the Greek Revolution*. 2 vols. Edinburgh: William Blackwood.

Finnegan, Ruth. 1970. *Oral Literature in Africa*. Oxford: Clarendon Press.

1977. *Oral Poetry: Its Nature, Significance, and Social Context*. Cambridge: Cambridge University Press.

Fish, Stanley. 1980. *Is There c Text in This Class?* Cambridge, Mass.: Cambridge University Press.

1985. Consequences. In Mitchell 1985a:106–31.

Fishman, Joshua A. 1976. Bilingualism with and without diglossia; diglossia with and without bilingualism. *Journal of Social Issues* 23:29–38.

Forbin, Count [N.D.L.A: de]. n.d. [=1820]. *Travels in Greece, Turkey, and the Holy Land in 1817–18*. London: Sir Richard Phillips.

Fortes, Meyer, and E. E. Evans-Pritchard, eds. 1940. *African Political Systems*. London: Oxford University Press for the International African Institute.

Foucault, Michel. 1971. A Reply to the Cercle d'Epistémologie, *Theoretical Practice* 3/4:112.

1979. Truth and Power. In Meaghan Morris and Paul Patton, eds., *Power, Truth, Strategy* (Sydney: Feral Publications), pp. 29–48.

Frake, Charles O. 1985. Cognitive maps of time and tide among medieval seafarers. *Man* (n.s.) 20:254–70.

Frankenberg, Ronald. 1985. Malattia come festa: sickness as celebration: Children's accounts of sickness episodes in a Tuscan community. Paper delivered at the annual meeting of the American Anthropological Association, Washington, D.C.

Frazer, James G. 1886. On certain burial customs as illustrative of the primitive theory of the soul. *Journal of the Royal Anthropological Institute* 15:64–104.

Freire, Paulo. 1970. *Pedagogy of the Oppressed.* Trans. Myra Berrgman Ramos. New York: Herder and Herder.

Friedl, Ernestine. 1962. *Vasilika: A Village in Modern Greece.* New York: Holt, Rinehart, & Winston.

1976. Remarks in Dimen and Friedl 1976:286–8.

Friedrich, O., and S. Burton. 1981. France's philosopher of power. *Time* 118:147–8.

Galaty, John G. 1979. Pollution and pastoral antipraxis: The issue of Maasai inequality. *American Ethnologist* 6:803–16.

1981. Models and metaphors: On the semiotic explanation of segmentary systems. In L. Holy and M. Stuchlik, eds., *The Structure of Folk Models* (ASA Monograph, 20) (New York: Academic Press), pp. 83–121.

1982. Being "Maasai"; being "people-of-cattle": ethnic shifters in East Africa. *American Ethnologist* 9:1–20.

Gallagher, Tom. 1983. *Portugal: A Twentieth-Century Interpretation.* Dover, New Hampshire: Manchester University Press.

Galt, Anthony H. 1982. The evil eye as synthetic image and its meanings on the island of Pantelleria, Italy. *American Ethnologist* 9:664–81.

1985. Does the Mediterraneanist dilemma have straw horns? *American Ethnologist* 12:369–71.

Garoufas, Dimitris, 1982. *Sarakatsaniki paradhosi: I klironomia mias panarkhaias filis.* Thessaloniki: Kiriakidis.

Geertz, Clifford. 1976. From the native's point of view: On the nature of anthropological understanding. In Keith H. Basso and Henry A. Selby, eds., *Meaning in Anthropology* (Albuquerque: University of New Mexico Press), pp. 221–37.

1983. *Local Knowledge: Further Essays in Interpretive Anthropology.* New York: Basic Books.

Gell, Alfred. 1985. How to read a map: Remarks on the practical logic of navigation. *Man* (n.s.) 20:271–86.

Gentile, Giovanni. 1963. *Studi vichiani.* 3rd edn. Ed. Vito A. Bellazza. Florence: Sansoni.

Georges, Robert. 1978. Conceptions of fate in stories told by Greeks. In Richard Dorson, ed., *Folklore in the Modern World* (The Hague: Mouton), pp. 301–19.

1984. The many ways of being Greek. *Journal of Folklore Research* 21:211–29.

Gerlach, Leither P., and Virginia H. Hines. 1970. The social organization of a movement of revolutionary chage: Case study, Black Power. In Norman E. Whitten and John F. Szwed, eds., *Afro-American Anthropology: Contemporary Perspectives* (New York: Free Press), pp. 385–401.

Giddens, Anthony. 1981. *A Contemporary Critique of Historical Materialism. Power, Property and the State,* vol. 1. London: Macmillan.

1984. *The Constitution of Society: Introduction to the Theory of Structuration.* Berkeley: University of California Press.

Gilmore, David D. 1982. Anthropology of the Mediterranean area. *Annual Reviews in Anthropology* 11:175–205.

Giovannini, Maureen J. 1981. Woman: A dominant symbol within the cultural system of a Sicilian town. *Man* (n.s.) 16:408–26.

Giuliani, Alessandro. 1976. Vico's rhetorical philosophy and the New Rhetoric. In Tagliacozzo and Verene 1976:31–46.

Gluckman, Max. 1963. Gossip and scandal. *Current Anthropology* 4:307–16.

Goldschläger, Alain. 1982. Towards a semiotics of authoritarian discourse. *Poetics Today* 3:11–20.

Gombrich, Ernst. 1984. *The Sense of Order: A Study in the Psychology of Decorative Art.* Ithaca: Cornell University Press.

Goody, Esther N. 1978. Towards a theory of questions. In Esther N. Goody, ed., *Questions and Politeness: Strategies in Social Interaction* (London: Cambridge University Press), pp. 17–43.

Goody, Jack. 1977a. Literacy and classification: On turning the tables. In Jain 1977a:205–22.

1977b. *The Domestication of the Savage Mind.* Cambridge: Cambridge University Press.

Gould, Stephen Jay. 1981. *The Mismeasure of Man.* New York: W. W. Norton.

Greene, Graham. 1943. *The Ministry of Fear: An Entertainment.* London: William Heinemann Ltd.

Grégoire, Henri. 1942. *Digenes Akritas: The Byzantine Epic in History and Poetry.* New York: The National Herald.

Greimas, Algirdas Julien. 1970. *Du sens: Essais sémiotiques.* Paris: Seuil.

1976. *Sémiotique et sciences sociales.* Paris: Seuil.

Greimas, Algirdas Julien and Joseph Courtès. 1979. *Sémiotique: dictionnaire raisonné de la théorie du langage.* Paris: Hachette.

Grillo, R. D., ed. 1980. *"Nation" and "State" in Europe: Anthropological Perspectives.* London: Academic Press. Introduction, by the editor, is pp. 1–30.

Grodzynski, Denise. 1976. Par la bouche de l'empereur (Rome IVe siècle). In J. P. Vernant *et al.*, *Divination et rationalité* (Paris: Seuil), pp. 267–94.

Guizot, François Pierre Guillaume, 1851a/1856. *Histoire de la civilisation en Europe depuis la chute de l'empire romain jusqu'à la revolution française.* 6th edn. Paris: Didier.

1874/1851b. *Histoire de la civilisation en France depuis la chute de l'empire romain.* 3rd edn. Paris: Librairie Académique Didier vol. 1.

Haller, Mark H. 1963. *Eugenics: Hereditarian Attitudes in American Thought.* New Brunswick: Rutgers University Press.

Hallowell, I. A. 1965. The history of anthropology as an anthropological problem. *Journal of the History of the Behavioral Sciences* 1:24–38.

Handler, Richard. 1984. On sociocultural discontinuity: Nationalism and cultural objectification in Quebec. *Current Anthropology* 25:55–71.

1985a. On dialogue and destructive analysis: Problems in narrating nationalism and ethnicity. *Journal of Anthropological Research* 41:171–82.

1985b. On having a culture: Nationalism and the preservation of Quebec's *Patrimoine. History of Anthropology* 3:192–217. (Objects and Others, ed. George Stocking; Madison: University of Wisconsin Press.)

Handman, Marie-Elisabeth. 1983. *La violence et la ruse: Hommes et femmes dans un village grec.* La Calade, Aix-en-Provence: Edisud.

Hanson, F. Allan. 1979. Does God have a body? Truth, reality and cultural relativism. *Man* (n.s.) 14:515–29.

—— 1983. Syntagmatic structures: How the Maoris make sense of history. *Semiotica* 46:287–307.

Harris, Marvin. 1968. *The Rise of Anthropological Theory: A History of Theories of Culture.* New York: Thomas Y. Crowell.

Harris, Roy. 1980. *The Language-Makers.* Ithaca: Cornell University Press.

Harrison, Jane Ellen. 1912. *Themis: A Study of the Social Origins of Greek Religion.* Cambridge: Cambridge University Press.

Hartog, François. 1980. *Le miroir d'Hérodote: essai sur la représentation de l'autre.* Paris: Gallimard.

Haviland, John Beard. 1982. El problema de la educación bilingüe en el área Tzotzil. *América Indígena* 42:147–70.

Hawkes, Terence. 1977. *Structuralism and Semiotics.* Berkeley: University of California Press.

Hazard, Paul. 1935. *La Crise de la conscience européenne (1680–1715).* Paris: Boivin.

Hegel, G. W. F. 1857. *Lectures in the Philosophy of History.* Trans. J. Sibree. London: Henry G. Bohn.

—— 1896. *Hegel's Philosophy of Right.* Trans. S. W. Dude. London: G. Bell & Sons.

Henderson, G. P. 1970. *The Revival of Greek Thought, 1620–1830.* Albany: State University of New York Press.

Herzfeld, Michael. 1976. *Categories of Inclusion and Exclusion in a Rhodian Village.* University of Oxford, D.Phil. thesis.

—— 1977. Ritual and textual structures: The advent of spring in rural Greece. In Jain 1977a:29–50.

—— 1979. Exploring a metaphor of exposure. *Journal of American Folklore* 92:285–301.

—— 1980a. Honour and shame: Some problems in the comparative analysis of moral systems. *Man* (n.s.) 15:339–351.

—— 1980b. On the ethnography of "prejudice" in an exclusive community. *Ethnic Groups* 2:283–305.

—— 1980c. Social borderers: Themes of conflict and ambiguity in Greek folk song. *Byzantine and Modern Greek Studies* 6:61–80.

—— 1980d. The dowry in Greece: Terminological usage and historical reconstruction. *Ethnohistory* 27:225–41.

—— 1981a. Meaning and morality: A semiotic approach to evil eye accusations in a Greek village. *American Ethnologist* 8:560–74.

—— 1981b. An indigenous theory of meaning and its elicitation in performative context. *Semiotica* 34:113–41.

—— 1982a. *Ours Once More: Folklore, Ideology, and the Making of Modern Greece.* Austin: University of Texas Press.

—— 1982b. Disemia. In Michael Herzfeld and Margot D. Lenhart, comps., *Semiotics 1980* (New York: Plenum), pp. 205–15.

—— 1982c. The etymology of excuses: Aspects of rhetorical performance in Greece. *American Anthropologist* 9:644–63.

—— 1983a. Semantic slippage and moral fall: The rhetoric of chastity in rural Greek society. *Journal of Modern Greek Studies* 1:161–72.

—— 1983b. Looking both ways: The ethnographer in the text. *Semiotica* 46:151–66.

—— 1983c. Interpreting kinship terminology: The problem of patriliny in rural Greece. *Anthropological Quarterly* 56:157–66.

1984a. The horns of the Mediterraneanist dilemma. *American Ethnologist* 11:439–54.

1984b. The significance of the insignificant: Blasphemy as ideology. *Man* (n.s.) 19:653–64.

1985a. *The Poetics of Manhood: Contest and Identity in a Cretan Mountain Village.* Princeton: Princeton University Press.

1985b. "Law" and "custom": Ethnography *of* and *in* Greek national identity. *Journal of Modern Greek Studies* 3:167–85.

1985c. Lévi-Strauss in the nation–state. *Journal of American Folklore* 98:191–208.

1986a. Within and without: The category of "female" in the ethnography of modern Greece. In Jill Dubisch, ed., *Gender and Power in Rural Greece* (Princeton: Princeton University Press), pp. 215–33.

1986b. Closure as cure: Tropes in the exploration of bodily and social disorder. *Current Anthropology* 27:107–20.

1986c. Of definitions and boundaries: The status of culture in the culture of the state. In P. P. Chock and J. Wyman, eds., *Discourse and the Social Life of Meaning* (Washington D.C.: Smithsonian Institute Press), pp. 75–94.

Hirschon, Renée 1978. Open body/closed space: The transformation of female sexuality. In Shirley Ardener, ed., *Defining Females* (London: Croom Helm), pp. 66–88.

1981. Essential objects and the sacred: Interior and exterior space in an urban Greek locality. In Shirley Ardener, ed., *Women and Space: Ground Rules and Social Maps* (New York: St. Martin's Press), pp. 72–88.

1983. Women, the aged, and religious activity: Oppositions and complementarity in an urban locality. *Journal of Modern Greek Studies* 1:113–30.

1985. The woman–environment relationship: Greek cultural values in an urban community. *Ekistics* 52:15–21.

Hirschon, Renée, and John R. Gold. 1982. Territoriality and the home: Environment in a Greek urban community. *Anthropological Quarterly* 55:63–73.

Hirschon, Renée and Thakurdesai, S. 1970. Society, culture, and spatial organization. *Ekistics* 30:187–96.

Hodgen, Margaret T. 1936. *The Doctrine of Survivals: A Chapter in the History of Scientific Method in the Study of Man.* London: Allenson.

1964. *Early Anthropology in the Sixteenth and Seventeenth Centuries.* Philadelphia: University of Pennsylvania Press.

Hoffman, Susannah M. 1976a. The ethnography of the islands: Thera. In Dimen and Friedl 1976:328–40.

1976b. Discussion of the film *Kypseli: Women and Men Apart – A Divided Reality.* In Dimen and Friedl 1976:382–4.

Hoffman, Susannah M., Richard Cowan, and Paul Aralow. 1974. *Kypseli: Women and Men Apart – A Divided Reality* (film). Distributed by the University Extension Media Center, University of California, Berkeley.

Holden, David. 1972. *Greece Without Columns: The Making of the Modern Greeks.* London: Faber & Faber.

Holmes, Stephen Taylor. 1981. The barbarism of reflection. In Giorgio Tagliacozzo, ed., *Vico: Past and Present* (Atlantic Highlands: Humanities Press), pp. 213–22.

Hoppál, Mihaly. 1979. Codes and/or cultures. In Peter Jozsa, ed., *Studies in Cultural Semiotics* (Budapest: Working Committee in Semiotics of the Institute of Culture of the Hungarian Academy of Sciences), pp. 5–32.

Houssaye, Henry. 1879. *Athènes, Rome, Paris: l'histoire et les mœurs*. Paris: Bibliothèque Contemporaine.

Houtondji, Paulin J. 1983. *African Philosophy: Myth and Reality*. Trans. Henri Evans. Bloomington: Indiana University Press.

Huxley, Aldous. 1932. *Brave New World*. London: Chatto & Windus.

Hvalkof, Søren and Peter Aaby. 1981. *Is God an American? An Anthropological Perspective on the Missionary Work of the Summer Institute of Linguistics*. Copenhagen: International Work Group for Indigenous Affairs.

Hymes, Dell. 1979. Foreword. In Basso 1979:ix–xviii.

——— 1981. *"In Vain I Tried To Tell You": Essays in Native American Ethnopoetics*. Philadelphia: University of Pennsylvania Press.

Iakovidis, Khristos. 1975. [Introduction]. *Neoklassika Spitia tis Athinas ke tou Pirea*. Athens: Dhodhoni.

——— 1982. *Neoelliniki arkhitektoniki ke astiki idheoloyia*. Athens: Dhodhoni.

Innis, Harold A. 1951. *The Bias of Communication*. Toronto: University of Toronto Press.

——— 1972[1950]. *Empire and Communications*. Revised by Mary Q. Innis; Foreword by Marshall McLuhan. Toronto: Toronto University Press.

Jackson, B. S. 1982. Structuralisme et "sources du droit." *Archives de Philosophie de Droit* 27:147–60.

Jackson, Michael. 1983a. Thinking through the body: An essay on understanding metaphor. *Social Analysis* 14:127–49.

——— 1983b. Knowledge of the body. *Man* (n.s.) 18:327–45.

Jain, Ravindra K., ed. 1977a. *Text and Context: The Social Anthropology of Tradition*. ASA Essays in Social Anthropology, 2. Philadelphia: Institute for the Study of Human Issues.

——— 1977b. Introduction. In Jain 1977a:1–8.

Jakobson, Roman. 1960. Linguistics and poetics. In Thomas A. Sebeok, ed., *Style in Language* (Cambridge, Massachusetts: MIT Press), pp. 350–77.

James, Wendy. 1977. The Funj mystique: Approaches to a problem of Sudan history. In Jain 1977a:95–133.

Jenkins, Romilly. 1961. *The Dilessi Murders*. London: Longmans.

Johnson, Bruce C. 1978. More on diglossia. *Language Sciences* 37:37–8.

Johnson, Douglas, 1963. *Guizot: Aspects of French History, 1787–1874*. London: Routledge & Kegan Paul.

Joseph, Brian. 1983. Language use in the Balkans: The contribution of historical linguistics. *Anthropological Linguistics* 25:257–87.

——— 1985. European Hellenism and Greek nationalism: Some effects of ethnocentrism on Greek linguistic scholarship. *Journal of Modern Greek Studies* 3:87–96.

Joseph, Roger. 1981. Vico and anthropological knowledge. In Giorgio Tagliacozzo, ed., *Vico: Past and Present* (Atlantic Highlands: Humanities), pp. 157–64.

Jusdanis, Gregory. 1987. East is east, west is west: It's a matter of Greek literary history. *Journal of Modern Greek Studies* 5:1–14.

Just, Roger. 1973. Some problems for Mediterranean anthropology. *Journal of the Anthropological Society of Oxford* 6:81–97.

Kabbani, Rana. 1986. *Europe's Myths of Orient*. Bloomington: Indiana University Press.

Kalonaros, Petros. 1941. *Vasilios Dhiyenis Akritas: ta emmetra kimena.* Athens: S. & P. Dimitrakos.

Karnoouh, Claude. 1985a. De l'usage du folklore ou les avatars du "Folklorisme." In M.-P. Canapa *et al.* 1985:49–62.

1985b. Une Genèse allégorique du politique: le folklore. *Revue française de science politique* 35:1064–79.

Karolidis, P. 1906. Kritike, istorike, ke topoghrafike simiosis epi tou meseonikou ellinikou epous *Akrita. Epistimoniki Epetiris Ethnikou Panepistimiou Athinon* 1905–6:188–246.

Karp, Ivan. 1978. *Fields of Change among the Iteso of Kenya.* London: Routledge & Kegan Paul.

Karp, Ivan and Martha B. Kendall. 1982. Reflexivity and fieldwork. In P. Secord, ed., *Explaining Human Behavior* (Los Angeles: Sage), pp. 249–73.

Karp Ivan and Kent Maynard. 1983. Reading *The Nuer. Current Anthropology* 24:481–503.

Kavadias, Georges B. 1965. *Pasteurs-nomades méditerranéens: les Saracatsans de Grèce.* Paris: Gauthier-Villars.

Kazantzakis, Nikos. 1953. *O Kapetan-Mikhalis.* Athens: Mavridis. (=*Freedom and death,* trans. Jonathan Griffin, Oxford: Bruno Cassirer, 1956.)

Kazazis, Kostas. 1966. Sunday Greek. *Papers for the Fourth Regional Meeting of the Chicago Linguistic Society* (Dept. of Linguistics, University of Chicago), pp. 130–40.

1981a. *Ellinas* vs. *Romios* anecdotally revisited. *Folia Neohellenica* 3:53–5.

1981b. Folk etymology with and without adaptation: Some Turkish loanwords in Greek. *Folia Slavica* 4:309–16.

1982a. Reanalysis in modern Greek women's surnames. *International Journal of Slavic Linguistics and Poetics* 25–6:233–8.

1982b. Partial linguistic autobiography of a schizoglossic linguist. *Glossologia* (Athens) 1:109–17.

Kedourie, Elie. 1970. *Nationalism in Asia and Africa.* New York: World Publishing Company.

Kendall, Martha B. 1981. Toward a semantic approach to terms of address. *Journal of Language and Communication* 12:237–54.

Kenna, Margaret E. 1985. Icons in theory and practice: An Orthodox Christian example. *History of Religions* 24:345–68.

Khrisanthopoulos, L. 1853. *Silloyi ton topikon tis Elladhos Sinithion.* Athens: Milt. K. Garpola.

Kingsbury, Henry O. 1984. *Music as a Cultural System: Structure and Process in an American Conservatory.* Ph.D. dissertation, Indiana University. To be published by Temple University Press.

Kiriakidou-Nestoros, Alki. 1978. *I theoria tis ellinikis laoghrafias.* Athens: Skholi Moraïti.

1985. L' idée du peuple dans les théories folkloriques de la Grèce moderne. In Canapa *et al.* 1985:62–9.

Knapp, Steven, and Walter Benn Michaels. 1985. Against theory. In Mitchell 1985a:11–30.

Kordatos, Yanis. 1972. *I kinoniki simasia tis ellinikis epanastasis tou '21.* Athens: Ekdhosis Dhiethnos Epikerotitos. 5th edn. Edited with an introduction by Than. Kh. Papadopoulos.

Kornaros, Vitsentzos. See Alexiou, Stylianos. 1980.

Kuklick, Henrika. 1984. Tribal exemplars: Images of political authority in British anthropology, 1855–1945. In George W. Stocking, ed., *Functionalism Historicized: Essays on British Social Anthropology. History of Anthropology* 2 (Madison: University of Wisconsin Press), pp. 59–82.

Kuper, Adam. 1985. The historians' revenge. *American Ethnologist* 12:523–8.

Kuter, Lois. 1985. Labeling people: Who are the Bretons? *Anthropological Quarterly* 58:13–29.

Labov, William. 1972. *Language in the Inner City: Studies in the Black English Vernacular*. Philadelphia: University of Pennsylvania Press.

Lagopoulos, Alexandros-Phaedon. 1980. Kinonio-simiotiki tou khorou: Tropi paraghoyis ke simiotikes astikes dhomes. In Karin Boklund-Lagopoulou, ed., *Simiotiki ke Kinonia* ([Athens]: Odhisseas), pp. 111–30.

Lakoff, George, and Mark Johnson. 1980. *Metaphors We Live By*. Chicago: University of Chicago Press.

Lambithianaki-Papadaki, Evangelia. 1972. *O sevdas tou delikani: To proksenio, o arravonas ke o ghamos sena [sic] khorio tsi Kritis*. Iraklio: no publisher given.

Lambrinos, Yorgos. 1947. *To dhimotiko traghoudhi*. Athens: Ta Nea Vivlia.

Lambropoulos, Vassilis. 1985. Toward a genealogy of modern Greek literature. In Margaret Alexiou and Vassilis Lambropoulos, eds., *The Text and its Margins: Post-Structuralist Approaches to Twentieth-Century Greek Literature* (New York: Pella), pp. 15–36.

Lambros, S. 1908. Monodhie ke thrini epi ti alosi tis Konstandinoupoleos. *Neos Ellinomnimon* 5:190–271.

Lane, Eugene N. 1975. The Italian connection: An aspect of the cult of Men. *Numen* 22:235–9.

Lang, R. Hamilton. 1887. On archaic survivals in Cyprus. *Journal of the Royal Anthropological Institute* 16:186–8.

Lawson, John Cuthbert. 1910. *Modern Greek Folklore and Ancient Greek Religion: A Study in Survivals*. Cambridge: Cambridge University Press.

Leach, Edmund. 1969a. Vico and Lévi-Strauss on the origins of humanity. In Giorgio Tagliacozzo and Hayden V. White, eds., *Giambattista Vico: An International Symposium* (Baltimore: The Johns Hopkins Press), pp. 309–18.

1969b. *Genesis as Myth and Other Essays*. London: Jonathan Cape.

1976. Vico and the future of anthropology. *Social Research* 43:807–17.

Lederman, Rena. 1980. Who speaks here? Formality and the politics of gender in Mendi, highland Papua New Guinea. *Journal of the Polynesian Society* 89:479–98.

Le Lannou, Maurice. 1977. *Europe, terre promise*. Paris: Seuil.

LeVine, Robert A., and Donald T. Campbell. 1970. *Ethnocentrism: Theories of Conflict, Ethnic Attitudes, and Group Behavior*. New York: John Wiley.

Lévi-Strauss, Claude. 1955. The structural study of myth. *Journal of American Folklore* 68:428–44.

1963a. *Structural Anthropology*. Vol. 1. Trans. Clare Jacobson and Brooke Grundfest Schoepf. New York: Basic Books.

1963b. *Totemism*. Trans. Rodney Needham. Boston: Beacon.

1964. *Le cru et le cuit*. Paris: Plon.

1966. *The Savage Mind*. Chicago: University of Chicago Press.

1968. *L'origine des manières de table*. Paris: Plon.

1974. *Tristes Tropiques*. Trans. John and Doreen Weightman. New York: Athenaeum.

1985. *The View From Afar*. Trans. Joachim Neugroschel and Phoebe Hoss. New York: Basic Books.

Levy, Harry L. 1956. Property distribution by lot in present day Greece. *Transactions of the American Philological Association* 87:42–6.

Lewis, Norman. 1978. *Naples '44*. New York: Pantheon.

Likiardopoulos, Yerasimos. 1983. *I "Romiosini" ston paradhiso: Simiosis ya mia kritiki tou neoellinikou andidhianooumenismou*. Athens: Erasmos.

Llewellyn Smith, Michael. 1965. *The Great Island: A Study of Crete*. London: Longmans.

Lloyd, G. E. R. 1966. *Polarity and Analogy: Two Types of Argumentation in Early Greek Thought*. Cambridge: Cambridge University Press.

Lloyd, P. C. 1965. The political structure of African kingdoms: An exploratory model. In Michael Banton, ed., *Political Systems and the Distribution of Power* (London: Tavistock: ASA Monogr., 2), pp. 62–112.

Lockwood, William. 1974. Bride theft and social maneuverability in western Bosnia. *Anthropological Quarterly* 47:253–69. (Special Issue: Kidnapping and Elopement as Alternative Systems of Marriage. Vol 47, 3 [July, 1974].)

Lodge, O. 1947. *Babin Den*: Midwives' day in Bulgaria. *Man* (o.s.) 47:83–5.

Loizos, Peter. 1975. *The Greek Gift: Politics in a Cypriot Village*. Oxford: Basil Blackwell.

1981. *The Heart Grown Bitter: A Chronicle of Cypriot War Refugees*. Cambridge: Cambridge University Press.

Loomis, Louise Ropes. 1906. *Medieval Hellenism*. Lancaster, Pennsylvania: Wickersham Press.

Lorenzatos, Zissimos. 1983. *The Lost Center and Other Essays in Greek Poetry*. Trans. Kay Cicellis. Princeton: Princeton University Press.

Lotman, Iurii M. 1985. The poetics of everyday behavior in eighteenth-century Russian culture. In: Nakhimovsky and Nakhimovsky 1985:67–94.

Lotman, Iurii M. and Boris A. Uspenskii. 1985. Binary models in the dynamics of Russian culture. In: Nakhimovsky and Nakhimovsky 1985:30–66.

Loukas, Georgios. 1874. *Filoloyike Episkepsis is ta Mnimia ton arkheon en to vio ton sinkhronon Kiprion*. Vol. 1. Athens: Nikolaos Rousopoulos.

Lynch, John. 1973. *The Spanish-American Revolutions, 1808–1826*. New York: Norton.

MacCannell, Dean, and Juliet Flower MacCannell. 1982. *The Time of the Sign: A Semiotic Interpretation of Modern Culture*. Bloomington: Indiana University Press.

Machin, Barrie. 1983. St. George and the Virgin: cultural codes, religion and attitudes to the body in a Cretan mountain village. *Social Analysis* 14:107–26.

Mackridge, Peter. 1985. *The Modern Greek Language: A Descriptive Analysis of Standard Modern Greek*. London: Oxford University Press.

Maris, Yannis. N.d. *Boomerang*. Athens: Atlandis.

McLuhan 1972: see Innis 1972.

McNall, Scott G. 1974. *The Greek Peasant*. Washington, D.C.: American Sociological Association.

1976. Remarks in Dimen and Friedl 1976:286–8.

McNeill, William H. 1957. *American Aid in Action, 1947–56*. New York: Twentieth Century Fund.

McQueen, Humphrey. 1984–5. Captain Cook did not discover Australia! *Austra-*

lian Book Review 67 (December 1984/January 1985):10–11. [Review of Watson 1984.]

Mahaffy, J. P. 1913. *Rambles and Studies in Greece*. New York: Macmillan.

Mailloux, Steven. 1985. Truth or consequences: on being against theory. In Mitchell 1985a:65–71.

Malinowski, Bronisław. 1935. *Coral Gardens and their Magic: A Study in the Methods of Tilling the Soil and of Agricultural Rites in the Trobriand islands*. Vol. 1. London: George Allen & Unwin.

Mandel, Ruth. 1983. Sacrifice and the bridge of Arta: Sex roles and the manipulation of power. *Journal of Modern Greek Studies* 1:173–83.

Mandouvalou, Maria. 1983. Romeos-Romios ke Romiosini. *Mandatoforos*, issue 32:34–72.

Maquet, Jacques. 1972. *Africanity: The Cultural Unity of Black Africa*. Trans. Joan R. Rayfield. London: Oxford University Press.

Marcus, George, and Dick Cushman. 1982. Ethnographies as texts. *Annual Review of Anthropology* 11:25–69.

Markides, Kyriacos C., Eleni S. Nikita, and Elengo N. Rangou. 1978. *Lysi: Social Change in a Cypriot Village*. Nicosia: Social Research Centre, 1.

Mears, Eliot Grinnell. 1929. *Greece Today: The Aftermath of the Refugee Impact*. Stanford: Stanford University Press.

Meeker, Michael E. 1979. *Literature and Violence in North Arabia*. Cambridge: Cambridge University Press.

Meraklis, Mikhalis G. 1984. *Elliniki laoghrafia: Kinoniki Singrotisi*. Athens: Odhisseas.

Merquior, José Guilherme. 1970. Vico et Lévi-Strauss: notes à propos d'un symposium. *L'Homme* 10:81–93.

Middleton, John, and David Tait, eds. 1958. *Tribes Without Rulers*. London: Routledge & Kegan Paul.

Mitchell, W. J. T., ed. 1985a. *Against Theory: Literary studies and the New Pragmatism*. Chicago: University of Chicago Press.

Mitchell, W. J. T. 1985b. Introduction: Pragmatic theory. In Mitchell 1985a:1–10.

Mol, J. J. ed. 1978. *Identity and Religion: International Cross-Cultural Approaches*. London: Sage.

Moss, David. 1979. Bandits and boundaries in Sardinia. *Man* (n.s.) 14:477–96.

Mosse, George L. 1985. *Nationalism and Sexuality: Respectability and Abnormal Sexuality in Modern Europe*. New York: Howard Fertig.

Mouzelis, Nicos P. 1976a. The relevance of the concept of class to the study of modern Greek society. In Dimen and Friedl 1976:395–410.

1976b. Remarks in Dimen and Friedl 1976:444–65.

1978. *Modern Greece: Facets of Underdevelopment*. London: Macmillan.

Mudimbe, Valentin Y. Forthcoming. Geography of a Discourse. *Final chapter of* Mudimbe, Valentin Y., *The Invention of Africa*. Bloomington: Indiana University Press.

Muecke, Stephen, 1983. Ideology reiterated. The uses of Aboriginal oral narrative. *Southern Review* (Adelaide) 16(1): 86–101.

Müller, Max. 1878. *Lectures on the Origin and Growth of Religion as Illustrated by the Religions of India*. London: Longmans.

1885. The savage. *Nineteenth Century* 17:100–32.

1897. *Contributions to the Science of Mythology*. Vol. 1. London: Longmans.

Nakhimovsky, Alexander D. and Alice Stone Nakhimovsky, eds. and trans. 1985.

The Semiotics of Russian Cultural History: Essays by Iurii M. Lotman, Lidiia Ia. Ginsburg, Boris A. Uspenskii. Ithaca: Cornell University Press.

Nanda, Serena. 1984. *Cultural Anthropology.* 2nd edn. Belmont, California: Wadsworth.

Needham, Rodney. 1971. Introduction. In Rodney Needham, ed. Emile Durkheim and Marcel Mauss, *Essay on Primitive Classification.* London: Routledge & Kegan Paul), pp. vii–xlviii.

1972. *Belief, Language, and Experience.* Oxford: Basil Blackwell.

Needham, Rodney, ed. 1973. *Right and Left: Essays in Symbolic Dual Classification.* Chicago: University of Chicago Press.

Nicholas, Ralph. 1966. Segmentary factional political systems. In Marc J. Swartz, Victor W. Turner, and Arthur Tuden, eds., *Political Anthropology* (Chicago: Aldine), pp. 49–59.

Nipperdey, Thomas. 1983. In search of identity: Romantic nationalism, its intellectual, political and social background. *In* J. C. Eade, ed., *Romantic Nationalism in Europe* (monograph no. 2) (Canberra: Australian National University: Humanities Research Centre), pp. 1–15.

Ong, Walter J. 1982. *Orality and Literacy: The Technologizing of the Word.* London: Methuen.

Onians, Richard Broxton, 1954. *The Origins of European Thought – about the Body, the Mind[,] the Soul, the World[,] Time, and Fate: New Interpretations of Greek, Roman, and kindred evidence[,] also of some basic Jewish and Christian beliefs.* Cambridge: Cambridge University Press.

Orlandos, Anast. 1969. To erghon tou Kendrou Erevnis tis Ellinikis Laoghrafias kata tin pendikondaetian apo tis idhriseos aftou (1918–1968). *Epetiris tou Kendrou Erevnis tis Ellinikis Laoghrafias* 20–1:5–14.

Orso, Ethelyn. 1979. *Modern Greek Humor: A Collection of Jokes and Ribald Tales.* Bloomington: Indiana University Press.

Orwell, George. 1945. *Animal Farm.* London: Secker & Warburg.

1956. *My Country Right or Left: The Collected Essays of George Orwell.* Eds. Sonia Orwell and Ian Ferguson. London: Secker and Warburg.

Owusu, Maxwell. 1978. Ethnography of Africa: The usefulness of the useless. *American Anthropologist* 80:310–34.

Pallis, A. A. 1959. *The Cretan Drama: The Life and Memoirs of Prince George of Greece, High Commissioner of Crete (1898–1906).* New York: Robert Speller.

Pandian, Jacob. 1984. *Anthropology and the Western Tradition: Toward an Authentic Anthropology.* Prospect Heights, Illinois: Waveland Press.

Papadopoulos, Stelios. 1985. La Découverte muséologique du paysan en Grèce. In Canapa *et al.* 1985:87–93.

Paparrhegopoulos, Konstandinos. 1925–32. *Istoria tou ellinikou ethnous.* 7 vols. 5th edn. Athens.

Papazisis, Dimitrios Tr. 1976. *Vlakhi (Koutsovlakhi).* Athens: no publisher named.

Pashley, Captain Robert. 1837. *Travels in Crete.* 2 vols. London: John Murray.

Pavlides, Eleftherios and Hesser, Jana. 1986. Women's Roles and House Form in Eressos, Greece. In Jill Dubisch, ed. 1986. *Gender and Power in Rural Greece* (Princeton: Princeton University Press), pp. 68–96.

Penniman, T. K. [1952] 1974. *A Hundred Years of Anthropology.* New York: Morrow.

Peradotto, John. 1983. Texts and unrefracted facts: Philology, hermeneutics and semiotics. *Arethusa* 16:15–33.

Peristiany, J. G. 1964. *The Social Institutions of the Kipsigis.* London: Routledge & Kegan Paul.

1965. Introduction. In J. G. Peristiany, ed., *Honour and Shame: The Values of Mediterranean Society* (London: Weidenfeld & Nicolson), pp. 9–18.

Peters, Emrys. 1967. Some structural aspects of the feud among the camel-herding Bedouin of Cyrenaica. *Africa* 37:261–82.

Petropoulos, Ilias. 1968. *Rebetika traghoudhia.* Athens: no publisher named.

Petrounias, Evangelos. 1978. The modern Greek language and diglossia. In Speros Vryonis, Jr., ed., *The "Past" in Medieval and Modern Greek Culture (= Byzantina kai Metabyzantina 1)* (Malibu: Undena), pp. 193–220.

Piault, Colette, ed. 1985. *Familles et biens en Grèce et à Chypre.* Paris: L'Harmattan.

Pitt-Rivers, Julian. 1971. *The People of the Sierra.* 2nd edn. Chicago: University of Chicago Press.

1977. *The Fate of Shechem, or the Politics of Sex: Essays in the Anthropology of the Mediterranean.* Cambridge: Cambridge University Press.

Pocius, Gerald L. 1979. Hooked rugs in Newfoundland. *Journal of American Folklore* 92:273–84.

Politis, Alexis. 1973. To dhimotiko traghoudhi: Kleftika. Athens: Ermis (Nea elliniki vivliothiki).

Politis, Nikolaos G. 1874. *Meleti peri tou viou ton neoteron Ellinon: Neoelliniki Mitholoyia.* Athens: Karl Wilberg & N.A. Nakis.

1914. *Ekloye apo ta traghoudhia tou ellinikou Laou.* Athens: Estia.

1918. Croyances populaires sur le rétablissement de la nation hellénique. *Revue de Grèce* 1:151–70.

Preziosi, Donald. 1979. *The Semiotics of the Built Environment: An Introduction to Architectonic Analysis.* Bloomington: Indiana University Press.

Price, Charles A. 1963. *Southern Europeans in Australia.* Melbourne: Oxford University Press.

Quigley, Carroll. 1973. Mexican national character and circum-Mediterranean personality structure. *American Anthropologist* 75:319–22.

Radcliffe-Brown, A. R. 1952. *Structure and Function in Primitive Society.* London: Cohen and West.

Reddy, Michael. 1979. The conduit metaphor. In A. Ortony, ed., *Metaphor and Thought* (Cambridge: Cambridge University Press), pp. 284–324.

Reisman, Karl. 1970. Cultural and linguistic ambiguity in a West Indian village. In Norman E. Whitten, Jr. and John F. Szwed, eds., *Afro-American Anthropology: Contemporary Perspectives* (New York: Free Press), pp. 129–44.

Ridgway, David, and Francesca R. Ridgway, eds. 1979. *Italy Before the Romans: The Iron Age, Orientalizing, and Etruscan Periods.* London: Academic Press.

Rorty, Richard. 1982. *Consequences of Pragmatism (Essays: 1972–1980).* Minneapolis: University of Minnesota Press.

Rosaldo, Michelle Z. 1980. *Knowledge and Passion: Ilongot Notions of Self and Social Life.* Cambridge: Cambridge University Press.

1982 The things we do with words: Ilongot speech acts and speech act theory in philosophy. *Language in Society* 11:203–37.

Safilios-Rothschild, Constantina. 1969. "Honour" crimes in contemporary Greece. *British Journal of Sociology* 20:205–18.

Sahlins, Marshall. 1976. *Culture and Practical Reason*. Chicago: University of Chicago Press.

1985. *Islands of History*. Chicago: University of Chicago Press.

Said, Edward W. 1975. *Beginnings: Intention and Method*. Baltimore: The Johns Hopkins University Press.

1978. *Orientalism*. New York: Basic Books.

1981. *Covering Islam: How the Media and the Experts Determine how we see the Rest of the World*. New York: Pantheon.

St. Clair, William. 1967. *Lord Elgin and the Marbles*. London: Oxford University Press.

1972. *That Greece Might still be Free: The Philhellenes in the War of Independence*. London: Oxford University Press.

Sakellarios, Athanasios A. 1890–91: *Ta Kipriaka*. 2 vols. Athens: no publisher named.

Salzman, Philip C. 1978a. Does complementary opposition exist? *American Anthropologist* 80:53–70.

1978b. Ideology and change in Middle Eastern tribal society. *Man* (n.s.) 13:618–37.

Şaul, Mahir. 1983. The mother tongue of the polyglot: Cosmopolitanism and nationalism among the Sapharadim of Istanbul. *Anthropological Linguistics* 25:326–58.

Schein, Muriel Dimen. 1975. When is an ethnic group? Ecology and class structure in northern Greece. *Ethnology* 14:83–97.

Schiffman, Harold. 1973. Language and politics in Tamilnad. In Edward Gerow and Margery D. Lang, eds., *Studies in the Languages and Cultures of South Asia* (Seattle: University of Washington Press), pp. 125–34.

1978. Diglossia and purity/pollution in Tamil. In Clarence Maloney, ed., *Language and Civilizational Change in South Asia* (Contributions to Asian Studies 11) (Leiden: Brill), pp. 98–110.

Schneider, David M. 1976. Notes toward a theory of culture. In Keith H. Basso and Henry A. Selby, eds., *Meaning in Anthropology* (Albuquerque: University of New Mexico Press), pp. 197–200.

Schwimmer, Erik. 1983. The taste of your own flesh. *Semiotica* 46:107–29.

Sciama, Lidia. 1981. The problem of privacy in Mediterranean anthropology. In Shirley Ardener, ed., *Women and Space: Ground Rules and Social Maps* (New York: St. Martin's Press), pp. 89–111.

Sebeok, Thomas A. 1978. *The Sign and its Masters*. Austin: University of Texas Press.

Seeger, Anthony, 1988. *Why Suyá Sing: A Musical Anthropology*. Cambridge: Cambridge University Press.

Seremetakis, Nadia. 1984. The eye of the other: Watching death in rural Greece. *Journal of Modern Hellenism* 1:63–77.

Shouby, E. 1951. The influence of the Arabic language on the psychology of the Arabs. *The Middle East Journal* 5:284–302.

Silverstein, Michael. 1976. Shifters, linguistic categories, and cultural description. In Keith H. Basso and Henry A. Selby, eds., *Meaning in Anthropology* (Albuquerque: University of New Mexico Press), pp. 11–55.

Skouteri-Didaskalou, Nora. 1984. *Anthropoloyika yia to yinekio zitima*. Athens: O Politis.

Smith, M. G. 1956. On segmentary lineage systems. *Journal of the Royal Anthropological Institute* 86:39–80.

Smolicz, J. J. 1985. Greek-Australians: A question of survival in multicultural Australia. *Journal of Multilingual and Multicultural Development* 6:17–29.

Sobré, Josip. 1980. Literature, diglossia, dictatorship: The case of Catalonia. *Ideologies and Literature* 3:51–67.

1983. The rise of modern Catalan. *Ideologies and Literature* 4:51–65.

Soteropoulos, S. 1868. *The Brigands of the Morea: A Narrative of the Captivity of Mr. S. Soteropoulos*. Trans. J. E. Bagdon. 2 vols. London: Saunders, Otley.

Sotiropoulos. Dimitri. 1977. Diglossia and the national language question in modern Greece. *Linguistics* 197:5–31.

1982. The social roots of modern Greek diglossia. *Language Problems and Language Planning* 6:1–28.

Spectator, The. 1900. Review of G. F. Abbot, Songs of Modern Greece. 3 November.

Stacy, R. H. 1977. *Defamiliarization in Language and Literature*. Syracuse: Syracuse University Press.

Stamatakos, Ioannis Dr. 1972. *Leksikon arkheas ellinikis Ghlossis*. Athens: Finiks.

Steiner, George. 1975. *After Babel: Aspects of Language and Translation*. London: Oxford University Press.

1976. A P.S. to Valesio. *Semiotica* 18:97–9.

Stewart, Charles. 1985. Nymphomania: Sexuality, insanity, and problems in folklore analysis. In Margaret Alexiou and Vassilis Lambropoulos, eds., *The Text and its Martins: Post-Structuralist Approaches to Modern Greek Literature* (New York: Pella), pp. 219–52.

Stirling, Paul. 1965. *Turkish Village*. London: Weidenfeld & Nicolson.

Stocking, George W. 1984. *Functionalism Historicized: Essays on British Social Anthropology*. (History of Anthropology 2.) Madison: University of Wisconsin Press.

Strathern, Marilyn. 1985. Kinship and economy: Constitutive orders of a provisional kind. *American Ethnologist* 12:191–209.

Struever, Nancy S. 1976. Vico, Valla, and the logic of humanist inquiry. In Tagliacozzo and Verene 1976:173–85.

1983. Fables of power. *Representations* 4 (Fall, 1983): 108–27.

Stuart-Glennie, J. S. 1896. The science of folklore, Greek folkspeech, and the survival of paganism. *Included in* Lucy M. J. Garnett and J. S. Stuart-Glennie, *New Folklore Researches: Greek Folk Poesy: Annotated Translations from the Whole Cycle of Romaic Folk-verse and Folk-prose*. Guildford: privately published.

Tagliacozzo, Giorgio, and Donald Phillip Verene, eds. 1976. *Giambattista Vico's Science of Humanity*. Baltimore: The Johns Hopkins University Press.

Tennant, F. R. 1968 [1930{1946}]. *The Sources of the Doctrines and the Fall and Original Sin*. New York: Schocken.

Thompson, Kenneth. 1963. *Farm Fragmentation in Greece*. (Research Monograph Series, 5). Athens: Center of Economic Research.

Thornton, Robert J. 1985. "Imagine yourself set down...": Mach, Frazer, Conrad, Malinowski and the role of imagination in ethnography. *Anthropology Today* 1(5):7–14.

Threadgold, Terry. 1986. Semiotics – ideology – language. In Terry Threadgold, E. A. Grosz, Gunther Kress, M. A. K. Halliday, eds., *Semiotics – Ideology – Language* (Sydney: Sydney Association for Studies in Society and Culture), pp. 15–60.

Todorov, Tzvetan. 1984. *The Conquest of America*. Trans. R. Howard. New York: Harper and Row.

Toye, Francis. 1962[1931]. *Guiseppe Verdi: His Life and Works*. London: Victor Gollancz [Heinemann].

Toynbee, Arnold J. 1922. *The Western Question in Greece and Turkey: A Study in the Contact of Civilizations*. London: Constable.

Tozer, Henry Fanshawe. 1869. *Researches in the Highlands of Turkey*. 2 vols. London: John Murray.

Tsigakou, Fani-Maria. 1981. *The Rediscovery of Greece: Travellers and Painters of the Romantic Era*. New Rochelle, New York: Caratzas.

Tsitsipis, Loukas. 1983a. Narrative performance in a dying language: Evidence from Albanian in Greece. *Word* 34:25–36.

1983b. Language shift among the Albanian speakers of Greece. *Anthropological Linguistics* 25:288–308.

Tsoukalas, Konstandinos. 1983. *Kinoniki anaptiksi ke kratos: singrotisi tou dhimosiu khorou stin Elladha*. Athens: Themelio.

Tylor, Edward Burnett. 1865. See: Tylor 1964.

1871. *Primitive Culture*. London: John Murray.

1964. *Researches into the Early History of Mankind and the Development of Civilization*. Abridged edition. Chicago: University of Chicago Press. (1st edn., 1865, London: John Murray.)

Tziovas, Dimitris. 1985. The organic discourse of nationistic demoticism: A tropological approach. In Margaret Alexiou and Vassilis Lambropoulos, eds., *The Text and its Margins: Post-Structuralist Approaches to Twentieth-Century Greek Literature* (New York: Pella), pp. 253–77.

Valesio, Paolo. 1976. The virtues of traducement: Sketch of a theory of translation. *Semiotica* 18:1–96.

1980. *Novantiqua: Rhetorics as a Contemporary Theory*. Bloomington: Indiana University Press.

Valetas, G. 1982. *Tis Romiosinis*. Athens: Filippoti.

Vaughan, Frederick. 1972. *The Political Philosophy of Giambattista Vico: An Introduction to La Scienza Nuova*. The Hague: Nijhoff.

van den Broek, Gerard. 1986. From Herbalists to Linnaeus: Natural classification and the classification of nature. *Recherches sémiotiques/Semiotic Inquiry* 5:176–95.

Vazouras, Aristotelis. 1974. *Ethima ke kratos is tin neoteran Elladha*. Athens: Papazisis.

Vico, Giambattista. 1744. *Principij di Scienza Nuova*. 3rd edn. Naples: Stamperia Muziana.

Vizandios, Dimitrios K. 1840. *Vavilonia*. 2nd edn. Athens: Kastorkhi.

Vlach, John Michael. 1984. The Brazilian house in Nigeria: The emergence of a twentieth-century house type. *Journal of American Folklore* 97:3–23.

Vlachos, Evan. 1976. Remarks in Dimen and Friedl 1976:286–8.

Wagner, Roy. 1975. *The Invention of Culture*. Englewood Cliffs, New Jersey: Prentice-Hall.

Walcot, Peter. 1970. *Greek Peasants, Ancient and Modern: A Comparison of Social and Moral Values*. New York: Barnes & Noble.

Wallace, Melanie. 1984. Death in Greece (Review Article). *Journal of the Hellenic Diaspora* 11:39–46.

Wallman, Sandra. 1978. The boundaries of "Race": Processes of ethnicity in England. *Man* (n.s.) 13:200–17.

Watson, Don. 1984. *The Story of Australia.* Melbourne: Nelson.

Webber, Jonathan. 1973. Review article. *Journal of the Anthropological Society of Oxford* 4:32–41.

Weber, Max. 1968. *On Charisma and Institution Building.* Selected papers, edited and with an Introduction by S. N. Eisenstadt. The Heritage of Sociology (series). Chicago; University of Chicago Press.

White, Hayden. 1978. *Tropics of Discourse: Essays in Cultural Criticism.* Baltimore: The Johns Hopkins Press.

Whorf, Benjamin Lee. 1956. *Language, Thought, and Reality: Selected Writings of Benjamin Lee Whorf,* John B. Carroll, ed. Cambridge, Massachusetts: MIT Press.

Wikan, Unni. 1984. Shame and honour: A contestable pair. *Man* (n.s.) 19:635–52.

Williams, Drid. 1977. The arms and the hands, with special reference to an Anglo-Saxon sign system. *Semiotica* 21:23–73.

Wilson, William A. 1976. *Folklore and Nationalism in Modern Finland.* Bloomington: Indiana University Press.

Winner, Irene Portis. 1977. The question of the Zadruga in Slovenia: Myth and reality in Žerovnica. *Anthropological Quarterly* 50:125–34.

Wolf, Eric R. 1982. *Europe and the People Without History.* Berkeley: University of California Press.

Woodhouse, C. M. 1986. Unbroken stones. Review of: Robert Browning, ed., *The Greek World: Classical, Byzantine and Modern* (London: Thames and Hudson). *Times Literary Supplement,* January 3 (no. 4318), p. 18.

Woolley, Leonard. 1954. *Digging Up the Past.* 2nd ed. London: Ernest Benn.

Zambelios, Spiridon. 1859. *Pothen i kini leksis "traghoudho"? Skepsis peri ellinikis piiseos.* Athens: P. Soutsas & A. Ktenas.

Zonabend, F. 1985. Du Texte au prétexte. La monographie dans le domain euro-péen. *Etudes rurales* 97–8:33–8.

Index

245